THE ONE YEAR®

Did You Know DEVOTIONS

NANCY S. HILL

TYNDALE KiDS

Tyndale House Publishers, Inc.
Carol Stream, Illinois

Visit Tyndale's exciting Web site at www.tyndale.com/kids

TYNDALE is a registered trademark of Tyndale House Publishers, Inc.

Tyndale Kids logo is a trademark of Tyndale House Publishers, Inc.

The One Year is a registered trademark of Tyndale House Publishers, Inc.

The One Year Did You Know Devotions

Previously published as *The One Year Book of Did You Know Devotions for Kids* by Tyndale House Publishers, Inc., under ISBN 0-8423-6184-7.

Designed by Ron Kaufmann and Jessie McGrath

The Library of Congress has cataloged the original edition as follows:

Hill, Nancy S., date.
  The one year book of did you know devotions for kids / Nancy S. Hill
    p. cm.
Includes bibliographical references and index.
  ISBN 978-0-8423-6184-2
  1. Devotional calendars—Juvenile literature. 2. Christian children—Prayer-books and devotions—English.
3. Curiosities and wonders—Juvenile literature. I. Title.
  BV4870 .H43 2002
242′.62—dc21   2002006747

ISBN 978-1-4143-1813-4

Printed in the United States of America

14   13   12   11   10   09
7   6   5   4   3   2

For my family—past sustenance,
present encouragement, and future inspiration—I love you all.
And for Zack, Maryn, Stacia, Kelsey, and Mathew:
You are my treasured gifts.

Contents

JANUARY
1. What money mistake did America make? 1
2. When can you buy an antique by scratching your nose?. 2
3. What's the background on "backlog"? 3
4. When do you "let the cat out of the bag"?. 4
5. How did a bathtub help solve a mystery? 5
6. How did cowboys get their meals "to go"?. 6
7. Why are girls' and boys' bikes different? 7
8. How did dead fish help improve frozen foods? 8
9. What's up with eyebrows? 9
10. How do you build a skyscraper with matchsticks?. 10
11. What really makes a bull charge at a red cape?. 11
12. When can books become a bother? 12
13. How did a medicine bottle turn into a toy?. 13
14. How did a church leader help invent bowling? .14
15. What can you do with a useless tunnel? 15
16. How could treason be committed during dinner?. 16
17. What causes bad breath? 17
18. Why were the police called to an exercise class? 18
19. Why isn't the bald eagle bald? 19
20. Why does a contest usually have first-, second-, and third-place winners?. 20
21. When was a sunny day bad for baseball? 21
22. Which fish takes aim at its lunch? 22
23. What did people do about their cuts before Band-Aids? 23
24. How did a little girl's letter change history?. 24
25. Why are barns red?. 25
26. Which sport started with a fruit basket? 26
27. Who was Chester Greenwood, and why did he cover his ears?. 27
28. Where did the first little red wagon come from?. 28
29. Who made the first metal detector? 29
30. When is it good manners to wipe your fingers on the tablecloth?. 30
31. Why do we call our favorite shopping place the "mall"?. 31

FEBRUARY

1. How did a mistake start the invention of the match? 32
2. When was a little girl sent through the mail? 33
3. Why did America destroy its own spaceship? 34
4. Why did a sculptor carve his statues smaller and smaller? 35
5. What should you know about mistletoe? 36
6. When was the last time you dropped your pencil and found $40,000? 37
7. Why would two brothers booby-trap their house? 38
8. Who called 9-1-1? 39
9. What can you do with a pack of camels? 40
10. Why are a cat's whiskers better than a man's? 41
11. Why do movie scenes start with a black-and-white-striped clapboard? 42
12. When can colors be confusing? 43
13. How did clay flowerpots help make buildings better? 44
14. Could you be found guilty by reason of rice? 45
15. Why were people buying raccoon tails? 46
16. How are crossword puzzles connected with Christmas? 47
17. Why did farmers have curfews? 48
18. Where were houses built roof-first and books read back to front? 49
19. Why did a priest decide to live with lepers? 50
20. Why did the United States have a one-day president? 51
21. Where does dew come from if it doesn't fall from the sky? 52
22. When can you strike a nerve at the dentist's office? .53
23. Which president had a giant bathtub? 54
24. Can you tell what a bird eats by looking at the bird? .55
25. How was the toothbrush invented? 56
26. What makes a Mexican jumping bean jump? 57
27. What did a president of the United States, a candy seller, and a stuffed animal have
    to do with a favorite children's toy? 58
28. Why do farmers want their calves to swallow magnets? 59

MARCH

1. Can a beaver make a tree fall in just the right spot? 60
2. Why keep a broken bell? 61
3. Why did a dog want to live in a graveyard? 62
4. Why would a bird need goggles? 63
5. How did Monopoly become a game? 64
6. Why is the Oscar named after a farmer? 65
7. Is there air pollution in outer space? 66
8. Why do people always get onto a horse from the left side? 67
9. What would you do if you went to a restaurant and the menu offered steamed
    kangaroo and rhinoceros pie? 68
10. Why does a pencil have six sides? 69
11. Why do we have white half-moon-shaped marks at the base of our fingernails? 70
12. Why is a bunch of lions called a "pride"? 71
13. Who was Dr. Pepper? 72
14. Why were the first napkins as big as towels? 73
15. What's the spin on revolving doors? 74
16. Why do we drive on the right side of the road? 75
17. How did a brilliant man's name develop into "dunce"? 76
18. Why did the Dutch build a memorial for a person who never existed? 77

19. Which country has a pancake party every year? 78
20. What do roofs and ears have in common? 79
21. Why would a man be glad to live in a cabinet? 80
22. When did paying a library fine make history? 81
23. What plant grows only after being burned by a fire? 82
24. What did a flag at half-mast used to mean? 83
25. Why aren't there any fleas at a flea market? 84
26. Are you seeing things? 85
27. Which flower looks like a lion's teeth? 86
28. When did people let their fingers do the talking? 87
29. Why did W. C. Fields open so many bank accounts? 88
30. Why was the general always absent during roll call? 89
31. Why would people be accused of stealing their own car? 90

APRIL
 1. When did spaghetti grow on trees? 91
 2. Why did a cookbook include a recipe for an explosion? 92
 3. Can someone be double-jointed? 93
 4. How can you read when you can't even see? 94
 5. When do parents want their kids to make noise? 95
 6. How could the idea of bungee jumping be over one hundred years old? 96
 7. If you burn your hand, what is the best thing to do? 97
 8. How did electricity surprise a whole crowd? 98
 9. Why do boys' and girls' shirts button on different sides? 99
10. Why were M&M's invented? 100
11. Why can't you feel your foot when it falls asleep? 101
12. Why are piano keys black and white? 102
13. Which cartoon was also a puzzle? 103
14. What really makes those noises you hear at night? 104
15. How was a person caught by a plane? 105
16. How did noodles get their names? 106
17. Why do our noses have little hairs in them? 107
18. Who froze the first Popsicle? 108
19. Why can dogs smell things better than people can? 109
20. Does an ostrich really bury its head in the sand? 110
21. How did riches escape a man who started a gold rush? 111
22. Why don't we eat goldfish? 112
23. How did golf courses end up with eighteen holes? 113
24. How did a fruit ruin a publicity stunt? 114
25. What causes gray hair? 115
26. Why were two security guards hired to stare up all day? 116
27. What are some predictable differences in people's hands? 117
28. When was Hollywood a happy little hamlet? 118
29. Why doesn't humble pie taste good? 119
30. How can you get to sleep without counting sheep? 120

MAY
 1. What do the letters IOU mean? 121
 2. Why has ironing always been a chore? 122
 3. How did the Jacuzzi get its name? 123
 4. When did a painting turn into a puzzle? 124

5. Is it possible to learn a language overnight? 125
6. How could you commit a crime with a pillow? 126
7. How can you move an elephant? 127
8. How did a toy stop an army? 128
9. How did the propeller of a ship help invent the cash register? 129
10. What haven't you noticed when watching the clock? 130
11. Why does a cat lick like that? 131
12. When did a softball player catch a flying baby? 132
13. Since fish are always in schools, aren't they smart? 133
14. How did the cavemen build their caves? 134
15. Why do chickens wear contact lenses? 135
16. If someone told you to be quiet, would you never speak again? 136
17. If you lived before locks were invented, how could you keep yourself and your
      things protected? 137
18. What kind of fire alarm would be foolproof? 138
19. What is a passport? 139
20. Why are the letters on a computer keyboard all mixed up? 140
21. Why were people lined up just to buy a ballpoint pen? 141
22. Which two letters have been left off the telephone, and why? 142
23. Why do rabbits wiggle their noses? 143
24. What misunderstanding created the piggy bank? 144
25. How can a plant get its own water? 145
26. When did the whole world have recess at the same time? 146
27. When did an umbrella make people laugh? 147
28. What lieutenant wouldn't stop fighting World War II? 148
29. Why did one letter take seven years to reach the White House? 149
30. What American pastime started with a garage door and a projector? 150
31. What is the surprise ingredient in your cereal? 151

JUNE
1. When was delivering mail a challenge for mail carriers? 152
2. What can happen if you have only one copy of your manuscript? 153
3. How did a nose and fingertips create measurements? 154
4. Why does metal feel colder than wood? 155
5. What billion-dollar industry was created from paper cups and milk shakes? 156
6. What popular game began on the grounds of a hotel? 157
7. Where does the term "hangnail" come from? 158
8. Where would you find a nest egg? 159
9. How did a captive audience escape from the singing emperor? 160
10. When was *Heidi* the most unpopular movie on television? 161
11. Why don't doctors wear white like nurses? 162
12. What do checkers and cookies have in common? 163
13. How did chop suey get its name? 164
14. Why did Cinderella wear glass slippers? 165
15. What made feeding babies more fun? 166
16. How did people wake up on time before alarm clocks? 167
17. How can you tell where a coin was made? 168
18. Why aren't there more green flowers? 169
19. Are you feeling red, pink, or yellow today? 170
20. What bird gives its babies up for adoption? 171
21. Why do golfers yell "fore"? 172

22. What happens when you grab a crab? 173
23. Why was a soft clay invented? 174
24. How did a bookmark become a special notepad? 175
25. How did Ping-Pong get its strange name? 176
26. What did kids in the past pay for their toys? 177
27. Why is purple the royal color? 178
28. Does your kitchen contain this invention? 179
29. Did you know that you've probably played with a toy called Gooey Gupp? 180
30. How can animals warn people of coming disaster? 181

JULY
1. What would you do if you were rolling across a slippery floor
   on skates that couldn't be stopped? 182
2. Will quicksand really swallow you up? 183
3. How does a mosquito choose its victims? 184
4. How could someone lose a three-mile-long painting? 185
5. Why wasn't the perfect book perfect? 186
6. How are "scratch 'n' sniff" products made? 187
7. What were cats once accused of causing? 188
8. Why did the barber need a pole? 189
9. Why are the sides of the boat called "port" and "starboard"? 190
10. Which city was named by the toss of a coin? 191
11. Why wasn't Miss National Smile Princess smiling? 192
12. Why was a statue dedicated to a bug? 193
13. How is Thomas Jefferson connected to the potato chip? 194
14. Why are detectives called "private eyes"? 195
15. What kind of puzzle took five years to solve? 196
16. What is the dollar bill saying with symbols? 197
17. How did an ocean liner get the wrong name? 198
18. How did the question mark get its strange shape? 199
19. What's the fastest-growing fungus in the world? .200
20. How did frogs fall from the sky? 201
21. Why isn't a fan really cooling the air? 202
22. Did George Washington really have wooden teeth? 203
23. Why do we call it the "funny bone" when it definitely isn't? 204
24. Which dogs were asked to dinner? 205
25. Did you know that you've probably used a cup named after a doll factory? 206
26. If a marble and a bowling ball raced down a ramp, which one would win? 207
27. Who had the biggest dollhouse ever? 208
28. When did a dog deliver mail? 209
29. Who invented raincoats? 210
30. How does a toad change its skin? 211
31. What does the pack rat pack? 212

AUGUST
1. How was the disposable razor invented? 213
2. How are a lemon seed and a drinking straw connected? 214
3. What do some of our nursery rhymes really mean? 215
4. When did one man with a good idea change an entire country? 216
5. Do boys and girls study differently? 217
6. Why was a man in a diving outfit working at a church? 218

7. What invention made grocery shopping easier? 219
8. Why did the rainmaker lose his job? 220
9. How was a wedding ring reclaimed after it was lost at sea? 221
10. Where does the asphalt go from a pothole? 222
11. Why was a bank alarmed about a withdrawal? 223
12. How do rocks travel in Death Valley? 224
13. How did a fire alarm improve baking bread?. 225
14. How do seeds always know to send their roots downward? 226
15. How did a war start the idea of a menu?. 227
16. Why is the ocean so salty? 228
17. Why is it impossible to buy fresh sardines? 229
18. How do you return the favor of a rescue? 230
19. Why don't birds seem frightened by scarecrows? 231
20. When were dirty tennis shoes helpful? 232
21. What does it mean to give someone the cold shoulder? 233
22. How did sideburns get their name? 234
23. Why don't birds get electrocuted when they sit on wires? 235
24. Who was Simon in the game "Simon Says"?. 236
25. Why do giraffes need such long necks?. 237
26. How was a sinking ship saved by a comic book?. 238
27. What's so great about grass? 239
28. When does a board game take a test? 240
29. How did they build a bridge across Niagara Falls?. 241
30. What trapped a fire truck? 242
31. What's the good of garlic? 243

SEPTEMBER
1. How do flies walk on the ceiling? 244
2. Why does aluminum foil have a shiny side and a dull side?. 245
3. Why do people say, "I'll eat my hat if I'm wrong"? 246
4. How is a pizza like the Italian flag? 247
5. Why do you shrink? 248
6. When did a fish lunch cost someone a big prize? 249
7. How does a beetle get a drink in the desert?. 250
8. When is it entertaining to have your face slapped? 251
9. Who missed a once-in-a-lifetime chance? 252
10. How does the telephone tell you the time?. 253
11. How did a spring become a toy? 254
12. Who didn't know about snow?. 255
13. What makes a small gift grand? 256
14. How did a dog help save a city? 257
15. How did stamp collecting start? 258
16. What secrets are some statues hiding? 259
17. Why does the man walk next to the curb when escorting a woman? 260
18. How was masking tape invented?. 261
19. What was brewing over the tea bag? 262
20. Why do men wear neckties?. 263
21. Why were wedding rings collected at a tollbooth? 264
22. Why does the Leaning Tower of Pisa lean? 265
23. Why do police cars use blue lights?. 266
24. Why couldn't the secretary of the U.S. Department of the Treasury buy dinner?. . .267

25. When didn't the son of the president of the United States listen to his father? 268
26. What's the story behind clean clothes? 269
27. Who wanted the same birthday present every year? 270
28. Why do people shake hands? 271
29. Why are veins blue when blood is red? 272
30. Who invented Frisbees? 273

OCTOBER
1. Which inventions were never used? 274
2. How was exercising turned into a game? 275
3. What's a "googol"? 276
4. When was a canteen alive? 277
5. What's it like to be swallowed by a whale? 278
6. Can a horse count? 279
7. What do a tree frog, an ant, and a warthog all have in common? 280
8. Is it "catsup" or "ketchup"? 281
9. Do you know what to do if you see someone choking? .282
10. How does a spider weave its web? 283
11. Can you guess which instrument used by doctors was made from a flute? 284
12. How did people make toast in the past? 285
13. Did you know that your stomach has acid in it? 286
14. Can animals get sunburned? 287
15. When was a toast a test? 288
16. Why don't dogs and cats cry? 289
17. Can a bird hear worms in the ground? 290
18. How did skipping a trip to the store change cookie baking forever? 291
19. What was the biggest goof never made? 292
20. Why is the bottom button of a man's vest left undone? 293
21. When did a solution lead to an even bigger problem? 294
22. Why would a family throw glass balls at a fire? 295
23. Why was someone ironing dollar bills? 296
24. Who tried to control the ocean? 297
25. How did a lost cabdriver help save a life? 298
26. What were sheep doing at the White House? 299
27. How was a whole country fooled? 300
28. How could you buy land from a cereal box? 301
29. How were Life Savers saved? 302
30. Why do birds fly in a V-formation? 303
31. How did a Christmas card lead to a unique advertising campaign? 304

NOVEMBER
1. What's the big secret behind Betty Crocker? 305
2. Where did Thomas Edison go on vacation? 306
3. When was the United States ruled by an emperor? 307
4. How did some prisoners dig themselves into deeper trouble? 308
5. Why does one eye work harder than the other? 309
6. What's the "hobo code"? 310
7. Why do some people have naturally curly hair? 311
8. Why do horses sleep standing up? 312
9. What kind of food was once sold with a pair of gloves so people could hold it? 313
10. What are some inventions made by kids? 314

11. Why was a 107-year-old lady supposed to go to first grade?. 315
12. How do animals help their friends?. 316
13. Why is fish served with lemon?. 317
14. What unusual tracks did a car leave on the road? 318
15. Why did a brand-new prison fail?. 319
16. Why won't a tire stay buried?. 320
17. Which word is used most in the English language?. 321
18. What treasure was found in a toolbox?. 322
19. Who was George Nissen, and why did he put a trampoline on top of his car? 323
20. When did children need to hunt for a home?. 324
21. What can go wrong with words? 325
22. What surprise was found in a closet?. 326
23. Why did people once hold parties just to watch someone vacuum? 327
24. Why was Florida so cold one Christmas?. 328
25. How can ants help with healing? 329
26. What is the five-year frog? 330
27. What did gloves say about hands? 331
28. Why would a house have two thousand doors? 332
29. Why did the richest woman in the world eat cold oatmeal? 333
30. What did you get if you ordered "bossy in a bowl"?. 334

DECEMBER
1. How did Kleenex find out that "the nose knows"? 335
2. How did the Jeep get its name? 336
3. What is the history of the sandwich?. 337
4. Why were windshield wipers invented?. 338
5. What's the story behind the Taj Mahal? 339
6. Does spinach really make you strong?. 340
7. How did foot powder win an election for mayor?. 341
8. Does sound always travel at the same speed?. 342
9. How did those sneakers get such a strange name? 343
10. Why do we call them "wisdom teeth"?. 344
11. What amazing number is always the same? 345
12. Why are traffic lights red, yellow, and green? 346
13. What do gold, tents, and a blacksmith have to do with your blue jeans? 347
14. Where did the dessert with the wiggle come from? 348
15. How can making a mistake make you money? 349
16. What toy was invented specifically to help students study?. 350
17. What does the X in "Xmas" stand for? 351
18. What job could you do if you couldn't hear or speak?. 352
19. Why did a school put a traffic light in its lunchroom?. 353
20. What letter is used most often in the English language? 354
21. Why wouldn't a locksmith give anyone his key? 355
22. Why did someone who never had to wash dishes invent the automatic dishwasher? . .356
23. How did Velcro get invented?. 357
24. Why do we call up-to-the-minute information the "news"? 358
25. How did a broken church organ inspire the creation of a Christmas carol? 359
26. What unusual item was once found in a bag of potato chips?. 360
27. Why is the White House white?. 361
28. Why would anyone collect chicken bones?. 362
29. What was so wacky about old-time wigs?. 363

30. Since earthworms have no legs, how do they move? 364
31. How did a weapon become a toy? 365

Bibliography 367
Scripture Index 393
Topical Index 397

January

What money mistake did America make?

ROMANS 12:2

The government thought of a new idea and manufactured a coin worth a dollar to replace the paper dollar bill. Called the Susan B. Anthony dollar, it had a picture of this woman on its face. She was well-known for her leadership in obtaining the right to vote for women. But the coin was very similar in weight, look, and size to a quarter. It was too easy to make the mistake of using the dollar coin to pay for something that should only cost twenty-five cents. Imagine the inconvenience of carrying twenty heavy, bulky coins instead of a twenty-dollar bill! People resisted using the coin, and finally the United States Department of the Treasury was stuck with 500 million unused Anthony dollars.

So what?

Sometimes changes are good, but sometimes they are not. The Susan B. Anthony dollar didn't make using money easier. Instead, it created more problems. But there's one change that is definitely worth it. The Bible tells us that our lives will change for the better when we become God's children. *It says:*

Don't copy the behavior and customs of this world, but let God transform you into a new person by changing the way you think. Then you will know what God wants you to do, and you will know how good and pleasing and perfect his will really is.   ROMANS 12:2, NLT

There's no mistake involved in letting God change you! Ask him to show you some of the changes he wants to help you make this year.

January

When can you buy an antique by scratching your nose?

PROVERBS 15:4

At an auction there is no price tag on the items for sale. An auctioneer stands at the front of the room, and people compete to buy an object by making signals that the auctioneer can see. This keeps the auction from becoming too confusing, because the auctioneer doesn't have to listen to the yelling of many voices shouting out suggested prices. By silently signaling, people can also bid without everyone else in the room knowing that they're interested in a certain object. But how do you know what moves to make? The most common signals for bidding are touching the nose or earlobe, wiggling the nose, lifting a hat, winking, nodding, or holding up a card that has your identification number on it. Do you have to sit totally still while visiting an auction if you don't want to bid? No, because people talk privately with the auctioneer beforehand and tell him which signal they will use. The movements of those people are the ones recognized by the auctioneer during the auction.

So what?

Sometimes, if we're not getting what we want, we show "signals" to other people. We frown or cry or say mean words. But there is a better way. *The Bible advises:*

Gentle words cause life and health; griping brings discouragement.
PROVERBS 15:4, TLB

When people receive pleasant signals from you, they will be more likely to help you or give you what you need. How about gently asking for God's help to delete those gripe-type words from your vocabulary?

January

What's the background on "backlog"?
PSALM 94:16-19

People say they have a "backlog" when they're behind in the work they have to do. They're usually trying to catch up or get it all done. But you might be surprised to know that "backlog" isn't a modern word. Its story comes from long ago in the days when the only way to heat a house was to keep a fire constantly burning in the fireplace. Making sure the fire lasted all night while people slept was a problem. Before going to bed, someone would put an enormous log, maybe as large as two feet thick, at the back of the fireplace. Smaller logs would be placed in front. Eventually the big log would heat up from the flames of the smaller kindling. Instead of bursting into flames itself, the log in back would slowly smolder all night long, making heat. In the morning, that log would have enough embers left to relight the fire. That's why a "backlog" stands for something that's left over or not all used up.

So what?

Sometimes we carry around a backlog of guilty feelings or hurts for things that happened in the past. It seems as if our bad feelings will never leave us—as if we'll be stuck with them forever. But God doesn't want us to bear that burden. *The Bible says:*

Who will be my shield? I would have died unless the Lord had helped me. I screamed, "I'm slipping, Lord!" and he was kind and saved me. Lord, when doubts fill my mind, when my heart is in turmoil, quiet me and give me renewed hope and cheer. PSALM 94:16-19, TLB

When you are God's child, you are entitled to his protection against your backlog of hurt, guilt, and fear. Call out to God, and he will fill you with "hope and cheer."

January 4

When do you "let the cat out of the bag"?
1 PETER 2:1

Maybe you're supposed to keep quiet about plans for a surprise birthday party, or your parents have asked you not to say anything yet about the new baby your family is expecting. But you forget (or ignore) what you've been told, and you share the news ahead of time. That's when someone may say that you "let the cat out of the bag." What does that mean? What cat? What bag? The answers come from history. It used to be the custom at county fairs for merchants to sell small pigs. After a sale, the merchants would tie up the animal and place it in a bag so the customer could carry it home. When he got the bag home, he would open it and release his purchase. Sometimes the customer would be surprised and dismayed to find that the merchant had been dishonest. Out of the bag would come the merchant's "secret," which had been hidden all the way home. He had not put an expensive pig in the bag, but— you guessed it—an ordinary cat. The customer paid a great deal of money, but the merchant kept the pig to sell again to someone else.

So what?
Keeping things hidden, whether an object or a fact about ourselves, almost always causes problems. It takes lots of energy to pretend to be calm when we're anxious, to act cheerful when we're sad, or to remember what gossip we whispered to whom. But how do you become a more honest person? *The Bible says:*

Get rid of your feelings of hatred. Don't just pretend to be good! Be done with dishonesty and jealousy and talking about others behind their backs. 1 PETER 2:1, TLB

We can stop pretending that we're good and let Jesus Christ make it true! He has the power to release all of the bad tricks in our bags and set us free.

January

How did a bathtub help solve a mystery?

JAMES 1:12

Archimedes, an early Greek scientist, was given a mystery to solve by the king. The king was afraid that his crown-maker had cheated. What if the man had added a cheaper metal into the crown, so he could keep the real gold for himself? Archimedes was supposed to prove whether the crown was pure gold or not, without destroying the crown in the process. Archimedes thought hard about a solution for this problem, but nothing occurred to him until he was taking a bath one evening. As he lowered his body into the tub, the water rose up around him. Suddenly he had a way to solve the puzzle! Archimedes realized that when something heavy is put into water, the same weight of water moves aside. So he began his science experiment by figuring out what the crown should weigh if it was pure gold. Then he put that amount of pure gold into the water, and when the water moved, he measured how much the moving water weighed. Next, he dropped the king's crown into water. When the water moved, he weighed again. Oops! This time the water was heavier than the first time. The crown-maker must have added some other cheaper, heavier metal, because the water weights didn't match. The king was right—his crown wasn't pure gold, and Archimedes proved it.

So what?

You can have a crown for free that is much more valuable than gold. How do you get it? *The Bible tells us:*

Happy is the man who doesn't give in and do wrong when he is tempted, for afterwards he will get as his reward the crown of life that God has promised those who love him. JAMES 1:12, TLB

This crown means you have a place in heaven reserved just for you. No one can steal it or replace it with something less. Give your life to God and claim your crown!

January

How did cowboys get their meals "to go"?
EPHESIANS 4:31-32

There were no fast-food drive-ins for cowboys, so they had to figure out how to take their own food along. Some cowboys cut meat into strips, dried it in the sun, and then carried it in their saddlebags until they were hungry. Cowboys from Argentina, called *gauchos,* had a slightly different way of "cooking" on the go. They placed raw meat strips under their saddles. By the end of the day, the meat was cooked by the heat from the horse's body and the friction of the saddle's movement. The strips were also tenderized at the same time by the rocking of the saddle. These meat strips had a Spanish name—*charqui,* meaning "dried meat." It might surprise you to know that we still eat this food. The beef "charqui" of yesterday is the beef "jerky" of today!

So what?
Meat is better when it's tender instead of tough. People are too. *The Bible says:*

Stop being mean, bad-tempered and angry. Quarreling, harsh words, and dislike of others should have no place in your lives. Instead, be kind to each other, tenderhearted, forgiving one another, just as God has forgiven you because you belong to Christ. EPHESIANS 4:31-32, TLB

We can ask Jesus to soften our hearts and make us sensitive to others. It will prepare us to do whatever he wants us to do, wherever he wants us to do it!

January

Why are girls' and boys' bikes different?

PSALM 95:4-5

Have you ever stopped to wonder why a girl's bike has the crossbar in a different place than a boy's? It has been proven that the ideal shape for a bicycle frame is a triangle or a diamond. Those shapes make the bike strong and able to support weight better. Boys' bicycles, with the crossbar parallel to the ground, are built for top efficiency. But girls' bikes are made differently for a historical reason. In the early 1890s, the crossbar was lowered for girls so that they could mount and pedal more easily while wearing their long skirts. Their bikes were called "safety bikes," and even though girls usually don't wear skirts when they ride bikes anymore (especially not long skirts), the design has never been changed. However, serious bikers, both male and female, use the male-frame bike when they are concerned about performance and durability.

So what?

Creating a way for girls to ride bikes comfortably was probably considered an impressive invention in its day. But what a tiny creation, compared to the works of the Master Inventor! *The Bible describes some of them:*

In his hand are the depths of the earth, and the mountain peaks belong to him. The sea is his, for he made it, and his hands formed the dry land. PSALM 95:4-5, NIV

Anything and everything man can create is so little in comparison to what God has done. Thinking about his awesome powers reminds us of how mighty he is and was and always will be.

January

How did dead fish help improve frozen foods?

TITUS 2:7

The story of frozen foods begins with fish. When Eskimos fish in the Arctic, the fish they pull out of the water freezes solid soon after hitting the fifty-degrees-below-zero air. In the early 1900s, Clarence Birdseye, a biologist, watched this happen and realized that freezing food quickly was the secret to good taste. The slow freezing process being used at that time damaged food's cells, which caused juices to leak out and the food to turn mushy and spoil. Anyone who tried to eat these bad-tasting early frozen foods never wanted to try them again. Not only that, but stores were supposed to buy expensive refrigeration equipment to stock the foods that no customers wanted to buy! So Birdseye started his own frozen foods company in 1922. Even though he eventually sold his company, his ideas and name remain part of frozen foods.

The first thing that was done to boost sales was to label the foods "frosted" instead of "frozen," because "frozen" reminded people of bad tastes. Then free refrigeration units were installed in eighteen grocery stores. But consumers didn't have freezers at home, so they had to eat the frozen foods the same day they were purchased. What really made frozen foods popular was World War II. Women were working and didn't have time to cook. Since canned foods used so much metal, which was needed for the war, frozen foods were available at less cost. It was even possible to rent space at a food locker to store frozen foods until they were needed. The popularity of frozen foods has grown over the years, and today the Birds Eye brand can be found in almost every grocery store.

So what?

The Eskimos probably weren't even aware that Clarence Birdseye was watching them, yet what he saw influenced his entire life's work. You may not have noticed it, but other people may be watching you. If they are copying you, what will they learn? If you'd like to be a good influence but you're not really sure how to go about it, the Bible gives you a great tip. *It says:*

Let everything you do reflect your love of the truth and the fact that you are in dead earnest about it. TITUS 2:7, TLB

Telling people what they should do isn't very convincing. We have the power to really make a difference in someone's life by showing how Jesus has changed us.

January

What's up with eyebrows?

ISAIAH 2:11-12

What happens when we raise our eyebrows? Unlike animals that depend more on hearing or smell, humans depend most on seeing. While animals flare their nostrils or raise their ears to heighten their alertness, we widen our eyes, dilate our pupils, and raise our eyebrows to see more clearly. It's a way our body tries to protect itself better.

Lowering our eyebrows in concentration is also a protection device, because a wrinkled brow makes the eyes' openings smaller. Our eyebrows also move because we have learned to communicate by making expressions with our face. Raised eyebrows can show surprise, questioning, disapproval, or interest.

So what?

Almost all of us know someone we disapprove of. We don't like the way that person talks or acts or looks. But we shouldn't be too quick to "raise our eyebrows" at this person. When we think we're better than someone else, we can get into serious trouble. *The Bible tells us:*

The day is coming when your proud looks will be brought low; the Lord alone will be exalted. On that day the Lord of Hosts will move against the proud and haughty and bring them to the dust.   ISAIAH 2:11-12, TLB

If we don't enjoy having someone "look down" on us, we shouldn't look down on anyone else.

January 10

How do you build a skyscraper with matchsticks?

PROVERBS 18:10

The first skyscraper was built from matchsticks and playing cards—at least in the architect's mind. In the late 1800s, William LeBaron Jenney finally solved the problem of how to build a structure with ten stories or more. Until then, builders had found that using brick walls would work only up to nine stories. The tenth story caused the whole building to crumble under its own weight. Jenney thought for months about how to overcome this puzzle, but without success. While relaxing, stacking matchsticks to make small boxes, he had an intriguing idea. Jenney covered his matchstick houses with playing cards and realized that this same process, using different materials, might be his answer. If he relied on steel beams for support and then added the bricks, the buildings might be strong enough to be built higher.

Following this blueprint, in 1885 Jenney oversaw construction in Chicago of the first skyscraper. The building, known as the Home Insurance Building, had only ten stories and was only 138 feet high, which is short compared to today's 1,454-foot Sears Tower. But that ten-story building is considered to be the father of skyscrapers. It was the addition of the extra floor that allowed Jenney to prove he could take buildings to new heights.

So what?

If your apartment or your doctor's office ended up being located in the first skyscraper, you would have to trust that the architect knew what he was doing. You would be going on faith that he hadn't made any mistakes and it would be okay to visit the tenth floor. God wants you to treat him that way also. He doesn't make mistakes, and he always knows what he's doing. In addition, he loves you so much that he will only do what is good for you. So you can trust God and have faith in his grand design. *The Bible promises:*

The name of the LORD is a strong fortress; the godly run to him and are safe. PROVERBS 18:10, NLT

January

What really makes a bull charge at a red cape?

PROVERBS 14:29

When a matador flashes a red cape in front of a bull, he's mainly giving the audience a "special effects" show. Perhaps afterwards, you might worry about wearing a red shirt or taking a red tablecloth on a picnic anywhere near where cattle roam. The matador would be proud that he caused such anxiety. That's because the red cape bothers us much more than it bothers the bull. When we see the color red, our blood pressure rises and our pulse speeds up. Red inspires us to be on alert because it is the color of blood, and blood is usually a sign of trouble or danger. The bull doesn't care about the color red. Bulls can't even see color—they're color-blind. The reason the bull charges at the matador is not because the cape is red, but because the cape is moving. Wave anything—in any color—at a bull, and he will get angry.

So what?

If the bull could only control his instincts and think, he could look ahead and figure out that being angry would be a big mistake. Showing anger ends in death by the matador's sword. If the bull could refuse to get upset, it's entirely possible that the matador would choose another bull that would put on a better show for the crowds. But bulls can't reason as we can. God gave us power over our impulses by giving us the ability to use our brains. *That is why the Bible tells us this:*

Those who control their anger have great understanding; those with a hasty temper will make mistakes. PROVERBS 14:29, NLT

Refusing to be angry is a choice. The more often we avoid anger, the less likely we are to be hurt by it.

January

When can books become a bother?
ISAIAH 34:16

Once there was a man whose goal was to own one copy of every book in the world. His name was Sir Thomas Phillips, and in the early 1800s he came as close as he could to doing that. He collected every printed paper available, even going so far as to gather other people's trash. Boxes of books were constantly being delivered to his house. Sir Thomas kept his books in boxes similar to coffins so they could be moved quickly in case of fire, which he greatly feared. But the books weren't organized, so he couldn't really use them. They were covered with dust and surrounded by logs, which Sir Thomas hoped would distract beetles from eating the covers and pages. He spent so much time and money collecting books that his daughters could afford to have only one dress each, and his family was always near bankruptcy.

When the floors of their house began to sag under the weight of all the paper, they decided they needed to move to a place with more room. It took 230 horses, 103 wagons, and 160 men to help move the books to the new house. Even then, some books were left behind, along with parts of wagons that broke because the books were so heavy. The final counting of Sir Thomas's collection was over 60,000 manuscripts and over a million books. What happened to all these books after Sir Thomas died? His family was still selling them at auctions a century later.

So what?

There was a lot of knowledge available to Sir Thomas in the books he had collected. But he was so busy gathering them, he didn't take the time to read them. Sometimes we allow our lives to be cluttered with busyness. We don't even take the time to read the one book that can teach us the most important things we'll ever need to know. *We are told:*

Search the Book of the Lord and see all that he will do; not one detail will he miss. ISAIAH 34:16, TLB

If you are searching the newspaper for good news or ads for free gifts, you're looking in the wrong place. There's no better source to find good news or free gifts than the Bible.

January

How did a medicine bottle turn into a toy?

JOHN 16:33

Childproof bottle caps have saved the lives of many children. But a Chinese company may have taken the idea of the childproof cap a little too far. Their aspirin bottle had thirteen separate moving parts, and it took thirty-nine steps to open the cap. As if that wasn't enough to keep children from opening the bottle, they replaced the tricky top with a new model every six months. Many people bought the bottles, but the company was surprised to learn why. Parents were buying them for their children to play with! The children liked trying to solve the puzzles.

So what?

Challenges can be fun when you're looking for something to keep you busy. But sometimes there are problems in life that aren't enjoyable. Maybe you're having problems in school, or with your family or friends. You feel that your burdens are too much for you to shoulder alone, and you're right. You need God's help. *He says:*

Here on earth you will have many trials and sorrows. But take heart, because I have overcome the world. JOHN 16:33, NLT

Ask God to walk with you through your troubles. His strength will comfort and support you.

January 14

How did a church leader help invent bowling?

JAMES 4:7-8

It is thought that bowling has been around since 5200 BC, because a stone ball and pointed stone pins were found in an Egyptian tomb. But bowling as we know it today began in the churches of fourth-century Germany. The people set up *kegles,* or war clubs, as pins. They would pretend that the pins were the devil. Using a rock or ball, they would try to knock down the pins. If they were successful, it was believed they were living a good life. If they failed, they thought it meant they had too many sins in their life. The number of pins used in German bowling was anywhere from three to seventeen until Martin Luther picked the number nine, which we began to use in the United States. The first indoor bowling alley was built of wood in London in 1450. Before that, a bowling "alley" was just the space between buildings or houses. Bowling balls were first made of stone, then wood, then iron, then rubber. They were just rolled off the palm of the hand, until two—and later three—holes were drilled. Eventually bowling was used as a way to gamble, so bowling "nine pins" was made illegal in 1839. Players avoided breaking the law by adding an extra pin.

So what?

No matter how many times we go bowling, we can't knock evil away. *There is only one good defense against sin, and the Bible tells us what it is:*

Humble yourselves before God. Resist the Devil, and he will flee from you. Draw close to God, and God will draw close to you. JAMES 4:7-8, NLT

God will strike down the devil if we call on God for protection.

January 15

What can you do with a useless tunnel?

MATTHEW 24:13

When you're working on a project, it's tempting to get sidetracked. But perhaps no one was more distracted than a man called William Henry "Burro" Schmidt. Schmidt was born in Rhode Island but went to California to prospect for gold. He was fortunate and did strike gold. But before he began to work his claim and dig further for gold, Schmidt got off track. He reasoned that he shouldn't begin mining his gold until he had built a tunnel through Copper Mountain. Then he could transport his gold directly to the road on the other side, to the smelter, where the gold would be purified. Schmidt began digging his tunnel in 1906, using just hand tools and, occasionally, dynamite. He worked alone, except for the company of his two burros, Jack and Jenny, which is how he got the name "Burro."

For the next thirty-two years, Burro dug, often in the dark, because there was not enough air in the tunnel for a candle to stay lit. He had set out to build his tunnel, and he wasn't going to quit. While Schmidt slowly dug through the mountain, all around him progress was taking place much more quickly. In 1938, after both a road and railroad tracks had been built over Copper Mountain, Burro finally reached the other side of the mountain. He was sixty-seven years old. But what can you do with a too-late, hand-dug tunnel? You can open it to the public as a tourist attraction, which is what Burro did for the next sixteen years until his death. He had earned a second nickname with his efforts: "The Human Mole," given to him by Robert Ripley from "Believe It or Not."

So what?

Even though Burro Schmidt may not have picked the most productive project, he has to be admired for his stubbornness and persistence. Once he got the tunnel idea in his head, absolutely nothing could stop him from finishing the task. That's the kind of devotion God would like to see in us concerning our faith. *He promises:*

Those who endure to the end will be saved. MATTHEW 24:13, NLT

We can learn from Burro's commitment. And with the Bible as our guide, we'll never need to worry about whether or not we're working on doing the right thing. We will be, so we should feel free to do it with all our might.

January 16

How could treason be committed during dinner?

LUKE 11:23

A traitor is someone who acts in a way that helps the enemy. There is no "middle ground"—you're either for or against your country. But what could you possibly do at the dinner table that would be considered an act of treason? If you lived in England in the seventeenth century, it was as simple as making a speech or a toast, or having a conversation over a drink. It wasn't even what you said—it was what you didn't say. There was a family named Stuart that had been banished from England. Some English people thought that the Stuarts should have been the real rulers of their country, and that it wasn't fair that they couldn't come back to England. So when people made toasts, they had a secret way of showing their support for the Stuarts.

In those days, tables were set with a small water bowl at each place so that the diners could rinse their fingers. If you were in favor of the Stuarts, as you raised your glass during a toast, you would be careful to hold it over your water bowl. That is how you showed that you were toasting the king "over the water," or across the ocean. Eventually the hidden meaning of the toast was discovered by those who didn't agree. As a result, water bowls were no longer put out on the tables. Even though the tradition of water bowls was brought back in later times, it is still considered an insult to have water bowls on the table when a British king or queen is dining.

So what?

Being a traitor is a serious offense. *When a person has Jesus as the Lord of his or her life, that person understands what Jesus meant when he said these words:*

Anyone who isn't helping me opposes me, and anyone who isn't working with me is actually working against me. LUKE 11:23, NLT

Because Christians are viewed as Jesus' representatives, our unkind acts can push people away from him. When others see that we're not trustworthy, they can become distrustful of God as well. There are many times each day when we can be a good representative of Jesus. Even the smallest bit of kindness and caring toward someone can end up being the exact invitation that person has been needing to join up with Jesus.

January 17

What causes bad breath?

JOB 12:10

There are four main reasons why your breath might be especially unpleasant in the morning. First, if your teeth have decaying food on or between them, your breath will smell bad. When you chew, talk, and swallow, saliva keeps your mouth moist and limits your bad breath, but those are things that we don't do while we sleep. Also, during the night, some of the skin inside your mouth is rubbed off and begins to smell. Add to this the fact that your stomach, which hasn't been given food to digest in a while, will churn and move during the night. This is normal activity that stirs up stomach gases, which rise to your throat. What you have eaten can also give you bad breath, but not because the odor is in your mouth. When you eat onions or garlic, their oils enter your bloodstream and get deposited in your lungs. When you breathe out, your breath will carry the smell of those oils mixed with carbon dioxide.

Mouthwashes can cover up, but not get rid of, bad breath. One man, Otto M. Dyer, was so worried about bad breath that he invented a breath-tester. He made a plastic mold that could be hidden in the palm. When he raised his hand to his mouth and coughed, he blew a puff of air into the plastic container, which sent some air to his nose so he could smell his own breath.

So what?

Every breath is a good one, even if it doesn't have the sweetest smell. Breath means life. Breathing is such an automatic part of our day, we seldom even think about it. Yet breathing is one of our most important bodily functions. Fortunately, we aren't responsible for keeping ourselves breathing, because trying to remember to take every breath would leave time for nothing else. God, as always, made plans to meet our needs. *The Bible tells us*:

In his hand is the life of every living thing and the breath of every human being. JOB 12:10, NRSV

God is so mighty. He is watching over everyone's breathing at the same time.

January

Why were the police called to an exercise class?

ACTS 1:24

Dr. Hunter was leading an exercise class for a group of elderly patients with arthritis. The senior citizens were supposed to raise their hands over their heads. That was a difficult exercise for them to do, so Dr. Hunter encouraged them by saying loudly, "Stick 'em up!" Just at that moment, someone walking by looked in the window. Soon the members of the exercise class heard sirens. Then police cars surrounded their building. It seems that the person looking in the window thought that he saw a robber holding up the whole class, yelling, "Stick 'em up!" The doctor explained that these oldsters were holding their hands up for their health, not for their safety. Finally the whole misunderstanding was straightened out.

So what?
People make mistakes. The person looking through the window thought he knew what was happening, but he didn't. Fortunately, God never makes mistakes. He always knows exactly what's going on. *The Bible says:*

Lord, you know everyone's heart. ACTS 1:24, NIV

If you're trying to do a good thing, God will know that you wanted to do well, even if it doesn't turn out right. He will understand what you meant to do. Even when you think no one could possibly understand, God does— every time.

January

Why isn't the bald eagle bald?

ISAIAH 40:31

It's common knowledge that birds have feathers. So why are we told that the national emblem is the *bald* eagle? Up close, the bald eagle has dark brown feathers on its body and white feathers on its head and tail. Long ago the word *balded* in Middle English meant "white fur or feathers." This bird was called the "balded" eagle, meaning the one with white head feathers. Through time, the word was shortened to *bald*. The bald eagle is a majestic and interesting creature. It takes only one mate for its whole life, and the pair builds only one nest. Every year the eagles add sticks to their nest, sometimes creating a home that weighs hundreds of pounds and measures almost ten feet across. The bald eagle was voted as the nation's official mascot in 1782. But if Benjamin Franklin had been given his way, the vote would have been different. His suggestion was that the best choice for an American symbol would be his favorite bird, the turkey.

So what?

No one can dispute that the eagle displays majesty and power, for its flight inspires awe and admiration. God understands the impact that the eagle can have on the people who see it. *That's why he refers to the eagle in these words of encouragement to us:*

But those who wait on the Lord will find new strength. They will fly high on wings like eagles. They will run and not grow weary. They will walk and not faint. ISAIAH 40:31, NLT

Any time you're feeling tired or discouraged, think of the eagle and spread your "wings." God's love will lift you up and carry you.

January

Why does a contest usually have first-, second-, and third-place winners?

ROMANS 2:7

If you think the answer to the above question is that the judges try to be kind by letting more than one person win, you're wrong. If you think more people will enter a contest if there are more prizes, that's not the reason either. The real reason will surprise you.

Long ago, in the 1600s, there was a horse race in England. The sheriff was in charge of the race and the prizes. He asked the silversmith to make a beautiful silver trophy for the winner. The silversmith went to work and returned to the sheriff with the trophy. But the sheriff didn't think it was grand enough for a prize. He told the silversmith to try again and sent him back to his shop. Later, the silversmith brought his second trophy to be inspected. Once again, the sheriff said no, the trophy wasn't quite good enough. The silversmith went back to work again. When he was finished making the third trophy, he took it to the sheriff, and this time, it was perfect. You would think the sheriff would have been happy, but instead he discovered he had a problem. He had three trophies now, but only one winner. The sheriff didn't want to waste the other two trophies, so he decided to have two more winners. Many people have gotten prizes because that sheriff was so picky!

So what?

Trophies are fun to win, but after time has gone by, they can get old and tarnished and rusty. God has promised us some prizes at the end of our lives, and they will never get old. *The Bible tells us:*

He will give eternal life to those who patiently do the will of God, seeking for the unseen glory and honor and eternal life that he offers.
ROMANS 2:7, TLB

The trophies of glory and honor and eternal life can't be looked at, held in our hands, or kept on a shelf. But they are the best rewards we could ever win, and they will belong to us forever.

January

When was a sunny day bad for baseball?
1 JOHN 1:9

It was a sports fan's dream come true—no more games canceled because of bad weather. The Astrodome in Houston opened in 1965. It was a huge stadium with clear plastic panels in the roof to let the sun in. Everyone was excited that the dome was finally built, and it wasn't until the first baseball game was played inside that people realized there was a problem. The skylights were letting in so much sunlight that when the players looked up, they kept missing the ball because of the glare. And the steel girders that held up the ceiling crisscrossed so much that the ball seemed to get lost in the air. No one had expected this mistake, and lots of people tried to think of a way to fix it. Maybe the players could use a neon orange ball. Perhaps special sunglasses could be used. The solution that worked was to paint all 4,596 ceiling panels a dark color. Then the glare was gone, and athletes could once again "Play ball!"

So what?

The Astrodome, which is huge, had a problem that was also huge. Yet the owners still were able to find a good solution. When you make a mistake, no matter how big it is, God can help you. And when you do something wrong, no matter how big your sin is, you don't have to figure out a way to fix it. The Bible already tells you what to do. You need to talk to God. *The Bible says:*

If we confess our sins to him, he can be depended on to forgive us and to cleanse us from every wrong. 1 JOHN 1:9, TLB

If you've done something wrong, make it right by going right to God.

January

Which fish takes aim at its lunch?
GENESIS 1:21

There is a type of fish that is called an *archer*. This fish has an interesting way of getting a meal. The archer likes to eat insects. The problem is, most insects are flying above the water's surface. But the archer has a solution. This fish swims to the surface of the water and puts its mouth near the top. Then the archer does something amazing. It spits a stream of water up into the air, and the water hits an insect flying by. The water knocks the insect into the water, and the archer is able to gobble it up.

So what?
The archer has a special talent. If you were in charge of giving talents to fish, would you have thought of making a fish that spits water? God's imagination is so much more creative than ours. God has made the world a fascinating place! *The Bible says:*

God created great sea creatures and every sort of fish and every kind of bird. And God saw that it was good.   GENESIS 1:21, NLT

We have fun looking at God's creatures too! When we see some of God's creation, we can tell that everything God did "was good."

January 23

What did people do about their cuts before Band-Aids?

PSALM 147:3

People used to help their cuts heal by smearing a cream made from the myrrh plant onto a piece of cloth and sticking the cloth to their skin with honey. Fortunately for us, Earl Dickson came up with a better idea in 1920.

Earl's wife was so clumsy that she was forever cutting herself while preparing meals. He usually bandaged her wounds by taping some gauze over the cuts. Earl decided to make some bandages that his wife could put on by herself when he wasn't home. He cut lots of pieces of tape, laid them sticky-side up on a table, and laid a patch of gauze on each one. He covered each bandage to keep the tape from drying out or sticking to itself. After that, when Earl's wife got hurt, she could just peel a bandage and stick it on. Earl's boss at Johnson & Johnson liked this new idea and began to sell the bandages, which they named *Band-* (because of the tape) *Aids* (for first-aid).

So what?

Today almost everyone uses Band-Aids to cover cuts. But sometimes it's not your body that needs fixing. Maybe your feelings are hurt or your heart is sad, and your pain is on the inside. That's when only God can help. *The Bible says:*

He heals the brokenhearted, binding up their wounds. PSALM 147:3, NLT

If you ask him to, God will cover your hurt with his love and protection until it is better—and he doesn't even need a Band-Aid!

January

How did a little girl's letter change history?
MATTHEW 18:10

When Grace Bedell, who lived in New York, was eleven years old, she wrote a letter to a very famous man. The letter told this man that he should grow a beard. Grace thought his face was too thin and that he would look better with a beard. One day, when this man came to Grace's city on a train trip, he asked to see her. Grace went to meet him, and when he saw her, he gave her a kiss and said, "You see, I let the whiskers grow for you, Grace." Who was the man? You've seen pictures of him yourself. His name was Abraham Lincoln.

So what?

You can imagine that it was quite exciting for Grace to learn that a president had listened to her. She couldn't help but feel important. But a president isn't nearly as powerful as God. Do you know what God thinks about children? Jesus explains to us how God feels. *Jesus says this:*

Beware that you don't look down upon a single one of these little children. For I tell you that in heaven their angels have constant access to my Father. MATTHEW 18:10, TLB

God loves everyone, but he especially loves children. And he always listens to their prayers.

God wants you to know that you are very important to him and that he always has time for you. He will never be too busy to pay attention to your feelings. God gives you, his child, a special place in his Kingdom. If you ever feel that your friends or parents aren't listening to you, or that you have problems that no one seems to be able to help you with, remember that you have someone on your side who will always make you his top priority. Tell God that you want him to be your Friend, and he will always be available for you to talk to him. You don't even have to write a letter to get his attention!

January

Why are barns red?

PROVERBS 3:9-10

So many barns are red that you might think someone long ago said, "Red is a cheerful color. Let's all make our farms prettier by painting our barns red." But that didn't happen at all. Actually, the weather is responsible for barns being red.

Back in the 1700s, farmers needed to protect their wooden barns from the warping and rotting that different kinds of weather can cause. After experimenting, farmers found a good mixture to paint on their barns. It was made from skim milk, lime, and a chemical called iron oxide. When these three things were mixed together and spread on wood, they dried to a plastic-like coating that lasted a long time. The iron oxide in the mixture was a reddish color, and it turned the wood red. Since almost everyone used this mixture, red-colored barns sprang up everywhere. Soon people got so used to seeing red barns that they became the custom.

So what?

Barns are places where people store crops and shelter animals. The Bible has something to say about filling barns. Barns are so large that it would take a long time to fill a barn completely from bottom to top. *But God's Word tells us:*

Honor the Lord by giving him the first part of all your income, and he will fill your barns with wheat and barley. PROVERBS 3:9-10, TLB

When we love someone, we want to share our things with that person. That's why we give to God first whenever we earn any money. We might not need wheat or barley, but God knows just what we do need. And when we give something to God, he promises to give back more than he gets—enough blessings to fill up a whole barn!

January

Which sport started with a fruit basket?

ECCLESIASTES 12:1

Football was played in the fall, and spring was the season for baseball. What kind of indoor ball game could be played in the winter? Dr. James Naismith, who worked at a Massachusetts YMCA in the late 1800s, came up with the answer.

Dr. Naismith nailed peach baskets to the balconies on each end of the gym. Players tried to throw an old soccer ball into the peach baskets. Fans watching the games sat in the balcony behind the baskets. To help their favorites win, when a ball came toward the basket, fans would slap the ball, kick it, or even hit it with umbrellas or sticks to help it land in the basket. Soon wire was put behind the baskets so the fans couldn't reach the ball. But when the ball hit the wire, it bounced off to unexpected places. The wire backboard was eventually changed to wood, and finally to glass. The baskets themselves were another problem. Janitors had to stand on a ladder through the whole game to throw the balls back out of the baskets! Soon a hole was made in the bottom of the baskets so the ball would come out. Then a trapdoor was made in the bottom of the basket that would open when a rope was pulled. Twelve years after basketball started, a net was made that the ball could fall through. The soccer ball was replaced with a bigger, lighter ball; and sneakers, which slid around on gym floors, were changed to shoes with better traction. Now players were ready to really play ball!

So what?

When you're young, God gives you lots of energy and the desire to jump and run and play until you've exhausted yourself. It's good for you to participate in sports, because that gives you the chance to use up energy in a fun way. But God doesn't want you to get so involved in the game that you lose sight of him. He wants you to play honestly and fairly and with kindness to your teammates and the other team. If you'll do anything to win, like cheating or injuring someone on purpose, you're forgetting God and not showing others that he is your main coach. *The Bible says:*

Don't let the excitement of being young cause you to forget about your Creator. ECCLESIASTES 12:1, TLB

You're never too young to show others how important God is to you.

January

Who was Chester Greenwood, and why did he cover his ears?

PROVERBS 16:28

Chester Greenwood just had to do something about his ears. They were embarrassing him because whenever it got cold (which happened often in Maine, where he lived) they would turn unusual colors like red, white, purple, or blue. Not only that, but he couldn't even try out the new ice skates he'd gotten for his fifteenth birthday because his ears hurt when they got too cold. Chester had tried wrapping a scarf around his head, but it was scratchy. He needed to come up with a better idea. Here is what Chester thought of next: He twisted some wire so that it went across the top of his head, and made a loop on each end near his ears. Then he asked his grandmother to sew some material onto the loops. She put black velvet on the inside by his ears, and beaver fur on the outside of each loop. She sewed the wire across Chester's hat to make it stay. When Chester went out to ice-skate, his ears stayed covered up and toasty for the first time. Soon lots of people in his town wanted ear warmers like Chester's, and he finally had to open a factory when he was nineteen just to make them all. Chester never dreamed that his funny ears would make him famous as the inventor of earmuffs!

So what?

God gave us ears for many good reasons. But one thing God *doesn't* want us to use our ears for is listening to gossip. If a friend tries to tell you a story about someone else, don't listen. Tell your friend you'd rather not hear it. *The Bible says:*

Gossip separates the best of friends.   PROVERBS 16:28, NLT

Help your friends stop gossiping about each other by refusing to listen, even if you have to wear earmuffs in the middle of summer!

January

Where did the first little red wagon come from?

GALATIANS 6:2

The first wagon for kids started out as a wooden tool cart. A man named Antonio Pasin, who had made a wagon for himself, soon found that all of his coworkers wanted wagons too. Antonio decided to sell his wagons, but he didn't want to use wood anymore. The new wagons should be made of steel and should be painted bright red. Antonio found a perfect but unusual place to get the steel for his wagons.

When automobiles were made in factories, their bodies were made of steel. The window parts had to be cut out of the big sheet of steel, and the cutouts became scraps that no one used. Antonio bought the window scraps, and they were exactly the right size for his Radio Flyer wagons. Most of the wagons were simple, but in 1936 a very fancy wagon was built. It was cream colored with red decorations, and it had a horn, a pasted-on dashboard that looked like a car's dashboard, shiny hubcaps, and even electric headlights. Since the Flyers were made out of car steel, it seemed only natural to make the wagon look like a car.

So what?

Antonio was doing a good thing when he made wagons for his friends. He helped them solve their problem of how to carry their tools. *The Bible tells us:*

Share each other's troubles and problems, and in this way obey the law of Christ. GALATIANS 6:2, NLT

Jesus wants us to try to help others whenever we can. Maybe we can help in a small way like helping someone who has trouble carrying groceries, or in a big way like sharing our groceries with someone who has a problem with homelessness and hunger. Every day, look for a new way to help someone who has troubles or problems, and you will find another way to please God.

January

Who made the first metal detector?
MATTHEW 7:14

In airports, people and their luggage must go through metal detectors before getting on the plane. The detectors look for items made of metal, so that no guns, bombs, or other weapons can be taken on a plane. Would it surprise you to know that someone thought of this idea long before the September 11, 2001, terrorist attacks? Actually, the idea of being able to detect metal came about more than two thousand years ago!

The inventor was a Chinese emperor. He stayed in his palace most of the time, but that didn't stop his enemies from trying to kill him. Once, when an enemy snuck into the palace, the emperor's doctor had to whack the enemy with his medical bag! A better way was needed to keep enemies out of the palace.

What the emperor invented was a door made of magnetite, a mineral that acts like a magnet. If anyone tried to come through the door wearing armor or carrying weapons made of metal, he wouldn't be able to enter the palace. He couldn't go through the door because he would be stuck to it!

So what?

The emperor's enemies had a hard time entering the palace. *And the Bible tells us that some people will have a hard time getting into heaven:*

The gateway to life is small, and the road is narrow, and only a few ever find it.   MATTHEW 7:14, NLT

The door to heaven can be found only by those who are sincerely looking for it. Searching for the way to heaven is something Jesus wants to help you do. He says, "I am the way. . . . No one can come to the Father except through me" (John 14:6, NLT). If you learn the way, you can make it your job to help your friends find Jesus too, for he is the only way to heaven.

January

When is it good manners to wipe your fingers on the tablecloth?

ROMANS 12:10

There are lots of very specific rules about how to behave at the table, including which fork to use or how to place your silverware when you're finished eating. Long ago, there were only a few rules. When we hear them now, we say to ourselves, "Well, of course, everybody knows that." But until the rules were made up, people could do whatever they wanted at the table. Here are some of the earliest suggestions about manners:

Don't sit on the table.
When you cough or sneeze, turn away from the table so that nothing lands on the tablecloth.
Don't put your whole hand into the serving pot. Just use three fingers.
Don't fish around for the biggest piece of meat—just take the first piece that you feel.
Don't lick your fingers when they're greasy. Wipe them on a cloth if there is one, and on the tablecloth if there's not.
Don't throw your chewed bones back into the pot.

So what?

These rules sound strange to us today, but they were the beginnings of good manners—attempting to be polite and kind to the people you are eating with, whether you know them or not. *The Bible tells us:*

Love each other with genuine affection, and take delight in honoring each other. ROMANS 12:10, NLT

When you use good manners, you are honoring those who are at the table with you. You are helping to make their meal more pleasant. Good manners can also help you make good friends.

January

Why do we call our favorite shopping place the "mall"?

PSALM 37:23

The word *mall* comes from the French word *maille,* which means "mallet." What in the world does a mallet have to do with shopping?

Long ago, there was a game like croquet that was played in Italy, England, and France. It was known as "palle maille," which meant ball and mallet. This game was played in an alley or a quiet street without traffic. People began calling these lanes *pall malls.* Businessmen realized that the players would probably buy something to drink after the game, so they opened shops around the edges of pall malls. More shops joined them, hoping to get business from the audiences that came to watch the games. After a while, no one played the game anymore, but the malls stayed full of shops, and people still enjoyed walking from store to store.

So what?

Maybe you haven't thought much about where your feet are taking you. Have you been spending your time running away from where you've just hurt someone's feelings, or stolen something, or told a lie? Perhaps you've walked up to someone to tell hurtful gossip, or walked through the mall spending money that you should have been saving, or walked over to a meeting place to join friends who aren't really good for you. If Jesus were following right behind you, would he be pleased with where you were going?

The Bible tells us:

The steps of the godly are directed by the LORD. He delights in every detail of their lives. PSALM 37:23, NLT

You can't go somewhere unless your feet go too. Ask Jesus to help you keep them pointed in the right direction, and he will guide you through every little detail of your life.

February 1

How did a mistake start the invention of the match?

PROVERBS 26:21

John Walker didn't mean to start a fire, but when he did, he invented the match. In 1827, he was working on an experiment, trying to make some explosives to be used in guns. John poured some chemicals together in a container and stirred them with a stick. When he pulled the stick out, John saw that some of the mixture was clinging to the end of his stick. He scraped the stick on the stone floor, trying to wipe it off, but the mixture didn't come off as he expected it to. Instead, it burst into flames!

After John got over his surprise, he got the idea of making smaller sticks with the chemical mixture on the end, and he amazed his friends by pulling these sticks, or matches, between rough paper and igniting them.

The matchbook was invented over sixty years later, in 1889, by Joshua Pusey. He put fifty matches inside a folding cover, but he made a big mistake. He put the striking surface *inside* the cover with the matches, which made the whole book catch on fire instead of just one match! Finally, the Diamond Match Company bought Joshua's idea and rearranged the matchbook with the striking surface *outside*. Many mistakes made the match!

So what?

Matches replaced coal and wood as an easier, faster way to start a fire. The Bible uses fire to explain to us why we shouldn't argue. *It says:*

A quarrelsome man starts fights as easily as a match sets fire to paper.
PROVERBS 26:21, TLB

Stay away from anyone who likes to argue, because he is trying to pull you into a fight. He knows you disagree with what he's saying, and he wants you to talk back to him. But if you do try to argue back, you will never convince this person that he is wrong. He will always find something else to say to keep you talking back. Just keep your opinions to yourself. Then he will go somewhere else to find his fight.

February

When was a little girl sent through the mail?
PHILIPPIANS 2:4

It was time for five-year-old May Pierstorff to visit her grandmother. May's parents wanted to have her ride the train, which was the best way to travel in 1914, but the ticket was way too expensive. So May's parents came up with another idea. There was a much cheaper way for May to get to Grandma's—through the mail!

May and her parents went to see the postmaster. He checked all the post office rules. A package could not weigh more than fifty pounds. That was fine, because May weighed just forty-eight pounds. The only live creatures that could be mailed were baby chicks. May's hair was yellow like a chick's, and she was still very young, so the postmaster said May could be called a baby chick. He put a label on May's coat, and a stamp on the label, and then May was driven to the train station. But May didn't sit with the people—she sat with the mailbags, where the man in charge of the baggage watched over her. When the train got to Grandmother's town, May was taken to the post office there. All the rest of the mail stayed at the post office overnight, but May was driven to her grandmother's house right away, as a very special delivery!

So what?
May's parents were pleasing God by going to so much trouble to let her visit her grandmother. *The Bible tells us:*

Don't think only about your own affairs, but be interested in others, too, and what they are doing. PHILIPPIANS 2:4, NLT

May's parents knew that her grandmother was probably lonely and missing her family. Perhaps her grandmother couldn't see well enough to travel, or was too weak to do so. May's parents were thinking of what would make her grandmother happy, so they sent May to visit even though they had to go through a lot of trouble to do it. From the verse above we know that God is pleased when we are thoughtful of others.

February

Why did America destroy its own spaceship?

2 CORINTHIANS 1:3-4

Your teachers and parents probably tell you often that you need to make sure your work is accurate and exact. Here's a good reason: In 1962, the space program launched a spaceship called *Mariner 1*. It was supposed to reach the planet Venus after one hundred days in space. Then it was to explore for the first time what was underneath the thick clouds surrounding Venus. It was a glorious, exciting plan.

When the day of the launch came, *Mariner 1* left the launching pad—and fell back to earth four minutes later. The computer had told the spacecraft to do the wrong thing. Why did the computer do that? Someone had programmed the computer with the wrong instructions. The big mistake was discovered to be one tiny line—a hyphen—that was left out. This one missing hyphen cost $18.5 million because *Mariner 1* had to be completely destroyed.

So what?

The man who made the mistake must have felt awful about what he had done. When we feel that bad, there's usually nothing we can do to make ourselves feel better. But if we turn to God during bad times, we will get help. *The Bible tells us:*

All praise to the God and Father of our Lord Jesus Christ. He is the source of every mercy and the God who comforts us. He comforts us in all our troubles. 2 CORINTHIANS 1:3-4, NLT

God will forgive you when you cannot forgive yourself. He will help you to see that no matter what you have done, he still loves you and always will. If you think that you can't face your family or friends because of something you said or did, tell God about it. He can help you deal with your troubles.

February

Why did a sculptor carve his statues smaller and smaller?

PSALM 139:14

Once there was a sculptor named Alberto Giacometti. He wanted to carve statues of human beings, but he wanted to leave out everything that wasn't important. He would begin by making a statue that looked like a normal person, only smaller. Then he would look at it and decide to chip first one part, then another part, off the statue. Alberto worked hard on making statues this way for four whole years. When he was finished, he had carved so much off of each statue that he could fit them all into six little matchboxes. People called them the "thin man" statues and collected them and put them in museums because they were so different from everyone else's.

So what?

We should be glad that God didn't think like Alberto the sculptor. When God was creating us, he gave us lots of "extras": We have eyes to see a sunset, ears to hear laughter, tongues to taste peppermint, and hands to pet kittens. *The Bible says:*

Thank you for making me so wonderfully complex! PSALM 139:14, NLT

God knew what we would need and what we would want, and he used his best ideas to make each of us.

February

What should you know about mistletoe?
PSALM 1:3

You've probably heard of the plant that people hang over the door at Christmastime and stand underneath to get a kiss. It's called mistletoe. But before it's picked to be hung up in our homes, mistletoe is doing something that's not so nice. Mistletoe is a parasite. It grows by sticking some roots into another plant or tree and stealing that plant's food.

The most interesting thing about mistletoe is how its seeds are spread. Some kinds of mistletoe have white, sticky berries that birds like to eat. The seeds are inside the berries, and when birds peck the berries open, seeds stick to their feet and beaks. After the birds have eaten, they fly away and wipe the seeds off on tree bark. That's where a new mistletoe plant will begin to grow.

There are thirty-five different kinds of mistletoe. One of the kinds has berries that get so full when they're ripe that they explode! The exploding berries shoot seeds as far as fifty feet, and another mistletoe can start where they land.

So what?
The Bible says that Christians are like trees that can't be harmed—even by a damaging plant like mistletoe. *It says this about God's people:*

They are like trees planted along the riverbank, bearing fruit each season without fail. Their leaves never wither, and in all they do, they prosper. PSALM 1:3, NLT

That's the kind of tree to be, because it is protected while it grows. If we read and follow God's Word, he will make sure that we are protected while we keep growing and learning more about him.

February **6**

When was the last time you dropped your pencil and found $40,000?

PROVERBS 16:16

That's exactly what happened to fourteen-year-old Todd Running one day at school in 1981. Todd's pencil rolled into the air-conditioning duct on the floor of his classroom. His summer math class got very exciting all of a sudden, because when Todd reached into the duct, he pulled out $100 bills—*lots* of them! Who would get to keep the money?

The teacher tried to claim it, because he had opened the rusty vents that morning to make the classroom cooler. The company that owned the trailer where the class was held said the money belonged to them. The school board said that it should be their money because they had scheduled the math class in the first place. The problem was finally taken to a judge.

The judge decided that Todd should have the money, because he was the one who actually found it. So what does a fourteen-year-old kid spend $40,000 on? Nothing. The judge gave Todd the money, but he put Todd's mother in charge of it until Todd's eighteenth birthday.

So what?

The day Todd found the money, he got double blessings from God. *The Bible tells us:*

How much better to get wisdom than gold, and understanding than silver! PROVERBS 16:16, NLT

Todd was doing what was most important by going to school to understand more and to become wiser. He never dreamed that he would get smarter and richer at the same time!

February

Why would two brothers booby-trap their house?

PSALM 124:7

Two grown brothers shared a house in the 1940s. The way the brothers lived, however, was very strange. Their house was filled from floor to ceiling with furniture, rags, newspapers, cardboard boxes, and car parts. The collection even featured fourteen pianos, thousands of books, and six United States flags. One of the brothers, Langley, liked to invent things. He tried to make a car motor that could run the electricity in the house, and to invent a vacuum that could clean pianos. The other brother, Homer, had been a lawyer until he got a disease that made him blind and nearly paralyzed. The brothers stayed in their house all the time. They boarded up the windows and had the water and electricity turned off. Langley went out only at night to get supplies.

People made up wild stories about hidden treasure in the house. After some thieves tried to break in, Langley began making tricky traps with all the junk in the house. He rigged wires and ropes so that garbage would fall on anyone who tried to enter. Finally, neighbors noticed that no one had seen either of the brothers in a long time, and they called the police. The police went into the house and found that the sick brother, Homer, had died in his bed. As they began to clear out the house, they discovered what had happened. Langley had accidentally gotten caught in one of his own traps and died first. Then, because Langley could no longer help, his brother, Homer, died as well.

So what?

When Langley was lying underneath his own trap, unable to get out, you can imagine how much he must have wanted someone to come along and free him. Sometimes we're caught in a trap of our own making. Maybe we've told a lie that has caused someone harm, or we've cheated and don't want anyone to know. We need God's help to correct our mistakes, and he's standing close by, ready to set us free. If you haven't already asked God to be a part of your life, that's the first step. You can invite him silently—right now, right where you are—and he will begin to share his power with you. Don't worry if you don't see immediate results. God cares for you so much that he will provide you with a solution to your problem—one that you can't even imagine yet. *We can believe in the promise that God will stay with us until we can say:*

We escaped like a bird from a hunter's trap. The trap is broken, and we are free! PSALM 124:7, NLT

February

Who called 9-1-1?

JOHN 14:13-14

Something was wrong. The emergency switchboard in Blacksburg, Virginia, received a 9-1-1 call, but no one on the other end said anything. Then a second call came in, also completely silent. Several similar calls followed. The call was traced to Linda and Danny Hurst's home. Sheriff's deputies had no idea what kind of situation would be waiting for them as they raced to the Hurst house. Guns drawn, they approached the residence. All seemed quiet. Further investigation showed that the Hursts weren't home, and no one else seemed to be there either. There was no evidence of burglary or foul play. How were the 9-1-1 calls being placed? The deputies finally solved the riddle. Near the telephone and answering machine, they found a hanging basket. And in the basket was a tomato that had become mushy and dripped on the machinery, causing a short that resulted in the 9-1-1 calls.

So what?

It's good to know that we can call 9-1-1 and get a quick response—even a tomato can get an answer! It should be much more important to us to know that we can get an answer from God when we call for his help. *Jesus said about God, his Father:*

You can ask for anything in my name, and I will do it, because the work of the Son brings glory to the Father. Yes, ask anything in my name, and I will do it!   JOHN 14:13-14, NLT

We don't even need a phone line to call God, because we have a prayer line. We should use it all the time—in calmness as well as crisis.

February

What can you do with a pack of camels?

PSALM 55:22

After a war with Mexico, the United States gained a half-million square miles of land. The land was like a desert and didn't even have a railway to help deliver supplies. Americans who had visited there thought the land was similar to land in the Middle East and suggested that using camels would be a good idea. Camels can close their eyes to keep out blowing sand, and they have two rows of eyelashes to protect their eyes. Camels can go a week without water, travel as many as forty miles in a single day, and carry a thousand pounds.

Congress voted to buy seventy-six camels in 1856. The camels came from Egypt and Turkey and arrived in Texas. The army was going to use the camels to move soldiers and supplies into the new desert territory. But then the problems began.

Soldiers were afraid of the camels, and so was every nearby horse. The veterinarian from Turkey who was hired to take care of the camels had no training. His method for curing a camel was to tickle its nose with a chameleon's tail. Soon it became obvious that the United States just wasn't prepared for the camel plan. The idea was good, but the results were disastrous.

After a while the Civil War started, and the army gave up on the camel idea. But what could be done with the camels? Someone made the suggestion that the camels could be used for delivering mail—a "Camel Express"! But that wasn't practical either, for the same reasons that the army couldn't use the camels. Eventually the camels were delivered (not through the mail!) to circuses and zoos.

So what?

Whenever something is too heavy for us to carry alone, we look around for help. Even though these particular camels couldn't be used as workers, people have long depended on camels as beasts of burden. Unfortunately, camels can't carry some of the heaviest burdens we encounter—like illness or anger or sorrow or fear. God does not expect us to shoulder these weights by ourselves. *The Bible tells us:*

Give your burdens to the Lord. He will carry them.   PSALM 55:22, TLB

One of the blessings of asking God into your life is the assurance that you won't be facing anything alone ever again. God will be with you whenever you cross a "desert" in your heart, lightening your load with his comfort.

February

Why are a cat's whiskers better than a man's?

PSALM 104:24

A man's whiskers can change his appearance and keep his face warm. If he shaves them off, all he loses is some hair. But cats depend on their whiskers for survival. Cut them off, and you could take away the cat's ability to care for itself. That's because the cat uses its whiskers to judge distances. The whiskers stick out from the cat's cheeks, upper lip, and forehead. The cat has very sensitive nerves where the whiskers meet skin. When something brushes against the tips of the whiskers, the cat's face feels it. Cats can tell from their whisker "antennae" how far away something is, which is important for an animal that pads around in the dark. If the tips of its whiskers are touching both sides of an opening, the cat can tell that the rest of its body won't fit through, and it avoids getting stuck.

So what?

If we were in charge of creating an animal like the cat, would we have had the good idea to give the animal such helpful whiskers? Probably not. God thought of a very creative way to help the cat protect itself. The cat is just one of the animals to which God gave amazing abilities. Nature is full of wonderful examples of God's planning. *Taking the time to notice them will help us realize:*

O Lᴏʀᴅ, what a variety of things you have made! In wisdom you have made them all. The earth is full of your creatures. PSALM 104:24, NLT

February **11**

Why do movie scenes start with a black-and-white-striped clapboard?

PSALM 119:126

Quiet on the set!" yells the director as the black-and-white-striped board is raised, clicked, and removed. The movie scene begins. As familiar as this process may be, the reason for using the clapboard is not as well known. The writing on the board tells filmmakers which scene is being filmed and how many times it has been repeated. But why do they open, clap, and shut the hinged board at each beginning? It's for matching the sound to the actions of a movie. It is important that actors' mouths move at exactly the same time as their words are spoken, and the clapboard is a way to test the sound. It is always closed as soon as the camera starts to roll, so that the sound technician can use this "snap" sound for reference. The technician makes sure that the sound of the clicking of the clapboard is heard when the film shows the hinged section being closed. This adjusts the rest of the sounds in the scene so that they, too, will be heard at precisely the right time.

So what?

Sometime or another we all feel like we're not matching up with the rest of the world. When we speak, no one seems to understand what we're trying to say. When we act, the results don't come out the way we expected. If you're frustrated and discouraged, call on God to be the director of your life. He will be glad to take action. *The Bible says:*

LORD, it is time for you to act.   PSALM 119:126, NLT

God's timing is never wrong. When you need to get your act together, he will help you match your actions with a pace that's appropriate for you.

February 12

When can colors be confusing?

JEREMIAH 29:13

More males than females suffer from color blindness, the inability to see colors. One out of every twelve men and one out of every two hundred women are color-blind. Color blindness may be hereditary, and it can show itself in several ways. Some people have trouble telling the difference between yellow and green, or red and green, because these colors appear gray to them. People who are completely color-blind see only shades of black and white. There are people who aren't even aware of their color blindness. They think that the gray they're seeing is called "red," and that everyone else is seeing gray too. As for animals, tests have shown that dogs and cats are completely color-blind. Horses, bees, and monkeys can tell the difference between some colors, and hens can tell all colors apart.

So what?

There are different ways to use your eyes to "see," regardless of your ability to tell colors apart. One kind of sight helps you to learn about the world through your eyes. With the other kind of "sight," you use your mind and spirit to understand more about the truth of God. *He says:*

If you look for me in earnest, you will find me when you seek me.
JEREMIAH 29:13, NLT

Search for God in Scripture and in the world. He will open your eyes to new and wonderful knowledge about himself.

February 13

How did clay flowerpots help make buildings better?

2 CORINTHIANS 12:9

Joseph Monier was trying to make a bigger flowerpot, but he learned how to build a bridge instead. He was in the gardening business and was having trouble making large flowerpots with clay. In 1849 he thought of covering some wire netting with concrete. He was very pleased with the results. Then he began thinking of other uses for his concrete. He tried using iron bars instead of wire netting and realized that large structures, like bridges and dams, could be strengthened. What made Monier's idea so valuable was that bars alone, or concrete alone, were not as strong as when the two were combined. As an added bonus, the iron bars didn't even rust when they were covered in concrete. Monier patented his idea, which provided a way to make better bridges and buildings.

So what?

Clay or cement, without mesh, can't withstand too much pressure and crumbles easily. Maybe you've been feeling a little like that lately. You're feeling a little shaky and worried, and you're wondering if sooner or later you're going to crack or fall apart. Strengthen yourself by asking God to help you. Nothing is too much for him to handle, and he invites you to come to him when you are weak. *He says:*

My gracious favor is all you need. My power works best in your weakness. 2 CORINTHIANS 12:9, NLT

Ask God to be the iron in your structure, and together you will form a super-strong combination.

February

14

Could you be found guilty by reason of rice?

1 CORINTHIANS 13:4-7

Courtroom justice used to have some strange customs. Long ago in China, the person on trial was given a mouthful of rice to prove his innocence or guilt. If he could swallow the rice, the verdict was "innocent." The Chinese believed that a guilty person, who was usually nervous and had a dry mouth, wouldn't be able to swallow the rice.

So what?

Does the way you behave every day identify you as being a follower of Jesus Christ? Would a judge and jury find enough evidence that you are obeying God's command to love your neighbor as yourself? How can you show this love? *The Bible gives us a checklist:*

Love is patient and kind. Love is not jealous or boastful or proud or rude. Love does not demand its own way. Love is not irritable, and it keeps no record of when it has been wronged. It is never glad about injustice but rejoices whenever the truth wins out. Love never gives up, never loses faith, is always hopeful, and endures through every circumstance. 1 CORINTHIANS 13:4-7, NLT

Do you believe that Jesus is God's one and only Son? If you do, let him forgive your sins and take control of your life. Then you will get a life sentence in heaven!

February
15

Why were people buying raccoon tails?

JOHN 8:12

In 1954 the price of raccoon tails went zooming from twenty-five cents to eight dollars a pound, and children began running around with bows and arrows, moccasins, and rubber knives. What was the cause of such strange behavior? Davy Crockett had arrived on the scene! Walt Disney Studios aired a one-hour television program called *Davy Crockett, Indian Fighter*. It was the first program of a three-part series, and no one, including Walt Disney himself, expected it to be very popular. But children loved the show, and that's when all the products began to be sold.

Before the year was over, the Davy Crockett theme song had been recorded by seventeen different artists. Crockett's picture appeared on lunch boxes, jigsaw puzzles, comic books, baby shoes, tablets, and anything else on which it could be printed. The most easily identified symbol of the Disney show was the raccoon cap that Crockett wore, with the tail down the back. Altogether, souvenir sales totaled more than 100 million dollars.

So what?

Perhaps you're like a lot of children and love to imitate what's popular. Doing that makes you feel like you're the same as everyone else. Part of growing up is deciding if the adults in your life that you're copying are leading you in the best direction. The only true guide for your life will always be Jesus. *He says:*

I am the light of the world. If you follow me, you won't be stumbling through the darkness, because you will have the light that leads to life.
JOHN 8:12, NLT

You don't have to worry about your security or well-being when you choose to follow Jesus. He never lies, he will never betray you, and he will always lead you to do the right thing. If you're saying to yourself, "Somebody would have to be superhuman to live up to that description," you're absolutely right! Jesus, not any television superhero, is the only true superhuman, for he is God. He lived on this earth as a human being for about thirty years, showing by his teachings and his miracles that he is a real superhero, and the only one worth following.

February

16

How are crossword puzzles connected with Christmas?

REVELATION 3:20

The first crossword puzzle was published in a small newspaper, *The New York World,* by Arthur Wynne for the 1913 Christmas edition. Wynne wanted something a little different for the issue, so he made a diamond-shaped puzzle that was similar to one he remembered his grandfather showing him. The readers loved Wynne's "word-cross."

People who had to travel by railroad in the 1920s became the crossword puzzle's biggest fans—so much so that dictionaries were provided on trains, and crossword puzzles were even printed on the backs of dining-car menus. In England, librarians blacked out copies of the crosswords so fanatics would return their newspapers. Germans dropped pamphlets over England during World War II that had crossword puzzles saying bad things about England. One time a minister even challenged his congregation to complete a crossword puzzle about his sermon!

So what?

Crossword puzzles give clues. It's your job to fill in the spaces with the word that you think the clue is describing. *Here's a clue for you, and the answer has five letters:*

Look! Here I stand at the door and knock. If you hear me calling and open the door, I will come in, and we will share a meal as friends.
REVELATION 3:20, NLT

Can you figure out who thinks you're so special that he stands outside your door, knocking and calling your name, and waiting patiently for you to answer? He won't enter without an invitation, but he wants you to know that he's ready to meet you anytime and give you gifts of peace, hope, and encouragement. Would it make any sense to "fill in the blank spaces" with the name of any friend of yours? No, because there isn't any human who could love you as much as this "mystery guest." Who is it? Open the door and see for yourself—his name is J-E-S-U-S.

February

Why did farmers have curfews?

JOHN 1:5

If your parents tell you when you need to come back home, they've just given you a "curfew." Where does that word come from? Back in medieval times, farmers would keep a fire burning in the fields or woods so they could stay warm in winter. For safety's sake, the fire was supposed to be put out after the day's chores were finished. But sometimes the farmers forgot, and an out-of-control fire would destroy everything in its path. A law was passed that required all open fires to be covered up at dusk. A bell would ring from the village church to remind everyone to *couvre-feu*—in French, this means "cover fire" and sounds very much like what we pronounce as "curfew." The British, who thought *couvre-feu* was a good idea, began to use the custom in their country and changed the spelling of the word. Eventually, the curfew came to mean the time when people should stop what they're doing and go home.

So what?

Most of us don't like being cold and in the dark. When darkness comes, we naturally gravitate toward the warmth of the light. Our souls are no different. When we are chilled with the dark feelings of hopelessness, helplessness, or fear, we long to see a flame's flicker. The Bible offers words of encouragement and invitation by teaching us that God's Son, Jesus, is light, and his light is much stronger than darkness. *It says:*

His life is the light that shines through the darkness—and the darkness can never extinguish it. JOHN 1:5, TLB

Don't settle for a small spark when you're discouraged. Remember that you have access to a bonfire!

February

Where were houses built roof-first and books read back to front?

DEUTERONOMY 7:9

The Chinese culture contains a long, rich history of traditions and customs that in some cases might seem the opposite of the ones we know. Until the modernization of China (and sometimes even now), when Chinese people met someone, they shook their own hand instead of their new acquaintance's. China had "lending libraries" on the street curbs, where children who couldn't afford to buy comic books could rent them long enough to sit by the booth and read them. Letters were addressed by putting on the top line the place where they were being sent, and writing the name of the person who was to receive it on the bottom of the envelope. It was acceptable to put the saucer on top of the teacup instead of beneath it, in order to keep the tea warm. Books started at the back and ended in the front. Houses were built from the top down.

So what?

Every country, as well as every generation, has its own customs. We owe much of what we know to our ancestors, who carefully passed on to us what experience had taught them. *The Bible tells us of our greatest heritage:*

Understand, therefore, that the Lord your God is the faithful God who for a thousand generations keeps his promises and constantly loves those who love him and who obey his commands. DEUTERONOMY 7:9, TLB

Start a custom of your own by passing on the legacy of God's love to someone else. It will be a lifesaving experience.

February 19

Why did a priest decide to live with lepers?

JOHN 10:11

It takes a very special person to devote his entire life to the service of others. Father Damien was one of those special people. From his teenage years, Joseph (Father Damien's name until he became a priest) was good at many tasks. He served his community as a painter, schoolteacher, cook, gardener, carpenter, and even doctor—whatever was needed. He and his brother studied together to become priests. Joseph's brother wanted to be a missionary, but he wasn't strong enough to work because of health problems. At twenty-two, Joseph became "Father Damien." He decided to serve as a missionary in his brother's place, and spent the next ten years in the South Sea Islands. He then volunteered to run a leper colony on the Hawaiian island of Molokai. Leprosy was believed to be a highly contagious disease, although now it is considered no more contagious than a common cold, and it is completely curable. At that time, however, not many people were willing to visit, much less live with, the lepers. The priest helped change their dirty, neglected colony into a tidy, pleasant village. Father Damien did eventually contract the disease himself after living with the lepers for ten years. On the last Sunday he was alive, the Gospel reading for the day was this: "I am the good shepherd. The good shepherd lays down his life for the sheep."

So what?

Father Damien is mentioned in history because he followed Jesus with his whole heart, soul, mind, and body in an attempt to be a "good shepherd." Not everyone can serve God in the same way as Father Damien. But we can look for opportunities to serve in our own ways. These are just a few suggestions: Make friends with the lonely new student at school. Carry a heavy bag of groceries for a disabled neighbor. Read to someone in a nursing home. Jesus laid down his life for us. If we follow him, God will be pleased by all of our efforts to take care of his "flock."

I am the good shepherd. The good shepherd lays down his life for the sheep. JOHN 10:11, NLT

February

Why did the United States have a one-day president?

JOHN 9:4

If you could be president of the United States for a day, what things would you do? David Rice Atchison had his chance in 1849. It was time to swear in the new president, Zachary Taylor. But Inauguration Day fell on a Sunday, and Taylor didn't want to be sworn in until Monday. The last president, James K. Polk, was finished with his duties on Saturday. What would happen on Sunday, March 4? It would be a day without a president, and that couldn't happen! The only way to fill the vacancy was to have the next official in line, President Pro Tem David Atchison of the Senate, take over for that day. Did Senator Atchison make a big difference to our country on that day? As it happens, he was exhausted from finishing all the business in Congress from President Polk's last day. On Saturday night, very late, David finally went home to sleep. He was so tired that "President" Atchison spent his entire one-day term on Sunday snoring away in bed!

So what?

Senator Atchison missed a once-in-a-lifetime chance of having the power and doing the work of the president of the United States. That's not very important, though, in comparison to having God's power behind us so we can do his work. We have that opportunity every day. *Jesus said:*

As long as it is day, we must do the work of him who sent me.
JOHN 9:4, NIV

You've been authorized to become God's representative today—will you take charge or waste the chance?

February

Where does dew come from if it doesn't fall from the sky?

ISAIAH 44:3-4

Most of us, when we see wet grass in the morning, imagine the dew falling softly during the night when we weren't looking. But dew doesn't "fall" at all. It comes from the air, but not like rain. Most of the time, air contains water vapor. At night, when the temperature cools down, the air can't continue to hold its moisture. A blade of grass, as it gets cooler, also cools the blanket of air surrounding it. When the air reaches a certain low temperature, called the "dew point," water from the air condenses onto the grass blade. But not all moisture on the grass is officially dew. The grass also draws water from the soil, and this moisture is pushed out through the blades. It would be possible to notice this process all day long, except that the heat of the day causes droplets to evaporate before they're completely formed.

So what?

Grass needs moisture to live, and so do we. Have you ever been so thirsty that just a swallow of water would be a real treat? God understands our physical needs. He uses the idea of thirst to let us know how abundantly he will bless us—not just with a drop or a swallow, but beyond our every expectation. *He says:*

I will give you abundant water to quench your thirst and to moisten your parched fields. And I will pour out my Spirit and my blessings on your children. They will thrive like watered grass, like willows on a riverbank. ISAIAH 44:3-4, NLT

God knows the needs of his children, both body and soul. You can count on him to nourish your soul with his constant, flowing love.

February

When can you strike a nerve at the dentist's office?

PSALM 59:9

The dentist offers you a shot of Novocain, which will make your mouth numb, but you're afraid. How will you be able to warn the dentist when he's hitting the nerve of your tooth if you can't feel anything? You worry that if he drills, the dentist will damage the nerve, and then you'll need even more work done on your tooth. Do you need to be upset about this? Absolutely not! When you experience a pinch of pain as the dentist works on your tooth, chances are very good that he's nowhere near the nerve. The most sensitive part of your tooth is where the enamel (the hard, white coating on your tooth) and the dentin (the tissue directly underneath the enamel) meet. If you told the dentist to stop there, he wouldn't be able to work on your tooth at all.

So what?

Being on guard all the time is very stressful. There are so many situations to protect yourself from during the course of a day. Sometimes you're so busy looking out for dangers that you don't have time to do anything else. It can make you angry and frustrated and sad that you don't have any time to relax or play. If you could, you'd love to hire someone to protect you from threats to your heart and soul and feelings, just as you would hire a bodyguard to protect your body.

There is good news. You can have protection for your soul, and it's free for the asking. *Each time you feel afraid, repeat to yourself:*

You, O God, are my place of safety.   PSALM 59:9, NLT

He is always watching out for you and will use his almighty power to defeat your fears, which can become your enemy. Don't let fear steal your peace of mind or your concentration. Instead, trust that God will clear your path so that you can continue to live your life knowing what pleases him and what does not.

February

Which president had a giant bathtub?
ISAIAH 1:18

In the 1800s, if you wanted to take a bath, you probably had to go downtown to do it. Most homes had no bathtubs, so the city provided a bathhouse where you could get clean. If you *were* fortunate enough to have your own tub, you would have taken your baths in the kitchen, where most bathtubs were kept.

The first tubs were around seven feet long and weighed as much as half a ton. The water for your bath came from the sink, but you had to heat it on the stove first before you poured it into the tub. Because it was expensive to fill up the tub, many people thought bathing was a luxury. So instead, they filled their tubs with dirt, growing vegetables and flowers there.

The White House bathtub had to be made even bigger than normal because President Taft, who weighed 350 pounds, once got stuck in it. The president ordered a new tub, which was so huge that when it was delivered, four grown men all climbed inside it at the same time and got their picture taken.

So what?
Imagine how good it felt to be clean in those days, whenever you finally did get around to taking a bath! Do you know that letting God make you clean inside feels even better than a bath? *In the Bible, God says:*

Come now, let us argue this out. . . . No matter how deep the stain of your sins, I can remove it. I can make you as clean as freshly fallen snow. Even if you are stained as red as crimson, I can make you as white as wool. ISAIAH 1:18, NLT

If he hasn't washed you clean yet, it's only because you haven't asked him to. God is waiting for you to come to him. How can you do that? Right now, right where you are, tell God that you want to be his child. Tell him you're sorry for the wrong things you've done and ask him to let you start over so that you can live out the plans he has for you.

February

Can you tell what a bird eats by looking at the bird?

MATTHEW 6:26

The answer is as plain as the beak on its face! A woodpecker's beak is long and strong enough to peck through the bark of a tree and reach inside for insects. Birds that eat seeds need short beaks to crack them open. The beak of a bird that eats meat, like an eagle, has a hook in it. That helps the bird rip up the meat into pieces small enough to swallow. What about the beak of a pelican? This bird eats fish, and there is a big pouch under its bill so that it can catch a fish by scooping it into the pouch. So looking at a bird's beak gives you a clue about what a bird will do!

So what?

Different birds eat different foods, and God makes sure that the foods they need are nearby. *Jesus tells us:*

Look at the birds. They don't need to plant or harvest or put food in barns because your heavenly Father feeds them. And you are far more valuable to him than they are. MATTHEW 6:26, NLT

When you see birds today, remember that God is watching over you even more than he watches over them.

February

How was the toothbrush invented?

PSALM 34:1-2

A prisoner, a bone, and a hog all helped to make the toothbrush. Long ago, before anyone had thought of a toothbrush, people kept their teeth clean by chewing on a stick until one end got soft and frayed like a brush. Sometimes they dipped a finger in chalk or salt and then rubbed their teeth. Toothpicks were another way to take care of teeth, and toothpicks were very fancy then. They were made of gold or jewels, and people would stick them in their hats or hang them on necklaces when they weren't using them. The first brushes came from China, where the Chinese made them out of hairs pulled from the backs of wild hogs. The invention of the toothbrush as we know it came from Joseph Addis. He worked on the toothbrush while he was in jail. First, he saved a bone from one of his meals and poked some holes in it. His prison guard gave him some bristles. Joseph tied the bristles into little bundles, cut them to make them even, put glue on the ends, and stuffed them into the holes.

So what?

Toothbrushes clean your teeth, but they don't do anything to improve the words that come out of your mouth. While you're making your teeth bright and shiny, think about polishing up what you say. *The Bible tells you how to do it:*

I will praise the Lord no matter what happens. I will constantly speak of his glories and grace. I will boast of all his kindness to me.
PSALM 34:1-2, TLB

Saying cheerful, encouraging, pleasant things will not only freshen your day, but everyone around you will feel refreshed also.

February

What makes a Mexican jumping bean jump?
ISAIAH 44:22

First of all, it isn't really a bean. It's a seed. It comes from a shrub in Mexico. And it doesn't really jump. It rolls and tumbles because there is a moth larva, or caterpillar, inside. The caterpillar drilled a hole to get into the seed, where it eats the inside. Eventually, the caterpillar becomes a moth and crawls back out of the hole.

But before the caterpillar goes to sleep, waiting to turn into a moth, it moves all around in the seed. Why? When the seed is in sunlight, it becomes too hot inside for the caterpillar. So the little creature tosses and turns until it can feel that the seed has rolled into some shade.

So what?
When a cloud covers the sun, the caterpillar probably enjoys being able to rest for a moment, because there is shade everywhere. Then the cloud blows away, the sun comes back out, and the caterpillar must start rolling again. People like the sun much more than the caterpillar does. We're happy when clouds move away and the world gets bright again. God talks about clouds when he tells us how he gets rid of our sins. *He says:*

I have swept away your sins like the morning mists. I have scattered your offenses like the clouds. ISAIAH 44:22, NLT

When you see a floating cloud, remember that the same God who sends the clouds skittering across the sky wants to dust your soul clean with just a puff of his holy breath. If you've never asked him to, why not ask him now?

February
27

What did a president of the United States, a candy seller, and a stuffed animal have to do with a favorite children's toy?

PSALM 135:13

When Theodore Roosevelt was president, he went hunting one day in 1902. A bear cub was captured and tied up for the president to shoot, but President Roosevelt said he would not kill the defenseless bear. The story became famous when it was reported in the newspaper and drawn as a cartoon.

A man named Morris Michtom owned a stationery and candy shop. His wife, Rose, sometimes made little stuffed bears, which they would put in the window of their shop. The Michtoms saw the cartoon about the bear, and that gave Morris an idea. He asked his wife to make some special bears like the one in the cartoon. Then Morris wrote a letter to the White House, asking if the new bears could be named after the president. President Roosevelt wrote back to Morris and said, "I don't think my name is likely to be worth much in the bear business, but you are welcome to use it." So Morris put the new bears in his shop window, next to the cartoon. The stuffed bears were called by the president's nickname: "Teddy's bear." We call them *teddy bears* today, and we celebrated their one-hundredth birthday in 2002!

So what?

It's fun to think about how names got started. Many times we don't even remember why we call something by a certain name. And sometimes names themselves get forgotten too. But there is one name that will always be remembered. *It says:*

Your name, O LORD, endures forever; your fame, O LORD, is known to every generation. PSALM 135:13, NLT

Because people have told each other about God for thousands of years, you know who he is today. If you tell others about Jesus, you can pass his blessings into the future.

February

Why do farmers want their calves to swallow magnets?

PROVERBS 27:23

Baby calves need a lot of attention. Their moms, the cows, must know this, because they take turns babysitting each others' calves. One cow will stay near a group of calves to watch them while the other cows graze farther away. After a while another cow will take over the babysitting job.

One thing the mother cows can't do is guard what their calves eat. For some reason, calves especially like to eat metal, like wire, staples, tacks, and nails. Farmers call this the "hardware disease," and they know how to solve the problem. When a calf is born, the farmer will often force it to swallow a magnet. All the metal that the calf eats will stay together in its stomach, stuck to the magnet.

So what?

Did you know that the Bible tells farmers they are to take good care of their animals? *This is what God's Word says:*

Be sure you know the condition of your flocks, give careful attention to your herds. PROVERBS 27:23, NIV

This is what the farmers are doing when they take good care of their calves. Whenever you are in charge of something, especially when you're taking care of your pets, it's important to give each job your whole attention. Do your best at every task, and you will be pleasing God.

March 1

Can a beaver make a tree fall in just the right spot?

PSALM 145:16

Lots of stories are told about the beaver, but not all of them are true. It is said that a beaver knows exactly where to chew a tree so that it will fall where the beaver wants it to. This is not true. The beaver doesn't have any idea where the tree will come down, and he has to be quick to get out of the way or risk getting hit.

It is true that beavers use their tails to help steer themselves when swimming. And beavers do slap their tails on the water to warn each other of danger. Also, once dams are built, beavers always repair them immediately if they come apart.

Some mother beavers keep their babies inside "houses" made of mud and sticks. The doors are underwater, so only beavers can swim in. Beavers don't get splinters when they chew wood, because they chew only live trees that hold lots of sap. The branches are then kept underwater, so the wood doesn't get dry enough to have splinters.

So what?

It's hard for us to understand how powerful God is and how he can take care of every creature in the whole world at the same time. As just one example, think about all the pets in your neighborhood. What if you had to take care of every one of them yourself? That would be quite a chore. Next, imagine that you were in charge of all the animals in your state—not just the pets, but also all the wild animals, like the beavers, squirrels, rabbits, prairie dogs, and foxes. You would have to spend all your time feeding and watching over all these creatures.

Now think about God. He takes care of all the animals in your city, in the whole country, and all around the world—not just for one day, but every day and night. And besides that, God pays careful attention to each human being on earth, too! *The psalmist David says this about God:*

You satisfy the hunger and thirst of every living thing. PSALM 145:16, NLT

God provides for all of his creation, including you! But sometimes he expects the human beings he created to do their part to help other living things. God wants to work through his children to satisfy everyone's hunger and thirst. Can you think of a human being or an animal creature that you can help?

March

Why keep a broken bell?

GALATIANS 5:13-14

There was a big crowd in front of the State House in Philadelphia. The new bell had arrived from England, and it was about to be rung for the first time. The bell ringer swung the clapper, the bell made a lovely bong—and then it cracked all the way up the side! Now it had to be fixed. A brass maker named Mr. Stow was hired to do the job. First he melted the bell, and then he remolded it. The bell was tested again. This time it just went *thud* when it was rung, so back to the shop it went. Again it was remade, and again it was rung. Finally it was perfect—which was a good thing, because this became the Liberty Bell that was rung in 1776 to gather everyone when the Declaration of Independence was read out loud for the first time.

In 1777, however, the Liberty Bell was in trouble again. Americans had to take it down and sneak it out of town at night to hide it from the British army, because the army would probably try to melt it and make bullets out of it. The bell stayed in the basement of a church for a year. Then it was brought back to Philadelphia and hung up again, to be rung on important occasions for the next fifty-seven years. But one day something amazing happened when it was rung. The Liberty Bell cracked again! What was really surprising was that it broke on exactly the same day, July 8, as it had cracked the first time—fifty-nine years earlier. It hasn't been rung since then, but it has been visited and admired by many Americans.

So what?

Liberty is another word for freedom. Some people say that they don't want to be Christians because they would have no freedom—there are too many rules to follow. But this is not true at all! *The Bible says:*

You have been called to live in freedom—not freedom to satisfy your sinful nature, but freedom to serve one another in love. For the whole law can be summed up in this one command: "Love your neighbor as yourself." GALATIANS 5:13-14, NLT

When we follow this one rule, we have true freedom and live in a way that pleases God.

March

Why did a dog want to live in a graveyard?
JOHN 3:16

Once there was a stray terrier named Bobby. He was adopted by Jock Gray, a policeman in Scotland, and as time went on, they were always seen together. When Jock died in 1858, Bobby was left all alone. The third day after Jock died, Bobby trotted up to the restaurant where he and Jock had often had lunch together. The owner threw him his usual biscuit, but Bobby didn't eat it. Instead, he carried his food back to Jock's grave and ate it there. Bobby came to the restaurant every day for the next fourteen years, and he always took his food back to his master's grave. Because everyone admired his loyalty, the townspeople took care of Bobby. He was given a license and a collar, shelter when it was cold, and plenty of food. Bobby was also allowed to be at the churchyard whenever he wanted (which was all the time). And when he died, the townspeople buried him in the best place—next to Jock.

So what?
Bobby was amazing because he wouldn't leave the man he loved: even after death, even though he didn't have to stay, and even though he was just a dog. God's love for us is much stronger than a dog's could ever be. *The Bible tells us:*

God so loved the world that he gave his one and only Son, that whoever believes in him shall not perish but have eternal life.   JOHN 3:16, NIV

God loves you so much that he allowed Jesus to die—the biggest sacrifice that could be made—so that you could become God's child. If you want a best friend whom you can always count on, tell God so. Invite God into your heart right now, and you can have his loving and faithful companionship from this moment on.

March

Why would a bird need goggles?

2 CORINTHIANS 5:7

Your eyes water when they are hit by a strong wind. You might have wondered whether this happens to a bird's eyes when it flies. The answer is no, because a bird's eyes are not made the same way as ours. Birds have an extra eyelid that we don't have. This clear eyelid is close to the beak in the corner of each eye. When the bird is not flying, the eyelid just slides over the eye when the bird blinks, wiping away dirt and soothing the eye with oil. But this unique eyelid, called a *nictitating membrane,* does something special when the bird flies. It sticks in a closed position, covering the eyes like a pair of goggles. Since the nictitating membranes are clear, the bird can still see through them.

So what?

God gave eyes to birds, animals, and people so that all creatures can see where they are going. We learn to trust our eyes to give us information about the world. But God asks us to go a step further. He asks us to believe in him *without* being able to see him. *The Bible says:*

We live by believing and not by seeing. 2 CORINTHIANS 5:7, NLT

If you were blind and your friend took your hand and led you into the living room, you would have to trust her word about where you were standing. You couldn't use your eyes to see where you were. God says that we can trust what he tells us to be true. So how about letting him lead you?

March **5**

How did Monopoly become a game?
LUKE 18:25

Sometimes dreams really do come true. Charles Darrow didn't have a steady job. During the Great Depression, no one had much money. Charles fixed appliances and even walked dogs to earn money for his wife and child. He dreamed of getting rich.

One night a friend brought a handmade board game called The Landlord's Game to Charles's house. Charles loved the game and decided to make one like it himself, with a few changes. He used linoleum for the game board and carved the game pieces out of wood. He used buttons for money. It took Charles a whole day to make one copy of the game, but his friends kept asking for the game and telling their friends how fun it was, so they wanted one too. Everyone enjoyed pretending to be very rich for a few hours.

Eventually, Charles offered to sell his game to the Parker Brothers Company. But they came up with fifty-two reasons why the game wouldn't sell. So Charles hired a printer and made five thousand copies of Monopoly. When these all sold, Parker Brothers changed their mind and bought the rights to Monopoly. Since The Landlord's Game had inspired Charles, Parker Brothers bought the rights to that game too. Then the company was free to make and sell copies of Monopoly, and Charles Darrow became rich.

People have played Monopoly in an elevator, in a tree house, underwater, on a balance beam, and on a fire truck. Once, in a college town, a whole block of streets was closed off and students played a life-sized Monopoly game. Bike riders with walkie-talkies told the players about each other's moves, and big foam-rubber dice were thrown from the third floor of a building.

So what?
When Monopoly became famous and Charles Darrow became rich, he may have thought he had it all. *But the Bible tells us:*

It is easier for a camel to go through the eye of a needle than for a rich person to enter the Kingdom of God! LUKE 18:25, NLT

People with lots of money need to be careful about becoming greedy or selfish or proud. All of those things could make them think that they don't need God. They may think that their money will take care of them. If you become rich, remember to stay humble, and then you won't have to worry about getting a camel squashed through a needle's little hole!

March

Why is the Oscar named after a farmer?
JOHN 6:40

The Oscar—that gold statue of a knight standing on a reel of film—is the trophy that entertainers win at the annual Academy Awards ceremony. The winners' names are kept secret until each envelope is opened onstage, and then they are presented with the trophy. But why is the statue named Oscar? It didn't even have a name until 1931. That's when Oscar Pierce, a wealthy Texas farmer, unknowingly entered the picture. His niece was the librarian for the Academy of Motion Picture Arts and Sciences. One day she casually mentioned that the knight on the statue looked a little like her Uncle Oscar. A newspaper reporter overheard her comment and published a story, including the information that "employees have affectionately dubbed their famous statuette 'Oscar.' " After that, the name became official, and it has been used ever since. By the way, the period during World War II was the only time the Oscar wasn't made of metal. Because of shortages, the Oscar was still awarded, but it was made of wood.

So what?
Years from now, Oscar statues will be sitting on a shelf or mantel somewhere, after the actors and actresses who won them have already died. We're not meant to stay on earth forever. We have an invitation to move to heaven. *Jesus says:*

It is my Father's will that all who see his Son and believe in him should have eternal life—that I should raise them at the last day. JOHN 6:40, NLT

When you ask Jesus into your life, a place is saved for you in heaven. That's a lot better than ending up on some dusty shelf!

March

Is there air pollution in outer space?

PSALM 19:1

There isn't any air in outer space, but there *is* trash! This litter comes from over 1,200 satellites that are orbiting around the earth. Parts of satellites like ceramic tiles, nuts, bolts, and other pieces of metal are now floating around in the galaxy. How do we know? NORAD, the North American Aerospace Defense Command, keeps track of the trash. NORAD is located in fifteen buildings underneath the Colorado Rockies and has computers that track space debris. Using telescopes, radios, and radar from around the world, NORAD keeps track of thirty thousand transmissions a day. NORAD's cameras, which are like telescopes, can take a picture of the light reflected by an object the size of a basketball from as far as twenty thousand miles away.

It's important to know where the trash is. Otherwise, it might be mistaken for an enemy missile. Or it might fall to earth and hurt someone. Neither of these things is likely to happen, though. Lots of the trash is over three thousand miles away from earth, and it will circle there in "deep space" for hundreds or even thousands of years. About once a day, some piece of the closer litter falls out of orbit, but it almost always burns up before it reaches the ground. Of course NORAD can't see everything—some objects are just too small—but amazingly, one researcher was able to watch a glove floating by.

So what?

We earthlings do not have the technology yet to clean up the trash we have left in space. When we know how to collect it, though, we should make sure that we remove all the waste materials that are floating around. Perhaps you will be the scientist who develops a trash-collecting system for space. *The Bible reminds us:*

The heavens tell of the glory of God. The skies display his marvelous craftsmanship. PSALM 19:1, NLT

We should work at keeping God's special gifts of creation clean!

March

Why do people always get onto a horse from the left side?

HOSEA 1:7

People sometimes think that a horse knows its left from its right, and that the horse likes being mounted from the left side. That's not true. Actually, horses are trained to expect to be mounted from the left. They are trained by riders who have been taught to mount on the left. Who started this custom, and why?

You have to go far back in history for the answer. When people carried swords as weapons, they carried them on their left side. Then if a man needed to pull out his sword, he would reach across his body with his right hand and grab the handle. If a rider mounted on the right side of his horse, his sword might poke the horse or get caught on the saddle. So instead, people always mounted from the left.

So what?

A person who had a sword and rode on a horse may have been more powerful than someone who walked unarmed, but riders who thought that they were completely protecting themselves were making a mistake. Power belongs to God. *He says:*

I will save them—not by bow, sword or battle, or by horses and horsemen, but by the LORD their God. HOSEA 1:7, NIV

God doesn't need any help from weapons, horses, or soldiers. Anyone who believes that a weapon makes him strong is forgetting where strength really comes from.

March

What would you do if you went to a restaurant and the menu offered steamed kangaroo and rhinoceros pie?

ROMANS 14:17

Francis Buckland would have picked up a fork right away, because he was used to having odd meals. When he was a boy, Francis's dad always used to tell him that he should never turn up his nose at a dish he'd never tried.

Francis loved studying animals, and he even took some of his pets with him when he went to college: a chameleon, a guinea pig, an eagle, a duck, a rat, a jackal, a hedgehog, a snake, a bear, and an old crocodile. Francis rode on the crocodile's back when it was alive and tasted it after it died. And Francis always seemed to have a little box in his pocket, where he kept toads or insects he had collected.

People started sending Francis strange insects or fish or lizards that they found. Francis learned what all the creatures' names were and wrote about them in magazines. He soon became famous.

He always kept his strange appetite, enjoying whale, deer soup, tortoise, ostrich, mice, Japanese sea slug, and even a giraffe that was killed in a zoo fire. What good did Francis do by eating all these strange dishes? He formed a club of people who volunteered to see whether humans could get used to eating strange animals. The answer to most of the meals was, "No way!"

So what?

Thinking about eating strange foods is fun, but it's not very important. *The Bible says:*

The important thing for us as Christians is not what we eat or drink but stirring up goodness and peace and joy from the Holy Spirit.
ROMANS 14:17, TLB

If you have some spare time, do something nice for someone else. God is pleased when you help not only someone who is hungry for food, but also someone who is hungry for kindness.

March 10

Why does a pencil have six sides?

JOHN 21:25

It was a compromise. A round pencil was easiest to hold, but it cost a lot to make. A square pencil was cheaper, but it was too uncomfortable to write with. The hexagonal pencil is a mixture of round and square—it's both inexpensive to make and comfortable to hold.

Who decided to make pencils yellow? Back in 1890, a company in Austria began making a very high quality pencil that everyone admired. Austria's flag was black and yellow. The pencil already came with black lead, so the wood part was painted yellow to match the flag. When other companies made pencils, they copied the yellow color, because everyone thought that the yellow Austrian pencils were the best.

Pencils have been around for a long time, and they write for a long time. The lead in most pencils can last long enough to draw a line thirty-five miles long.

So what?

John was one of the authors in the Bible who wrote down some of the things that Jesus did. *John said:*

Jesus did many other things as well. If every one of them were written down, I suppose that even the whole world would not have room for the books that would be written. JOHN 21:25, NIV

If pencils had existed back then, and if John had written down every single thing about Jesus, just imagine how many pencils he would have used up!

March
11

Why do we have white half-moon-shaped marks at the base of our fingernails?

MARK 4:26-27

These marks are called *lunules,* and they are caused by the fact that your nail is only loosely attached to your finger there. Air is trapped between your nail and your finger. The rest of your nail is pinker because the fingernail is attached tightly to your finger, and you are seeing the blood in your finger through your clear nail.

Now check your nails for white spots. If you see one, that is where you bumped your nail while it was being formed and getting ready to grow. It takes your nails six months to grow, so you will be watching that white spot move slowly closer to the tip of your nail for a long time. One day the spot will be clipped off when you cut your nails. If you have a ridge in your nail, you must have been sick while that part was being formed. The ridge will stay on your nail, growing closer to the tip, for the next six months.

There are some other things you might want to know about nails. Your nails grow slower in winter and faster in summer. It takes a toenail four times longer to grow than a fingernail. A hangnail doesn't really have anything to do with hanging. It is named from the Old English word *ang,* which means pain—and that's what a hangnail gives you! Finally, the middle fingernail grows faster than any of the others, and the hand that you use the most is the hand that has faster-growing fingernails.

So what?

God takes care of many things for us that we can't do for ourselves. We can't make our nails grow, or keep ourselves breathing while we are asleep, or make saliva come into our mouths to keep them moist. We can't turn day into night or make the rain fall. God knows we need these things, and he makes sure that we get them. *Jesus tells us:*

A farmer planted seeds in a field, and then he went on with his other activities. As the days went by, the seeds sprouted and grew without the farmer's help. MARK 4:26-27, NLT

That's what a loving God we have! He keeps our bodies, and our world, running for us, because we would be helpless without him.

March

Why is a bunch of lions called a "pride"?

ISAIAH 9:6

Long ago in England, the rich people didn't have much to do. To keep themselves entertained, they invented a game to play while they were sitting around. They decided to make up special names for groups of animals. It was boring to say "a group of lions," or "a group of seals," so they chose fancier words. They decided that a group of lions would be called a *pride,* and seals in a group would be called a *pod.* Some of the other names they made up were a *parliament* of owls, a *rafter* of turkeys, a *kindle* of kittens, a *hover* of trout, and an *exaltation* of larks. All of these names were printed in books, because people wanted to know how to speak and act like the rich people who made up the names. Soon many people began using the game names, and that is why today we still say a *gaggle* of geese and a *covey* of quails.

So what?

Jesus has many names, but his names were not made up for fun. We are taught to call Jesus by these names because each one helps us to know him better. *The Bible says:*

These will be his royal titles: Wonderful Counselor, Mighty God, Everlasting Father, Prince of Peace. ISAIAH 9:6, NLT

Jesus' names explain his love for us and how he can help us.

March

Who was Dr. Pepper?

PROVERBS 1:23

Dr. Charles Pepper was the owner of a drugstore, and he had a beautiful daughter. His employee, Wade Morrison, fell in love with the daughter. Dr. Pepper didn't like this romance, so Wade moved to Waco, Texas, and opened his own drugstore. Wade often told Charles Alderton, the pharmacist in his store, about his broken heart.

One of Charles's jobs was to make drinks at the soda fountain. Charles saw that people were tired of the same old drinks, so he experimented with mixing flavors together. One combination of tastes became very popular with their customers, and Wade and Charles named the drink "Dr Pepper." (By the way, the soft-drink name doesn't use a period after *Dr.*) They thought it might make the real Dr. Pepper like Wade more. He never did, though. Charles Alderton, who actually invented the drink, just wanted to be a pharmacist, so it was Wade who became rich as the head of the Dr Pepper Company. Dr Pepper is the oldest major soft drink in America. It was introduced to the nation at the World's Fair in 1904.

So what?

If the soda-fountain man poured a cool drink for you on a hot day, it would make your life nicer for a few minutes. But God can make your life better forever. *The Bible says:*

Come here and listen to me! I'll pour out the spirit of wisdom upon you and make you wise. PROVERBS 1:23, NLT

Visit the Bible more often than the soft-drink machine, and you will fill yourself up with what's really important.

March **14**

Why were the first napkins as big as towels?

1 JOHN 1:9

If you had no fork or spoon to eat with, your hands would get pretty messy. That's why the first napkins, used by the Romans, Egyptians, and Greeks, were as big as towels. These napkins also came in handy for drying your hands after dipping them in the bowls of perfumed water at the table. And when you were finished with your meal, there was plenty of room to carry your leftovers home in your napkin.

Napkins got smaller after silverware became popular and eating wasn't as messy. The napkin got its name from an old word that meant "a little tablecloth"—*naperon.* This is also how we got the word *apron.* Over the years, both the napkin and the apron have helped to make eating a much neater event!

So what?

We use napkins to keep our mouth and hands clean. But how can we make our soul clean? The truth is, we can't. Only God can do that. *The Bible tells us:*

If we confess our sins to him, he can be depended on to forgive us and to cleanse us from every wrong. 1 JOHN 1:9, TLB

March

What's the spin on revolving doors?

JOHN 14:6

As you push your way through a revolving door, do you ever wonder why it's there? It's not used to count people, or to keep them from crowding together through the doorway. So why does it turn around instead of opening like a regular pull-open door? And why do some buildings have revolving doors, while others don't? The revolving door's only purpose is to conserve energy—not yours, but the building's. The air pressure outside a building is different than the air pressure inside. This difference causes air to gush from the inside to the outside, or from the outside to the inside, whenever a regular door is opened. When cold air flows in, the building's furnace tries to warm it up. When hot air flows in, the building's air conditioner tries to cool it down. The building doesn't know that the blast of air is only temporary, so energy is wasted as it tries to change the air's temperature. A revolving door never lets a clear, strong gust of air into the building, so there's no change in air pressure, no gust of wind, no change of temperature, and no waste of energy.

So what?

Revolving doors are fun to push around and around. But sometimes it seems like your life keeps you going in circles that are not fun. Every time you clean your room, it gets messy again. Whenever you promise yourself you won't tell another lie, maybe you hear one coming out of your mouth. Your intentions to save your allowance are ruined when you spend it all again. *If you begin to feel that you're stuck in life's revolving door, listen to Jesus:*

I am the way, the truth, and the life. No one can come to the Father except through me. JOHN 14:6, NLT

When we open our hearts to Jesus, our challenges will not all disappear. But with him, we have the promise that he will be with us in our troubles and take us safely through the door of eternal life.

March

Why do we drive on the right side of the road?
MATTHEW 7:13-14

Although no one seems to know for sure, it appears that shields, wagons, and horsewhips are three reasons we drive on the right side of the road in America. In Roman times, long before America existed, soldiers carried their shields in their left hands, so they always tried to pass strangers on the right. Later, teams of wagon horses were led by the right hand down the road as a man walked in front of them. He wanted passing wagons to be on his left so he could make sure the horses didn't get too close. During the days of the covered wagons, which rarely had front seats, the driver sat on the back of the left rear animal. Since the driver was usually right-handed, sitting far to the left allowed him to manipulate the whip more easily and reach all the animals. In addition, he often carried a rifle in his left arm, aimed toward the left, so the trigger could be fired quickly with his right hand. Because the driver could see the wagon wheels better on the left side of his wagon, he could make sure that his wheels didn't lock with another wagon's if he kept his own to the right.

So what?

People need to pay attention when they're driving. It's necessary to know where you're going and to keep your eyes on the road. Getting to heaven is like that too. *The Bible tells us:*

You can enter God's Kingdom only through the narrow gate. The highway to hell is broad, and its gate is wide for the many who choose the easy way. But the gateway to life is small, and the road is narrow, and only a few ever find it. MATTHEW 7:13-14, NLT

When you're traveling in an unfamiliar place, it takes concentration to stay on the right road. Are you watching your way to heaven as carefully? If not, ask God to be the navigator for your soul, and he will show you the way.

March

How did a brilliant man's name develop into "dunce"?

1 PETER 4:12-14

We use the word *dunce* to mean someone who is ignorant, and we picture from old times a child sitting in a corner of the schoolroom with a tall triangular hat on his head, being made fun of by other students. The word *dunce*, though, actually refers to one of the most brilliant scholars of the Middle Ages. His name was John Duns Scotus, and he wrote about logic, theology, metaphysics, and grammar. He attended Oxford University, Cambridge University, and the University of Paris. How did such an educated man become associated with stupidity? It was a matter of politics. The king of France and the pope had a fight over taxes. John Duns Scotus took the pope's side, so Scotus was banished from France. Two centuries later, the leaders who liked the king of France were still angry with Scotus. They attacked his writings and his decision to side with the pope. They said that anyone who believed in John Duns Scotus was a "Duns man," which was shortened to "dunce."

So what?

Many people throughout history have been persecuted for their beliefs. Those with strong opinions are most likely to be punished, because they are easy to identify. If you follow Jesus, you may get the same kind of treatment and trouble. So why would anyone want to follow him, just to be humiliated? The Bible has an answer. *It says:*

Don't be bewildered or surprised when you go through the fiery trials ahead, for this is no strange, unusual thing that is going to happen to you. Instead, be really glad—because these trials will make you partners with Christ in his suffering, and afterwards you will have the wonderful joy of sharing his glory in that coming day when it will be displayed.
Be happy if you are cursed and insulted for being a Christian, for when that happens the Spirit of God will come upon you with great glory.

1 PETER 4:12-14, TLB

If you're going to stand strong for something, doesn't it make sense to stand for a cause that will bring you eternal rewards?

March

Why did the Dutch build a memorial for a person who never existed?

ISAIAH 7:14

Have you ever heard about the little Dutch boy who put his finger in the dike, or wall, to keep the ocean from flooding his city? The storybook figure was created in 1865 by Mary Maples Dodge as she told the story of Hans Brinker in her book *Silver Skates*. Americans believed the tale. They began touring The Netherlands, asking to see the dam where the story occurred. The Dutch people got tired of telling the tourists that the story was make-believe, because the tourists wouldn't listen. Finally, in 1950, the Dutch gave in and built a statue showing the little Dutch boy stopping the water with his finger. The Americans were happy to visit the memorial, and the Dutch were happy to collect the tourists' dollars.

So what?

The curious Americans who traveled to Holland expected to find proof that the story of the Dutch boy was true. When they didn't see any, they asked someone to point the way. In this case, even with the "proof" of the statue, tourists didn't really find the truth. But that's not how it is with God. He provided his "proof" right at the beginning. *The Bible says:*

The Lord himself will choose the sign. Look! The virgin will conceive a child! She will give birth to a son. ISAIAH 7:14, NLT

Jesus and the Bible will never prove false or fictitious. You should never feel foolish for having faith that God's Word is true. God's Word is the only absolutely permanent truth that exists on earth.

March
19

Which country has a pancake party every year?

2 CORINTHIANS 6:4-5

Lent is a special time for Christians. It comes in the spring, and people give up certain foods to remind them of when Jesus wandered in the wilderness. Some of the things that are given up are eggs, milk, and fats. Those are exactly the same ingredients that go into pancakes. So in England, people go crazy for pancakes on the day before Lent, using up all the groceries that they won't be needing for a while.

In fact, they have an official Pancake Day, and they celebrate by playing pancake games. One is toss-the-pancake: Someone tosses a pancake up high, and kids jump up to grab it. In another race, women holding frying pans with pancakes in them must run to the finish line while flipping the pancakes up into the air. People say that they run the pancake race to copy a lady who heard the bells announcing the beginning of church and ran to the chapel with a frying pan still in her hand.

England is not the only country where people do strange things with pancakes. In 1984, in Vermont, a giant pancake was made out of two and a half tons of pancake mix. It used 150 pounds of syrup and over 1,000 pounds of butter. It was so big that they needed a helicopter to flip it!

So what?

Christians have always set aside time to glorify God, even when it meant making a sacrifice. God doesn't promise that life will constantly be easy if you are a Christian. But he does promise that he will be your strength through everything that happens to you. *In the Bible, Paul says:*

In everything we do we try to show that we are true ministers of God. We patiently endure troubles and hardships and calamities of every kind. We have been beaten, been put in jail, faced angry mobs, worked to exhaustion, endured sleepless nights, and gone without food.
2 CORINTHIANS 6:4-5, NLT

There will always be troubles on earth because earth isn't heaven, but you can count on God not to leave you to go through your problems alone.

March

What do roofs and ears have in common?
ROMANS 10:16-17

How did the word *eavesdropping* come to mean secretly listening to something that isn't being said to you, and is probably none of your business? Long ago, houses didn't have gutters on the roofs to let the rainwater drain away from the building. Instead, houses had overhanging roofs that came out far over the walls. These eaves kept the rainwater from dripping close to the house. There was a space under the eaves where a person could stand without getting wet, which was called the eavesdrop. If a person was listening at a window, he was probably standing within the eavesdrop area, and was therefore called an "eavesdropper."

So what?

You make choices every day about what you're going to listen to. *The Bible says:*

Not everyone welcomes the Good News, for Isaiah the prophet said, "Lord, who has believed our message?" Yet faith comes from listening to this message of good news—the Good News about Christ.
ROMANS 10:16-17, NLT

If you've ever thought that you're tired of hearing about Jesus, think about this. Would you get tired of hearing someone tell you how handsome, beautiful, rich, kind, charming, or popular you are? In God's eyes, you are such a special person that he let his much-loved Son die for you. You are so unique and valuable to God that he wants you to be in heaven with him one day. No one will ever love you as much as God does. Trust in him and listen to the Good News—every word you'll hear about God in the Bible is true.

March 21

Why would a man be glad to live in a cabinet?

2 CORINTHIANS 5:1

Patrick Fowler lived in a cupboard, which is a type of cabinet, and it saved his life. The cupboard was less than six feet high, and he stayed inside it for four years. Patrick was an English soldier stationed in France during World War I, fighting against the Nazi German soldiers. He got separated from the rest of his army and had to wear an ordinary coat instead of a uniform to disguise himself as he walked around. If the German soldiers had noticed him, he would have been killed.

A French woodcutter saw Patrick and decided to help him by allowing him to hide in a cupboard in someone's house. Patrick came out of the cupboard only at night to eat, stretch, or go to the bathroom. Sometimes German soldiers visited the house to drink coffee, but they never knew that Patrick was in there. Once, when the owners of the house had to move, a German soldier helped carry the cupboard. He didn't even notice how heavy it was with Patrick still inside. Another time, the Germans began to search for enemies, and Patrick disguised himself as a woman of the village so the soldiers wouldn't find him. One time Patrick ducked under a haystack to hide. The soldiers stabbed the haystack with pitchforks, but they missed Patrick. The Germans finally retreated from France. Then, after four years of hiding, Patrick was safe at last.

So what?

Patrick needed the cupboard to stay safe. But the door could have broken, or the wood could have rotted away, or his hiding place could have been destroyed by fire. And then Patrick wouldn't have been safe anymore. *The Bible tells us that we have much more than a piece of furniture to depend on:*

We know that when this earthly tent we live in is taken down—when we die and leave these bodies—we will have a home in heaven, an eternal body made for us by God himself and not by human hands.

2 CORINTHIANS 5:1, NLT

No matter what happens to us or our bodies on earth, if we belong to God we have the promise of living with him in heaven forever. People could never build a place as wonderful as heaven, and people can't destroy what is waiting for us there. Only God could make such a perfect place where his children will always feel peaceful and protected.

March

When did paying a library fine make history?

JOHN 3:14-17

In 1823 a man borrowed a book from the medical library at the University of Cincinnati. Nothing was unusual about that—until later. Much later. One hundred and forty years later, to be exact, when the borrower's great-grandson, Richard Dodd, discovered the book, walked into the library, and returned it for his great-grandfather, who had passed away. The fine, which was more than two thousand dollars, was forgiven, so it did not have to be paid. But as far as anyone knows, it still stands as the fine for the longest-overdue book in America.

So what?

Richard did an unusual thing by caring enough to try to pay what his relative owed. There are quite a few people who probably try to avoid paying their own debts, much less someone else's. We might think that if we heard of someone who was willing to pay the debts of everyone on earth, that would be impossible to believe. It would be too much generosity for us to understand. But that's exactly what Jesus did when he died on the cross for us. *He said:*

I, the Son of Man, must be lifted up on a pole, so that everyone who believes in me will have eternal life. For God so loved the world that he gave his only Son, so that everyone who believes in him will not perish but have eternal life. God did not send his Son into the world to condemn it, but to save it. JOHN 3:14-17, NLT

The sins of the world were too great—we could never repay God for them. But Jesus released us from our debt and made it possible for us to go to heaven. The Bible tells all about God's love for us and is one book that will never be overdue.

March
23

What plant grows only after being burned by a fire?

ISAIAH 43:2

A forest fire usually destroys all the plants and trees in its path and prevents regrowth in that area for a while. In South Africa, however, there is a plant called a *protea* that can grow only if there is a fire. The head of this strange national flower contains the seeds, which can stay tightly sealed in a hard shell for almost twenty years. The shell doesn't open until it's scorched and the fire is over. The light, fluffy seeds are then blown to the ground by the wind, where they begin to grow.

So what?

The Bible tells Christians:

When you walk through the fire, you will not be burned; the flames will not set you ablaze.   ISAIAH 43:2, NIV

Christian people don't have special fire-resistant bodies. What the Bible means is that if you believe in Jesus Christ, the devil cannot take your soul, no matter how hard he tries to lead you away from God. You will be able to walk through all the devil's tricks by holding on to Jesus, and your soul will not be touched by evil, even though it rages all around you.

March 24

What did a flag at half-mast used to mean?

ROMANS 6:4

When the American flag flies at half-mast, we know that someone important to our country has died and America is paying its respects. But originally a half-raised flag had a different meaning. The custom started on ships as far back as the 1600s. When a ship was made to surrender, it flew its flag at half-mast as proof that it was being forced to show that the enemy was superior. It was a sign that room was being made at the top of the flagpole to put the victor's flag up above. After the conquered ship reached the shore, the flag stayed at half-mast as a gesture of honor and respect for the sailors who had died trying to defend the ship. Any other type of death on board was also signaled by a half-mast flag. By the 1700s, the tradition was being copied on land. The flag at half-mast was first a sign of defeat, but later became a sign of honor.

So what?

The cross on which Jesus was crucified had the same change of meaning. When Jesus died on the cross, it was only human to assume that death had conquered him. For three days the cross stood as a reminder to everyone that anyone who believed in Christ had been defeated by his death. People thought that the disciples should surrender their beliefs and admit that they had been wrong. Then came the turnaround—Jesus Christ rose again! Not only did he come back to life, but he let his followers know that they, too, could have a fresh chance. *The Bible says:*

We died and were buried with Christ by baptism. And just as Christ was raised from the dead by the glorious power of the Father, now we also may live new lives. ROMANS 6:4, NLT

The cross became a symbol of honor: Christ had kept his word. He was truly the Son of God, and his promises of a new life for us were proved beyond doubt. The cross serves as a symbol honoring Christ's death, just as the half-mast flag honors the death of a beloved citizen.

March

Why aren't there any fleas at a flea market?

2 TIMOTHY 2:15

Flea markets are groups of booths, usually outdoors, that sell a variety of goods at discount prices. Why do we call this meeting place a "flea" market? You might think that it refers to dirty conditions at the market that could attract fleas and other bugs. But that's not the case. The word *flea* is really supposed to be a different word—we've just mispronounced it. It started in New York at one of the first outdoor markets called the Vallie Market. A sign was made to help people find the location, but the sign turned out to be too small for the whole name to fit. The painter abbreviated the name and wrote it as "Vle. Market." People started calling it the "vlee" market because that's what the sign seemed to spell. The words "vlee market" were repeated often and began to sound like "flea market." Now every open-air market is referred to by this strange label.

So what?

It's funny how even our smallest and most casual actions can have such a big impact. The person who made the sign reading "Vle. Market" probably never even thought twice about what he had written. He certainly had no idea that years later the term used for outdoor markets would still be based on the abbreviation on his simple sign. You never know when things that seem unimportant will turn out to be important. That's especially true when we tell others about God and his Word. *And that's why the Bible tells us:*

Work hard so God can approve you. Be a good worker, one who does not need to be ashamed and who correctly explains the word of truth.
2 TIMOTHY 2:15, NLT

By keeping your eyes on the details, you will have the assurance that you did your best and created a lasting impression.

March

Are you seeing things?

MATTHEW 7:1-5

What are those annoying little dots and threads that drift around in your eyesight? You try blinking, rolling your eyes, and looking somewhere else, but they don't disappear. They're known by a name that truly describes them— "floaters"—and you're stuck with them for life. How did they get inside your eyes? While you were in your mother's womb, blood was carried to your eye by the hyaloid artery. When your eye finished developing normally, this artery shriveled up and disintegrated into floating pieces that were then permanently caught in your vision. Floaters can increase with age. Tiny veins on the retina often rupture or leak, causing more blood to drift through the vitreous humor, which is the transparent jelly-like fluid that fills the eyeball behind the lens.

So what?

The Bible has an interesting observation about irritating objects in the eyes. Even though floaters can't be removed, we'd take them out if we could because they're occasionally bothersome. In the same way, we tend to be bothered by faults we see in someone else, and we'd like to get rid of them. *This is why the Bible cautions us:*

Stop judging others, and you will not be judged. For others will treat you as you treat them. Whatever measure you use in judging others, it will be used to measure how you are judged. And why worry about a speck in your friend's eye when you have a log in your own? How can you think of saying, "Let me help you get rid of that speck in your eye," when you can't see past the log in your own eye? Hypocrite! First get rid of the log from your own eye; then perhaps you will see well enough to deal with the speck in your friend's eye. MATTHEW 7:1-5, NLT

27
March

Which flower looks like a lion's teeth?
JOB 11:13-17

Two common flowers got their names from the way they look. The dandelion is technically a weed that flowers into a white feathery ball. In French, its fluffy seeds were described as *dent de lion,* which translates to "teeth of the lion." Although dandelions aren't eaten by lions, they do remind people of the way a lion's teeth look. Another flower with an interesting name is the daisy. Daisies open up in the morning, showing their bright yellow centers. In the evening, they close. That's why the English, in the language spoken years ago in Great Britain, called them the "daeg-eseage," which meant "day's eye."

So what?

Daisies don't have a choice about whether or not to "open their eyes" in the morning. But people do have a choice. God knows that we enjoy waking up to the light of day after the dark of night. The Bible tells us how we can keep spiritual light with us both day *and* night. *It says:*

If only you would prepare your heart and lift up your hands to him in prayer! Get rid of your sins and leave all iniquity behind you. Then your face will brighten in innocence. You will be strong and free of fear. You will forget your misery. It will all be gone like water under the bridge. Your life will be brighter than the noonday. Any darkness will be as bright as morning. JOB 11:13-17, NLT

Beginning life with Jesus is like the dawning of a new day!

March

When did people let their fingers do the talking?

PROVERBS 20:11

Fingerprinting is not a modern idea. In Babylonia, authors pressed their fingerprints into clay tablets to prove whose work it was and to prevent forgery. The Chinese put thumbprints on their official documents long ago. One man in India, however, was responsible for the first modern use of fingerprinting in 1858. William Hershel was in the Indian civil service when he used oil ink to take the palm print, which also included the fingers, of a local worker who had agreed to supply some metal for a job. Hershel wasn't trying to identify the man; he just wanted to impress on the man that he couldn't back out of the contract. Hershel then began a registry of fingerprints by taking samples from his coworkers and friends. In 1877, Hershel used fingerprints for official reasons. He wanted to keep army personnel from getting their paychecks twice. Fingerprinting was also used to stop prisoners from hiring someone else to serve their sentences. But Hershel didn't think of the possibilities of finding criminals. That idea came along later, after a man named Sir Francis Galton made a huge fingerprint collection. Scotland Yard was impressed and decided to use fingerprinting as a way to catch criminals.

So what?

To a fingerprint expert, your hands can identify you. To others, your hands can also reveal who you really are. Most of us say a lot about ourselves by what we do with our hands. *The Bible says:*

Even children are known by the way they act, whether their conduct is pure and right. PROVERBS 20:11, NLT

If a little boy throws rocks at a dog every day on the way home from school, you can tell that he's not a kind person. In the same way, hands that give out sandwiches at a homeless center "say" something different than hands that burglarize cars. Let your hands identify you as someone who works for God.

March

29

Why did W. C. Fields open so many bank accounts?

PROVERBS 3:24-26

W. C. Fields was a famous actor, but he wasn't always as confident as he appeared to be in his old movies. He had many difficulties when he was young, including poverty and hunger. Because of this, he had a fierce fear of being broke. He often had nightmares about being penniless, alone, and chased by the police in a strange city. Fields came up with a plan to comfort himself. In every new city where he traveled, he opened a bank account under a false name, possibly to feel safer, and deposited whatever money he had with him at the time. Sometimes it was a few coins, sometimes it was fifty thousand dollars. Fields probably felt more secure knowing he could withdraw some of his money from almost any bank. He once told a friend that he had opened more than seven hundred accounts. Unfortunately, Fields kept such poor records that only twenty-three accounts could be traced after his death in 1946. It is estimated that $1.3 million of his money was never found.

So what?

It didn't do Fields much good to spend his life accumulating money and storing it away. He was putting his faith in his possessions, expecting them to bring him security and peace. But Fields's nightmares kept occurring because his trust was misplaced. *The Bible says:*

When you lie down, you will not be afraid; when you lie down, your sleep will be sweet. Have no fear of sudden disaster or of the ruin that overtakes the wicked, for the LORD will be your confidence and will keep your foot from being snared. PROVERBS 3:24-26, NIV

The only true way to feel safe is to put your trust in God. He can, and will, take care of you much better than you could ever take care of yourself.

March

Why was the general always absent during roll call?

ISAIAH 49:15-16

During World War II, General Douglas MacArthur meant a great deal to the people of the Philippines because he helped protect their country. When the general was recalled from the Philippine Islands in 1942, he made his famous promise, "I shall return." General MacArthur kept his word and came back two years later to liberate the Philippines from the Japanese. In gratitude, the Congress of the Philippines honored General MacArthur by promising to call out his name from that day forward at every parade roll call of the Philippine army. When the general's name was spoken, a senior officer would answer, "Present in spirit." This gesture touched General MacArthur deeply. He cried when he heard of the plan, something he hadn't done since he was a boy. General MacArthur visited the Philippines one more time at the age of eighty-one, and true to their word, the citizens called out his name during roll call as they had been doing for the last thirty-six years. The people of the Philippine Islands were as faithful to General MacArthur as he had been to them. Once again the general cried.

So what?

It was very meaningful to General MacArthur to be remembered. We like being remembered too. Sometimes we may wonder if God has forgotten us. It seems as if we're all alone, and we wonder if we've been abandoned. But we have God's promise that he will not leave us. His assurances are found time and time again in the Bible. *The next time you are doubting God's interest in you, remember what he has said:*

I will not forget you! See, I have engraved you on the palms of my hands. ISAIAH 49:15-16, NIV

God's own Son, Jesus, will return for you—that's a promise!

March 31

Why would people be accused of stealing their own car?

PSALM 139:13

That's what almost happened to Richard Baker and his wife. After shopping, they unlocked their car in the parking lot and drove away. Richard noticed that his seat had been pushed back farther than he had left it, but he fixed it and forgot about it. Then his wife asked whose sunglasses were in the car. She found other things in the car that she didn't recognize either. Finally she said, "This isn't our car!" Richard stopped the car, got out, and checked the license plate. She was right—it was someone else's car!

They drove back to the shopping center, where they saw the police in the parking lot. The police were talking to the owner of the car Richard and his wife were driving—everyone thought it had been stolen. Richard got out and explained that this car looked exactly the same as his car, and his key had worked in the lock. The police officer found that Richard's key worked in both cars, and so did the other owner's key. But the most amazing thing of all was that both men had the same last name—Baker—even though they had never met! And the whole mix-up happened on April Fools' Day!

So what?

Maybe sometimes you feel you are like one of those cars: that you are nothing special in God's eyes, and that he probably can't even tell you apart from anybody else. But you're wrong! God knows exactly who you are because he created you! *You can say to God:*

You made all the delicate, inner parts of my body and knit me together in my mother's womb. PSALM 139:13, NLT

God knew who you would become long before you were even born. He has given you a combination of talents and abilities that don't match anyone else's. God created you with everything you would need to become the special person that you are today. No one else on earth is exactly like you. God planned it that way, and that's why he loves you so much.

April **1**

When did spaghetti grow on trees?
JOHN 8:31-32

Did you know that spaghetti noodles don't grow on trees? Apparently lots of people weren't aware of this fact, and they proved it on April Fools' Day, 1957. An English current-events television program called *Panorama* chose to show an unusual news story on April 1, the traditional day for playing pranks. Viewers watched pictures of women picking long noodles off the limbs of trees and drying the spaghetti in the sun. The narrator, a much-trusted broadcaster, calmly told about the annual spaghetti harvest taking place on the border of Switzerland and Italy. He ended his report by commenting on the goodness of homegrown spaghetti. Some people thought a joke shouldn't be played on a serious news show, and others thought the joke was funny. But many viewers sent in requests to the television show, wanting to know how they could attend the spaghetti harvest themselves next year.

So what?

Sometimes it's hard to tell what's really true. Although the spaghetti harvest was a harmless joke, people are capable of deceiving you in wicked ways as well. But you can trust Jesus to tell the truth. *He says:*

You are truly my disciples if you keep obeying my teachings. And you will know the truth, and the truth will set you free. JOHN 8:31-32, NLT

April

Why did a cookbook include a recipe for an explosion?

PSALM 19:12

Just because it's written in a book doesn't always mean that it's true. People put books together, and people can make mistakes. A big mistake was made in 1978. A publishing company named Random House printed a cookbook. In the cookbook was a recipe for caramel slices. In the recipe, something very important was left out. It was a simple ingredient—water. If you tried to make the caramel slices without water, the way the recipe was printed in the book, one of the ingredients—a can of condensed milk—could explode. To correct their mistake, Random House asked for all ten thousand copies of the book to be returned. Hopefully, they received them all, or else a cook intending to make a treat for a surprise could have a bigger surprise than he expected!

So what?

No one knew that the mistake in the cookbook was there, but when it was found, the publisher wanted to change it. That's what we should do. *Like King David in the Psalms, we should ask God:*

How can I know all the sins lurking in my heart? Cleanse me from these hidden faults. PSALM 19:12, NLT

God will help you see the things in you that he wants you to change—and with his help, you can do it!

April

Can someone be double-jointed?

EPHESIANS 5:30

You've probably heard some people say they're double-jointed because they can bend their fingers or toes in extraordinary ways. Since a joint is sort of like a hinge, to be truly double-jointed someone would have to have two of their bones fastened together by two different "hinges." That never happens. No one is really double-jointed. So why can they bend more than you? The joints (or hinges) between bones can bend because they are made of ligaments, which are tough tissues. Sometimes these ligaments become permanently stretched. When that happens, the joint can bend farther than normal. That makes people think that they are double-jointed.

Speaking of joints, your jawbone has an interesting one. Maybe you assume that when you open your mouth, both your upper and lower jaw move. That's not true. The lower jaw is the only part that is movable. To test this, try to move your upper jaw while keeping the rest of your head still. It can't be done.

Another fact about bones that you may not know is that bones are *not* the hardest part of your body. Your tooth enamel—the white covering on your teeth—is harder than your bones. The difference is that a bone can grow to repair itself, but teeth can't.

So what?

The Bible tells us that if we belong to Jesus:

We are members of his body, of his flesh, and of his bones.
EPHESIANS 5:30, KJV

This is another way of saying that we are important to him, and he will take special care of us. No one wants to break a bone on purpose. We try to take care of our bones because they are important to our bodies.

April

How can you read when you can't even see?

ISAIAH 42:16

Even a sixteen-year-old can change the whole world! Louis Braille did. And Louis had been blind since the age of three.

When Louis Braille was a small boy, he used to spend lots of time in his father's saddlery shop. One day Louis snuck into the shop by himself and tried to copy what he had seen his father do, cutting leather with a sharp knife. The knife slipped, and Louis stuck himself in the eye. Eventually, his other eye became affected also, and he ended up completely blind.

Louis went to a school for the blind to try to learn to read, but it was very hard. There were only fourteen books in the whole school, and they weighed twenty pounds each! The letters in these special books were just like regular letters, except much larger and puffed up from the page. Imagine having to feel the letter *w* with your fingers, or the letter *r*, or the letter *a*, and how long it would take to feel a whole word. But things changed when Louis was fifteen. Charles Barbier invented a writing system using raised dots on paper. His soldiers needed to be able to read in the dark so the enemy wouldn't see them. Mr. Barbier brought his system to the school that Louis was attending. When Louis tried it, he knew it was too complex. So he improved the system by making it simpler. Finally, there was a way for the blind to read, and it is named for the boy who figured it out: the Braille system.

So what?

If you close your eyes for fifteen minutes, you will discover that being blind can be scary and dangerous. You need someone to help you. *God says:*

I will lead the blind by ways they have not known, along unfamiliar paths I will guide them. ISAIAH 42:16, NIV

You can depend on God to lead you down the paths he wants you to take, even if there are times that you can't see, or understand, what he's doing. He will lead you by what he says in his Word, the Bible, and also by what older Christians teach you—your mom and dad or your Sunday-school teacher, for instance. God will never let you get lost. He will always know exactly where you are, and he will be watching over you.

April
5

When do parents want their kids to make noise?

PSALM 71:17

Imagine that you are a young African boy sitting in a tree house. You are beating on a drum made from a tin can with animal skin stretched over the top. You beat the drum all day because your father has asked you to. Are you in the tree house because you were making too much noise at home? No. Actually, you are doing a valuable job. When you beat your drum, you are scaring monkeys away from eating your father's crops.

In Africa, as you get older, you may still be beating a drum, but now you will be making it talk. You will be given a special drum for sending messages. It is called a *lunga,* and it looks like an hourglass. You hold the lunga under your arm and squeeze it to make different sounds as you beat. Then you learn to make your drum talk by hitting it with your hand, your fingers, or a drumstick. First, you have to learn the names of people in your family—each one has a different beat. Then you learn to beat the names of all the leaders in your tribe. After practicing for a long time, you'll be able to beat out words and sentences to send messages to other people in Africa who will be happy to hear your noise.

So what?

The most important message you can give people is that Jesus loves them. You can share with them the Good News of Jesus by what you say, by your kindness, through what you write, or even by beating a drum. Maybe you'd like to find a way to show someone how much God has blessed you, and start telling the story now. *Then someday you can say:*

O God, you have taught me from my earliest childhood, and I have constantly told others about the wonderful things you do.
PSALM 71:17, NLT

April

How could the idea of bungee jumping be over one hundred years old?

2 SAMUEL 24:14

Almost everyone has heard of the sport of bungee jumping, where a person fastens herself to a long rubber strap and jumps off some high place. The bungee jumper falls down fast, but the strap bounces her back up before she hits the ground.

Bungee jumping is not a modern idea. A Frenchman named Mr. Carron first thought of it in 1891. He made a metal capsule that could carry fifteen people, so a whole group of people could ride at the same time. They each had their own cushioned chair to sit in, and on the floor was a mattress with bouncy springs almost two feet long. The capsule was going to be dropped from the top of the Eiffel Tower in Paris. On the ground below would be a sixty-yard-deep pool shaped like a funnel.

So what?

Fortunately, no one ever took the capsule ride, because this idea could have been very dangerous. We get no guarantees with the plans that people make for us—only with God's plans. *A Christian says:*

Let us fall into the hands of the LORD, for his mercy is great. Do not let me fall into human hands.   2 SAMUEL 24:14, NLT

Be careful about trusting every word or idea people tell you. The best plan is to trust God first in everything.

April

If you burn your hand, what is the best thing to do?

REVELATION 22:17

Should you put ice on it, soak it in cold water, or smear it with butter? Butter is not the right answer, although lots of people think it is. Butter can have germs in it that might make the burn infected. Butter won't prevent a scar either. Putting ice on it is also a wrong answer because ice can stick to your skin. The best thing to do for a burn is to run cool water over it, maybe for as long as an hour. Running water works better than soaking with water in a bowl. This is the best way to help prevent a scar and take the pain away. When your hand feels like it's on fire, think of a house that's on fire—what puts it out? Not ice, not butter, but water. You should do the same as the firefighters do, and run for the water.

So what?

When you burn yourself (which doesn't happen often) or when you are thirsty (which happens every day), you are happy to find water. The Bible tells us that learning about God is as satisfying as a glass of cool water when your mouth is very dry. *Jesus says:*

Let the thirsty ones come—anyone who wants to. Let them come and drink the water of life without charge. REVELATION 22:17, NLT

Just as our bodies would die without water, so our souls would die without God. Remember that God is ready and waiting to hand you a cold drink of love every time you decide you are thirsty to learn more about him.

April

How did electricity surprise a whole crowd?
ISAIAH 9:2

Imagine that you are in charge of getting people's attention at a fair. Electricity has just been invented, and most people are not used to seeing anything light up. What would really surprise them?

The Edison Electric Lighting Company thought of a good plan. They hired a man to hand out their business cards near the gate. What made this man special was the fact that the Edison Company figured out a way to make the helmet he was wearing light up. Wires that ran underneath the man's jacket were connected to the helmet. Under the heels of his boots, he had some copper plates. There were also copper plates hidden in the ground underneath his feet. When the man stepped on these plates, touching them to the plates on his boots, his helmet lit up. The man secretly kept moving on and off the plates, making it look like his helmet went on and off all by itself. This was very shocking to people. At that time, because electricity was so new, it seemed like magic. Some people were so fascinated with the lighted helmet, they wanted to buy one to use around the house. They had no idea how complicated electricity really was.

So what?

Seeing an electric light for the first time must have been very exciting. Even though we see electricity all the time and are used to it, there is another kind of light that can be very exciting. *The Bible says:*

The people who walk in darkness will see a great light.   ISAIAH 9:2, NLT

If you tell someone about Jesus, and they have never heard of him before, it could be like turning on an electric light in a dark room. Tell the story. God will decide when to turn on the power in that person's life.

Why do boys' and girls' shirts button on different sides?

MATTHEW 6:3-4

We all have buttons on our clothes. Have you ever noticed that boys' buttons are different from girls' buttons? It's not the size or shape or color of the buttons that makes them different—it's where they are. A boy's buttons are sewn on the right flap of his shirt, because most boys are right-handed and they use their right hand to button up. Girls' shirts have the buttons sewn on the left flap. Since most girls are right-handed, too, why are their buttons sewn on the left?

Long ago, buttons were very expensive, so only rich people had them on their clothes. Rich ladies did not dress themselves then; they had maids who got them dressed. The maid needed to have the buttons near *her* right hand as she stood in front of the lady to button her up, so the buttons were sewn on the left side. Even though most girls now dress themselves, the buttons have never been changed.

So what?

Both of your hands can be used for much more important things than buttoning. You can use your hands to help others. *The Bible says:*

When you give to someone, don't tell your left hand what your right hand is doing. Give your gifts in secret, and your Father, who knows all secrets, will reward you. MATTHEW 6:3-4, NLT

This means that it is very important not to brag or show off when you are helping. Try to be so quiet about helping that no one even notices! Put away your little brother's toys, but don't mention it. If the trash can is full, empty it without being asked. Even if you don't get thanked or praised for your help, keep doing nice things. God will see you, and that's what counts.

April

Why were M&M's invented?

PHILIPPIANS 2:9

Long ago, candy was just a small piece of a loaf of sugar, cut off with scissors. Then candy got fancier, and people began making different kinds of candy for different reasons.

One favorite candy was invented during a war. Soldiers in 1940 needed a treat that they could carry in their pockets that wouldn't get their fingers sticky. Two men, Bruce Murrie and Forrest Mars, made a bite-sized chocolate candy that had a hard, colored coating. They named it after their initials: M&M's.

Other candies got their names from real people, too. Leo Hirschfield invented a chocolate candy and named it after his six-year-old daughter, Tootsie. The candy? A Tootsie Roll. Most people think that the Baby Ruth candy bar was named after the famous baseball player Babe Ruth. That's not the true story. This candy bar was named after a little girl, Ruth Cleveland. What made her special enough to have a candy bar named for her? She was the daughter of President Grover Cleveland.

So what?

You've probably told at least one of your friends how good one of these candies is. It's natural to want to tell someone else about good things! Then your friend learned the name and remembered it, too. That's how it is with Jesus. *The Bible tells us this:*

God exalted him to the highest place and gave him the name that is above every name. PHILIPPIANS 2:9, NIV

People who hear about Jesus and get to know him grow to love him. Then they tell their friends about Jesus. When you tell someone the name of a new candy, you are sharing a sweet treat that lasts a few minutes. Telling your friends about Jesus can sweeten the rest of their lives.

April

Why can't you feel your foot when it falls asleep?

1 THESSALONIANS 5:17

Almost everyone has had this experience—after sitting still for a while, when you get up your feet feel numb. People often say that their feet are asleep. But feet can't really sleep. What is happening, and why?

Your body is full of nerves, which are like fibers or wires. These nerves send information to your brain from different locations, and the brain sends back directions. For example, if you step on hot pavement with bare feet, your foot sends a message to your brain that says "Hot!" Your brain then sends back "Move!" The nerves that connect your brain to your body run very close to the surface of your skin at certain places. If you happen to be pushing on the skin near one of these nerves by sitting on your feet, the nerve becomes squeezed shut. No signals can pass to or from the brain, so that part of your body seems disconnected. When you move to a different position, the nerve you were pinching opens up, and you begin to feel again.

So what?

Prayer is the way messages are sent to and from God. *The Bible tells us:*

Keep on praying.   1 THESSALONIANS 5:17, NLT

That is how we keep our souls from falling asleep and how we can get directions from God. Pray all the time, and your connection with God will always stay open.

April

Why are piano keys black and white?
EPHESIANS 5:19

If you were in charge of deciding what two colors to make the keys on a piano, which would you choose? Black and white may seem boring, but there are good reasons why they became the piano's colors.

Piano makers knew that the keys had to be strong enough to last a long time. They had to be made of something that could be polished easily, and they had to be pretty to look at. Long ago, the best material for this job was ivory. That's what the lower-level keys were made from. For the upper-level keys, piano makers had a riddle to solve: What feels smooth, polishes well, lasts long, and is the opposite of ivory in color? The answer turned out to be ebony wood, which is black. Now you know why people sometimes say they "tickled the ivories" when they were playing the piano.

So what?

God knows that people enjoy music, and he likes for us to use music to praise him. *The Bible gives these guidelines:*

Sing psalms and hymns and spiritual songs among yourselves, making music to the Lord in your hearts. EPHESIANS 5:19, NLT

Whether we write songs for God or play instruments or sing or just hum a tune in our minds, God likes to know we are thankful and enjoy thinking about him.

April 13

Which cartoon was also a puzzle?

PSALM 27:9

Once there was an artist named Al Hirshfeld who drew cartoons for newspapers. In 1945, Al was very excited when his daughter Nina was born, and to celebrate, he started hiding the name *Nina* in his cartoons. Everybody who saw his cartoons began to love the game of finding the name.

After a while Al thought it was time to stop hiding his little girl's name, but he was wrong. He left Nina out once, and he got letters from lots of people asking him where the Nina was and saying that their families were arguing over where they thought they saw it. So Al put the Nina back into the cartoons. Another time Al's daughter asked him to hide the name of her friend Liza in a cartoon too. Al did, but he never imagined what would happen next. People began sending flowers and telegrams to his house, and Al and his wife were astonished to discover that the readers all thought a new baby named Liza had arrived!

This little game of hiding the name Nina has helped our country in some serious ways. The Pentagon used the Nina cartoons to study different ways to camouflage things. Air Force pilots looked for the name as practice for spotting targets on the ground.

So what?

Christians have something even more important to look for than a little girl's name. *We ask God:*

Oh, do not hide yourself when I am trying to find you.   PSALM 27:9, TLB

And God has promised that he never will hide from us. When we look for him, he will make sure that we find him. God doesn't play hide-and-seek!

April

What really makes those noises you hear at night?

JOB 11:18-19

Many children are sure they hear noises at night—and they're right! Sometimes children are afraid that the noises are made by scary monsters—but they're wrong about that. Actually, it is the wooden furniture in the house and the wooden boards in the walls, ceilings, or floors that make the noises. Are they noisy because someone is using them? No! The wood makes noises all by itself as it changes in size.

When the air is hot or damp, the wood puffs up a little. When it's cold or dry, the wood shrinks a little. As the wood gets a tiny bit smaller or bigger, it creaks. These noises happen during the day, too. But at night you are quieter, so you notice the noises more.

So what?

When you feel afraid, especially at night, you can always pray. If you ask God to comfort you, he will. *The Bible says:*

You will look about you and take your rest in safety. You will lie down, with no one to make you afraid. JOB 11:18-19, NIV

You will feel safer when you ask God to be near you.

April

How was a person caught by a plane?
PSALM 119:117

Captain Hedley was in trouble. World War II was raging, and he was an American pilot riding as the passenger in a two-person plane with an open roof. The plane was fifteen thousand feet up in the air, and Germans were firing at it. The pilot flying the plane dove almost straight down, trying to avoid being shot. Captain Hedley, in the backseat, wasn't prepared for the plane to dive. He was pulled right out of his seat into the sky. The pilot knew he couldn't help his friend, so he just kept the plane going down for hundreds of feet and then straightened the plane. But then the most amazing thing happened! The plane was going down so fast, it created suction in the air, which means that the air was pulling on everything behind the plane's path. Captain Hedley was caught in this suction as he fell, and he was pulled back onto the plane. He grabbed the tail of the plane and clung to it with all his might. He was finally able to crawl back into his seat, and the plane landed safely in American territory.

So what?
Sometimes we may be in danger of falling into evil. Our friends might be trying to talk us into doing something wrong. We may be tempted to break one of God's laws by telling a lie or stealing. *Those are the times when we need to pray:*

Hold me safe above the heads of all my enemies; then I can continue to obey your laws. PSALM 119:117, TLB

God will hear your prayer and give you his strength and hold you up, just the way he did for Captain Hedley and his plane.

April **16**

How did noodles get their names?
MATTHEW 1:23

If you like Italian food, then you know that noodles come in all different shapes and sizes and that they each have their own name. But you probably don't know what the names mean, or how well they describe the way the noodles look. *Lasagna,* the large flat ruffled noodle, means "baking pot"—which is what you need to cook it in. *Cannelloni* means "big pipes." *Manicotti* means "little sleeves." *Ravioli* stands for "little turnips." *Macaroni* is named for small cookies, called macaroons. *Spaghetti* means "little strings." *Linguine* stands for "small tongue." The noodle that wins the prize for the most unappetizing name is *vermicelli,* which means "little worms." The next time you have Italian food, try to guess which noodle is in it—just from the way it looks.

So what?
Names tell us a lot, like the noodle names, which describe how something looks. The Bible says that before Jesus was born, his father was told that one day people would call Jesus by another name. This new name would describe who Jesus was. *Joseph was told:*

They will call him Immanuel—which means, "God with us."
MATTHEW 1:23, NIV

The people who knew who Jesus was would someday give him another name. The new name would let everyone know he was the true Son of God, living on earth among us. Then no one would have to wonder anymore if Jesus was truly the Savior.

April

Why do our noses have little hairs in them?

PSALM 104:24

The hairs in your nose act like a screen, stopping what shouldn't go into your lungs, and letting clean air through. There are so many tiny hairs in your nose that they look like a carpet. Your nose makes liquid mucus, which wets the hairs. Then you breathe in, and dust particles in the air get stuck on the moist nose hairs. Your nose also helps your lungs by warming the air while you breathe it in.

There's something else that's interesting about breathing. Babies can breathe and swallow at the same time, which helps them eat. But after the age of about seven months, little ones lose this ability. Just try to breathe through your nose and swallow, too. You can't! You must do one or the other.

(By the way, your nose keeps growing your whole life.)

So what?

If you were in charge of making people, would you have thought of giving each person a carpet in the nose? We should be very thankful to God, because when he made us, he paid attention to the littlest details to make our bodies work. He thought of everything! *The Bible says:*

O Lord, what a variety of things you have made! In wisdom you have made them all. PSALM 104:24, NLT

God is so smart, he can keep track of everything in the universe at the same time, even the little specks of dust that float toward our noses!

April 18

Who froze the first Popsicle?

PROVERBS 25:25

Can you imagine inventing something wonderful, without even knowing that you're doing it? That's exactly what happened to eleven-year-old Frank Epperson in 1905. He decided to fix himself a drink by stirring soda water and flavored powder together with a mixing stick. Frank left his glass out on the back porch, completely forgetting that it was there. That night, the temperature got unexpectedly cold. When Frank found his glass outside the next morning, he saw that the drink had frozen with the stick still in it. Eighteen years later Frank remembered this incident and started producing Epsicles, named after himself. We know Frank's invention by another name—a combination of *lollipop* and *epsicle*—the Popsicle! Originally Frank produced these frozen treats in seven different fruit flavors. Today we can get Popsicles in over thirty flavors.

So what?

Popsicles taste great on a hot day. *The Bible talks about that feeling when it says:*

Good news from far away is like cold water to the thirsty.
PROVERBS 25:25, NLT

If you know someone who lives far away from you, or someone who is lonely, you can brighten that person's day just by making a phone call or sending a letter. Sharing some happy news is a great way to give someone special a treat that will last a lot longer than a Popsicle.

April

Why can dogs smell things better than people can?

1 CORINTHIANS 4:7

In each nostril, or nose hole, humans have an area of cells that have just one job—to smell things. Dogs' noses have these cells in them also, but they have twenty times more "smell cells" than people do, and they can cover an area five times the size of ours. Because the dog's smell cells are so concentrated, a dog can smell things much better than we can.

Dogs' noses are remarkable in another way. No two noses are alike. Dogs can be identified by their noseprints, just like people can be identified by their fingerprints. At one time, dogs' paws were used for identification, but it has been found that the nose is much more accurate. So it is the dog's nose that is inked and pressed against paper to show people which dog they are buying or selling.

So what?

No matter how hard you try, you'll never be able to smell as well as a dog can. God has decided that a dog's nose will always be better than a person's. But you are superior to the dog in many other ways—and that is God's plan too. God chooses what you look like and what talents you have. He starts your body working when you are born, and he knows how many breaths you will take before you die. That's why you shouldn't brag, even when you think you are the best at something. It is God who gives you the power and ability. *The Bible asks:*

What makes you better than anyone else? What do you have that God hasn't given you? And if all you have is from God, why boast as though you have accomplished something on your own? 1 CORINTHIANS 4:7, NLT

Remember, God deserves the credit for all your achievements.

Does an ostrich really bury its head in the sand?

PSALM 9:9

Almost everyone has heard the story of how an ostrich hides his head in the sand when he's afraid. We laugh at the ostrich; just because his head is underground, he thinks no one can see the rest of him! But actually, ostriches are smarter than that. They do put their heads down, but not to hide their eyes. When the ostrich senses danger, he flattens his neck across the sand, which makes the rest of his body look like a bush. He is hoping his enemy won't notice he's there. If the enemy gets too close, the ostrich will get busy. He will hiss, kick, peck, or outrun his enemy. He can run up to sixty miles an hour and can travel twenty-five feet each time he takes a step. The ostrich's legs are so strong that if he kicks you, you can be killed. If an ostrich doesn't like you, you have more reason to hide than he does!

So what?

If you are ever feeling afraid, remember this:

The Lord is a refuge for the oppressed, a stronghold in times of trouble.
PSALM 9:9, NIV

A *refuge* is a place where you can go to feel protected, and a *stronghold* is like a fort. Someone who is *oppressed* is worried. God wants you to know that you can always come to him when you are in trouble, and he will help you.

The ostrich didn't think up ways on his own for how to protect himself. He had to depend on the instincts God gave him so he would know what to do. Since God made sure that even the ostrich had some help, you can be sure that he has a good plan for you, too. Just ask him to show you what it is.

April

How did riches escape a man who started a gold rush?

GALATIANS 6:9

George Harrison of Australia and George Walker of England started one of the world's largest gold rushes. The year was 1886, and the place was South Africa. The two men made a report about a "payable gold field" that they had discovered. When word got out, nearby Johannesburg grew from a sleepy collection of shacks and tents to an important city. Gold diggers arrived from around the world during the next three years. The gold vein was fifty miles long and served as the world's leading gold source for the next thirty years! Later, even more land was discovered to contain gold—more than three hundred miles and eight hundred tons of gold. Walker should have been unbelievably rich since he and Harrison started the whole search, but for unknown reasons, he sold out too soon. In exchange for his claim of gold deposits, Walker received less than fifty dollars.

So what?

George Walker gave up too soon and missed out on a great reward. He obviously couldn't see far enough ahead to feel confident that if he stood firm, he would receive a prize far beyond his biggest dreams. God tells us that believing in Jesus and staying committed to him will bring us the reward of heaven, which is so spectacular we can't begin to imagine it. *The Bible encourages us when it says:*

Let us not get tired of doing what is right, for after a while we will reap a harvest of blessing if we don't get discouraged and give up.
GALATIANS 6:9, TLB

Stake your claim on Jesus, because he promises us valuable blessings.

April

Why don't we eat goldfish?

PROVERBS 20:15

Many years ago the Chinese figured out that raising their own fish for food would be a smart and inexpensive idea. They needed a fish that was hardy and could live well in shallow water with little oxygen. The best candidate was the goldfish, at the time a greenish-bronze member of the carp family. As the Chinese continued to breed the fish, its color began to turn golden. People began to admire the goldfish for its looks, and they became interested in keeping the fish as decorations for their garden ponds. Once the wealthy filled their ponds with goldfish, the fish became very popular. Europeans also wanted goldfish as pets, and the Chinese found that there was more money in raising the fish for their beautiful color than for their taste. Hatcheries for raising goldfish developed quickly, and in just a short time there were more than one hundred varieties of goldfish—but not enough buyers. Goldfish became ordinary and inexpensive, but we still keep them as pets. Some goldfish have been known to live for more than fourteen years!

So what?

People have always admired things of beauty. Imagine their delight when they first saw the shiny, wriggling, sparkling goldfish! Yet eventually the glamour and appeal of these special fish tarnished.

Nothing on earth is meant to last forever. The Bible tells us what should be important to us as Christians. *It says:*

Good sense is far more valuable than gold or precious jewels.
PROVERBS 20:15, TLB

Don't be distracted by glitz and glitter; concentrate on learning all you can from God's Word, because that's what gives you wisdom and makes you rich in spirit.

April

How did golf courses end up with eighteen holes?

JOB 18:7-10

Most golf courses are made up of eighteen holes. But that's not how early courses were designed. Originally, each course had a different number of holes to play. The number of holes at each location depended on how much land was available to build the course. The first golf course, Saint Andrews in Scotland, had only eleven holes. But the golfers played each hole twice, so a game at Saint Andrews was twenty-two holes long. After a while, course designers made some of the holes harder by making them longer. Other holes were left out, and by 1764 a total round was set at eighteen holes.

Perhaps the strangest golf courses, along with the most unusual jobs, were created during World War II. The United States was concerned for the security of its airplane-manufacturing plants. So grass was grown on the roofs to create an illusion for enemy pilots. From the air it appeared that they were seeing only golf courses. And the odd jobs? People were hired to play on these courses to complete the creative scenery.

So what?

One of the goals of every golfer is to avoid the sand traps that engulf the ball and make playing harder. Life has pitfalls, and the consequences of falling into them are much more serious than in a golf game. *The Bible tells us that a person who rejects God will have problems:*

The vigor of his step is weakened; his own schemes throw him down. His feet thrust him into a net and he wanders into its mesh. A trap seizes him by the heel; a snare holds him fast. A noose is hidden for him on the ground; a trap lies in his path. JOB 18:7-10, NIV

Are you practicing your actions in life as carefully as some people practice their golf game? Ask God to guide you through life's course, and you will avoid getting trapped.

April 24

How did a fruit ruin a publicity stunt?
ROMANS 12:15

It seemed like a good idea at the time. In 1915, Wilbert Robinson, manager of the Brooklyn Dodgers, agreed to do a publicity stunt. The plan was for an airplane to fly overhead and drop a baseball to Wilbert, who would try to catch it. The pilot was Ruth Law, a famous aviator. She was supposed to receive a baseball at the airport from someone on the team, but no one had arrived to deliver the ball by take-off time. The plane's mechanic offered Ruth a nearby substitute, which she took on the flight and later dropped as planned.

Down below, Wilbert was waiting, but he missed the round object. Instead, it hit him on the head. Wilbert began screaming that he was dead—he had stinging, blinding liquid dripping into his eyes, and big hard chunks of something were falling from his head. He panicked, thinking that blood was flowing from his skull, which he thought had just cracked into pieces. It took a few minutes for Wilbert to realize what the mechanic had given Ruth to drop from her plane. Instead of a baseball, Wilbert had just been hit by a large grapefruit!

So what?
When Wilbert was bonked on the head with the grapefruit, the first reaction of the crowd in the stadium was probably to laugh. We are, after all, human. But this wasn't funny to the baseball manager. As the spectators were being amused, Wilbert was experiencing terror. The Bible reminds us to consider the other guy's feelings. *It says:*

When others are happy, be happy with them. If they are sad, share their sorrow. ROMANS 12:15, NLT

Feeling what other people are feeling may not always be our natural response, but we can learn to do it. We can have compassion for others, because God has taught us compassion by his example.

April 25

What causes gray hair?

PROVERBS 16:31

As you get older, gray is not a color that's added to your hair—it's color that's subtracted. When you're young, your body manufactures pigment, or color, that enters each of your hair shafts through the follicles in your scalp. This pigment, called melanin, supplies your hair with its natural color. As you age, melanin production slows down, and the hair shafts become more clear than colored. Less color means the hair shafts will look more white or gray when light strikes them. Getting gray hair takes a while because hair grows only about a half-inch each month. If it seems to you that someone's hair "turned gray overnight," you've probably witnessed a case of an inflamed scalp. The gray hairs are most resistant, so they will stay in the scalp. The darker hairs fall out more quickly, so what's left on the head suddenly looks grayer or whiter than before.

So what?

Gray hair can mean more than just getting old and forgetful. The world might tell you that it means you're getting feeble and washed-out, but the Bible tells another story. *It says:*

Gray hair is a crown of glory; it is gained by living a godly life.
PROVERBS 16:31, NLT

Respect the wisdom of your grandparents and elders, and feel free to cherish your own silver hair when you get it! If you dye your hair instead, you may be covering up one of your most valuable features.

April 26

Why were two security guards hired to stare up all day?

PSALM 46:1-3

At the John Hancock Tower in Boston, two full-time guards spend all their time staring straight up through their binoculars. What are they looking at? Their job is to report any cracks or discolorations in the more than ten thousand windows throughout the sixty-story building. Such diligence is necessary. The Hancock Tower has a historic problem with its panes. Construction on the building started in 1968 and was completed four years later. It still couldn't be used for another four years because of a mysterious problem. The windows kept popping out by the dozens—large four-by-eleven-foot panes that shattered to the ground. Once all the windows were replaced with huge four-hundred-pound sections of thick tempered glass. But the new windows popped out also. When Boston was hit by seventy-five-mile-per-hour winds, sixty-five windows exploded and hundreds more were damaged as the glass flew. When a fourth of the windows were boarded up as architects tried to decide what to do, the Tower was nicknamed the "Plywood Palace." It was determined that the sway of the building was putting too much stress on the windows, so gigantic weights were used to anchor the building from the inside. Even though this improved the problem, guards remain posted as an extra safeguard.

So what?

Maybe sometimes you feel a little like the John Hancock Tower. You have so many stresses, and are being pulled in so many directions, that you are having trouble keeping all the pieces of your life together. God doesn't want you to feel this way. He knows that you can't enjoy life when you're constantly upset or worried. He wants more for you. Maybe you can't change the circumstances around you, but you can get relief. *Rely on this fact:*

God is our refuge and strength, always ready to help in times of trouble. So we will not fear, even if earthquakes come and the mountains crumble into the sea. Let the oceans roar and foam. Let the mountains tremble as the waters surge! PSALM 46:1-3, NLT

God will help to carry your burdens for you if you let him. Don't be afraid to ask him, because once you have, you won't need to feel fragile during life's strong winds.

27 April

What are some predictable differences in people's hands?

PSALM 102:25

Although there are exceptions to every rule, there are some interesting comparisons between the male and female hand. If you watch people's hands carefully, you may notice for yourself that these "rules" are often true. Test them!

1. A man's ring finger is longer than his index finger, or pointer. A woman's pointer is longer than her ring finger.
2. If you ask people to show you their hands, a man puts his hands out with the palms up. A woman turns her palms down.
3. If a man is looking at his fingernails, his hand is usually turned up with his fingers curled. A woman turns her palms down and holds her fingers straight.
4. On both men's and women's hands, their middle finger is almost always as long as their palm is wide.

So what?

What we humans do with our hands is nothing compared to what God does with his. *The Bible praises God's handiwork when it says:*

In the beginning you laid the foundations of the earth, and the heavens are the work of your hands. PSALM 102:25, NIV

If someone told you that you had to copy the world that God made, how would you do it? How could you make a star? Or a mountain? How would you make a flower open up or give a dog its bark or get a cloud to hang in the sky? What would you do to get a river to flow? God knows how to create all of these things and how to keep them working. Our job is simply to enjoy them and to thank God for creating them.

April

When was Hollywood a happy little hamlet?

JOB 28:12-13

Did you know that Hollywood was intended in its beginning to be a model community for very conservative nondrinkers? It was founded by the Wilcox family, who bought the land in 1886. The name *Hollywood* was picked by Mrs. Wilcox. She had been seated on a train next to a woman who had a summer home near Chicago by that name, and Mrs. Wilcox liked the sound of it. Imagine a community with no crime—not even a jail—and where the mayor worked as a volunteer. For almost twenty years Hollywood was a hamlet of five hundred residents with no bigger problems than how to keep sheep away from the town square.

In 1903 Hollywood became a city, and in 1910 it merged with Los Angeles. The first film studio moved there in 1911. By the 1920s it had turned into the nation's movie capital for two reasons. First, the weather made a longer filming season possible. Second, movie executives were often worried about breaking the law by using someone else's work without permission. Hollywood was close enough to Mexico that they could cross the border for safety if necessary. Films were first called "movies" by the people of Hollywood because filming required such constant movement and activity. The "Hollywood" sign started out as "Hollywoodland," an advertising gimmick for a realty firm. The last four letters fell off, and "Hollywood" was left on the hillside.

So what?

Many aspiring actors and actresses flock to Hollywood in hopes of gaining fame and fortune. To some, becoming well-known must seem like the ultimate success. But the Bible advises us to strive for something more valuable. *It says:*

Do people know where to find wisdom? Where can they find understanding? No one knows where to find it, for it is not found among the living. JOB 28:12-13, NLT

Don't spend your time looking for spotlights to bring you happiness or wealth—search the Scriptures instead.

April 29

Why doesn't humble pie taste good?

MATTHEW 6:19-21

When we were forced to admit that we were wrong about something, it used to be said that we had to "eat humble pie." What we really meant is that we were made to feel less proud of ourselves. But this is not what the phrase was intended to say. The word *humble* comes from the Latin word for *earth*, which is *humus*. We usually think of someone humble as "down to earth," or not acting with too much pride. But the phrase "eating humble pie" comes from a very different history. It doesn't have anything to do with the word *humble* as we know it today. Long ago, people who were poor had to eat some undesirable parts of animals in their meat or pot pies because they couldn't afford better meats. Their pies often contained such ingredients as the umbilical cords of animals. The rich would have nothing to do with this "umble" (as in "umbilical cord") pie. If you were forced to eat "umble pie," it didn't mean you were humble. It meant you were poor.

So what?

Maybe you can identify with the people who had to eat "umble pie." Perhaps your family does not have as much money as your friends' families do, and you wish you had more. Before you make the mistake of thinking that lots of money means lots of security, the Bible has some wise words for you. *It says:*

Don't store up treasures here on earth, where they can be eaten by moths and get rusty, and where thieves break in and steal. Store your treasures in heaven, where they will never become moth-eaten or rusty and where they will be safe from thieves. Wherever your treasure is, there your heart and thoughts will also be.   MATTHEW 6:19-21, NLT

God wants you to know that your heart is much more valuable than what's in your wallet. Who you are does not depend on what you own. Concentrate on multiplying your love for God, and he will work on multiplying your blessings.

April

How can you get to sleep
without counting sheep?

PSALM 3:4-6

The clock is ticking, everyone else is asleep (at least it seems that way), and you're staring at the ceiling in the dark, getting more tense by the minute. All of us have experienced this type of sleepless night once in a while. But there are steps you can take to avoid being awake too many nights—and they don't involve counting sheep. First, set a schedule and try to stick to it. Get up and go to bed at the same times each day, even on weekends and holidays. If you're positively not sleepy one evening, ask your parents if you can get out of bed to do something that relaxes you, like soaking your feet in hot water for ten minutes. (Soaking your feet moves blood from your brain to your feet, making your thoughts less active.) Exercise on a regular basis: the best times are mornings or late afternoons. Stay away from the caffeine in sodas and try to eliminate things that irritate you while trying to go to sleep—like a bright light or a dripping faucet.

So what?

There's another way to get to sleep—talk to God. *The Bible says:*

I cried out to the Lord, and he heard me from his Temple in Jerusalem. Then I lay down and slept in peace and woke up safely, for the Lord was watching over me. And now, although ten thousand enemies surround me on every side, I am not afraid. PSALM 3:4-6, TLB

If you feel worried or afraid, allow God to listen as you tell him about it. Ask him to take charge of whatever seems overwhelming to you. It pleases God when you show your trust in him. You can rest quietly without doing any counting except counting on God to bring you peace.

May 1

What do the letters IOU mean?

ROMANS 13:8

If you borrow money from someone, you might give that person an informal receipt with the letters IOU written on it. You intend these letters to stand for "I owe you." That's not, however, what these three letters originally meant. In the past, someone writing this type of receipt would print, "I owe unto . . ." and then add the name of the person who lent the money. "I owe unto" was abbreviated through time as IOU.

So what?

What comes after your IOUs? *The Bible says:*

Pay all your debts.   ROMANS 13:8, NLT

Some people don't repay money they owe because they say to themselves, *I need the money more than the other people do. They won't miss it. I can do more good with the money than they would.* But God doesn't want you to think that way. He doesn't want you to be dependent on anyone but him. He wants you to keep your word, repay the money quickly, and be free from every obligation. When you keep your word, you can have respect for yourself and receive the respect of others. You'll find that the next time you need to write an IOU, it won't be a problem, because everyone will know that you quickly repay any money that you borrow.

May

Why has ironing always been a chore?

2 CORINTHIANS 4:8-9

If you've ever tried to iron clothes but haven't had much success, remember that it used to be worse! At first, Greeks rolled heated iron bars across their clothes, and Romans used metal hammers to beat wrinkles out of material. Then, Vikings rocked an upside-down-mushroom-shaped iron across their damp clothes—multiple pleats were a sign of Viking wealth, because the poor didn't have enough time or servants to have pleats pressed into their clothes. By the 1400s, wealthy people in Europe used "hot box" irons. These irons were filled with a hot brick or hot coals. The poor used a flat piece of metal with a handle, heating the metal by returning it to the fire many times.

But different designs for irons caused problems. The fire-heated irons got soot or ashes on the clothes. The gas-heated irons of the 1800s could leak or even explode. By 1882 the first electric iron was patented by Henry Weely, but it took a long time to heat up, and not many people had electricity. It wasn't until 1926 that the steam iron made its first appearance.

So what?

The worst part of ironing is that it isn't permanent. That's why we have so many permanent-press fabrics today. No matter how beautifully you iron out the wrinkles on clothing that is not permanent press, the wrinkles return after the clothes are worn. Life is like that. You try your best to straighten out the "wrinkles" in your life: your troubles, your fears, and your weaknesses. But it seems that as soon as you smooth those creases, other areas appear that need work. Don't get discouraged. *The Bible tells us:*

We are pressed on every side by troubles, but we are not crushed and broken. We are perplexed, but we don't give up and quit. We are hunted down, but God never abandons us. We get knocked down, but we get up again and keep going. 2 CORINTHIANS 4:8-9, NLT

Ask God to keep you pressed close to him.

May

How did the Jacuzzi get its name?
JOHN 5:7

Did you know that the popular whirlpool tub called a Jacuzzi has its history in airplanes and arthritis? The Italian family of Candido Jacuzzi came to America in 1917. They began manufacturing equipment for airplanes, but they left the aviation business after a monoplane they had designed crashed with fatalities. The family then invented a water-injection pump for swimming pools. Candido's young son, Kenneth, had rheumatoid arthritis. One day Candido was watching Kenneth get help for his illness in a hospital whirlpool. Candido saw that the pump in the whirlpool was similar to the pump his family made, so he developed a home version of the whirlpool and sold it through medical stores. Hollywood, with its health-oriented residents, started a Jacuzzi trend by installing the tubs in their homes and by later purchasing portable versions. In 1975 the Jacuzzi family sold their business for seventy million dollars, but they will always be connected to the tubs by their name.

So what?
The Bible tells of an ill man who told Jesus:

I have no one to help me into the pool when the water is stirred up. While I am trying to get there, someone else always gets in ahead of me. JOHN 5:7, NLT

Jesus healed this man when he saw that the man couldn't reach the water. Candido found his life's work by trying to help his son get to the water. Jesus filled the ill man's need; Candido filled his son's need. If you're looking for a way to make your life meaningful, these are good examples to follow. If you look for and find a need that you can help fill, you will discover that you're helping yourself as well.

May

When did a painting turn into a puzzle?

EZEKIEL 34:16

First, the painting disappeared completely. A painter named Angelica Kauffman owned *St. Jerome,* by Leonardo da Vinci. When Kauffman died in 1804, the painting was discovered to be missing. For ten years, no one could solve the mystery. Then one day, Cardinal Joseph Fesch was touring through the antique shops of Rome and stumbled across a box. Its lid was made from the painting of St. Jerome, but the section containing Jerome's head was not on the box. The cardinal bought the box anyway. A few months later, in another shop, Cardinal Fesch found a head that looked similar to the one missing from the painting. When he took it home, he was excited to see that it matched exactly. The pieces of the puzzle were finally reunited!

So what?

It was very unlikely that the two pieces of the painting would ever be rejoined. Yet it happened. Maybe you've wandered far away from Jesus' teachings, and you think there's no way to get back. But putting things back together is Jesus' specialty. No matter how far away you are or how long you've been hidden, if you want to join Jesus again, he can find you. *The Bible says:*

I will search for my lost ones who strayed away, and I will bring them safely home again. I will bind up the injured and strengthen the weak.
EZEKIEL 34:16, NLT

If you feel like you're lost and you need to come home to Jesus, tell him about it. He will help to fit you back where you belong.

May

Is it possible to learn a language overnight?

PROVERBS 2:6

Joseph Caspar Mezzofanti always had something to say. He was a talented communicator, who by age twelve could already speak eight different languages. The Italian boy wanted to be a priest, but he wasn't old enough. He decided to study more languages until he was ordained. In 1833 the pope called Joseph to the Vatican, where Joseph served as head librarian before being promoted to a cardinal. Through it all, Joseph became well known for his ability to understand the confessions of foreign prisoners who spoke different languages.

The cardinal's most impressive achievement involved two foreigners who were scheduled for execution the next day for their crimes. Joseph prepared himself by learning their whole language in just one night so that they could speak to him freely before their death. In total, Joseph knew thirty-eight languages perfectly. He learned Chinese, the most difficult, in only four months. Joseph understood a total of seventy languages. Most amazing of all, he had never left the country of Italy, where he was born.

So what?

The fact that Joseph could communicate with so many people is amazing. It didn't matter so much what he said—people were just impressed that he could say it at all. If Joseph was amazing, God is astounding. God speaks to every person on earth, and every single one knows exactly what God is saying. *But in addition, the Bible tells us:*

The Lord grants wisdom! From his mouth come knowledge and - understanding. PROVERBS 2:6, NLT

God is the perfect communicator, and listening to him through Bible reading and prayer will help you to perfectly understand him.

6
May

How could you commit a crime with a pillow?

MARK 4:23-24

You've been sleeping on a new pillow, but the crackling from the tag is driving you crazy. You decide to cut it off. Suddenly you see those words: "Do not remove under penalty of law." What will happen if you snip it with the scissors? Will the police or the FBI come knocking on your door? Will cutting the tag cause some kind of unforeseen harm to the pillow or to you? Don't worry or lose any sleep. The warning on the tag isn't directed at you. It's addressed to the manufacturers and sellers of your pillow. Some time ago the people who stuffed upholstered articles didn't always use the materials they were supposed to. The tag was meant to make them comply with safety laws. The law insists that the contents of your pillow be listed on the tag so that you'll know what you're buying. The sellers are the ones who aren't allowed to remove it.

The tag that seemed such a threat to you is actually there for your protection. Once you take your purchase home, you may do whatever you'd like with the tag. Newer tags, by the way, now say, "Under penalty of law this tag is not to be removed, except by the consumer." The consumer, of course, is you, the customer—the one who uses or consumes the product.

So what?

If a threat from a pillow can make us take notice, why aren't we paying more attention to a message that comes straight from God? *He has said:*

If you have ears, listen! And be sure to put into practice what you hear. The more you do this, the more you will understand what I tell you.
MARK 4:23-24, TLB

God wants you to focus on a real danger—that you'll miss out on a lifetime of blessings. The next time you lay your head on your pillow, don't worry about the tag. Instead, create in your mind a label for yourself: "Do not remove from God." And be sure you follow that instruction!

May

How can you move an elephant?

PSALM 32:9

It takes a long time to understand an elephant. That is why, in Asia, a young boy is given his own baby elephant to make friends with and be buddies with throughout his life. The boy learns that elephants use their trunks the way humans use their hands—the trunk is raised to say "hi," the trunk strokes another elephant that's sick, or the trunk swings from side to side to show worry. Elephants talk, too—with snorts, growls, and squeaks—and each sound means something different. An elephant even blows its trunk like a horn to make people move out of the way. Elephants are very light sleepers—they sleep only about an hour a day. They snore very loudly when they do go to sleep.

After the boy learns these things, it is time for the elephant to learn from the boy. Riding on the back of his elephant, the boy teaches it that a touch on its back means *stop,* pressing its right ear means *turn right,* pressing its left ear means *turn left,* and a pat on the head means *kneel.*

Now the boy-and-elephant team are ready to work. The boy rides his elephant while the elephant pulls heavy logs from place to place or knocks over small trees. At one time elephants were even ridden into war like tanks. But elephants didn't do well in battle, because they were too peaceful. They would run away from a fight, and they stepped on whoever was in their way, even their masters.

So what?

Training animals is a hard job, because the trainer is trying to make them do something that they're not used to doing. *The Bible tells us:*

Do not be like the horse or the mule, which have no understanding but must be controlled by bit and bridle or they will not come to you.

PSALM 32:9, NIV

This means that God wants you to come quickly and willingly to him. He doesn't want you to have to be dragged or pushed by your parents. Once you learn of God's greatness, you'll *want* to run to him, because you know he will be waiting to show you his plan for you, which is the very best plan.

May

How did a toy stop an army?

HEBREWS 13:6

Once, three little boys with a toy cannon stopped a whole army. Two groups of soldiers were practicing war games in Louisiana in 1944. The Blue Team was sneaking around in the woods. Nearby, three boys were playing with their toy cannon. It fired carbide gas and was very loud. The boys fired the cannon in the direction of the Blue Team, not even knowing that they were there. The Blues heard the boom and didn't know who was shooting at them. They returned fire, shooting blanks (not real bullets) at the boys. The boys and the army shot at each other for almost half an hour. Finally, everyone discovered that five hundred tanks, jeeps, and trucks, plus a lot of men, had been kept busy by three boys and a toy.

So what?

Sometimes you may feel like you are battling something much greater than you are, just like the boys were "fighting" against a whole army. Maybe it's your math class, or a school bully, or trying to learn to live with your parents' divorce. When you feel weak and powerless and unable to change things, you can turn your troubles over to God. He is stronger than any problem. *The Bible reminds us how to count on him when it says:*

The Lord is my helper, so I will not be afraid. What can mere mortals do to me? HEBREWS 13:6, NLT

God is mightier than anything on earth, even the biggest cannon ever built. He will bless you with hope, comfort, and help that go far beyond what any human could provide.

May

How did the propeller of a ship help invent the cash register?

LEVITICUS 19:13

A man named James J. Ritty, who owned a business in Ohio, had a big problem. He owned a store, and his employees were taking money that didn't belong to them. Mr. Ritty had no good way to keep track of the money his business was making. This upset Mr. Ritty so much that he took an ocean cruise to feel better.

While he was on the ship, Mr. Ritty noticed a machine that was counting how many times the boat's propeller went around. A counting machine was just what Mr. Ritty needed! He was so excited about it that as soon as the ship reached shore, Mr. Ritty turned right around and went home again without spending even one night of his vacation there. The year was 1879, and soon Mr. Ritty had designed and started selling the cash register. Some registers were made with a bell that would ring every time the drawer was opened. Anyone trying to sneak money out of the drawer would suddenly have everyone else in the store looking at him. One kind of cash register was even called the "thief catcher."

God tells us that workers have the right to keep the money they have honestly worked for. So, of course, Mr. Ritty was right to keep his employees from stealing his money.

So what?

When you get your first job, you'll want to be the kind of worker your boss can trust, not someone he or she always has to keep an eye on. And if you're a boss yourself someday, be sure to treat your employees fairly. *The Bible explains:*

Do not cheat or rob anyone. Always pay your hired workers promptly.
LEVITICUS 19:13, NLT

Whether you grow up to be a boss or an employee, remember to respect the people who work with you, and give them what rightfully belongs to them.

May

What haven't you noticed when watching the clock?

ECCLESIASTES 3:1

We spend a lot of time looking at the faces of clocks. Here are some facts about clocks that you may not have noticed.

Many clocks use Roman numerals to show the hour. In school, you are taught that the number four is written as IV. But look carefully at the number four on clocks or watches that have Roman numerals. Many times the four is written with four straight lines. Why? Long ago, a French king named Louis XV had a watch. Whenever he looked at it, he got the IV (four) and the VI (six) mixed up. The king sent his watch back to the watchmaker and asked that the four be changed to look different from the six. Naturally, everyone wanted to copy what the king was doing, so many clocks and watches began to use the four lines instead of the IV, and the custom still exists.

Check the faces of clocks and watches that are being advertised in newspapers, on TV, or in stores. If the clock has hands, most likely the hands will be set at 8:20 or 10:10. Why? One rumor says that clocks are set at 8:20 because that is when President Lincoln died. But he was actually shot around 10:00 at night and died around 7:30 in the morning. The real reasons why clocks and watches often say 8:20 or 10:10 are not very exciting. When the hands are placed in either of these positions, the clock looks more pleasing because it looks balanced. The other reason is that most watchmaking companies put their names near the bottom of the face. So the hands of the clock need to be set in a position that does not cover up the name of the company.

So what?

We use time to help keep our days in order. It would be very confusing if kids went to school and came home at a different time each day. Suppose there were no schedule for when your favorite TV show would come on! What if you never knew whether your next meal would be served in five minutes or five hours? God keeps his world in order by regularly giving us day and night, winter and summer. *The Bible says:*

There is a right time for everything.   ECCLESIASTES 3:1, TLB

Use time to help you keep track of what you're doing, and make sure to include time for God!

11

May

Why does a cat lick like that?

MATTHEW 23:26

Cats have everything they need to set up their own Laundromats. They lick their fur to clean themselves, and it works very well because of their tongues and their saliva. The saliva of a cat has a kind of detergent in it, which keeps their fur washed and smelling sweet. The cat's tongue is rough, so when the tongue rubs over the fur, it pulls out dead hair and dirt. But licking helps cats in other ways, too. The saliva acts like a little shower when the weather is hot, helping the cat stay cool. Also, when the sun shines on a cat's fur, it makes Vitamin B, which the cat digests from licking itself. Licking fur also helps a cat to hunt, because after licking itself, the cat gets rid of its natural odor. When the cat, especially a wild cat like a lion, tries to hunt, other animals can't smell it coming.

So what?

Cats clean only the outside of their bodies. But people need to think about being clean on the inside, too. That's where our hearts and souls and feelings and personalities are. While it's important to be neat and clean on the outside, it's even more important to be clean on the inside—that's where God looks! He checks to see if you are loving and kind and honest. That's what makes you bright and shiny clean to him. *The Bible tells us:*

First wash the inside of the cup, and then the outside will become clean, too. MATTHEW 23:26, NLT

When you are full of God's love on the inside, it will shine out of you, and you will look wonderful.

May

12

When did a softball player catch a flying baby?

DEUTERONOMY 33:27

Tom Deal was disappointed in himself. One afternoon, Tom had been play-ing softball, and he had missed a fly ball that should have been easy to catch. Because Tom missed the ball, his team lost. When he went to sleep that night he was still thinking of that bad catch. The next morning, Tom had something else to think about. He heard crying, and when he looked out the window, he saw that a baby in the apartment across the street was crawling out onto the balcony. The balcony was on the third floor, and the baby was heading straight for the railing. Tom dashed across the street and rang and rang the doorbell, but nobody answered. When Tom looked up, he could see that the baby was crawling right through the railing! Tom stretched out his arms and leaped forward—just in time to catch the falling baby.

So what?

Years from now, no one will remember whether Tom caught the baseball or not. But that baby's family will always remember that Tom was there to save their child. Lots of times we feel like failures because of little things that didn't work out right. But when we believe in Jesus Christ, we can be free from disappointment about things that really don't matter. That's because we've taken care of the most important thing. *The Bible says:*

The eternal God is your refuge, and his everlasting arms are under you.
DEUTERONOMY 33:27, NLT

This verse tells us that God promises to catch us in his arms no matter what.

May 13

Since fish are always in schools, aren't they smart?

PSALM 103:2

When fish travel in groups, we call that group a school. Maybe that's why we expect fish to be smart—but they really aren't.

A good place to go fishing is on a bridge, because fish are attracted to the water below bridges. The water there is shady and dark. Plankton, which is a kind of plant, collects on bridges under the water, so the fish have plenty to eat. Because bridges are usually built at the narrowest part of a river, fish enjoy the way the water flows faster there.

While you're hooking a fish and pulling it out of the water, the other fish are watching. Why don't they swim away so they won't get caught also? When they see a fish struggling, the other fish get upset and try to hide. That's when they seem smart. But as soon as you pull the fish out of the water and out of sight, within a minute the other fish forget about danger and come swarming back.

So what?

The Bible tells us it is smart to remember what God does:

Praise the LORD, I tell myself, and never forget the good things he does for me. PSALM 103:2, NLT

If you forget how good God has been to you, you might become afraid. You might think that God has left you all alone and that you have no one to protect you. But the Bible tells you that you don't need to be afraid and that you can prove it to yourself by listing all the ways God has already helped you. If you don't forget like the fish do, you won't be hooked by fear.

May
14

How did the cavemen build their caves?

1 PETER 2:4

Did cavemen have to chip away rocks and dirt until they had a hole big enough to live in? Not at all. The only thing the cavemen had to do before they moved into a cave was to find one. So how did the caves get there in the first place? The rain made them! There is a soft rock called limestone that is full of tiny holes. Rainwater dribbled through those holes for thousands of years and washed away the rock in between the holes. Finally there was just one big hole, and the hole was full of water. After the water drained out, the cavemen moved in.

So what?

Having a house already made of stone was convenient for the cavemen. *Rocks are hard and sturdy, and that is why the Bible says:*

Come to Christ, who is the living Foundation of Rock upon which God builds. 1 PETER 2:4, TLB

You can always count on the promises of Jesus. If you make your relationship with Jesus the most important thing in your life, God will build you strong and sturdy.

May
15

Why do chickens wear contact lenses?

PSALM 146:8

Why would anyone buy contact lenses for a chicken? Contacts usually make vision better. But the contacts that chickens wear make their eyesight *worse*.

Chickens often fight with each other to try to establish who is boss and to pick on the weak chickens. To keep them from fighting, their owner will sometimes put contact lenses in their eyes to make the chickens' vision blurry. Then they don't know which other chickens they are looking at, and they don't attack each other. Also, the chickens wearing contacts have to look at the ground very closely to find their food. When a chicken keeps its head down, that means it doesn't want to fight, so the other chickens tend to leave it alone.

So what?

Contact lenses affect the way people (or chickens!) see with their eyes. But to see and understand things better with your *heart*, you need God's help. *The Bible promises this:*

The LORD opens the eyes of the blind.   PSALM 146:8, NLT

If you are confused or doubt God's promises, it's as if your soul is blind to God's goodness. Ask God to help, and he will make his love clear to you. Try it and SEE!

May 16

If someone told you to be quiet, would you never speak again?

ECCLESIASTES 3:1, 7

Everyone has been asked to be quiet at one time or another, but Mrs. Regnier, a French lady, didn't like being told to hush—she REALLY didn't like it. She had been speaking to her husband, and he said in an irritated way, "Be silent, woman, you talk nonsense." Mrs. Regnier got angry and left the room. She didn't speak to her husband for days.

Feeling bad, Mr. Regnier went to his wife and apologized. But she just stared at him and stayed silent. She wouldn't speak to anyone else either. When her daughter asked her for permission to marry, Mrs. Regnier wouldn't even say the one word *yes*. She just nodded to her daughter. After her one moment of anger, Mrs. Regnier never allowed herself to make a sound to anyone, for any reason, ever again for as long as she lived.

So what?

Mrs. Regnier did not do the right thing. *The Bible says:*

There is a time . . . to be quiet and a time to speak up.
ECCLESIASTES 3:1, 7, NLT

If Mrs. Regnier had tried to be kind, she wouldn't have made everyone around her unhappy for so long. Her family wanted her to talk again, and they tried to tell her so. But she showed her family selfishness instead of giving them love. If someone says something mean to you, don't say something mean in return. That is a time to be silent. As soon as you can, think of something nice to say and say it. That is when it's good to speak. Learning the right times "to be quiet" and "to speak up" will make you happy, and it will make other people happy with you.

17

May

If you lived before locks were invented, how could you keep yourself and your things protected?

PSALM 4:8

It wouldn't be easy. In early times, a tree with a hole in it made a good place to hide valuables, and you could roll a heavy rock in front of your cave door so no one would be able to come in. If your home was built into the side of a cliff like the homes of the Pueblo Indians, you would drop a ladder out the door during the day and pull it back in at night. You could also build your house on stilts, where it was hard for everyone, including you, to get in.

People eventually started living in log houses, which were smaller than most houses today but similar in style to many contemporary homes. In the early days of log houses, you could have rolled a big log against the door to keep enemies out. But that worked only as long as you were inside. If you wanted to leave the house, there would be no one inside to put the log in place. You can imagine how convenient and comforting it was to finally have a lock!

So what?

Sometimes, though, people put too much importance on keeping possessions inside and strangers outside. Perhaps you know people who have spent lots of money on security systems and special fences. No matter how much we try to protect ourselves, we won't ever feel completely safe if we just depend on things that humans have created. *The Bible says:*

You alone, O Lord, will keep me safe.   PSALM 4:8, NLT

God is the only one who can really protect you.

May 18

What kind of fire alarm would be foolproof?

JAMES 3:5-6

Someone pulls the fire alarm. The trucks roar out of the firehouse, honking and flashing, and speed to where the alarm was set off. Ready to help, the firefighters jump off the truck. That's when they discover that this was only a false alarm. About one-fourth of all fire alarms are false alarms. Sometimes people make a game or a dare out of setting off the alarm, which is not a mature thing to do, for it wastes both time and money.

Lawrence Hartshorn had an idea about how to stop false alarms. He made a large booth, which looked like a huge lipstick holder, and put the alarm system inside. Someone wanting to pull the alarm had to go inside the booth and lock the door behind him. Otherwise the alarm wouldn't go off. How did that help stop false alarms? Whoever was in the booth had to stay there for at least five minutes before the door unlocked itself. During that time, the police and firefighters would probably arrive. If you were just playing a joke, you couldn't run away and hide. Everyone would know it was you. The booth was put outside a school in Rhode Island, where kids had been pulling alarms for fun. The false alarms stopped, and the alarm booth passed its first test.

So what?

A real fire can spread quickly and destroy everything it touches. That is why firefighters are in such a hurry to get to the scene, not stopping to find out first if the alarm is false. The Bible tells us that gossip is a lot like fire. *It says this:*

The tongue is a small thing, but what enormous damage it can do. A tiny spark can set a great forest on fire. And the tongue is a flame of fire. JAMES 3:5-6, NLT

When you repeat a rumor about someone, it can quickly get out of control, just like a fire. Soon everyone believes that the rumor is true, and the person you're talking about gets hurt. Don't use your tongue to tell stories about anyone. After all, God wants you to help people, not hurt them.

May

What is a passport?

ISAIAH 6:8

When people travel to foreign countries, they have to take along a passport. A passport is a document that has your name and picture on it. It tells what country you live in, and sometimes it names what countries you are allowed to visit.

Long ago, if you traveled from one place to another, people might try to rob you or bother you in some other way. So the leader of your country would give you some type of identification to prove that he was sending you and that you should be allowed to keep going. In Egypt, for example, the pharaoh would give you a long shield to carry. It had his name written on it, so everyone would know you had the pharaoh's permission to travel. In other countries, the ruler would give you a ring stamped with the official seal. In Europe, you would be given a letter handwritten by the authorities. Often the people traveling were pilgrims—Christians who were going to visit holy cities. They would show their letters and promise a reward to anyone who let them pass. The reward was that when the pilgrims reached their destination, they prayed for all of the people who had allowed them to keep going.

So what?

Passports in ancient times were a way of proving that someone important had sent you on an errand. *If you want to do something for the most important ruler of all, say to God the same thing that the prophet Isaiah said:*

Lord, I'll go! Send me.   ISAIAH 6:8, NLT

God loves to hear those words. He may bring people into your life who are not Christians, so that you can tell them about Jesus. Perhaps God wants someone lonely to feel his love, and he will ask you to do something kind for that person. Wherever God needs you, he will send you. And each person you meet might say, "I know who gave you your passport! You came from God!"

Why are the letters on a computer keyboard all mixed up?

JAMES 2:8

When we talk about computer or typewriter keyboards, we may use the made-up word *qwerty*. That's because *Q, W, E, R, T,* and *Y* are the first six letters on the top row of the keyboard. The letters are arranged strangely for a good reason.

The first typewriters had all the letters arranged in alphabetical order. The letters were easy to find, but the keys kept getting jammed. The letters that people needed to use most often were too close together, and the metal arms, which used to stamp the letters, caught on each other and couldn't type. So now the most-wanted letters have been separated far apart from each other. The idea started with the typewriter, but when computers were invented, the keyboards were made to match the old typewriter arrangement so that people could type the same way on either machine.

Rules are made to make things easier. Because every keyboard uses the *qwerty* rule, people don't have to learn new places for the letters every time they want to type. There are little rules, like *qwerty*, and there are much more important rules.

So what?

The Bible says this about rules:

If you really keep the royal law found in Scripture, "Love your neighbor as yourself," you are doing right. JAMES 2:8, NIV

If everyone followed this rule, the world would be a peaceful place. You can't be selfish or greedy when you are thinking of someone else's feelings first. If no one were selfish, there would be no reason to fight with anyone. Obeying the rule of treating others the way you'd like them to treat you makes life easier for everyone. But even if you're the only person trying to follow this rule, you should never stop.

May

Why were people lined up just to buy a ballpoint pen?

PROVERBS 3:3

Making a ballpoint pen that worked was a big problem for a long time. A ballpoint pen has a tiny ball in the writing tip that rolls the ink out of the pen and onto the paper. But many early ballpoint pens didn't work because the ink smeared on the paper or leaked out of the pen, and the balls often got stuck and wouldn't roll at all.

By 1945, a man named Ladislaus Biro had made a ballpoint pen that was supposed to be able to write underwater. A big department store in New York announced that it would be selling the new pens for $12.50 each. People stood in line to buy the pens and bought 25,000 of them. But the pens still didn't work very well, and many people returned them.

Finally, after four more years, Patrick Frawley improved the ink and began selling a ballpoint pen called "Papermate." Since so many people were still suspicious of the way ballpoint pens had made such a mess by leaking, Mr. Frawley told his salespeople to run into the offices of department stores and scribble with the pen on an executive's white shirt. The salesman would then guarantee to buy the man an expensive new shirt if the scribbles didn't wash out completely. The ink all came out of the shirts, so people began buying the pens again.

Then along came a man named Marcel Bich. For two years, he studied ball-point pens with a microscope. Then he made the "Ball-point Bic." Maybe you've noticed that some Bic pens also say *Biro*. That's to remind you of who really began the ballpoint.

So what?

People like good pens because when we write something important on paper, it lasts longer than if we just say it. *That is why the Bible tells us:*

Let love and faithfulness never leave you; bind them around your neck, write them on the tablet of your heart. PROVERBS 3:3, NIV

We don't really have a tablet of paper in our hearts. The Bible uses those words to show how important love and faithfulness are to God, and how important it is that we remember to put them into practice.

May

Which two letters have been left off the telephone, and why?

PSALM 34:11

The letters are Q and Z. (Could you tell without looking?) If you want to play a joke on a friend, tell them they will win a prize if they can call the numbers right away that match up to the letters FUN-QUIZ. No one can do it because of the missing letters!

Now here's another test question: Which two numbers on the telephone have no letters at all? The answer is the 0 and the 1. Long ago, the phone company decided to keep the numbers 0 and 1 free for special phone numbers. You can use 0 to call the operator, and 1 for emergencies (9-1-1), directory assistance (4-1-1), or to start a long-distance call. There are ten number buttons on the phone—numbers 0 to 9. Because 0 and 1 are special, that left only eight number-buttons free for letters. Each number could have three letters, but there would still be two letters left over. Q and Z were the unlucky letters to be dropped.

So what?

The telephone is useful because it allows us to hear from people who aren't near us at the moment. The telephone can bring us news and information. The Bible also brings us news and information, which is much more important than what a neighbor might tell us. The Bible is a message from God. *It says:*

Sons and daughters, come and listen and let me teach you the importance of trusting and fearing the Lord. PSALM 34:11, TLB

As many times as you answer the phone each day, open the Bible and read a verse or two—then you'll really be getting good answers!

May 23

Why do rabbits wiggle their noses?
MATTHEW 24:42

A rabbit has lots of control over the muscles and nerves in its nose. The rabbit can wiggle its nose all the way to the tip, which very few animals can do. When its nose is wiggling, the rabbit is searching in every direction for the smell of danger. It's a good thing for rabbits that they have such powerful noses, because being able to discover enemies ahead of time is important.

The rabbit also depends on its ears for protection, and that's why its ears are so large. Try it yourself. Cup your hands behind your ears, and you will hear better. The rabbit can also turn its ears toward a noise without moving its head, so it can hear very well.

A rabbit's ears and nose are valuable because the rabbit's enemies are wildcats, wolves, and coyotes. Since the rabbit can't outrun any of these animals, it needs to get a head start.

So what?

God gives the rabbit lots of help to stay alert, because being alert keeps it alive. As God's children, we need to stay alert too. We shouldn't get lazy and skip church on Sundays, or tell ourselves that it won't hurt us to break just one little rule or tell a teeny-tiny lie. *The Bible reminds us:*

Keep watch, because you do not know on what day your Lord will come. MATTHEW 24:42, NIV

We need to keep watching and guarding against temptation, so that we'll be ready to meet Jesus when he comes back to earth. Bible reading and prayer help us to be aware of danger just like the nose and ears help a rabbit.

What misunderstanding created the piggy bank?

1 TIMOTHY 6:18

No one really invented the piggy bank, even though the pig is the most popular container for saving pennies. It's not because pigs like to eat coins, or because pigs are expensive to feed. In the beginning, real pigs had nothing whatsoever to do with where people kept their money.

In the 1600s, almost every container in the home was made from a special kind of clay, because it was cheap and sturdy. A clay jar or bowl was used for storing extra coins. The name of the special clay that containers were made from was "pygg," so people talked about putting their money in their "pygg" or "pyggy" bank. Many years later, when potters were asked to make a "pyggy" bank like in the good old days, almost everyone had forgotten about the clay called "pygg." The potters made what they thought they were asked to create— a bank in the shape of a *pig*. Banks that looked like pigs soon became very popular, and people have enjoyed the potters' mistakes ever since.

So what?

The Bible tells us not to keep every penny of our money. *In one of the letters in the Bible, Paul wrote to a pastor named Timothy, giving him these instructions for his people:*

Tell them to use their money to do good. They should be rich in good works and should give generously to those in need, always being ready to share with others whatever God has given them. 1 TIMOTHY 6:18, NLT

Be on the lookout for ways that your money can do more good than just sitting in a pig!

May

How can a plant get its own water?

2 CORINTHIANS 4:14

Every day, kids get up from where they're sitting to get themselves a drink of water. But did you know that there is a plant that can get its own water too? When the ground is dry and there is no moisture, the resurrection plant shrivels up, curls its leaves around the fruit in its center, and turns brown. Its roots pull up out of the ground, and it looks completely dead. But the resurrection plant is only hibernating. Because its roots aren't connected to the ground, the plant can be blown by the wind. It can travel for miles. The plant rolls along until it reaches a moist place. Then it sticks its roots into the ground, uncurls its leaves, and turns green. When the water is gone, the resurrection plant curls up and rolls along again, keeping its baby fruit protected inside its crumpled leaves.

So what?

It's amazing that God has created a plant that can look dead but can come back to life. But God has done something much more amazing than that! *The Bible tells us:*

We know that the same God who brought the Lord Jesus back from death will also bring us back to life again with Jesus.
2 CORINTHIANS 4:14, TLB

God has made it possible for us to live forever in heaven, if we trust Jesus to forgive us for our sins. What a wonderful thing to know! It's more important—and impressive—than knowing about a plant that turns from brown to green.

May
26

When did the whole world have recess at the same time?

EPHESIANS 4:4

One day five million kids went out to play at the same time. Of course, they weren't all playing on the same playground. Kids from all fifty states and forty other countries took part in the idea started by one physical education teacher, Len Saunders, from New Jersey.

Len thought that a worldwide recess would be a good way to celebrate exercise. He called it Project ACES, or "All Children Exercising Simultaneously." Schools in many parts of the world made plans to fill their playgrounds with kids at a certain time. But in Australia and Japan, it is the middle of the night when it is daytime in America. How did those kids join in the fun? They set their alarm clocks to wake them up and went to their school yards in the dark!

Started in 1989, Project ACES continues to grow every year.

So what?

Being a Christian is like being part of the recess project. There are Christians all over the world who all believe the same things even though they don't speak the same language. *The Bible tells us:*

We are all parts of one body, we have the same Spirit, and we have all been called to the same glorious future. EPHESIANS 4:4, TLB

Imagine what it would be like if every Christian in every country decided to light a candle at the same time. What a glow of God's love!

May 27

When did an umbrella make people laugh?

PSALM 69:7

When Jonas Hanway walked around London with his umbrella in the eighteenth century, he always caused a big commotion. Some people laughed at him. They made fun of him because at that time umbrellas were just for women. Umbrellas were mainly used to shade ladies from the sun and were made of colorful cloth and trimmed in gold or silver. In fact, the word *umbrella* comes from the Latin word *umbra,* meaning "shade." The men of London thought Jonas was being silly.

Other people got angry with Jonas. Coach drivers were upset because they were afraid that if he showed people that they could walk in the rain, no one would pay for a carriage to take them anywhere. Church people said that Jonas was being disrespectful, because they thought that when God made it rain, he wanted people to get wet.

Jonas paid no attention to what people said. He carried his umbrella everywhere he went. When he had visited Portugal, Jonas had learned that umbrellas were given to royalty as gifts and that whenever Portuguese sailors landed in another country, they would jump out of their ships and hold an umbrella up over their captain's head so everyone would understand that he was in charge. Jonas Hanway liked the Portuguese ideas and decided to prove to the English people that umbrellas were for everyone, in all kinds of weather. Finally, after thirty years, lots of English people began to carry umbrellas, and no one laughed at Jonas anymore.

So what?

Jonas believed in the umbrella so much, he didn't pay any attention to the people who made fun of him. Sometimes, as God's children, we have to do the same thing. There are people who don't believe in Jesus. They may want to make you feel bad. But stay strong, and don't pay attention. *You can be proud to say to God:*

I am mocked and cursed and shamed for your sake. PSALM 69:7, TLB

God will protect you much more than the umbrella protected Jonas.

May

What lieutenant wouldn't stop fighting World War II?

LUKE 12:2-3

You have to admire the man for his obedience. Japanese Lieutenant Hiroo Onoda was ordered not to surrender to the enemy during World War II. He didn't—even thirty years after the war was over. Onoda was left by his countrymen on the Philippine Islands with the promise that they would come back. The war ended, Japan surrendered, and papers were dropped on the island explaining to their soldiers that they should come out of the jungle. But Onoda thought the announcements were a trick and ignored them. He lived in the jungle from 1945 to 1974, until a young Japanese explorer told the loyal lieutenant that the war was over. Even then Onoda wouldn't believe it. He said he would only surrender after receiving word from his former commanding officer. Fortunately, the man was still alive. He was brought to the island, and only then did Onoda accept the truth.

So what?

Because Onoda stayed hidden, he missed years and years of a better life. He made things much harder on himself than they had to be. Sometimes we think that if we hide from God, we will be better off, because we don't really believe that God is our friend. *But Jesus tells us in the Bible:*

The time is coming when everything will be revealed; all that is secret will be made public. Whatever you have said in the dark will be heard in the light, and what you have whispered behind closed doors will be shouted from the housetops for all to hear! LUKE 12:2-3, NLT

It is impossible to hide from God. He already knows the worst things about you, and yet he promises to love you no matter what you have done. If you are weary of ducking, dodging, and hiding, come out into the freedom of the light of God's love by asking his forgiveness. He will give you a clean soul and a fresh start.

May

Why did one letter take seven years to reach the White House?

MATTHEW 7:7-8

During the Vietnam War, a soldier named George Mellendorf was distressed about how long it was taking to send and receive his letters. At that time, travel and communication were difficult. Nevertheless, George decided to try to do something about it. He went straight to the top, sending a letter of complaint to the President of the United States, Richard Milhous Nixon. George's letter said: "Dear President Nixon: It seems nobody cares if we get our mail. We are lucky to get it twice a week. Sir, someone is not doing their job." George didn't get an answer to his letter, written in January of 1971, that year or the next year or the next. Apparently, everything possible was already being done to improve the mail service, but things still remained tough. George's letter didn't actually arrive at the White House until 1978, more than seven years after it was sent.

So what?

Surely George was hoping that he would get a fast answer to his letter. It probably crossed his mind that he was not important enough to be "worth" the efforts of the president of his country.

Jesus is the most important, most exalted, and highest ranking person who ever existed. But you never have to worry about getting his attention. You have his promise to count on, and Jesus never goes back on his word. *He said:*

Keep on asking, and you will be given what you ask for. Keep on looking, and you will find. Keep on knocking, and the door will be opened. For everyone who asks, receives. Everyone who seeks, finds. And the door is opened to everyone who knocks. MATTHEW 7:7-8, NLT

You are so important to God that he will always answer you. If you haven't already, ask him to open the door to his kingdom for you, so you can see for yourself.

May

What American pastime started with a garage door and a projector?

1 TIMOTHY 4:14-16

What was Richard Hollingshead Jr. doing in his driveway that night in Camden, New Jersey, in 1932? He had put a screen in front of his garage door, fastened a projector to the top of his car, and then sat in the front seat to watch home movies. That's how the first drive-in movie was born. Hollingshead began planning how to market his new idea. He tested his car under a sprinkler to make sure the movie could be seen in the rain, and he planned to serve snacks. In 1933 he began to build his dream. His "Automobile Movie Theatre" had parking for four hundred cars on a lot the size of a football field. Guardrails kept the cars from rolling off the seven slanting rows.

The drive-in was a big success. After the Great Depression, people loved movies as an escape from their dreary lives, and they gladly paid the one-dollar fee per car. The biggest problem Hollingshead had to overcome was the sound for the movie. In the beginning, small speakers were placed on the ground under each car, but the sound coming through the floorboards wasn't satisfactory. Next, big speakers on each side of the screen let everyone hear—even those in the neighborhood who didn't want to listen. Finally, speakers that could be hung on car windows proved to be a success. In the 1950s, there were more than five thousand outdoor theaters. But when television appeared on the scene, people stopped going to drive-ins so regularly. While there are still a few drive-in theaters scattered across the country, they've lost the widespread popularity they once enjoyed.

So what?

It's not easy being a trendsetter. People tend to think you're odd, and they often don't hesitate to point that out. But if you have a good idea, pursue it. God may be speaking to your heart. *The Bible says:*

Be sure to use the abilities God has given you. . . . Put these abilities to work; throw yourself into your tasks so that everyone may notice your improvement and progress. Keep a close watch on all you do and think. Stay true to what is right and God will bless you and use you to help others. 1 TIMOTHY 4:14-16, TLB

Work hard, pray hard, and expect big results.

May

What is the surprise ingredient in your cereal?

JEREMIAH 31:3

Did you know that we actually eat pieces of iron on a regular basis? Since our bodies need iron to help oxygen get to our muscles, many cereals are "iron-fortified"—and they really mean it. It's added to cereal in the form of tiny metal filings. You can even see the slivers sometimes by taking an extremely strong magnet and plunging it into the box. The magnet will attract these specks, and you'll be able to inspect them. Although it doesn't sound very appetizing, eating the metal shavings is harmless.

So what?

God was the one who designed metal to be attracted to a magnet. If he had wanted to, he could have made us unable to resist him by creating us to be pulled to him against our will. But God gave us hearts and souls and emotions, which make us different from mere animals. He also gave us the freedom to choose whether or not to follow him and become part of his family. If we are attracted to God, it is because we realize that he has something very special that we need. *God says:*

I have loved you, my people, with an everlasting love. With unfailing love I have drawn you to myself. JEREMIAH 31:3, NLT

There's no need to wait. Right now you can draw near to God. He is the only source that can fortify your life with the strength and power and love you need to live.

June 1

When was delivering mail a challenge for mail carriers?

JOHN 20:30-31

Rural Free Delivery Service began, first as an experiment in 1896, and later as an official service of the United States Post Office Department in 1902. In the early 1900s, it was a real challenge to be a rural mail carrier. Driving up to a farmhouse, the mailman never knew where he'd be putting the mail. He could find any type of container waiting for him—an ordinary basket, or something a little more imaginative, like an old tire or a cigar box or an oil can. At each stop, the mailman had to leave his truck, hunt for the place, and hope that the rain or snow didn't destroy letters that weren't protected from the weather. In 1902, Congress authorized a standard-size mailbox, but the postmaster general had to sift through proposed plans for the next thirteen years before postal worker Roy Joroleman came up with the winning design seen everywhere today.

That doesn't mean that mail carriers always have it easy now. People still find ways to modify their mailboxes. Lee Patterson of Montana built his box fourteen feet in the air. As a basketball player, he enjoyed jumping for his letters. The postman, however, wasn't thrilled about having to stand on the roof of his truck to complete his job.

So what?

We depend on mail carriers to deliver messages to us. You've probably waited anxiously for the mail now and then, anticipating something important. Wouldn't it be great if everyone was that eager to read the Bible? It contains the most important written message anyone could receive, because the words are from God, who is our Creator and the Creator of the whole universe! *The Bible says:*

Jesus' disciples saw him do many other miraculous signs besides the ones recorded in this book. But these are written so that you may believe that Jesus is the Messiah, the Son of God, and that by believing in him you will have life. JOHN 20:30-31, NLT

God wants you to love and enjoy his words in the Bible. The message was sent special delivery just for you.

June

What can happen if you have only one copy of your manuscript?

MATTHEW 24:35

Before the days of copiers and computers, writing could be a risky business. Take Thomas Carlyle, for instance. He had written a book in the 1830s called *The French Revolution.* He wanted the opinion of one of his good friends, John Stuart Mill. So he sent the manuscript to Mr. Mill for review. Mill had to leave his house for a period of time, and while he was gone, the maid lit a fire in the grate. What did she use for fuel? The manuscript, of course, which she thought was scrap paper. Thomas Carlyle had to rewrite the whole book!

So what?

Carlyle's creation couldn't be counted upon to last—it was created by a human being, with the weaknesses and faults that all people and their creations have. Don't depend on anything to last forever unless it comes from God. *God is the only one who can promise:*

Heaven and earth will disappear, but my words will remain forever.
MATTHEW 24:35, NLT

The Bible has the only words that were available yesterday, are available today, and will be available forever.

June

How did a nose and fingertips create measurements?

ISAIAH 40:12

Where would you go to see the one, the only, the original metric meter? One actually does exist, and it's kept in Paris. It's made of platinum alloy, and all meters around the world are measured to its markings. We can thank Napoleon for the metric system. He wanted to find a way to unite all the countries he had conquered so that the people would have a common form of measurement. Napoleon's scientists devised the meter by determining that it was one ten-millionth of the distance between the North Pole and the equator. They weren't completely exact with that calculation, but they did establish a length everyone could use.

The meter was a big improvement on the yard, which King Henry VIII declared to be precisely the distance between the tip of his (and only his) nose and the tips of his outstretched fingers. An inch was supposed to be the width of a thumb—any thumb. You can see the problem. A foot was as long as a person's foot, and a cubit, which was an even older measurement, was the length between the elbow to the tip of the middle finger.

The word *meter* comes from the Greek word *metron,* which means "measure." The meter made measuring a lot simpler for everyone.

So what?

No matter what we try to measure, our efforts will always fall short compared to God's standard. *The Bible says:*

Who else has held the oceans in his hand? Who has measured off the heavens with his fingers? Who else knows the weight of the earth or has weighed out the mountains and the hills? ISAIAH 40:12, NLT

As humans, we can only measure those things that God has already created. His might is beyond measure!

June 4

Why does metal feel colder than wood?

REVELATION 3:15-18

Have you ever noticed that whenever you touch a piece of metal, it feels cool? Try it now by feeling a doorknob, and then touching the wooden door to which the knob is attached. What makes the difference in the temperature? Metal is a good conductor of heat, which means that heat moves through it quickly. When you touch metal, it immediately pulls heat from your hand. This makes your skin feel cool. It's not really that metal itself is cold. It's just better at taking heat away from you.

So what?

God uses an example about temperature to teach us how to live. *He says:*

I know all the things you do, that you are neither hot nor cold. I wish you were one or the other! But since you are like lukewarm water, I will spit you out of my mouth! You say, "I am rich. I have everything I want. I don't need a thing!" And you don't realize that you are wretched and miserable and poor and blind and naked. I advise you to buy gold from me—gold that has been purified by fire. Then you will be rich. And also buy white garments so you will not be shamed by your nakedness. And buy ointment for your eyes so you will be able to see.
REVELATION 3:15-18, NLT

God wants you to be totally committed to him. We often say that people who are totally committed to serving God are on fire for him. If we don't get excited about living for God and doing things for him, then we're just lukewarm. God is not pleased with lukewarm Christians. It's the ones who are on fire that he promises to help. He will give us everything we need. The things he promises to give us (gold, white garments, and ointment) will make us rich and wise spiritually. Being lukewarm about the way you feel toward God will make you miserable. But being on fire for God, now that's the way to go!

5

June

What billion-dollar industry was created from paper cups and milk shakes?

HEBREWS 13:5

Ray Kroc was a paper-cup salesman. To sell more cups, he tried to think of more ways for people to fill up his cups. When he learned about a machine called a Multimixer, which made malted milk shakes, Ray began selling those machines. That's how he ran across the McDonald brothers, who were running a hamburger stand that used eight Multimixers—enough to make forty milk shakes at once! Ray visited the restaurant in California to see how it was being run, and he was very impressed.

Unlike most restaurants, they didn't have carhops come to your car window to take your order or use dishes that had to be washed. They offered a limited menu of nine ready-to-go items at reasonable prices: hamburgers were fifteen cents, french fries were ten cents, and milk shakes were twenty cents. A platter toasted twenty-four buns at the same time.

In 1954, Ray began franchising the McDonald's concept in exchange for giving the brothers a percentage of the income from these new restaurants. The brothers chose not to build more restaurants themselves, saying that they had all the money they needed, and they didn't want the headaches that came with expanding. Under Ray's direction, the first new McDonald's opened in Des Plaines, Illinois, in 1955. In 1961, the brothers sold all McDonald's rights to Ray.

So what?

Despite the fact that Ray Kroc became a rich man, neither Dick nor Mac McDonald ever expressed regret for selling their fast-food concept. The McDonald brothers came up with a winning combination for selling fast food, but even more valuable was their decision to sell McDonald's. They had learned a rich lesson that money can't buy: They were happy with their lives. *The Bible says:*

Stay away from the love of money; be satisfied with what you have. For God has said, "I will never fail you. I will never forsake you."
HEBREWS 13:5, NLT

God wants us to take the time to count our blessings instead of our bucks.

June

What popular game began on the grounds of a hotel?

HEBREWS 13:8

If you were visiting Carter's Lookout Mountain Hotel in Tennessee in 1926, you could do something that no one else in America had ever done before. Garnet Carter, the hotel's owner, had just invented this activity for his guests. No one could guess what a popular fad it would become or how profitable it would be. What was keeping the residents of the hotel so busy? Miniature golf, which Carter called "Tom Thumb" golf after the little person in the P. T. Barnum circus. When Carter saw how many people wanted to play, he started the Fairyland Manufacturing Company, which made courses at other locations in one week's time for two thousand dollars. By 1930, two hundred thousand people were working in the miniature golf industry. People began to think that this was an easy way to get rich quickly, and soon there were so many golf courses that players became bored with the game, and the fad died—except as a children's amusement.

So what?
The public often changes its mind in a hurry. They may love something, hate something, or seesaw back and forth between the two. Whenever you're trying to decide what people want, don't put your complete trust in what appears to be true at the moment. In fact, throughout life, you really can't trust anything to be absolutely unchangeable except God's love for you. *The Bible says:*

Jesus Christ is the same yesterday, today, and forever.   HEBREWS 13:8, NLT

You never have to worry about fads, cycles, or trends with God's love. It will never change or disappear.

June

7

Where does the term "hangnail" come from?

MICAH 7:8

Sometimes on the sides of your fingernails, extra bits of dry, brittle skin stick out. They look and feel like a short needle, and we call them "hangnails." Hangnails are one of those annoying little problems that everyone has experienced. They take up a tiny amount of space, but they deliver an attention-getting sting. If you're thinking, like most of us, that the name comes from the skin "hanging" from your fingernail, you'd be incorrect. The name comes from the Old English words for a corn on the toe: *ang,* which stood for "pain," and *naegl,* which meant "nail," because people thought the corn looked like the head of a nail. After a while, the words blurred together in sound, and the meaning grew to include fingers.

So what?

When a hangnail is hurting us, we know what to do about it. But sometimes the hurt doesn't come from a place you can pinpoint. You just know it's a dull, sad ache in your heart. God knows about that feeling, and he knows how to heal it. *He wants you to say:*

When I sit in darkness, the Lord himself will be my Light.   MICAH 7:8, TLB

Let God blow away the clouds of gloom that may sometimes sting your heart and keep you from feeling joyful. He will be your companion and your comforter, and he'll help you to have many bright tomorrows.

June

Where would you find a nest egg?

LUKE 12:34

You might hear people who are trying to save money say that they're making a nice little "nest egg" for themselves. What do they mean? Unless you're a farmer, you may not be aware that there really is such a thing as a nest egg, but it has nothing to do with money. Long ago, farmers who raised chickens would put a fake egg, sometimes made of porcelain, in the nest with the hen. This was supposed to encourage her to lay more eggs than she otherwise would. We've borrowed the words, and the idea. If we put a little money away, maybe it will turn into more as we get used to adding to it.

So what?

It's good to put money aside, but it's not so good to do it if accumulating money is what you care about most. Don't forget the value of being a friend and sharing and loving and giving. Those are the things that lead to many joys and blessings. In the long run, caring about others gives us more happiness and satisfaction than money could ever give.

It's good advice to collect the friendship of many people as carefully as you collect pennies. The Bible talks about keeping a balance. *It says:*

Wherever your treasure is, there your heart and thoughts will also be.
LUKE 12:34, NLT

If you consider your greatest treasure to be the love that you give and receive, you'll always be wealthy in spirit.

Ju n e

How did a captive audience escape from the singing emperor?

GALATIANS 5:22-23

You would think that being emperor of Rome would be enough for any man. But not so for Nero. His most-desired goal was to become a singer. He took lessons and then chose to have his first recital in Naples, where things did not go well for him. The earth shook with a tremor during the performance, and several people left while Nero was still singing. Apparently used to more loyalty than this, Nero arranged to have the gates locked so that his future audiences would be sure to stay. Some of the men got so tired of applauding, they jumped over the walls. A woman was not so fortunate—she gave birth in the stands. Three other men came up with a creative plan to get the guards to let them out of the gates. One man played dead, and the other two volunteered to carry him out.

So what?

Nero tried to force his singing on people, but it didn't work. You can't make someone like you. But when you are close to God, you will be given some tools to attract people. *The Bible says:*

When the Holy Spirit controls our lives, he will produce this kind of fruit in us: love, joy, peace, patience, kindness, goodness, faithfulness, gentleness, and self-control. GALATIANS 5:22-23, NLT

We'd all enjoy having friends with these qualities—how about letting God develop these qualities in you?

June 10

When was *Heidi* the most unpopular movie on television?

PSALM 91:14-16

Imagine that you're the television executive in charge of making a programming decision. You've been broadcasting a football game. There is one minute plus five seconds left in the game. The score is 32 to 29. A movie is scheduled to begin in one minute. What will it be—the end of the football game, or the beginning of *Heidi?* One unfortunate executive made the wrong choice in 1968 during the Oakland Raiders and New York Jets game. Viewers called the station trying to figure out why the football players had disappeared and a little girl from the Alps had arrived on the screen. Football fans were especially upset when they found out what happened in that last crucial minute on the football field. The Oakland Raiders, who had been behind, made two touchdowns and won the game! Fourteen years later, fans still hadn't forgotten—that game still stood as a gigantic blunder of sports broadcasting. *Sports Illustrated* magazine even made an award, the "Heidi Award," to give to the worst sports programming of 1968.

So what?

The hard thing about making a decision is that it comes with a result. It's obvious that the programmer who decided to show *Heidi* wasn't very popular for an awfully long time. There is a big decision for you to make that will affect the rest of your life. You need to decide whether to follow Jesus or not. If you decide that you will, the results will be spectacular. *In Scripture the Lord says:*

I will rescue those who love me. I will protect those who trust in my name. When they call on me, I will answer; I will be with them in trouble. I will rescue them and honor them. I will satisfy them with a long life and give them my salvation. PSALM 91:14-16, NLT

Making the decision to follow Jesus will bring you everlasting joy that will be far more exciting than watching a winning touchdown.

11

June

Why don't doctors wear white like nurses?
ISAIAH 1:18

Nurses have worn white throughout history. The color white seems pure and is proof of cleanliness, because you can see immediately when it gets dirty. Doctors, on the other hand, have worn many uniform colors. Surgeons started with white, but switched to a spinach green color in 1914 when it was decided that red blood against white cloth was especially startling and alarming. The green background dulled the red color, but it still looked too harsh under the operating-room lighting that came into use after World War II. The green was toned down at that time to a "misty" color. Around 1960 the color changed again—this time to a "seal blue." Why? The blue color looks better on television monitors, which have become a part of operating rooms as surgeons record their operations for teaching purposes.

So what?
Red against white makes a very striking contrast. Maybe that's why God uses these colors as examples when he offers his purity to you. *He says:*

No matter how deep the stain of your sins, I can remove it. I can make you as clean as freshly fallen snow. Even if you are stained as red as crimson, I can make you as white as wool. ISAIAH 1:18, NLT

There is no such thing as being too dirty from your sins for God to love you. Ask him to clear your conscience, clean your soul, and claim your heart.

June 12

What do checkers and cookies have in common?

JOHN 1:1-3

Americans are actually responsible for two products that we've probably all assumed came from China. One is the fortune cookie, and the other is the game of Chinese checkers.

The fortune cookie that we're used to, with the paper fortune wrapped in dough, was created in 1916 by George Jung, a Chinese immigrant to America. He was a noodle maker who wanted to give the customers in Chinese restaurants something fun to do while they waited for their food to be prepared. Even though in China there was already a custom of putting messages—such as birth announcements—into cakes, and there was also a flat wafer cookie, Jung was the one who thought of putting the two ideas together. Although later Jung printed predictions, fortunes, and proverbs on the papers, the first fortune cookies contained verses from the Bible.

As for Chinese checkers, the game started in Europe in the late 1800s. It was called "Halma." By the 1930s, Americans were playing the game with some changes. It is believed that the name "Chinese checkers" came from the star-shaped game board on which colored marbles are moved. Apparently the star reminded people of the star on the design of the Chinese flag. The Chinese people do play Chinese checkers. They were taught by the Americans and Japanese, who learned it from the English!

So what?

Human beings have a natural curiosity. We like to know how things got started. If you've found yourself wondering how the world began, you've probably heard two stories. One is that everything fell into place by itself, and the other is that God made it all. To find out for sure, consult the only true reference book. *The Bible says:*

Before anything else existed, there was Christ, with God. . . . He created everything there is—nothing exists that he didn't make. JOHN 1:1-3, TLB

Begin with this truth, and your spiritual life will be started on a firm foundation.

June **13**

How did chop suey get its name?

ECCLESIASTES 7:1

No one seems to know exactly who invented chop suey, but everyone agrees that it was first made in America. One story says that long ago, a Chinese diplomat was visiting the United States. Some of his American friends asked him to make a Chinese meal that they could sample. The Chinese man couldn't find the same ingredients in America that he had used when making meals in China, so he asked his cook to gather up some American foods and put them in a pot. Then they added some tangy Soya sauce (which few Americans had tasted yet), served the dish, and created a taste sensation.

Another story suggests that a Chinese cook was feeding gold miners. He threw together all the leftovers, and chop suey was born.

And what about the name *chop suey?* There are several ideas about where the name came from. The *chop* could have come from chopsticks or from our English word *chop,* meaning to cut into small pieces. The *suey* could have started as a mispronunciation of "Soya" sauce. Or the term *chop suey* might have come from the Chinese words *tsa sui,* which means a mixture of various bits and pieces, and sounds like "chop suey" in English.

So what?

If you like to eat chop suey, then you're probably glad when you hear its name. The words *candy, present,* and *vacation* may make you feel happy too. But words like *homework, shots,* or *punishment* might make you uncomfortable. When people hear your name, do they feel happy or upset? Do they admire you, or do they want to stay away from you? *The Bible tells us:*

A good name is better than fine perfume.   ECCLESIASTES 7:1, NIV

When you are kind and fair, people will welcome you and your name, because you will be pleasing to them, just like the finest perfumes.

June 14

Why did Cinderella wear glass slippers?

ECCLESIASTES 9:10

The story of Cinderella has been told for hundreds of years. It's been told in many different countries, including China, England, Germany, and France.

In 1697, a Frenchman named Charles Perrault wrote the Cinderella story in his own language. In the earliest Cinderella stories, her shoes were made of gray and white squirrel fur. The French word for fur is *vair.* Charles wrote that Cinderella's shoes were made of *verre,* which sounds the same, but is spelled differently and means "glass." Ever since, American children have pictured a sparkling glass slipper left behind on the palace stairs.

So what?

It is not clear if Charles Perrault (or another French writer before him) changed the word *fur* to the word *glass* on purpose, or if the word was changed because of a mistake in spelling. Whatever the case may be, no one had any idea that this change would become so famous. If it was a mistake, the translator would probably be embarrassed to know about it. *The Bible says:*

Whatever you do, do well.   ECCLESIASTES 9:10, NLT

People often look at your actions to see what kind of person you are. So double-check that homework, and put some extra effort into your chores. Do your work so that your example will shine as much as that "glass" slipper did.

June
15

What made feeding babies more fun?

PSALM 71:5

Before 1900, if you had a baby in the house, you had a mess in the kitchen. That's because you had to strain your baby's food before every meal so it would be mushy enough to be eaten without teeth.

Dorothy and Dan Gerber were tired of fixing meals for their baby, Sally, but store-bought baby food could only be purchased with a prescription and was very expensive. Sally's grandfather owned a vegetable canning plant, so her parents suggested to him that they begin making their own foods. The first five kinds were peas, spinach, prunes, carrots, and vegetable soup.

The Gerbers were pleased with the new products and knew that other parents would buy them if they just knew about them. So Dan came up with an idea to help sell the baby food. He put an ad in *Good Housekeeping* magazine, making this offer to parents. They could buy six jars of baby food for only one dollar if they would send in the name of their grocer. Dan then went to each grocery store and showed how many people had sent in the grocer's name—people who would buy the baby food if they could find it in the store.

Then the Gerbers had a contest to see who could draw a healthy, happy baby for the picture on the Gerber baby food jars. One lady, Dorothy Hope Smith, decided to send in a drawing, but she didn't finish it. She told the Gerbers she would work on it some more if they wanted to use it. But the Gerbers loved the drawing just the way it was and used it on every jar. The Gerbers eventually made more than 187 kinds of foods for babies.

So what?

Babies trust their parents to feed them only what is good for them. The babies don't ask questions or examine the food—they just open their mouths. As God's children, we can have that kind of faith in him. *It pleases him for us to say:*

O Lord, you alone are my hope; I've trusted you from childhood.
PSALM 71:5, TLB

No matter how old you get, God wants you to accept every blessing he sends with the complete trust of a baby taking food from a spoon.

16

June

How did people wake up on time before alarm clocks?

ISAIAH 60:1

How would your family wake up on time without an alarm clock? Long ago, there was no such thing, so inventors worked on different ways to get people to open their eyes. They tried many things, like a machine that sprinkled cold water on the sleeper, or a bed that tipped up and slid the sleeper out. Monks would light a candle and stick it between their toes before going to sleep. When the candle had burned down far enough for the flames to touch their toes, the monks knew it was time to wake up.

In 1882, Samuel Applegate thought there must be a way to be awakened more pleasantly. His idea was to attach a cord to a clock. When the time was right, the clock would release the cord, which ran to a big frame hanging over the bed. Dangling from the frame were sixty corks, which dropped onto the sleeper.

So what?

Many of us don't like getting up early, and if someone wakes us up, we often act grouchy instead of being happy to have the time to start the day with God. *The Bible tells us:*

Arise, my people! Let your light shine for all the nations to see! For the glory of the Lord is streaming from you. ISAIAH 60:1, TLB

God is pleased when we are cheerful, because that means we are so full of his love that we have some extra to give away. If you start someone's day by giving that person a smile, your day will go better too.

17

June

How can you tell where a coin was made?

ACTS 3:6

If you want to find out where a coin was made (or *minted*), here's how you can do it: If the coin has a little letter *D* stamped on it, the coin was minted in Denver. An *S* means it came from San Francisco. If there is no small letter on the coin, it was made in Philadelphia.

Here are some more fun facts that you may not know about our coins:

Every face on every United States coin is always turned to the left, with one exception. That is the penny, on which President Lincoln's face is looking to the right.

The penny and the nickel have smooth edges, but dimes and quarters have grooves around theirs. There is a reason for this. Long ago, coins were made of valuable metals like gold and silver. Dishonest people sometimes tried to carve some of the metal off coins before spending them. That meant that they weren't paying the storekeeper as much metal as he was supposed to get. It was a way of cheating. Pennies and nickels were not made of valuable metals, but dimes and quarters had real silver in them. So the government put notches on the edges of dimes and quarters. If anyone tried to shave some of the silver off, it would show, because the grooves would be gone. Just in case you're wondering, quarters have 119 notches, and dimes have 118!

So what?

Sometimes people make the mistake of thinking their money is the most valuable thing they have. But that's not true. Jesus wants to give us much more than money. If you belong to him, you have the present gift of his love and the future gift of heaven. You have talents that he has given you. You also have kindness and cheerfulness to give away to others—and those qualities can't be priced. They may be the most valuable presents that you give to someone on a day when that person is discouraged. *When a poor man asked the apostle Peter for money, Peter told him:*

Silver or gold I do not have, but what I have I give you.   ACTS 3:6, NIV

What did Peter have? He had the ability to pray for sick people. And he was able to help a lame man walk by calling on Jesus' name. Share your caring heart, and share your helping hands. Those are the possessions that make you truly rich!

June 18

Why aren't there more green flowers?

ISAIAH 61:11

We enjoy the pretty colors of flowers, but the colors are not there just to please us. They have a more important purpose. To make more plants, pollen has to be carried from one flower to another flower just like it. Flowers need insects to step on them so that the pollen will stick to their feet and come off on the next flower they land on. Their bright colors help attract insects. Bees like yellow and blue flowers. Butterflies are attracted to all bright colors. The plants that flower at night usually have very pale blooms so that moths can see them in the dark. Not many insects or birds are attracted to the color green, so there are not many green flowers.

So what?

It is exciting and pleasing to us when a garden grows. *The Bible tells us:*

The Lord will show the nations of the world his justice; all will praise him. His righteousness shall be like a budding tree, or like a garden in early spring, full of young plants springing up everywhere.
ISAIAH 61:11, TLB

God's garden of love will attract even more people than a flower garden does. God used one of the most beautiful places on earth, a garden, to describe for us how wonderful the world will be one day, when everyone will know about him.

June **19**

Are you feeling red, pink, or yellow today?

PSALM 30:11

You may not realize it, but colors can affect the way you feel. Scientists have tested people's reactions to colors, and they found some interesting results. Yellows and oranges make people feel happier, warmer, and more active. Red is an even stronger color in this group; in fact, red is such a strong color that it can make some people feel nervous. Blues and greens are calming colors. They make your blood pressure, heart rate, and breathing go slower. Another color that can help make you feel peaceful and quiet is pink.

If you were decorating a fast-food restaurant, which colors would you choose to use? The next time you go for a hamburger or a pizza, notice the walls and decorations—even the signs out in front of the restaurant. Most fast-food places stay away from greens, pinks, and blues, because these colors make people, as well as their appetites, slow down. Oranges and yellows are the best colors to inspire people to eat a lot, eat faster, and leave sooner; that way, there is room for even more customers to come in and do the same thing.

So what?

Colors may temporarily change our moods, but there is something much more lasting than paints or crayons to change our personalities. God wants to help you change in ways that are positive and permanent. *The Bible lets us know that God can do this:*

You have turned my mourning into joyful dancing. You have taken away my clothes of mourning and clothed me with joy. PSALM 30:11, NLT

If something is bothering you, don't just look for a cheerful room to make you feel better. That won't work for very long. Instead, take your problem to God. When he helps you, it won't be just temporary!

June

What bird gives its babies up for adoption?
PSALM 27:10

One day a cardinal was sitting on her eggs in her nest. She flew away for a moment, and when she came back to her nest, there was an extra egg in it. She didn't seem to notice, because she sat on all the eggs, including the new one. That was good news for another bird called the cowbird. Cowbirds never build nests of their own, and they never help raise their own families. Instead, they sneak into other birds' nests and lay their eggs there. Baby cowbirds hatch faster than most other birds, so the tiny cowbird is often the first chick the foster parents see. These parents feed the little cowbird even though it doesn't look like the other babies.

So what?
The cowbird didn't take care of her baby herself, but she made sure that someone else would do it. That baby bird would grow up never knowing its real parents, but it would still be provided for. These birds have shown us something about God's love. *The Bible tells us:*

Even if my father and mother abandon me, the Lord will hold me close.
PSALM 27:10, NLT

Maybe you or some of your friends have only one parent or don't live with either Mom or Dad. God wants to be like a Father. He wants to take good care of his children and give them all the love they have been missing. Just as the cowbird grows up and has someone to take care of it, even without its parents, so you and your friends can live a happy life, leaning together on God's love.

June

Why do golfers yell "fore"?

ISAIAH 52:12

When you're out on a golf course, you will hear a lot of golfers yelling the word *fore* and then hitting the ball. Why did they pick the number four, and why aren't they getting in trouble for screaming it?

Actually, it doesn't mean a number at all. Golfers are really copying something soldiers from long ago used to do. Soldiers had to stand in rows when they shot their guns at the enemy in a war. The back row of soldiers needed to warn the soldiers in the front row to move out of the way so they wouldn't get hit by bullets from behind. The soldiers would yell, "Beware before!" which meant "Get out of the way or you'll be shot!" Then the front row would kneel down, and the back row could shoot over their heads. But after a while the soldiers got tired of yelling the whole warning, so they shortened it to "Before!" and finally to just "Fore!" So when a golfer swings at the ball, he will yell "fore" to say, "Everybody, get out of the way of my golf ball, just in case it might hit you!" This is one time when it isn't considered rude to shout; instead, it's the most polite thing to do.

So what?

The Bible says:

The LORD will go before you, the God of Israel will be your rear guard.
ISAIAH 52:12, NIV

When you are God's child, it is better than having a whole row of soldiers behind you to protect you. Because God loves us, he gave us the Bible to tell us every way to keep ourselves safe. The Bible doesn't shout, but what it has to say is loud and clear.

June

What happens when you grab a crab?
MATTHEW 10:29-31

When you go for a walk on the beach, you're likely to find several empty crab shells on the shore. You might wonder what caused so many crabs to die. The truth is, nothing did. Each shell is like an empty house that a crab has already moved out of. Crabs grow bigger all the time, and their shells are too hard and stiff to stretch. The crab becomes really cramped and finally has to push off its old shell and grow a new one that fits him better. But the shell isn't the only part of a crab that can come off. Crabs can do a special trick to help protect themselves. If you grab a crab by one of his legs, he will just drop it off in your hand and scurry away. He can always grow a new one.

So what?

God's design for the life of a crab is fascinating. He gave each crab a sense of how to survive best. But crabs are not nearly as important to God as we are. He has made even more careful plans for our lives. *The Bible reminds us:*

Not even a sparrow, worth only half a penny, can fall to the ground without your Father knowing it. And the very hairs on your head are all numbered. So don't be afraid; you are more valuable to him than a whole flock of sparrows. MATTHEW 10:29-31, NLT

If God is paying so much attention to how a little bird flies or where a little crab lives, imagine how much more he cares about you, his child! God knows so much about you that he even keeps track of how many hairs you have. Even you don't know that number, and it's your own head! Because God knows more about you than you know about yourself, you can trust that he is always watching over you with love.

Why was a soft clay invented?

PSALM 90:17

We usually don't think of school and playing as being the same thing. But in 1955, something to be used for playing was invented because of a need in a classroom of young children. A teacher in New Jersey was not happy with the regular clay her nursery school students had to play with. It was too stiff, too dry, and too difficult for her students to use. She told her brother-in-law about this problem, and he began experimenting. He came up with a grayish-white clay that was softer and easier to mold into shapes. People in schools started using it, and one day during a demonstration, a department store became interested in buying the new clay. That's when it began being sold as a toy, after the colors red, yellow, and blue were added. Have you guessed what this new product was named? When you're in the toy store, look on the shelf for Play-Doh.

So what?

God has plans for each of us, and no matter how small our tasks may seem, he has a reason for having us do them. Using Play-Doh in nursery school may not seem important, but perhaps God is helping a child learn to create something with her hands, because she will one day become a sculptress. Only God knows what our talents are. *We should pray this prayer:*

May the Lord our God show us his approval and make our efforts successful.   PSALM 90:17, NLT

He will send us to people who will help us get the training we need for the job he wants us to do.

June 24

How did a bookmark become a special notepad?

ROMANS 8:28

Arthur Fry had a problem. When he sang in church, the bookmarks he used kept falling out of his hymnal. Arthur worked for a company that made different kinds of glue, and he remembered a mistake that one of the workers had made that just might come to his rescue. That scientist, Spencer Silver, had been trying to invent a very strong glue, but it didn't work. Instead, he ended up with a very *weak* glue: It stuck things together, but they could easily be pulled apart again. What good was glue that didn't stick forever? Arthur Fry thought he knew. He got some of the glue and spread it on his bookmarks. Sure enough, the glue was so weak that it stuck only as long as Arthur wanted it to. When he wanted to move the bookmarks, they came out easily without ruining the pages of the book. From a mistake, something good had just been invented. We call it the Post-it note.

So what?

The Bible says:

We know that God causes everything to work together for the good of those who love God. ROMANS 8:28, NLT

For his children, God will make sure that something good comes out of anything bad, and that something right comes out of anything wrong. That's a promise. Maybe the good thing will be difficult for you to find, but if you look long enough, you will discover it every time.

25 June

How did Ping-Pong get its strange name?

1 CORINTHIANS 3:8

The Gibb family was bored one rainy day, so they decided to make up a game to play indoors. They put a pile of books on the middle of the dining room table to build a little wall. They used cigar-box lids for paddles and tried to hit balls of string back and forth across the table.

The balls of string didn't work very well, so they tried corks. The corks were such a strange shape that they were hard to hit. And the little rubber balls that they tried to use next were too heavy to hit quickly. Finally the father, James Gibb, thought of using hollow balls, which were lightweight and bounced well.

The paddles needed to be improved next. Instead of using the heavy cardboard cigar-box lids, the Gibbs made a paddle that looked like a little drum with a very long handle. Later, newer paddles were made of flat wood, but they were still too smooth.

The paddle problem was finally solved—because of a headache! A man named E. C. Goode, who liked the game, went into the drugstore to find some medicine for his headache. What he found instead was a rubber mat with little rubber spikes on it. He thought it would be perfect for giving the paddles some grip. He bought the rubber mat, took it home, cut it to the shape of the paddle, and glued the pad to the wood.

The game, which the Gibb family called "Gossima," has stayed much the same since then, except for its name. It has also been called "wick-wack," "whiff-whaff," and "click-clack." The name that finally stuck was "Ping-Pong" because it sounded like the ball as it bounced back and forth.

So what?

The inventors of Ping-Pong had to work out many problems before the game was playable. If they had given up instead of working through the troubles, they never would have succeeded. *The Bible tells us:*

The one who plants and the one who waters work as a team with the same purpose. Yet they will be rewarded individually, according to their own hard work. 1 CORINTHIANS 3:8, NLT

When you have a goal, keep trying to reach it. If you fall down and fail, get up and try again. The harder you work, the more ways God will find to reward you.

June
26

What did kids in the past pay for their toys?

LUKE 12:15

Long ago, kids had to make most of their own toys. The store of Sears, Roebuck and Co. didn't even have a toy section in its catalog. But the catalog of 1897 did list a few toys, and here are some examples of their prices: You could buy a pair of ice skates for 62 cents. A fancy harmonica was 22 cents, a rocking horse was 75 cents, and a catcher's mitt was 20 cents. If you wanted a toy broom, it cost 9 cents. A baseball cost 79 cents, and a toy wagon was as little as $1.15. Wouldn't it be fun to go shopping today at yesterday's prices?

So what?

If you don't have all the toys you want, don't be sad or jealous. *Jesus said:*

Don't always be wishing for what you don't have. For real life and real living are not related to how rich we are.   LUKE 12:15, TLB

Jesus is telling us that we can be very poor and still be a treasured child of God. It doesn't matter how many things we own. What matters is how much we love God. The more we love him (the one who already loves us), the less we need possessions to make us happy.

27 June

Why is purple the royal color?
JOHN 19:2-3

You have to go way back in history to see why purple is a special color. In Roman times, there was only one way to make the color purple, which the Romans called *purpura*. In the Mediterranean Sea, there was a certain underwater creature called a shellfish. These shellfish grew small bumps, or cysts, on their bodies. Inside the cysts was a very small amount of the substance that the Romans used to mix up a batch of purple dye. Because it was so hard to collect the ingredients for purple dye, not very much of it was made, and it was extremely expensive to buy. Since people needed lots of money to purchase purple, this color was usually worn only by the rich and famous. Naturally, the richest and most famous people in the country were the king and queen, so they were able to wear the most purple.

So what?
Before they put Jesus to death on the cross, soldiers made fun of him. *The Bible tells us:*

The soldiers made a crown of long, sharp thorns and put it on his head, and they put a royal purple robe on him. "Hail! King of the Jews!" they mocked, and they hit him with their fists. JOHN 19:2-3, NLT

During the days when Jesus lived, people thought that kings were very powerful. The soldiers put the purple robe on Jesus for a joke. They wanted everyone to wonder why Jesus didn't use his power to stop his own death. But we know that Jesus was dying on purpose. We know that Jesus is not only the King of the earth, but the King of the whole universe and all of Creation. It was not a little piece of purple cloth that made Jesus our King, but Almighty God, the Father himself.

June

Does your kitchen contain this invention?
PSALM 31:23

Earl Tupper—does his name sound familiar? You probably have something of his in your kitchen, because Earl Tupper created—you guessed it—Tupperware. He started out his sales career as a boy, selling vegetables that other kids had grown because he could make more money by doing that than by growing the vegetables himself. As an adult, Tupper worked for DuPont and had a mail-order business on the side, selling toothbrushes and combs. When his business allowed him to retire from DuPont, he began experimenting with a plastic-type material called polyethylene. He succeeded in 1945 with an invention he called Poly T. It was a big improvement over the plastic of the late 1930s, which cracked because it was so stiff. He decided to sell plastic dishes and containers. To avoid high advertising costs, a woman named Brownie Wise developed Tupperware "parties," which became the best way to sell his new product. Women hosted their neighbors and friends at home demonstrations. The first piece of Tupperware was a seven-ounce bathroom tumbler glass. Then came bowls with airtight lids. Everybody wanted some, from institutions to corporations to museums. Tupper became wealthy, selling out to Rexall Drugs in 1958 for sixteen million dollars.

So what?

If you have something tucked away in a Tupperware container, you've already decided it's worth making sure you can save it. God has only one thing he wants saved. *The Bible tells us:*

The LORD preserves the faithful. PSALM 31:23, NIV

A Tupperware container can save something for a while, but God's saving of your soul will endure throughout eternity. Let God become your Keeper!

June 29

Did you know that you've probably played with a toy called Gooey Gupp?

ECCLESIASTES 7:8

A man named James Wright was trying to make something to replace rubber, but what he invented wasn't strong like rubber, even though it stretched and bounced. It wasn't perfect, but Gooey Gupp was fun. If Gooey Gupp was pressed onto a newspaper, it copied the words and pictures. Nobody bought Gooey Gupp when it was first sold in toy stores. But then Peter Hodgson found Gooey Gupp while he was shopping one day. He liked it so much, he bought the company. Then he changed the name and the package. He made the package look like a TV screen, with a boy and girl looking at a red egg inside the TV. And what was in the red egg? Its new name was Silly Putty. Lots of kids have played with it, and grown-ups have even used Silly Putty for some unexpected jobs. When the astronauts of Apollo 8 needed a way to keep their tools from floating around, a gob of Silly Putty stuck the tools back where they belonged.

So what?

If Gooey Gupp had been thrown away just because it wasn't exactly like rubber, lots of kids over the years would have missed the chance to enjoy Silly Putty. *The Bible tells us:*

Finishing is better than starting.   ECCLESIASTES 7:8, NLT

Before you give up on a good idea, or even a job your parents ask you to do, give it your best effort. You never know when you might come up with something wonderful!

June

How can animals warn people of coming disaster?

COLOSSIANS 1:28

One day in 1974, the Chinese people noticed that their animals were acting strangely. Geese that normally flew, wouldn't. Hens didn't rest like they usually did. Pigs were biting each other's tails, and snakes that were supposed to be hibernating came out of the ground. Even dogs that had been trained to obey their masters refused to follow commands. Finally someone figured out what was wrong with the animals. Hundreds of thousands of people left their homes and went to another place.

Two days later, the whole world understood. The animals were heroes. Because of the animals' strange actions, the Chinese people were warned that an earthquake was coming.

So what?

Many people were warned by the animals in time to escape harm. Christians need to do some warning of their own, just as the disciples did. *As the Bible says:*

Everywhere we go, we tell everyone about Christ. We warn them and teach them with all the wisdom God has given us. COLOSSIANS 1:28, NLT

The Chinese people were probably very grateful to the animals that kept them from ending up in a dangerous situation. When you tell people about Jesus, you may be saving them from the dangerous situation of dying without knowing him. Imagine how thankful your friends would be if you introduced them to Jesus, and they discovered that they could have eternal life!

July
1

What would you do if you were rolling across a slippery floor on skates that couldn't be stopped?

MATTHEW 16:19

Long ago, that was Josef Merlin's problem. He was an instrument maker who was invited to a costume ball. He wanted to capture everyone's attention with a spectacular outfit, so he wore something no one had seen before: roller skates! Playing his violin as he skated, Josef zoomed through the door and across the ballroom. He didn't realize until too late that there was no way to turn around or stop on the metal wheels. He crashed right into a huge mirror, which shattered into many pieces.

Because Josef got hurt, no one was very interested in trying out roller skates again for a long time. Every once in a while, someone would tinker with inventing another kind of skate, but it wasn't until 1863 that a rich man named J. L. Plimpton, who missed ice-skating, found an easy way to skate on land. His skates had two wooden wheels side-by-side on the front, and two wooden wheels side-by-side at the back, with rubber springs. Later, another inventor improved these skates by making adjustable skates that could be fitted to the shoe by turning a key. After that, if you saw a kid with a key on a necklace, it was a sure sign that he loved to skate!

So what?

Kids liked to show off their skate keys because they were proud to let everyone know that they had roller skates. When you become God's child, you have something much better to be proud of. *God promises:*

I will give you the keys of the Kingdom of Heaven. MATTHEW 16:19, NLT

When Jesus died on the cross, he made it possible for us to go to heaven. So when people wear a cross, it's likely that they're proud to show that they have the key to heaven.

July

Will quicksand really swallow you up?

PSALM 27:5

You've stepped into some quicksand. It's thick and soupy, and it seems to be creeping up your legs. You can picture yourself being sucked under the surface in minutes, just like in the movies. You begin to struggle, but that makes you sink even faster. Are you doomed? Not if you understand what quicksand really is.

Quicksand is usually found around rivers, where the banks are made of clay or soft dirt. You might step onto a patch of quicksand, thinking it's just regular sand, because it looks the same. The difference is that in quicksand the sand is actually floating on water. When you step into quicksand, the sand on the water can't hold you up, so you sink down into it. What most people don't realize is that quicksand behaves like water—you can float on it. If you ever find yourself in quicksand, the best thing to do is to stay calm and try to lie on your back. Then slowly roll toward shore.

So what?

Even though you can get out of quicksand, it is still scary when you take a step and unexpectedly start to sink. You don't feel safe. *God understands this, and that's why the Bible reminds us:*

He will set me on a high rock.   PSALM 27:5, TLB

When you step on a rock, it is solid. It will hold you up. God wants you to think of him as your Rock. He will hold you up and keep you safe.

July

How does a mosquito choose its victims?

PHILIPPIANS 2:14-16

You're having a great time at a picnic, and all of a sudden you hear that familiar buzz near your ear. The mosquitoes have found you!

Researchers have found out some interesting facts about mosquitoes. First, mosquitoes are attracted to the color blue more than any other color. If you're eating bananas, mosquitoes love the odor that comes from your skin. Mosquitoes would rather bite children than adults. And mosquitoes are attracted to lighter-colored people. So if you are a blond boy wearing blue jeans and eating a banana, watch out! The mosquitoes are coming for you!

There's one other thing that you should know about mosquitoes. They would rather bite pigs, cattle, dogs, and horses than people. If you live on or near a farm, you may want to see if you can set up your next picnic near a barnyard. Then you'll have a better chance of avoiding those pesky little pests!

So what?

When we hear the buzzing of the mosquito, it is not a pleasant sound. We don't want to be near the tiny insect that is making that noise. Sometimes, when we complain, we probably sound like mosquitoes to God. He doesn't like the sounds we are making. We need to remember to praise God for all the blessings in our lives, instead of pointing out everything that we think is wrong. *The Bible reminds us:*

In everything you do, stay away from complaining and arguing, so that no one can speak a word of blame against you. You are to live clean, innocent lives as children of God in a dark world. . . . Let your lives shine brightly before them. Hold tightly to the word of life, so that when Christ returns, I will be proud that I did not lose the race and that my work was not useless. PHILIPPIANS 2:14-16, NLT

July 4

How could someone lose a three-mile-long painting?

PSALM 8:3-4

Historians still don't know what happened. In the mid-1800s, an artist named John Banvard decided to paint a landscape of the Mississippi River. He wanted to show everything he saw along twelve hundred miles of the river. He spent one year rowing, camping, and making sketches. Then he built a studio in Kentucky large enough to house his long canvas, which he wound around large spools. It took Banvard five years to complete his painting, which included scenes of Indian settlements, riverboats, a shipwreck, and local forts. Completed in 1846, the painting was exhibited across America and Britain. People would gather all along the tour to watch Banvard spend two hours unrolling his canvas. The artwork, titled "Panorama of the Mississippi," was updated through the years. In 1862, for example, the painter added another section showing part of the Civil War. The wear and tear of traveling caused the painting to begin falling apart. Eventually, portions of the painting were cut out to make backdrop scenery for theaters. Banvard died in 1891, but no one knows what happened to the rest of his painting after his death. Not one picture of it remains to show Banvard's contribution to American art.

So what?

Everyone was amazed at how large and lifelike Banvard's painting was. But the painting was only a copy of the "real thing" that we see growing and changing around us every day. Isn't a tree that buds more fascinating than a painted one that never changes? And what could be more magnificent in size than the sky at sunset? *The Bible says:*

When I look at the night sky and see the work of your fingers— the moon and the stars you have set in place—what are mortals that you should think of us, mere humans that you should care for us?
PSALM 8:3-4, NLT

God not only pays attention to us but also makes it clear that we are his most important creation. What an honor to be the central subjects in God's artistic panorama!

July
5

Why wasn't the perfect book perfect?

PSALM 94:16-19

Once a publishing house with a good reputation, the University Press of Glasgow, Scotland, set out to publish a completely error-free book. The process was started by six proofreaders, who look for mistakes as their daily job. They used their experience to check and recheck every page for mistakes. Next, each page of the book was publicly posted at the University, and a reward was offered to students or teachers who could find any errors. After two weeks and many corrections, the publishers printed the book, feeling fairly sure that the manuscript was flawless. But they were wrong. Several mistakes appeared in the finished book. The first error was spotted on the first page in the first sentence!

So what?

Ever had a day like that? No matter how hard you try to make things go smoothly, something goes wrong from the very first. Your alarm doesn't go off. The shirt you wanted to wear to school has a spot on it. You miss the bus. The dog ate your homework. The list can be endless. But are you doomed to be battered and tossed around by every event that comes along? King David in the Bible went through many struggles also. First he tells us about his troubles. Then we learn what he did about them. Finally he gives us a prayer to use when we're feeling anxious. *He starts:*

Who will protect me from the wicked? Who will be my shield? I would have died unless the Lord had helped me. I screamed, "I'm slipping, Lord!" and he was kind and saved me. Lord, when doubts fill my mind, when my heart is in turmoil, quiet me and give me renewed hope and cheer. PSALM 94:16-19, TLB

God has the perfect way to help us handle our less-than-perfect lives.

July

How are "scratch 'n' sniff" products made?
PROVERBS 27:9

Kids love the bright-colored fruit stickers that smell like oranges, watermelons, and strawberries. Women who want to try before they buy appreciate the perfume samples handed out at the store or tucked inside a magazine. Its technical name is *microfragrance* or *microencapsulation,* but it is popularly known as "scratch 'n' sniff." How does it work? The idea is to keep a fragrance contained until someone wishes to smell it.

The people who make scratch 'n' sniff products start with a tiny plastic capsule, too small to see. The scent is enclosed in the capsule by mixing perfume oil with water to form tiny droplets. These drops are sprinkled on a surface and then coated with plastic. The droplets are sometimes heated and sometimes left alone until they have set in the plastic. Then a coat of resin is applied, which sticks the whole thing to paper. When the paper is scratched, or a sticky seal is broken, the capsules release the fragrance.

The idea was developed in the 1960s by the 3M company. At one time there was even a scratch 'n' sniff movie. Members of the audience were given sheets with numbered samples. When the movie screen showed number three, for instance, everyone would scratch number three and then smell roses, or popcorn, or whatever scent matched the picture on the screen.

So what?
God made all of our senses, so he knows how pleasant it is for us to smell something fragrant. He meant for us to enjoy our sense of smell and to be delighted with an appealing scent. *He uses the following comparison to encourage us to use kind words:*

Friendly suggestions are as pleasant as perfume.   PROVERBS 27:9, TLB

You don't ever have to be critical or stern, bossy or spiteful when you speak to someone. Instead, find a way to deliver your message with peaceful words, encouraging words, and words of hope and help. The people who hear you will listen much more carefully—drawn to your kindness in the same way that they would move toward the smell of fresh-baked cookies.

July

What were cats once accused of causing?
ISAIAH 42:16

Between 1334 and 1351 there was an outbreak of bubonic plague, also known as the Black Death or Black Plague. As much as 75 percent of Asian and European populations died. How could this have happened? The main problem was that the people had no idea how the disease was spread. At first they worried that cats were responsible. Thousands of cats were killed in the hopes that the disease would be stopped. But the disease spread faster than ever. Finally people began to realize that killing cats was the worst thing they could have done. The bites of fleas caused the plague. The fleas stayed on rats, and the rat population grew bigger quickly when the natural predators of rats—the cats—had been eliminated. It was determined that all garbage should be burned every day. That way there was less to attract the rats. This practice eventually allowed the disease to fade away.

So what?
During the time of the plague, the people didn't know what to do. They panicked and selected the most disastrous course of action. Maybe that has happened to you. Perhaps you are so overwhelmed by what's happening to you that you don't know which way to turn. You've tried to fix the problem, but it's just gotten worse. You would love to be rescued by someone. *You long to hear words like these:*

I will lead the blind by ways they have not known, along unfamiliar paths I will guide them; I will turn the darkness into light before them and make the rough places smooth. These are the things I will do; I will not forsake them. ISAIAH 42:16, NIV

If any human being tells you these things, that person will be misleading you, and you will be disappointed again. These words come from God, and he is the only one who can guarantee that he can really do these things. Ask God to be your guide and protector. He wants to walk with you through your dark times and take you into his light, where he can cure you with his love.

July

Why did the barber need a pole?

PSALM 19:1, 3-4

The red-and-white pole in front of the barbershop was not created just to be a decoration. It had a special meaning for the people who went to the barber during the Middle Ages. At that time, barbers did more than cut hair—they served as doctors and dentists, performing surgery and tooth removal. They even practiced bloodletting, which involved putting leeches on the skin to suck out some blood, supposedly taking poisons out of the body. The barber pole tells the story of the bloodletting process. The tools the barber needed were basins to catch the blood and hold the leeches, a pole for the patient to grasp tightly, and lots of white linen bandages. After this procedure, barbers would hang the cloth bandage strips outside the shop on the gripping pole.

Historians disagree on where the red-and-white colors came from. Some say the bandages were bloody, and the pole was white. Others think that the bandages were washed and hung out to dry on the pole, which was painted red to hide any blood stains. In either case, the strips would spin in the wind and form swirls of red and white. Because not many people in the 1700s could read, the barber pole was an advertisement everyone could understand. In later times, when cleanliness became more important, the barber pole was merely painted red and white to create the familiar symbol. Originally the leech bowl was put on top of the pole, but through the years it came to be represented by a ball.

So what?

Barbers used the barber pole to advertise their services. God has his own advertising. *The Bible reminds us of this when it says:*

The heavens tell of the glory of God. The skies display his marvelous craftsmanship. . . . They speak without a sound or a word. . . . Yet their message has gone out to all the earth.   PSALM 19:1, 3-4, NLT

If you were walking past a store that had a window display showing a miniature, moving version of sunrises, sunsets, sparkling stars, and a glowing moon, you would be fascinated. You would probably go inside the store to see what other amazing things were inside. Every day you have access to the gigantic, original version of this display of earth's beauty. It's yours for free, to admire and stand in awe of what God can do. God's universe is the best advertising you'll ever see.

July

Why are the sides of a boat called "port" and "starboard"?

PSALM 107:23-31

The right side of a boat is called "starboard." Long ago, Viking ships had a large oar for steering called a steering paddle or board. It was always attached on the right side because most people are right-handed. This prompted people to call the right side the "steerboard" side. It eventually became the word we use today. The left side of a ship is called the "port" side. Some people say that's because the big oar on the right side kept boats from pulling up to the land, dock, or port near the right side—the oar was always in the way. Since the left side of the boat was the side that had to be used when going into port, it became the "port" side. Others say the original word for the left side was "larboard," meaning "empty side." Although the reason for the name "port" is unclear, we do know why portholes, the windows on boats, are round instead of a square or oblong shape. It has to do with the stress that is put on a ship from bobbing up and down on the ocean. This motion tends to make the outer covering of the ship "stretch." Corners on the windows would bear most of this stress and might cause the walls of the ship, or the glass in the windows, to crack. A round window distributes the stress evenly. Also, long ago when the window rims were spun out of bronze or iron on a lathe, circles were naturally easier to shape than a square.

So what?

We trust that ships are sturdy enough to keep us afloat. But our safety doesn't depend on metal and wood. *The Bible brings this to our attention when it says:*

Some went off in ships. . . . They, too, observed the LORD's power in action, his impressive works on the deepest seas. He spoke, and the winds rose, stirring up the waves. Their ships were tossed to the heavens and sank again to the depths; the sailors cringed in terror. They reeled and staggered like drunkards and were at their wits' end. "LORD, help!" they cried in their trouble, and he saved them from their distress. He calmed the storm to a whisper and stilled the waves. What a blessing was that stillness as he brought them safely into harbor! Let them praise the LORD for his great love and for all his wonderful deeds to them. PSALM 107:23-31, NLT

God constantly surrounds us on all sides, both port and starboard.

July

Which city was named by the toss of a coin?

PROVERBS 16:33

The only thing they couldn't agree on was a name. Two men were developing a community in Oregon. The property was 640 heavily wooded acres at the mouth of the Willamette River. Asa Lovejoy and Francis Pettygrove were planning the streets and building the first houses in their new city, which still had no name. Lovejoy wanted the city to be named Boston, in honor of his home state of Massachusetts. Pettygrove had another idea. They finally decided that the only fair thing would be to toss a coin. Pettygrove won. He wanted to name the city after a city in his home state of Maine, so the new Oregon city became Portland.

So what?

At some time or another you may have felt like these two developers. You just couldn't decide what to do and figured tossing a coin would give you as good an answer as any other. But as God's child, you never need to feel so alone that you have to let a piece of metal decide what you'll do. *The Bible tells us:*

We toss the coin, but it is the Lord who controls its decision.
PROVERBS 16:33, TLB

God, not a coin, is in control of your life. Through prayer, he will guide your every decision.

July
11

Why wasn't Miss National Smile Princess smiling?

JOHN 15:9-11

Miss Moya Ann Church was happy. She had just been voted Miss National Smile Princess for National Smile Week. But it was hard for her to smile that week. First, Moya lost her crown within a minute after being chosen. Without explanation, her crown was later found in a trash pile. But that was only the beginning of her troubles. Someone spilled coffee on her expensive dress and sash, which permanently spoiled them both. Next, she was locked out of her own house by mistake. Then her car broke down, so she had to call for help. When she came back to her car, she found that she had been given a parking ticket. Finally, Moya's week as the National Smile Princess was over. Her picture was taken one last time, and then she missed catching her train on the way home.

So what?

If you let your happiness depend on the events of your day, it can disappear in a moment. The only way to remain happy is to have your peace of mind dependent on your relationship with Jesus. *He says:*

I have loved you even as the Father has loved me. Remain in my love. When you obey me, you remain in my love, just as I obey my Father and remain in his love. I have told you this so that you will be filled with my joy. Yes, your joy will overflow! JOHN 15:9-11, NLT

Add some joy to your day and put a smile on your face by letting Jesus love you and by loving him back!

July 12

Why was a statue dedicated to a bug?

JOEL 2:25

Things couldn't have been worse. In 1915 the farmers in Enterprise, Alabama, were losing one-third of their cotton crops, and all hope of planting more, to the insect called the Mexican boll weevil. With their livelihood all but destroyed, you would think that the town of Enterprise would never want to see another boll weevil again. Instead, three years later, they built a bronze statue honoring the boll weevil in the town square. Why? Farmers realized that they could no longer depend on just one crop. After the boll weevil did its damage, there was a big change in the crops that were planted. Farmers began to diversify by growing corn, hay, potatoes, peanuts, and sugar cane. This led to prosperity for everyone and gratitude to the bug that started it all.

So what?

Nothing is too difficult for God. He can turn every bad thing into something good. *He says:*

I will give you back the crops the locusts ate!   JOEL 2:25, TLB

Whatever your hardship may be, never underestimate God's ability to make something good come out of it!

July 13

How is Thomas Jefferson connected to the potato chip?

MATTHEW 4:4

Everyone seemed to enjoy the thick-cut french fries that Thomas Jefferson introduced to America from France in the 1790s. Everyone, that is, except one customer in a restaurant at the Moon Lake Lodge in Saratoga Springs, New York. Native American chef George Crum was losing his patience with this particular customer. Chef Crum had been sent back to the kitchen with a plate of his thick-cut fries. The critical customer had complained that the fries weren't thin enough. Another batch was prepared, served, and again rejected. Crum tried one more time, but decided to exaggerate. He sliced the potatoes so thinly that they couldn't even be pierced with a fork. Then he soaked them in ice water for half an hour. After he fried and salted them heavily, he presented them to the customer—who loved them! First named "Saratoga chips" in 1835, the treat later became known as "potato chips." Crum was eventually able to open his own restaurant, specializing in—you guessed it—potato chips!

So what?

Some people, like Crum's customer, can be annoyingly demanding about their food. They inspect it for freshness, fat content, nutritional value, color, and flavor. Although eating is an enjoyable part of life, just like anything else, it can sometimes distract you from what's really important. If you study the menu longer than you study the Bible, there's something you should know. *Jesus quoted Deuteronomy 8:3 from the Old Testament when he said:*

People need more than bread for their life; they must feed on every word of God. MATTHEW 4:4, NLT

If you fill your soul before you fill your stomach, you will feel better about both.

July 14

Why are detectives called "private eyes"?

PSALM 130:6

Allan Pinkerton made spying his business. The first case he cracked involved counterfeiters. At the time, he wasn't even a detective, but he decided he could make a living at it. In 1850 he started the Pinkerton National Detective Agency. He taught America to call detectives "private investigators" or "private i's" for short. To go along with the term *private i,* Pinkerton used a wide-open eye as the logo for his company, with "We Never Sleep" as the slogan. After a while, detectives became known as "private eyes." Pinkerton went on to become President Lincoln's bodyguard and to serve as head of the Secret Service during the Civil War.

So what?

When something grabs your interest, you tend to be more alert than when you're bored. The ever-open eye of the Pinkerton Detective Agency suggested that he would always be curious about what you were doing—enough to keep him awake at night. *The Bible talks about the anxiousness of waiting through the night for something special or important when it says:*

My soul waits for the Lord more than those who watch for the morning. PSALM 130:6, NRSV

It is that excitement, eagerness, and attention that pleases God. If you are always looking forward to what God is planning for you next, you won't miss the blessings he wants to give you.

July
15

What kind of puzzle took five years to solve?

ROMANS 2:6-7

Workers building a new road near one of the great Pyramids in 1954 uncovered something unusual. Under a hill of sand, they found many stone blocks. Under those blocks, there was a "box" carved into the limestone. In the box were 1,224 pieces of wood, lots of rope, and some reed mats. The wood pieces were stacked in thirteen layers. What had the workers discovered? Ahmed Youssef, an Egyptian master restorer, had the answer. Each piece of wood had a hieroglyphic picture on it that described where it belonged. The oldest puzzle in the world was waiting to be assembled! Ahmed spent a year and a half taking the wood out of the box and restoring the rotted or bent pieces. It took four more years to put all the pieces in order, because only ropes or pegs held them together. Finally, a wooden picture of a funeral barge, or boat, became apparent. The more-than-four-thousand-year-old puzzle had finally been solved.

So what?

Making your way toward heaven is similar to waiting for Ahmed's puzzle to be solved. You know the end will be great, and you're excited about seeing it for the first time. But you know you have to wait patiently. Ahmed was rewarded with a completed puzzle. God will give you the best reward of all for not giving up on your quest to do his will. *The Bible says:*

He will give each one whatever his deeds deserve. He will give eternal life to those who patiently do the will of God, seeking for the unseen glory and honor and eternal life that he offers. ROMANS 2:6-7, TLB

Dig into the Bible, and you'll find all the pieces you need for your journey toward heaven.

July
16

What is the dollar bill saying with symbols?

PROVERBS 15:3

Have you looked carefully at a dollar bill lately? Did you notice all the symbolism? If not, you might want to take a second look. It may seem strange that an American bill would have a pyramid on it, but it's there in the middle of a circle. The pyramid is supposed to symbolize the strength and permanence of our country. Look closely, and you'll notice that the pyramid is unfinished. It means that America looks forward to growth and perfection in the future. There's also an eye at the top of the pyramid. That's the overseeing, all-seeing eye of God. The words *Annuit Coeptis* are a Latin reference to God, meaning "He has favored our undertakings." At the bottom of the circle are the words *Novus Ordo Seclorum,* also Latin, meaning "A new order of the ages" and intended to show hope for the new American era. Finally, there's the Roman numeral MDCCLXXVI inscribed on the base of the pyramid. That's 1776—the beginning of the "new era" of America's independence from England.

The other circle is just as interesting. The eagle holds an olive branch that has thirteen leaves and thirteen berries, standing for the original thirteen colonies. In the other claw are thirteen arrows. The olive branch means peace; the arrows mean war. The eagle's head is turned toward one and away from the other, indicating early America's hope for peace.

So what?

The designers of the dollar bill had obviously read their Bibles. *The Bible says:*

The LORD is watching everywhere, keeping his eye on both the evil and the good. PROVERBS 15:3, NLT

God sees everything—your pain, your joys, your fears, your laughter. He wants to be with you today and in your future. He is absolutely trustworthy and totally willing to be your comfort and stronghold. Turn your responsibilities and burdens over to him, and he will bear them with you, and even for you.

July

How did an ocean liner get the wrong name?

LUKE 9:56

Sir Thomas Royden didn't choose his words carefully enough in 1934. Sir Thomas was the director of the British Cunard transatlantic ocean liners. A new ocean liner was almost ready to be launched. It just needed a name. Sir Thomas had decided that the new vessel should be christened as the *Queen Victoria*, after a much-loved former Queen of England. But Sir Thomas needed to ask permission from the king who was presently ruling. King George V received a visit from Sir Thomas, who asked the king if the new ocean liner could be named "after the greatest queen this country has ever known." King George loved the idea, and referring to his own wife, Mary, he replied, "That is the greatest compliment ever paid to my wife. I'll ask her." Sir Thomas knew right then that he should never mention whom he was originally thinking of, and that he would be naming the new ship the *Queen Mary*.

So what?

Sir Thomas was probably relieved that his error wasn't discovered. Maybe you've had a similar experience: You escaped an embarrassing moment without being discovered, or you made a mistake around someone who was compassionate and didn't hold it against you. It's a great relief to realize you won't be punished in the way you know you deserve.

That's how you feel when you accept Jesus into your life. The all-powerful, almighty, exalted Lord has the power to crush any of us in an instant for all the sins we've committed. But God is not like that. *The Bible tells us:*

The Son of man is not come to destroy men's lives, but to save them.
LUKE 9:56, KJV

As you probably know, there is a big difference between mistakes and sins. All of us make mistakes, and God understands that. But all of us also do things that are the opposite of the way God has commanded us to live. These wrong things, called sins, have to do with our relationships with people and with God. But even the sins we commit can be forgiven. That's why God sent his Son, Jesus, to our world. He came to help us—to save us from being destroyed. Maybe you'd like to thank God for understanding your mistakes. Maybe you'd also like to ask him to forgive you for your sins.

July 18

How did the question mark get its strange shape?

JAMES 1:5

The question mark is one of the most strangely shaped punctuation marks. Who decided what it would look like and why? The story of the question mark starts back in the time when Latin was the standard language. After each question, the Latin word *questio* (question) was written. That was a lot of work. As an alternative, people started using the abbreviation *QO* at the end of every question. The problem with that was that the reader would often think the *QO* was part of the spelling of the word before it. This was very confusing. Soon people began writing the *Q* above the *O*, lined up like a mathematical fraction. As time passed, the shape of the *Q* became more and more eroded, and the *O* turned into a simple dot. The result of these changes was the question mark as we know it today.

So what?

Asking questions is how we learn. A very important question we should ask is, "How can I accomplish God's plan for me?" The Bible tells how to find out. *It says:*

If you need wisdom—if you want to know what God wants you to do— ask him, and he will gladly tell you. He will not resent your asking.
JAMES 1:5, NLT

Every question that you ask God is a good one, because, as Creator of the universe, he is the ultimate authority for every answer.

July **19**

What's the fastest-growing fungus in the world?

JAMES 5:7

If you've ever planted a garden, you know that it usually takes a lot of patience to wait for the plants to grow. It might surprise you to know that in Brazil there is a fungus that takes only twenty minutes to be full grown. This fungus is called the stinkhorn, and it starts its growing by absorbing water extremely quickly. The water fills up the dried-up fungus so fast that if you're standing nearby, you will hear a crackling noise while the fungus grows about an inch every five minutes. But that isn't the only unusual thing about the stinkhorn. Immediately after it finishes growing, the fungus starts to rot. Rotting is the fungus's way of spreading its seeds. The bad odor attracts flies, and the flies crawl on the fungus, where spores stick to their feet. Wherever each fly goes next, another fungus will begin.

So what?

It's fun and exciting when you don't have to wait for something. But things in real life usually take a lot longer to develop than the stinkhorn does. Most of the time we need to be patient. Having patience is a good thing to practice. *The Bible says:*

Be patient, like a farmer who waits until the autumn for his precious harvest to ripen. JAMES 5:7, TLB

Whether you are waiting for Jesus to come back to earth, which is what the verse above is about, or waiting for God to answer a prayer, you need patience. If you are praying for something to happen, wait for God's answer. There will be one, even though it may not happen as fast as you would like. God knows what answer you need to have. You can trust that he always hears you and that he always answers at the best time and in the best way.

July

How did frogs fall from the sky?
1 TIMOTHY 4:14

When it hails, it's hard enough to keep from getting hit by the "ice rocks" that are falling from the sky. But what if you had to dodge falling frogs, too? That's exactly what happened one day in Iowa in 1882.

During a hailstorm, the air is very cold up in the clouds, so the raindrops freeze and come down as ice pellets called hail. Meanwhile, strong winds are blowing up and down between the earth and the sky. On this day, the wind blew so hard that it picked up some small frogs and whisked them into the clouds. The raindrops began to freeze on the frogs, and they were coated with ice until they turned into hail as big as five inches across. Then the froggy ice cubes fell back to earth, where the amazed people of Iowa discovered them.

Finding that they were up in the clouds probably made the frogs pretty confused! Frogs are jumpers, but they had definitely never jumped *that* high before. Sometimes we are like those frogs. We get used to being ordinary and doing things the same way everyone else does them. When we have a chance to do something special, or we get an idea that no one else has ever thought of, we tell ourselves, *Oh, I'm sure I could never do that. No one else has ever done it before.* And we give up before we've even tried.

So what?
Whenever you get a different kind of idea than you've had before, remember that God may be giving it to you as a challenge to use your talents in a new way. If God could lift those frogs into the clouds, he can help you to be the first person who lives on the moon or the person who invents ice cream that doesn't have to be frozen or . . . you name it. *The Bible says:*

Do not neglect your gift. 1 TIMOTHY 4:14, NIV

Maybe the only reason it's never been done before is that no one else has the special abilities God has given you!

21 July

Why isn't a fan really cooling the air?

PSALM 65:7

On a hot day, the idea of cooling off in front of an electric fan sounds inviting. We sit very close to the fan and count on it to make us more comfortable because we think it's going to lower the air temperature. But that's not really what happens. A fan can actually make a room hotter because of the warmth of the running motor. Fans don't cool the temperature of the air at all—they just blow the same hot air around. So why does a fan make us feel better? The fan moves air against our skin, which causes perspiration to evaporate. If we couldn't sweat, our body temperature would rise so high that we would die. We have sweat glands all over our body, but the largest ones are in our palms, forehead, armpits, and the soles of our feet. We notice our perspiration the most in those places. Even though the air temperature doesn't get cooler when a fan is blowing, we feel cooler as evaporation occurs and our body temperature drops.

So what?

In the same way that you can look forward to your body feeling better in front of a fan, you can look forward to refreshment for your spirit in the presence of God. If you dream of having some "cooling-off" time from your busy schedule, ask God to blow his soothing breath into your soul to calm you down. *In the Bible, David says this about God:*

You quieted the raging oceans with their pounding waves and silenced the shouting of the nations. PSALM 65:7, NLT

If you spend just a few minutes talking with God each morning, he will give you the peace that you need. He will help you to stay cool and comfortable, inside and out, all day long.

Did George Washington really have wooden teeth?

PROVERBS 25:19

Imagine that you had only one tooth in your mouth. If you were a baby, it probably wouldn't matter. But what if you were a grown-up? That's what happened to George Washington. His teeth started falling out when he was about twenty-two, and he had only one left by the time he became president. President Washington tried many different ways to replace his teeth. Although he never had wooden teeth, which is a story many people have heard, he did have teeth carved from elk's teeth or ivory. There were hinges between the top and bottom sets, and he had to bite down all the time just to keep his mouth from flying open. It was hard to talk and hard to eat. At one time, President Washington had a set of dentures with a special hole so that the one tooth he still had could poke through. He tried to keep them smelling clean by soaking them in wine, but instead the fake teeth just turned black and got mushy. In 1796, the dentist had to pull out President Washington's last tooth, and the president kept his tooth in a gold locket attached to his watch chain. When the time came for the president to have his portrait painted, cotton was pushed under his lips so that he would look like he had teeth. But the cotton made his mouth puff out too far. Look at the picture on a dollar bill, and you can see for yourself.

So what?

What can we learn from George Washington's troubled teeth? *The Bible mentions bad teeth when it says:*

Putting confidence in an unreliable person is like chewing with a toothache or walking on a broken foot. PROVERBS 25:19, NLT

That means that if we depend on someone who can't be trusted, we could be hurt or disappointed. And even trustworthy people will sometimes let us down. We should depend most on God to help us. He'll never let us down!

July

Why do we call it the "funny bone" when it definitely isn't?

PROVERBS 17:22

Not only is it not funny, it's not even a bone! Along the upper arm bone, there's a nerve that runs underneath the arm. When it reaches the elbow, the nerve is very close to the skin. When you bump your elbow, you hit the nerve, and that is why it hurts. The upper arm, where the nerve is, has a big bone that's called the *humerus* bone. The name of the bone sounds the same as the word *humorous,* which means funny. People used to believe that it was the "humorous" bone that hurt when it was hit, so it got nicknamed the funny bone.

So what?

The first time you heard someone say he bumped his funny bone, you probably wondered how it felt. You might even have wanted to bump your own because it sounded like fun. *The Bible tells us:*

A cheerful heart is good medicine, but a crushed spirit dries up the bones. PROVERBS 17:22, NIV

It is good for us to be cheerful and to laugh. We like the feeling of being happy, and God planned that our happiness would be healthy for us. So go ahead—have a few chuckles. But don't expect to get them from hitting your funny bone!

2 4
July

Which dogs were asked to dinner?
PROVERBS 12:10

If you had ever been invited to eat dinner in Paris with a very wealthy man named Lord Egerton, you would have been in for a big surprise. Lord Egerton always had twelve guests for dinner, and every one of his guests had four legs!

Lord Egerton loved his dogs and insisted that they eat at the table with him. Twelve dogs sat in twelve chairs with napkins tied around their necks. The dogs were very well behaved, because they had been trained to have the same table manners as people. If one of the dogs forgot to be polite at the table, the next night it had to eat alone in another room. Its chair stayed empty until it showed it was sorry for misbehaving, and then it was allowed to return to its seat. After dinner, Lord Egerton would go for a ride in his carriage, and the dogs would go too. But even then the dogs got special treatment, because they each wore four little boots to keep their feet from getting muddy.

So what?

Lord Egerton's story is funny because he pampered his pets a little too much by treating them like people. *But the Bible tells us:*

The godly are concerned for the welfare of their animals.

PROVERBS 12:10, NLT

God expects us to be kind to all of his creatures. Do your best never to injure or neglect your pet, but don't worry too much about teaching him to use a fork. Your pet would probably be just as pleased with a nice dog biscuit.

July 25

Did you know that you've probably used a cup named after a doll factory?

ISAIAH 58:11

Long ago, when people were away from home and wanted a drink of water, they could go to the middle of their town, where there would be a large tub full of water with a big spoon to scoop and drink from. Everyone used the same dipper, so it was never very clean. A young man named Hugh Moore had an idea about how to fix this problem. He invented a machine that would give people a drink of water with a fresh cup each time for a penny. But people didn't use Hugh's machine, because they couldn't understand why they should pay for water when they could already get it free from the tub. Finally, laws were passed making it illegal to drink from dippers and spread germs and disease.

Hugh Moore saw then that he didn't need to sell fresh water anymore; what people really needed were his paper cups. He began selling them to restaurants and soda fountains, and even to ice cream factories so kids could have a small cup of ice cream all to themselves. As his cups became more famous, Hugh began to look for a catchy name for them. Next door to his business was a doll factory. He asked the doll maker if he could borrow the name, and the doll maker said yes. That is why, when you use a paper cup, you may be drinking from a Dixie cup, which got its name from the Dixie Doll Company.

So what?

Our bodies need water to stay alive. If we had to find a new place to get water every day, we would be worried all the time about where our next drink would be coming from. God understands how hard that would be. *That's why he says:*

You shall be like a watered garden, like a spring of water, whose waters never fail. ISAIAH 58:11, NRSV

God is telling us that when we depend on him, we don't need to worry. He will make sure we always have what we need, including plenty of water.

26

July

If a marble and a bowling ball raced down a ramp, which one would win?

HEBREWS 12:1

We all know that a bowling ball weighs a lot more than a marble. But if you drop them both at the same time from a tall place, which would reach the ground first? An Italian scientist named Galileo wondered about this question. He decided to do tests to find the answer. Because he lived so long ago, there wasn't a stopwatch to use as a timer. And everything that was dropped down would fall too quickly to measure. How could he make a decision? Galileo decided to roll things down a ramp to see which ones won the race. He understood that gravity, which is the force that pulls things toward the earth, would have the same pull on big items and small items. To prove this, Galileo made his own timer: He counted drops of water as they fell into a container while two objects rolled down the ramp. Which object won the race? The answer is—it was a tie, and it always will be—even if you put a marble and a bowling ball in the race. That's how gravity works.

So what?

Christians run a different kind of race. We are not rolling downhill and competing against a bowling ball or a marble. Instead, we are running toward the goal of becoming more like Jesus and eventually going to live with him in heaven. *The Bible says:*

Lay aside every weight and the sin that clings so closely, and let us run with perseverance the race that is set before us.   HEBREWS 12:1, NRSV

We need to drop the heavy sins that hold us back, and race on, letting nothing stop us until we cross the finish line in heaven.

July 27

Who had the biggest dollhouse ever?

JOHN 14:2

Queen Mary loved to play with dollhouses when she was a little girl. But she was fifty-seven years old when she got the best dollhouse of all as a present. The people of her country, England, spent four years and one million dollars to build it. The dollhouse is over eight feet long and five feet deep, and it has three stories. Everything in the house is very tiny, but it really works. Hot and cold water run out of faucets made of real silver. Pieces of hot coal heat the ovens in the kitchen. An elevator goes up and down, light switches turn on the lights, and each door has a key that really locks it. Copies of the famous royal jewels are kept in a safe that can be opened only if you know the combination. A record player plays records one inch across. Cars that really run, including a Rolls-Royce, are in the garage. And a drawer underneath the doll house has a pop-up garden. Lots of workers carefully built Queen Mary's dollhouse, which is still kept at Windsor Castle, where everyone can enjoy looking at it.

So what?

Jesus said:

There are many rooms in my Father's home, and I am going to prepare a place for you. JOHN 14:2, NLT

Jesus was talking about heaven, God's house. If Queen Mary's amazing dollhouse was made by people here on earth, imagine what God's house must be like! After all, Queen Mary ruled only the small country of England—God is the King of the whole universe, including all the land, the oceans, and even the stars. Think about the most wonderful place you can picture, and then remember that heaven will be so great that you can't even picture it!

July
28

When did a dog deliver mail?

1 THESSALONIANS 5:14

Mail carriers usually have to watch out for dogs to keep from getting bitten while trying to deliver the mail. But what happens if the mail carrier *is* a dog?

Let's look back to the 1800s in Calico, California. One day the town's postmaster found a black-and-white stray shepherd dog that he adopted and named Dorsey. The shepherd dog would follow the postmaster from house to house whenever it was time to deliver the mail. When the postmaster got sick and couldn't go on his mail route, he got an idea. He made two saddlebags for Dorsey that draped across the dog's back. He attached a note to Dorsey's collar, asking people to please take out their mail from one of Dorsey's pouches and to put the mail they wanted delivered in Dorsey's other pouch. Then the postmaster sent Dorsey out. Sure enough, Dorsey went to all the right addresses. After that, Dorsey got a mail route of his own. Although he was a friendly dog, he would never stop to play until his letters were delivered!

So what?

We can learn a good lesson from Dorsey. Because he loved his master, he wanted to help him. If you love Jesus, you will want to help him—and help other people, too. *The Bible tells us:*

Take tender care of those who are weak.   1 THESSALONIANS 5:14, NLT

If you can help a weak or sick person with a chore, do it. Volunteer even if you haven't been told—some people are too shy or embarrassed to ask. Helping others is a great way to show Jesus that you love him.

July

Who invented raincoats?

MATTHEW 5:40

Until a man named Charles Macintosh invented it, there was no such thing as a raincoat. People wore coats made of cotton. But when it rained, these coats got wet and so did all the clothes underneath. Macintosh knew that rubber was waterproof and that rubber could be made into a liquid called latex. If only a cotton coat could be dipped into latex, it would be waterproof. But the coat would be very uncomfortable to wear, because when latex dries, it becomes very stiff. Imagine trying to wear a coat that was soft when you put it on, but soon became as hard and as tough as a car tire!

Macintosh had to find a way to keep the latex soft, and he finally discovered it—by mistake. He accidentally dropped latex on the top of a cabinet. The cabinet already had turpentine on it, and Macintosh was surprised to see that the latex stayed soft after it touched the turpentine. He mixed some latex and turpentine together and then tested his discovery by dipping coats into it. He had found the way to make a coat weatherproof *and* wearable. That's why the first raincoats were called "mackintoshes."

So what?

People love staying dry in the rain! Once you've had a raincoat, it would be hard to give it up. But sometimes that's what God wants his children to do. *He tells us:*

If you are ordered to court and your shirt is taken from you, give your coat, too.   MATTHEW 5:40, NLT

God is using the shirt and coat as an example. He means that he wants us to be ready to do something extra. He wants us to give generously, even if we're poor, and to work cheerfully, even if we're tired.

July

How does a toad change its skin?
EPHESIANS 4:24

It may surprise you to know that toads and frogs don't keep the skins they were born with. Our skin stretches, but theirs doesn't. As they get bigger, amphibians grow a new skin inside the old one. When the old skin is so tight that it needs to come off, how does the toad make the change? It's not like taking off a coat, because there aren't any zippers or buttons. Instead, the toad knows a good trick. It takes very deep breaths and holds them in, puffing up its body. Then it lets out the air and starts all over. Finally, the skin bursts down its back. That's when the toad wiggles and pulls its front feet out of the skin. Once its front feet are free, the toad uses them to pull off the rest of the old skin. In case you're wondering why we don't see old toad skins all over the ground, it's because the toad doesn't litter. It gets rid of the old skin by eating it.

So what?

When you become God's child, you become a new person. All your old sins and faults no longer count. You get rid of them, just like an old toad's skin and start over with God's forgiveness. *The Bible says:*

Yes, you must be a new and different person, holy and good. Clothe yourself with this new nature. EPHESIANS 4:24, TLB

The new skin of the toad fits better and feels better. Your new Christian "skin" will make you feel better too, and it will set you free. You won't have to be anxious or worried or guilty anymore!

July 31

What does the pack rat pack?

1 CORINTHIANS 14:40

When your bedroom looks like a big collection of junk, you might be a lot more like a rat than you think. A person who saves everything, even if it isn't useful, is often called a pack rat. Why? There really is a rat with that nickname. Its actual name is the wood rat, and it does save things, carrying them back to its nest. This small rat likes to stockpile coins, buttons, pieces of glass, foil, nails—anything that attracts its attention. If it could somehow find its way into your house (which seldom happens), it would carry things out. You could be missing your eyeglasses or a piece of silverware and never suspect that your possessions had moved to the middle of a rat's nest. The wood rat is also sometimes called the trader rat, because while the little rat is busy carrying a treasure away, it might spy something even better. Then it drops the first thing and grabs the new one, hurrying back to the nest. Take a look at your bedroom. Could someone call it a pack rat's nest? Maybe it's time to tidy up a little!

So what?

Have you ever thought about how much easier it is to get dressed in the morning if you already know where your clothes are? Or how difficult it is to find a certain book in the library if it isn't put on the shelf in order?

God created the world and the whole universe in an orderly way, so that everything is in its place and keeps moving. He is a God of order. He even wants our church services to be orderly. *This is what the Bible tells us about that:*

Let all things be done decently and in order.   1 CORINTHIANS 14:40, NKJV

Wherever we are, we can follow God's example of orderliness. If we all behaved like the pack rat does, stuffing things away where they don't belong or always looking for something to trade, we would be constantly mixed up. When our belongings are out of place, our minds are probably cluttered too. Make room in your brain for important thoughts by making space for your possessions in your room!

August 1

How was the disposable razor invented?

JUDE 1:20

Men have been trying to get rid of their whiskers for many, many years. They have used sharpened rocks as razors and clam shells for tweezers. Even the name "barber" comes from an old Latin word, *barba,* which means "beard." But it took just one man in the 1800s to change the history of shaving.

His name was Mr. King Gillette, and he was a salesman with big hopes for being successful. He was trying to think of a product that everyone needed: something that they could use for a while, throw away, and then buy again. Mr. Gillette wanted people to buy their replacements from him.

The answer came to him one morning when he wasn't expecting it. He was shaving, and his razor was so dull that it wasn't working well. He would have to take it to a barber and have it sharpened. Mr. Gillette thought to himself, *Wouldn't it be nice if there were a razor that you could just throw away when it got dull?* He liked this new idea so much, he began to work on it right away. It took six years to find just the right parts. Finally, Mr. Gillette invented the disposable razor and became wealthy, just as he had dreamed he might.

So what?

Mr. Gillette found a good way to improve the razor. Things can always be improved in some way. People can always be improved too, because no one is perfect yet. *The Bible tells Christians the most important way that they can improve:*

You, dear friends, must continue to build your lives on the foundation of your holy faith. And continue to pray as you are directed by the Holy Spirit. JUDE 1:20, NLT

Talking to God—praying—will make you a better person every time.

August

How are a lemon seed and a drinking straw connected?

JOHN 17:3

Strangely enough, the hole in the first straws was designed to be just narrow enough to keep a lemon seed from getting stuck inside it. That's because lemonade was a very popular drink when Marvin Stone made the first paper straw in 1888.

Mr. Stone enjoyed his drinks very cold, which meant that the glass was uncomfortable to hold. He had tried the only solution available for a straw at the time—a wild grass stalk, which was hollow. But these stalks made the drinks taste odd. And when they dried, they either cracked or got dusty.

Mr. Stone thought of a better way. He took a long, skinny piece of paper, wound it around a pencil, dotted the end of the paper with glue, and pulled the pencil out. He made several of these tubes, just for himself. But when other people saw Mr. Stone's straws, they wanted to try one too. Mr. Stone owned a factory, so he instructed all of his employees to roll straws. The workers made the straws out of wax-coated paper so they wouldn't get soggy when wet. Mr. Stone sold many of his simple straws. Lots of fancier straws have been tried since then. Mr. Stone himself invented a double-barreled straw—two straws stuck together so you could drink twice as much. Other inventions were a glass with a straw built in; loop-the-loop straws; and chocolate-, vanilla-, or strawberry-flavored straws. But the plain, simple straw has lasted longest.

So what?

If you could choose a type of straw to use right now, would you pick the double-barreled one, the loop-the-loop, or the flavored? If you could choose another straw tomorrow, you would probably want to choose a different kind. Sometimes choices can be confusing, and it's hard to decide between them. The Bible helps us with many of the choices we have to make—choices about what's right and what's wrong, what pleases God and what does not please him. *There is one choice that's very easy to make, because Jesus tells us there is only one way to get to heaven:*

This is the way to have eternal life—to know you, the only true God, and Jesus Christ, the one you sent to earth. JOHN 17:3, NLT

August

What do some of our nursery rhymes really mean?

ISAIAH 57:15

Do you believe that people really used to jump over candles? That's what the story of "Jack be nimble, Jack be quick, Jack jump over the candlestick" is all about. People thought you were lucky if you could jump over a candle without touching it. And you were unlucky, of course, if you got burned!

Another nursery rhyme is about muffins: "Hot cross buns, hot cross buns; one a penny, two a penny, hot cross buns." Near Easter time, buns, or muffins, were iced with the shape of a cross to remind people of how Jesus died for them. While they were still warm, the buns were sold out on the street to people walking by. The vendors would say the "Hot Cross Buns" rhyme to attract attention.

And what about "Pop Goes the Weasel"? The weasel in this rhyme is not an animal at all. Long ago, "weasel" was another name for an iron that had to be heated on the fire. When people ran out of money, they would trade in their irons at a pawnshop for some extra money. This was called "popping" the iron or "weasel."

And what is the "tuffet" that Little Miss Muffet sat on? A tuffet was a little cushion. People used to play a game at parties, sort of like musical chairs, and they sang the "Little Miss Muffet" rhyme.

So what?

We often say things, like nursery rhymes, without really knowing why we say them. Maybe you've done that recently. Maybe you were angry and said something mean to someone you love. You're not even really sure why you said it. You didn't mean it, and now you feel awful. What can you do to fix this mess? Apologize. If you are too proud to say "I'm sorry," you won't be pleasing God. *If you do apologize, you'll feel better, because God tells us:*

I refresh the humble and give new courage to those with repentant hearts. ISAIAH 57:15, NLT

Ask God for some of that new courage, and then be sure you are truly sorry (repentant) when you ask your loved one for forgiveness.

August 4

When did one man with a good idea change an entire country?

JOB 29:15

The year was 1869, the country was Japan, the man was an American minister named Jonathan Scobie, and the idea was a rickshaw. A rickshaw is a small carriage that is pulled along by a person holding two long handles. The carriage has two wheels and a hood that can be pulled up in unpleasant weather.

Reverend Scobie invented the rickshaw for a very personal reason. His wife was an invalid and couldn't walk well, so he needed a way to help her travel through the city. After Reverend Scobie and his wife started using their rickshaw, other people in their church started building their own rickshaws, and soon many Japanese people had new jobs pulling rickshaws through the city of Yokohama. The Japanese word for this vehicle was *jinrikisha—jin* means "a man," *riki* means "power," and *sha* means "carriage." It was shortened in English, but any way it's said, it was a very successful idea.

So what?

God wants us to help people, just as Jonathan Scobie helped his wife. If you are blessed with good eyesight, offer to read to someone who can't see. If your hearing is fine, try to learn sign language so that you can help someone who's deaf understand what's being said. If you have good handwriting, volunteer to write a letter for someone whose hands are shaky. God is always pleased when you share your blessings. *Look for ways that you can help others, so you can say:*

I served as eyes for the blind and feet for the lame. JOB 29:15, NLT

Small things can make a big difference in someone's life. Reverend Scobie and his rickshaw prove it!

August

Do boys and girls study differently?
PROVERBS 24:5

It may surprise you to know that boys and girls differ when it comes to studying, and that the time of day in which you choose to study can make a difference about how much you learn. A psychologist at Ohio State University has studied studying, and he has found something interesting. Boys can usually study quite well when there is talking going on in the background. The older boys get, the more the background noise helps them study. Girls, on the other hand, usually need quiet to study well. That's because girls tend to be more sensitive to language, so they have more trouble concentrating on their studies when they hear background talk.

As for the time when you study—not long before you go to bed is the best time, because the shorter the time between when you study and when you go to sleep, the better it is. The next day you will remember more of what you learned the night before.

So what?
Just studying school subjects is no guarantee that you will be wise. But the more you study, the more knowledge you are giving yourself; and the more information you have, the better you will be able to make wise decisions. *The Bible says:*

A wise man is mightier than a strong man, and a man of knowledge is more powerful than a strong man. PROVERBS 24:5, NLT

Brain power can make you strong. Go for it!

August 6

Why was a man in a diving outfit working at a church?

1 CORINTHIANS 3:11

People in England saw just such a man for six years at a very famous church called Winchester Cathedral. Why was he there?

Underneath the cathedral there was a peat bog, which is like a giant mud hole. Over many years, the building had been slowly sinking, and the foundation was now under water. William Walker, who was a deep-sea diver, was hired to swim under the building and stop it from sinking down any further. Mr. Walker kept diving over and over. He dug out the peat bog a little at a time and replaced it with 115,000 concrete blocks, 25,000 bags of concrete, and almost a million bricks. Mr. Walker saved the cathedral, and the king of England thanked him when the work was finished.

So what?

A foundation is made up of the rocks or cement that the rest of the building sits on. The foundation that people build can sometimes get weak, like it did in the cathedral. *The Bible says:*

No one can lay any other foundation than the one we already have— Jesus Christ. 1 CORINTHIANS 3:11, NLT

This means that you can count on Jesus to be a permanent foundation for your life. What he says will never wash away, sink, or crumble. Build up your trust in Jesus, and he will hold you firmly.

August

What invention made grocery shopping easier?

PROVERBS 24:27

If you saw two folding chairs facing each other, what would that make you think of? It made Sylvan Goldman think of the answer to a problem.

He owned a chain of grocery stories in Oklahoma, and he noticed that his customers needed a better way to take their groceries to the counter. His customers sometimes carried baskets, but the items they collected made the baskets too heavy. Mr. Goldman was thinking about this problem while he walked to work, and that's when he saw the two chairs on someone's lawn. His idea was this: Why not put wheels on the chairs, put wood across the two seats that are facing each other, and surround the whole thing with wooden sides like a crib? Then it would be like a baby carriage that customers could fill with groceries!

Mr. Goldman built his shopping carts and began to park them in his stores. But he had one more problem to solve—his lady customers were tired of pushing baby carriages and didn't want to push grocery carriages, too. So Mr. Goldman hired some women to just push the shopping carts around his store, until everyone got used to using them.

So what?

Mr. Goldman was always looking for ways to make his stores better, even when he wasn't working. He found a good way. *The Bible tells us that it's smart to improve your business as much as you can:*

Develop your business first before building your house.
PROVERBS 24:27, NLT

If you aren't trying your best when you do a job for someone, don't expect to make any money. If you don't spend time studying, don't expect to get a good grade. Work hard first, like Mr. Goldman, and you could end up with a shopping basket full of blessings!

August

Why did the rainmaker lose his job?

EZEKIEL 34:26

How do you know when you've had too much of a good thing? The city of San Diego found out the hard way in 1915 when Charles Hatfield offered the city council a chance to fill up the nearby water reservoir, which had never been more than one-third full. Hatfield considered himself a rainmaker, and he gave the city a special offer. If he caused rain, the city would pay him $10,000; if no rain came, no payment would be expected. The council agreed and hired Hatfield. He built a tower near the reservoir and put some of his specially mixed chemicals on the top. Four days later, it began to rain. Five days after that, steady rain was falling over the whole county, and it lasted for ten more days. So much rain fell that the water rushed through downtown San Diego, stopping business. Rivers overflowed; roads were shut down; buildings were swept away.

The rain finally stopped when the reservoir was only five inches away from overflowing. The long-term effects were that the trains didn't run for at least a month, more than two hundred bridges were ruined, and fifty people died.

Hartfield felt that he had kept his bargain and was shocked when the city council said he would not be paid unless he could prove he was the cause of the rain. That was basically impossible to prove, so Hatfield never got paid.

Could rainmaking be scientifically done at that time? Not really. In earlier days, people thought that explosions could cause rain because they often noticed a downpour after a battle. But it was only after the mid-1940s that "seeding" was developed. A pilot can spray powdered dry ice or carbon dioxide into fluffy cumulus clouds, which are the only kind that will respond. As moisture collects around these particles, they become too heavy to stay in the clouds, and the liquid falls as rain or snow.

So what?

When the ground is dry, rain is very exciting. God understands this feeling and uses rain to explain his blessings. *He says:*

I will send showers, showers of blessings, which will come just when they are needed. EZEKIEL 34:26, NLT

Turn your face up toward heaven, and let the good things God wants to do for you pour down over you like showers of blessings.

August

How was a wedding ring reclaimed after it was lost at sea?

PSALM 49:15

Prince Urussof was a worried newlywed. He and his bride were on their honeymoon, sailing on the Black Sea. The prince was remembering a family story passed down to him about wedding rings. The belief was that if you lost the ring, you lost the bride. That's what was troubling him—his bride's ring had just slipped off her finger and fallen into the sea. How could he get it back? Although he tried to think of a way to retrieve the ring, it seemed impossible. So he settled for the next best thing. He went up and down both shores of the Black Sea, buying the properties that touched the shores. The prince spent forty million dollars making deals with hundreds of owners. Now he "owned" the Black Sea and everything in it—including the wedding ring at the bottom. After the prince's death, his descendants no longer needed the ring, so they sold the Black Sea properties for eighty million dollars, a one hundred percent profit.

So what?

The prince spent lots of money and effort trying to "recover" the lost wedding ring. It makes a charming tale because we all like to think love is so strong that someone will go to the ends of the earth to preserve it. But there is a much more powerful love story that involves each one of us. When you die, your body will be covered with earth, just as the ring was covered by water. But the valuable part of you—your soul—will be raised to heaven because of the death of Jesus. He paid the highest price—his very life—to regain your soul, which would have been "lost" without him. *The Bible says:*

God will redeem my soul from the power of death, for he will receive me.
PSALM 49:15, TLB

That's the greatest love of all.

August

Where does the asphalt go from a pothole?

ISAIAH 35:8-10

Let's talk road maintenance. We've all seen those rubber reflectors that are embedded in the road. They were invented in 1934 to help drivers stay on course at night, and they're referred to as "cat's eyes." Inside the rubber casing is yellow-colored glass that attracts the light coming from a car's headlights. Cat's eyes are basically maintenance-free for two reasons. First, the rubber case is used to protect the glass from cracking when a tire rolls over it. Second, the cat's eyes are designed to be "self-cleaning." The pressure of a tire pushes the rubber case against the glass eye, and the rubber moves across the glass, wiping it clean.

Potholes, however, are another story. They can't take care of themselves. They're caused mainly by moisture that is absorbed by the asphalt: add to that the freeze-thaw cycle, traffic wear, and chemicals, and soon the pavement crumbles from within. It's easy to figure out how potholes are filled up, but how are potholes emptied out? Where does all the asphalt go that used to be in the potholes? It's a combination of conditions that removes the broken asphalt. Vehicle tires scatter it, rain carries it away, and wind pushes it onto the road shoulders.

And what about those manholes? Why are the covers round, instead of square or oblong? No matter which way it's turned, the round manhole cover can't fall through the hole; it's kept in place by a lip rimming the inside of the hole.

So what?

As you travel daily on patched and potholed roads, keep this glimpse of the road to heaven in your head:

A main road will go through that once deserted land. It will be named the Highway of Holiness. Evil-hearted people will never travel on it. It will be only for those who walk in God's ways; fools will never walk there. Lions will not lurk along its course, and there will be no other dangers. Only the redeemed will follow it. Those who have been ransomed by the LORD will return to Jerusalem, singing songs of everlasting joy. Sorrow and mourning will disappear, and they will be overcome with joy and gladness. ISAIAH 35:8-10, NLT

Keep Jesus as your destination, and you'll travel on with confidence!

11
August

Why was a bank alarmed about a withdrawal?

COLOSSIANS 1:20-23

Many times a day, people go into the bank, fill out a slip of paper, and receive cash from their accounts. Imagine Ron Schatz's surprise when he did just that one day, but the next thing he knew, he was in big trouble! The police had been called by secret alarm, and the person they wanted to arrest was Ron. He had no idea what he had done wrong. It took a while to straighten out the story. The teller had pressed the silent alarm button after turning over the slip of paper Ron had handed her and seeing the words, "This is a holdup" written on the back. She had no way of knowing that Ron hadn't written the message. It was discovered that the whole stack of withdrawal slips on the counter, one of which Ron had filled out, had the same words printed on the back—someone's idea of a practical joke.

So what?

Look at the chain reaction just a few words on a piece of paper could cause! But the actions of Jesus, and the news of his sacrifice on the cross, can have a much more startling effect. They can change your whole life. *The Bible tells us:*

It was through what his Son did that God cleared a path for everything to come to him . . . for Christ's death on the cross has made peace with God for all by his blood. . . . You were his enemies and hated him and were separated from him by your evil thoughts and actions, yet now he has brought you back as his friends. He has done this through the death on the cross of his own human body, and now as a result Christ has brought you into the very presence of God, and you are standing there before him with nothing left against you—nothing left that he could even chide you for; the only condition is that you fully believe the Truth, standing in it steadfast and firm, strong in the Lord, convinced of the Good News that Jesus died for you, and never shifting from trusting him to save you. COLOSSIANS 1:20-23, TLB

Act as quickly on reading the words above as the teller did when she read the note. You won't be protecting mere money—you will be moving to save your soul for all eternity.

August

How do rocks travel in Death Valley?

MATTHEW 28:2

Death Valley is a place of extremes, because it is the driest, hottest, and lowest location in America. There is a three-mile-long, dried-up lake bed in Death Valley, and all across it, rocks and stones leave small paths behind them in curved, zigzagged, or straight patterns. The rocks aren't alive, of course, yet they travel across the lake bed. How?

Dr. Robert Sharp, a geology professor, decided to find out about the roaming rocks. He put tags on thirty stones of different sizes and shapes. He hammered spikes into the ground where the rocks were sitting, and then he studied what happened for the next seven years. Twenty-eight of the stones did indeed move, sometimes more than six hundred feet. Sharp matched the movements with the weather conditions and found that the rocks moved due to wind and rain. Even though Death Valley gets less than two inches of rain a year, the raindrops make the smooth clay in the lake bed very slick. The wind then blows the rocks across the slippery surface, sometimes as fast as three feet per second.

So what?

The sight of these "moving rocks" is amazing, because we expect rocks to stay put. We know that ordinarily they don't move on their own. That's precisely why a big rock was put in front of Jesus' tomb when he died. It was even guarded, to keep the disciples from pushing it away. The rock was supposed to be proof that Jesus didn't rise from the dead. But God keeps his promises. *The Bible says:*

Suddenly there was a great earthquake, because an angel of the Lord came down from heaven and rolled aside the stone and sat on it.
MATTHEW 28:2, NLT

Desert rocks that move on their own are fascinating, but an angel perched on a dislodged rock, telling others that Jesus is alive, is a true miracle!

August

How did a fire alarm improve baking bread?
MATTHEW 7:9-11

If it wasn't for an unexpected fire alarm one day in 1949, you most likely wouldn't be able to enjoy fresh-baked rolls with your meals at home very often. Almost everyone appreciates the taste and smell of this type of bread, but very few people have the extra hours needed to mix, knead, and let the dough rise. That was Joe Gregor's problem. He had spent many hours experimenting, trying to figure out how to shorten the time needed to bake rolls. He was having no success. Joe, a volunteer fireman in Florida, was baking another batch of rolls when the fire siren screeched. Joe quickly pulled the rolls out of the oven, dumped them on the counter, and raced to the fire. When he returned, he inspected the white, cold, plastery dough he had left behind. Rather than throwing it away, Joe decided to reheat the oven and finish baking his bread. To his surprise, the rolls turned out perfectly. After experimenting a little more to determine the exact times and temperatures, Joe spread the word about how bakers could do all the beginning work of making bread, and then leave the last, best part for their customers to finish.

So what?
We often wonder if God will answer our prayers. Sometimes we're suspicious of someone who promises to love us no matter what, because it's so hard for us to love that way. Jesus understands our doubts and impatience. He is also, by the way, aware of our fondness for bread. *That's why he gives us reassurance in this way:*

You parents—if your children ask for a loaf of bread, do you give them a stone instead? Or if they ask for a fish, do you give them a snake? Of course not! If you sinful people know how to give good gifts to your children, how much more will your heavenly Father give good gifts to those who ask him. MATTHEW 7:9-11, NLT

God holds the perfect recipe for our lives, and his timing is never wrong. He hears our prayers more quickly and answers them more abundantly than a whole ovenful of quick-bake rolls.

August
14

How do seeds always know to send their roots downward?

EPHESIANS 3:17-19

When you're planting, there's no way to figure out which side of the seed will be growing the roots. Yet you never see a plant pushing its roots toward the sun and its leaves into the ground. How does it happen that the plant always grows right-side-up? In the ground, the seed first sends out a root. Then it sends out a stem shaped like a hook. The root points down; the stem points up. Scientists call the root development "positive geotropism" and the stem growth "negative geotropism." When the stem breaks through the earth and starts to grow toward the sun, its "hook" straightens out, and that's called "phototropism." But the secret to the seed has a much simpler name than its scientific labels. It's called gravity.

The root pushes toward the center of the earth, moving with the pull of gravity. The stem pushes away from the pull of gravity, toward the earth's surface. That's why you don't see any upside-down gardens. On earth, seeds are always predictable, growing in the same order, in the same way. It's only in outer space, where there is no gravity, that seeds would have no clue how to grow. There, a seed could grow in any direction.

So what?

Roots grow in the right direction so that plants will survive. We need to grow toward God so that our souls can survive. *The Bible says:*

I pray that Christ will be more and more at home in your hearts as you trust in him. May your roots go down deep into the soil of God's marvelous love. And may you have the power to understand, as all God's people should, how wide, how long, how high, and how deep his love really is. May you experience the love of Christ, though it is so great you will never fully understand it. Then you will be filled with the fullness of life and power that comes from God. EPHESIANS 3:17-19, NLT

All of God's children gathered together will make a gorgeous garden!

15

August

How did a war start the idea of a menu?

DEUTERONOMY 30:19-20

When your family is trying to decide which restaurant to go to, you can thank the French Revolution for giving you a choice. What do a war and a restaurant have to do with each other? Before the revolution you could eat away from home, but the taverns served only one dish at one specific time. You could also go to a cook shop, where they would sell you some already-cooked meat to take home for a meal. Along came a Frenchman named Boulanger, who sold soups. He called his shop *Restorante,* the French word for "restorative." In other words, you could restore or get back your strength, health, or energy by swallowing his hot broths. From that French word we get the word "restaurant." Boulanger offered several different kinds of soups, which made his the first eating place to offer a menu.

It was the French Revolution, however, that changed "eating out" forever. Before the revolution, wealthy French people had highly talented cooks working for them in their homes. After the war, the wealthy lost their money, leaving lots of cooks unemployed. These chefs began to work for local restaurants, or opened up their own, until there were more than five hundred restaurants in France by 1804.

So what?

We are free to choose whatever pleases us in a restaurant. We are also free to choose whether we will follow God. *Moses said:*

Today I have given you the choice between life and death, between blessings and curses. . . . Oh, that you would choose life, that you and your descendants might live! Choose to love the LORD your God and to obey him and commit yourself to him, for he is your life.
DEUTERONOMY 30:19-20, NLT

You could search for the rest of your life, but you'll never find a better deal on any other menu.

August

16

Why is the ocean so salty?

PSALM 119:117

Sea water collects its salt by starting in rivers, which flow against land along their way to the sea, pulling minerals from the ground. Rain falling on the land washes more minerals into the rivers. Rivers also rush along on tops of rocks, washing even more minerals downstream into the ocean. But not all bodies of water have the same amount of salt. If the sea water has a river near its shore, the sea water will be less salty, because there is so much fresh river water being added in. If the sea water is shallow, it will be more salty because of evaporation. When the sun dries up water, the water leaves its salt deposits behind.

The Dead Sea, for example, is very salty because it is surrounded by a dry desert and has lots of evaporation. The Dead Sea contains so much salt—about 25 percent—that it is almost impossible to drown in its waters. The salt makes the water "heavy," which makes the swimmer's body light in comparison. Your body will stay close to the surface of the water and not sink. Average sea water has only about 3.5 percent salt, but it is still easier to stay afloat in any sea water than in a freshwater lake or pool. By the way, can you guess why rain is not salty when it falls, even if it is collected from salty water? It's because the salt is too "heavy" to rise with the water vapor that evaporates from the ocean.

So what?

In the same way that salt can keep you floating above danger in the water, God can keep you floating above danger in life. *Just ask him to help you by saying with the psalm writer:*

Hold me safe above the heads of all my enemies; then I can continue to obey your laws. PSALM 119:117, TLB

When someone rescues you so that you are safe, you naturally want to do something extra for that person in return. Your loyalty to God for keeping you safe will please him greatly.

August

Why is it impossible to buy fresh sardines?
MATTHEW 4:19

Have you ever tried asking for fresh sardines at the supermarket seafood counter? If not, save yourself the embarrassment. They will never have any. That's because there is no such fish as a sardine. Yes, you can buy a can labeled "sardines," but that name applies to the fish only *after* they're packed in oil in a can.

Sardine cans are really filled with any one of twenty-one species of small fish. Every country is allowed to define what kind of fish its "sardines" will be.

So what?

Each country sends fishermen out to catch the small fish that will be sold as sardines. Jesus used the job of fishing to show how much more important our work can be when we work for him. *He said:*

Come, be my disciples, and I will show you how to fish for people!
MATTHEW 4:19, NLT

Instead of bringing in a fish for canning, imagine the satisfaction of helping people land in heaven someday—what a great catch!

August

How do you return the favor of a rescue?

LUKE 6:38

The year was 1965. It took only an instant. Four-year-old Roger Lausier was playing in the sand on a beach by the ocean, and then he vanished. He had waded into the ocean and stepped off a ledge into deep water over his head. When he opened his mouth to yell, the water began to choke him. At that instant someone grabbed him and pulled him up. Alice Blaise saved Roger's life after seeing the boy disappear—something his parents had missed by being distracted for just one moment. Roger's parents were grateful to Alice because they got their son back.

The family continued to vacation year after year at that same beach near Salem, Massachusetts. Nine years later, when Roger was thirteen years old, he had become a very good swimmer. One day that summer, Roger noticed a man out in the ocean who was struggling and yelling for help. Roger took his air raft and floated it beside him as he swam to reach the man. With Roger's help, the man was able to lay across the raft and be towed to shore. Only after the rescue did Roger find out the identity of the man: He was Alice Blaise's husband.

So what?

When Alice pulled little Roger from the waves, she didn't know her actions would be returned in the rescuing of her husband a number of years later. But that's how God works. *He promises:*

If you give, you will receive. Your gift will return to you in full measure, pressed down, shaken together to make room for more, and running over. Whatever measure you use in giving—large or small—it will be used to measure what is given back to you. LUKE 6:38, NLT

God kept his word in an unusual way as he returned to Alice her gift of life to Roger. The gift came back when God allowed Roger to grow up and give the gift of life to Alice's husband.

A u g u s t

Why don't birds seem frightened by scarecrows?

PSALM 145:13

It's not unusual to see a scarecrow with birds perched along its arms. You have to wonder why the farmers go to all that trouble if the crows aren't even afraid.

Many years ago some scarecrows were made because the farmers were scared. They worried about evil spirits. They thought they could protect their crops from any damage by putting two branches together in the shape of a cross and sticking the cross into the ground. Then, to camouflage the cross, they hung old clothes over it.

Other farmers used scarecrows because they really were having trouble with the birds. It was so bad that they planted four seeds in each hole—two for the birds, one for the worms, and one to grow. Native Americans sometimes had a real man stand in the middle of their fields, waving and throwing rocks. That's probably where they got the idea to make a scarecrow that looked like a person.

The scarecrows actually did keep those pesky crows away for a while. But it wasn't the way the scarecrow looked that bothered the birds. The smell of humans clung to the newly hung clothes and kept the crows out of the fields. After wind, rain, and fresh air swept the scent away, the birds saw that the scarecrow never moved, so they weren't scared anymore.

So what?

Anything that human beings make won't offer permanent protection. No law, weapon, or barrier lasts forever. Only God's protection can be counted on to last throughout eternity. *The Bible says:*

Your kingdom is an everlasting kingdom. You rule generation after generation. PSALM 145:13, NLT

Nothing can keep you away from God's love when you give your heart to him.

August

When were dirty tennis shoes helpful?
PSALM 91:11-13

A dirty tennis shoe is responsible for helping to keep your favorite couch clean. The owner of the shoes was wearing them one day in 1953 when she was assisting in the research lab at the 3M company. The 3M researchers were experimenting with some chemicals they planned to use on aircraft. Some of the chemical spilled onto the research assistant's tennis shoe, and it wouldn't come off. No matter how dirty the shoe got, the spot where the chemical dropped stayed clean. Patsy Sherman saw what happened and was fascinated by what she saw. She and Sam Smith, another chemist at 3M, worked together to develop a flourochemical that could repel oil and water from fabrics. And that's how Scotchgard was invented. Scotchgard, which has been on the market since 1956, coats materials, repels stains, and helps fabrics, including the fabrics on furniture, stay cleaner and last longer.

So what?

If your sneakers are Scotchgarded, you feel free to walk around. You're not worried about getting them so dirty you can't wear them anymore. As God's children, we have "Scotchgard" for our hearts as well as our feet. In a very special way, God protects our souls from being soiled or damaged, and he guards our footsteps, too. *The Bible says:*

He orders his angels to protect you wherever you go. They will steady you with their hands to keep you from stumbling against the rocks on the trail. You can safely meet a lion or step on poisonous snakes, yes, even trample them beneath your feet! PSALM 91:11-13, TLB

Only God's power can perfectly protect our steps and keep us spotless!

August 21

What does it mean to give someone the cold shoulder?

PROVERBS 25:17

When we are given the cold shoulder, we are ignored or snubbed or not welcomed warmly. It's almost as if someone is turning his back on us. But the "shoulder" referred to in this saying does not mean a person's shoulder. It stands for the shoulder of an animal.

During the Middle Ages, the shoulder of an animal was the least-wanted part for food. The shoulder would be the most likely piece to be a leftover. When poor people would beg for a meal, they would often be given a shoulder that hadn't even been warmed up. On occasion, even rich people would receive this meal. If you were visiting someone's castle, and he felt that you had stayed long enough, he might order a cold shoulder of mutton to be served to you. This would be a hint that he was ready for you to leave.

So what?

The Bible has a very straightforward comment on this subject. *It advises:*

Don't visit your neighbors too often, or you will wear out your welcome. PROVERBS 25:17, NLT

God is the only one who will never grow tired of spending time with you. He invites you to enjoy his company and encourages you to stay forever. Make your friendship with God grow stronger by talking to him in prayer all the time. The more often you visit him through prayer, the more welcome you'll feel in his house.

August

How did sideburns get their name?

HEBREWS 6:12

The name for that extra hair growing in front of men's ears has gotten tangled up through time. You may think that the *side* in *sideburns* comes from the fact that the hair is located on each side of a man's face. But that leaves no explanation for the second half of the word, *burns*. The real reason we use the word *sideburns* is because during the Civil War, there was a general who was fond of wearing his hair this way. His name was Ambrose E. Burnside. Somehow through the years his name was turned around, but he is the gentleman credited with starting the fashion all the same.

So what?

We copy fashion trends to show that we admire a certain style or identify with a certain group. Imitating fads is amusing, but it's a shallow way of "belonging." The Bible encourages us to be much more serious when choosing a whole lifestyle for ourselves. We are to look beyond the present and think about what will be happening in the future. *The Bible explains:*

Knowing what lies ahead for you, you won't become bored with being a Christian, nor become spiritually dull and indifferent, but you will be anxious to follow the example of those who receive all that God has promised them because of their strong faith and patience.
HEBREWS 6:12, TLB

Enjoy changing and experimenting with your "outside," but make sure that your "inside" stays close to God.

August

Why don't birds get electrocuted when they sit on wires?

1 CHRONICLES 29:11

Electricity finds the shortest way to travel between two places. Usually this means that the electricity runs down one wire to the appliance, like a television or a lightbulb, and back through another. That round-trip is called "completing a circuit." But if something is in the way of this path, the electricity will take a shortcut to get where it wants to go. For example, if you are standing in a puddle and touching an electrical wire, the electricity will flow through you, through the puddle, and down into the ground. When electricity passes through your body, it can kill you. That's why it is so important to treat electricity carefully.

In the case of a bird perching on the wire, the bird is not touching water or anything else that would make the electricity take a shortcut. So the electricity just stays on its original path, and the bird can sit on the wire as long as it wants without being harmed.

So what?
We know how powerful electricity is. It can light up a whole city at once. But electricity doesn't even come close to the power of God. *King David said to God:*

Yours, O LORD, is the greatness, the power, the glory, the victory, and the majesty. Everything in the heavens and on earth is yours, O LORD, and this is your kingdom. We adore you as the one who is over all things. 1 CHRONICLES 29:11, NLT

God doesn't just run lights or televisions or microwaves. He runs the sun, the moon, the stars, the waterfalls, the planets, the universe. At the same time, he watches over every person on earth. It's hard to imagine how great God is!

August

Who was Simon in the game "Simon Says"?

DEUTERONOMY 5:32-33

The Simon in the game "Simon Says" really could say something, because he was an actual person. He was the social director in charge of keeping people entertained at a resort in the early 1900s. He helped his guests develop a fondness for the English game of Wiggle Waggle, but he changed the name to Do This, Do That. The point of the game was that Simon was in charge. If he told you to do something, you needed to do it exactly, or you were out of the game. If you acted without his permission, you were out also. The guests started calling the game "Simon Says."

So what?

The goal of the game "Simon Says" is to be the best listener and therefore the one who obeys most exactly. If winning a game seems important, how much more valuable it is to listen to God and obey him exactly. *We are told in the Bible:*

You must obey all the commands of the LORD your God, following his instructions in every detail. Stay on the path that the LORD your God has commanded you to follow. Then you will live long and prosperous lives in the land you are about to enter and occupy.

DEUTERONOMY 5:32-33, NLT

Use all your listening and understanding skills to play "God Says" each day, and you will always be a winner.

25
August

Why do giraffes need such long necks?
EPHESIANS 3:12

A giraffe can see an enemy coming from far away because its eyes are so high up. The giraffe can reach far above where most animals can, so it usually has plenty of leaves to eat from the tops of trees. The only trouble a giraffe has with his long neck is bending down to drink. To reach the water with its mouth, the giraffe spreads its front legs far apart and lowers its head between them. Giraffes must stay on guard against enemies, so they almost never lie down. Giraffes get only about twenty minutes of deep sleep by taking five-minute naps several times throughout the night. When baby giraffes are born, they fall five feet to the ground, but they are not hurt. In fact, a baby giraffe is standing up within thirty minutes and running with the other giraffes when it's only about ten hours old! Don't worry about the little giraffes being too small to take care of themselves—young giraffes grow incredibly fast, sometimes as much as a whole inch in just two hours!

So what?
God gave the giraffe a way to get close to the tasty leaves at the top of a tree. We don't need leaves to eat, but we do need God's love. His Son, Jesus, gave us a way to get close to God. *The Bible tells us:*

Because of Christ and our faith in him, we can now come fearlessly into God's presence, assured of his glad welcome. EPHESIANS 3:12, NLT

Having Jesus in our heart is like having someone to lift us up to the treetops, even right up to heaven, so that we can get as close to God as we want!

August
26

How was a sinking ship saved by a comic book?

PSALM 93:4

In 1964, a cartoon character saved a real ship from sinking. It wasn't Popeye who lifted the ship out of the water, or Superman who blew it to shore. The heroes of this story were Donald Duck and his nephews Huey, Dewey, and Louie.

A ship was coming into the harbor near Kuwait, getting ready to unload the six thousand sheep it was carrying, when it began to sink. The people on land were very worried that the sheep would drown in the water and make it too dirty for drinking. There didn't seem to be any way to stop that from happening. Then a Danish engineer named Karl Kroyer remembered a comic book from 1949 that he had read. In the book, Donald Duck and his nephews had found a sunken yacht and had brought it to the top of the water by filling it with Ping-Pong balls. Karl decided that this plan was worth trying. So he had twenty-seven billion plastic balls stuffed into the bottom of the ship. Amazingly, the ship stopped tilting and floated safely to shore. Donald Duck saved the day!

So what?

Karl Kroyer probably got a lot of admiration for being able to control the ship. But imagine if he had been able to control the ocean! *The Bible says:*

Mightier than the violent raging of the seas, mightier than the breakers on the shore—the LORD above is mightier than these!
PSALM 93:4, NLT

Only God can control the sea. Not only that, but God created the ocean in the first place. He made every grain of sand on its shores, and he even knows exactly how many grains there are. That's a lot more amazing than Ping-Pong balls!

27
August

What's so great about grass?
ISAIAH 40:8

Toward the end of a summer of mowing, you may be wondering just exactly whose idea it was to plant grass all around a house. Actually, yards have existed since 400 BC, but grass was used only as a background to show off the garden and flowers. Until the 1800s, people admired long grass combined with wildflowers. But you can thank nineteenth-century Europe for starting the idea of mowing yards. At that time rich and poor alike began enjoying lawn games like golf and bowling, so both castles and cottages were soon surrounded with pretty playing fields. Besides, low grass made it easier to see who was approaching, serving as an early warning of intruders.

Much later, as people began moving into the suburbs, they were anxious to match their neighbors' yards, and grassy lawns became a status symbol. In early history, unless you had a flock of sheep that could constantly eat the lawn, grass had to be cut with a sickle. Then, in 1830, Edwin Budding invented a rotary push mower. The large version was horse drawn and not popular, because the loose pieces of sod dug up by the horses' hooves ruined the job. People gradually accepted the small, human-powered push mower. It was almost one hundred years later, just after World War I, when Edwin George took the engine from his wife's washing machine and attached it to the back of his mower, creating the first gas-powered version.

So what?

If you stopped taking care of your lawn, it would eventually decay, die, and return back to dirt. The rains would come and wash the dirt away, and the wind would blow away the dust. *The Bible says:*

The grass withers, and the flowers fade, but the word of our God stands forever. ISAIAH 40:8, NLT

Sometimes we spend more time taking care of our yards than our souls. Take notice of your efforts, and make changes now if you need to. It doesn't make much sense to take good care of the "grass" if the soul is in danger of drying up and withering away.

August

When does a board game take a test?

1 JOHN 4:1-2

It's the middle of winter, and you've been stuck in the house for days because of rain or snow. Christmas has come and gone, you're tired of playing with your new toys, and you're really bored. You happen to see a television commercial for a new board game, and all of a sudden it seems to be a terrific idea to buy one. Your attention wasn't grabbed by chance—it was done on purpose.

Toy companies know that after Christmas, it's hard to sell new toys. So that's the time toymakers concentrate on trying to sell board games to the bored. But not just any board game will do. The Milton-Bradley Company actually makes a game pass a test before the company will start selling it. Here are the things that Milton-Bradley wants to know: Is playing the game fun? Does the game have a reward at the end? Is the game too easy, so that it's not enough of a challenge? Is it so hard that players will get frustrated and want to quit? Will people want to play it more than once? If the game passes these tests, the company will try testing your willpower to see if they can persuade you that it's a game you just have to buy.

So what?

Games aren't the only things that need to be tested. *The Bible tells us to test things we hear to see whether they're true or not:*

Dear friends, do not believe everyone who claims to speak by the Spirit. You must test them to see if the spirit they have comes from God. For there are many false prophets in the world. This is the way to find out if they have the Spirit of God: If a prophet acknowledges that Jesus Christ became a human being, that person has the Spirit of God.
1 JOHN 4:1-2, NLT

Get to know God's book, the Bible, and then no one will be able to trick you.

August

How did they build a bridge across Niagara Falls?

AMOS 5:24

Once there was a kite that helped build a bridge. It's true! Between Canada and the United States is a wide waterfall called Niagara Falls. It flows so swiftly that it's like fifteen million water hoses shooting out their fastest water. Long ago, before there were so many buildings and so much traffic, people could hear the water whooshing down from as far as twenty miles away. Around 1848, people decided they needed a way to get across Niagara Falls to the other side. They needed a bridge. How could they build one when they couldn't reach across? A boat certainly wouldn't get across the rushing water; it would just be pushed over the falls. The answer was to have a contest—a kite-flying contest! A young boy named Homan Walsh was able to sail his kite across Niagara Falls. (He won a prize of five dollars.)

A heavy rope and some cables were tied to the kite string. Then it was pulled back across the falls, dragging the first supplies for the new bridge along with it.

So what?

The Niagara waterfall is so powerful that it frightens people. They know that if the water ever washed over them, they couldn't stand up against it. God used the example of rushing water to tell how he wanted us to behave. *He said:*

I want to see a mighty flood of justice, a river of righteous living that will never run dry. AMOS 5:24, NLT

God wants so many of his people doing so many good things that the rest of the world won't be able to resist him.

August

What trapped a fire truck?

PSALM 24:7

The firefighters in Stratford, Connecticut, had a big problem that was sort of a mystery. When the alarm sounded and the truck started to roar out of the firehouse, the overhead door would close, blocking the truck from leaving. The firefighters would have to stop, get the door open, and then get going. Obviously, something had to be done.

The people who had installed the door were called to come for an inspection. The mystery was finally solved. The fire truck's radio came on whenever the truck was started. The radio sent a signal that was exactly the same as the one that the garage door opener used. The garage door couldn't tell the signals apart. So when the firefighters started the truck, the door went down.

So what?

Firefighters have very important jobs, so it's a serious matter when a closed door blocks their path. It means they can't answer a call for help. Whenever you call for Jesus, nothing will stop him from coming to you. *The Bible says:*

Open up, ancient gates! Open up, ancient doors, and let the King of glory enter. PSALM 24:7, NLT

No gate, door, or lock can stop Jesus. The thing he wants most is to be with you.

31

August

What's the good of garlic?

PSALM 104:14

Try this strange experiment: Rub a piece of garlic on the bottom of your foot. In just a few minutes, your breath will smell like garlic. How does this happen? The oil in the garlic goes through your skin. It enters your blood, and the blood goes into your lungs. When the air comes out of your lungs through your mouth, so does the strong smell of garlic.

Why would anyone want to use a plant that smells like that? Throughout history, garlic has been used for many jobs. At one time it was rubbed on meat to keep the meat from spoiling. Garlic has also been used as a cure for more than sixty different sicknesses. It was even used at one time to help with snakebites. Garlic was thought to cure the flu. People would boil it in water and breathe the steam to clear up stuffiness in the nose. Actually, garlic really did help with many of these situations. It's true that garlic kills germs—even better than some antibiotics. Doctors in World War I even wiped garlic into soldiers' wounds because it helped keep infection away. But garlic is not just for people—cats and dogs love the taste, and most of their canned food has garlic in it.

So what?

God cares so much for us that he created many plants to help us. *The psalm writer says this about God:*

You cause grass to grow for the cattle. You cause plants to grow for people to use. You allow them to produce food from the earth.
PSALM 104:14, NLT

Garlic is just one of the creations God gave to us to make our lives better.

September

1

How do flies walk on the ceiling?

PSALM 17:5

If you have imagined that a fly has suction cups on its feet, you're getting the wrong picture. A fly that stuck itself to the ceiling with suction wouldn't be able to fly away quickly, which you know a fly can do if you've ever tried to swat one. The truth is that the fly has small claws, like a lobster's, on each of its six legs. These claws can grab the rough surfaces on the ceiling. The fly also has pads, called *pulvilli,* on the end of each leg. These pulvilli are fuzzy and covered with a sticky goo, allowing the fly to stay on metal or glass as well as ceilings.

So what?

People don't have the same ability as flies do to walk on ceilings. But that doesn't mean that God has neglected us. Far from it! God watches over us everywhere we walk. *If we choose to follow God and obey his teachings, we can say to him, as David said in one of his psalms in the Bible:*

My steps have stayed on your path; I have not wavered from following you. PSALM 17:5, NLT

God gave the fly sticky feet to hold it up. For us, though, God himself holds our feet to make sure that we stick to his paths of safety.

Se**2**mber

Why does aluminum foil have a shiny side and a dull side?

MARK 13:37

If you're good at noticing things, you may have discovered something unusual about aluminum foil—one side is shiny, and the other side is dull. Some people say the shiny side is supposed to be closest to the food. Others think the dull side is supposed to face the food. Who is right? Neither one. It makes no difference when you're cooking. Actually, no one made the two sides different on purpose—it just happens when the foil is made.

Foil starts out as a big block of aluminum. It is flattened with a roller until it is long and thin. Then, two sheets of foil are put through the rollers back-to-back at the same time. The big, heavy rollers are very smooth and shiny, so the sides of the foil that touch the rollers also get smooth and shiny. The sides of the foil that are pressed against each other don't get polished by the rollers, so those sides stay dull.

So what?

If you have noticed that the two sides of foil don't look the same, you are an alert person. Jesus wants us to be alert—to be aware of what is going on around us. The more you see, the more you learn. One of the things he warned his followers about was to be watching and waiting for him to come back. *Jesus said about himself:*

What I say to you I say to everyone: Watch for his return!
MARK 13:37, NLT

Even before Jesus comes back, he wants us to watch out for times when temptations come to do something wrong. Being observant about little things, like aluminum foil, is good practice.

September

Why do people say, "I'll eat my hat if I'm wrong"?

2 TIMOTHY 1:13

Many times we say words or phrases without really knowing where they came from, why we say them, or what they used to mean. When people say, "If I'm wrong, I'll eat my hat!" they aren't really talking about what sits on their heads.

Long ago, there was a terrible-tasting food made from eggs, dates, and veal. It was called *hattes*. When you were promising to do something, you'd say you absolutely would or "eat hattes" as your punishment. When nobody cooked that dish anymore, people forgot what it was but still promised to eat hattes. Eventually people just thought it meant the hats we wear.

So what?

It really doesn't matter that people forgot what *hattes* meant, because a dish of food is not very important. You wouldn't want to forget how to get to your house, though, or how important it is to stay away from a hot stove, which can burn your hand. Some things are very important, and those are the things we should be sure to remember. *The Bible tells us:*

Hold on to the pattern of right teaching you learned from me. And remember to live in the faith and love that you have in Christ Jesus.
2 TIMOTHY 1:13, NLT

There is nothing more important to remember than that Jesus came to save us. We need to have faith in him and believe that he loves us. And we need to do our part to make sure that no one ever forgets about his love or about his ability to save us.

September 4

How is a pizza like the Italian flag?

MATTHEW 4:4

Pizza is the Italian word for "pie." The bottom of a pizza is made of yeast dough, which would bake into a regular round loaf of bread if the toppings didn't hold the bread down. People have been making pizza in Italy since the 1400s, but it wasn't until 1889 that tomatoes and cheese were added. A baker named Raffaele Esposito was making a pizza for the queen of Italy, and he decided to use ingredients that were the colors of the Italian flag. So he added red tomatoes, white mozzarella cheese, and green basil leaves.

Pizza came to America in 1905, when the first pizza parlor was opened in New York City, and twenty-five years later, bakers began twirling the dough up in the air to shape it. Was this because twirling made the pizza taste better? Not at all. It just made the show better for customers who were watching the pizzas being made.

So what?

Once Jesus was in the desert, where he didn't eat for forty days. Knowing Jesus was very hungry, the devil tried to tempt him. The devil asked Jesus to turn some stones into bread, so that there would be food to eat. *But Jesus said:*

No! The Scriptures say, "People need more than bread for their life; they must feed on every word of God." MATTHEW 4:4, NLT

Before you bite into that pizza, take care of the more important things first. If you have done anything wrong, ask God to forgive you. Then thank him for caring enough to fill your stomach with a meal and for filling your life with his goodness. Most kids will tell you that they can never get enough pizza, and most Christians will tell you that they can never get too much of God's love.

September

Why do you shrink?

EPHESIANS 6:1

Gravity pulls us to the earth, and it squishes the cartilage, or rubbery parts, between our bones. When we stand up, our bones push hard against each other. But when we lie down, our cartilage expands again like a sponge. This allows our bones to spread out a little, and that means that we are taller in the morning than at night—by about three-tenths of an inch.

The same thing happens to astronauts in space. Since there is no gravity in space, the bones of the astronauts stay more spread apart. For a while when they return to earth, they can be as much as two inches taller. Eventually gravity presses them back to their normal size.

So what?

At about the age of forty, though, an interesting thing begins to happen to all of us. We begin to shrink permanently. The cartilage between our bones gets smaller. Every ten years, we get shorter by four-tenths of an inch. So while you are busy growing taller, your parents may be shrinking!

Even if you end up being taller than your parents, God still wants you to respect them. *The Bible says:*

Children, obey your parents because you belong to the Lord, for this is the right thing to do. EPHESIANS 6:1, NLT

September

When did a fish lunch cost someone a big prize?

LUKE 24:38-39

Fishermen are often teased about exaggerating the size of fish they supposedly caught. We laugh when they can't prove how big the fish was. But once, an eleven-year-old boy named Jackie Johnson really did have a fish story to tell. He and his dad were fishing from the shore of a lake in Florida. Jackie caught a bass and pulled it in. He and his father must have been surprised when they weighed the fish, because the bass weighed almost twenty-three pounds. That's a big fish! Jackie and his dad had a wonderful meal after they cooked Jackie's fish.

Later, Jackie found out that the largest fish ever caught in that lake weighed twenty-two pounds, four ounces, and it had been caught nearly fifty years before, in 1932. Ever since, there had been a prize offered to anyone who could beat that record, but Jackie no longer had the fish for the officials to weigh. He and his dad had had no idea they were eating such an expensive lunch!

So what?

God knows that people often need proof before they will believe something. That is one reason Jesus came back to life after he died on the cross. He appeared to his followers to show them that he really was alive again. *He asked:*

Why are you frightened? . . . Why do you doubt who I am? Look at my hands. Look at my feet. You can see that it's really me. Touch me and make sure that I am not a ghost, because ghosts don't have bodies, as you see that I do! LUKE 24:38-39, NLT

God wants us to be absolutely sure that Jesus is his Son. And that's no fish story!

September

How does a beetle get a drink in the desert?
JOHN 4:14

When you're thirsty, you can fill a glass of water at the sink. But most animals and insects have to work hard to find their water. One insect, the African beetle, has found a very strange place to look for water: It drinks fog from the air.

The beetle, which lives in the Namib Desert, cannot fly. It buries itself under the sand most of the time so that it is not too hot during the day or too cold at night. Very little rain ever falls on the Namib Desert. But about once a week, heavy fog from the nearby sea hangs over some areas of the desert. When the fog comes, the beetle crawls out from under the sand, climbs up to the top of the highest pile of sand it can find, and then waits for water droplets to collect on its shell. The beetle has little grooves on its shell that are just right for the water droplets to slide down, and they end up in the beetle's mouth.

So what?
We all need water. No matter how many times we drink, we know we'll get thirsty again sooner or later. But Jesus talked of another kind of water. *He said:*

Those who drink of the water that I will give them will never be thirsty. The water that I will give will become in them a spring of water gushing up to eternal life. JOHN 4:14, NRSV

When Jesus gives something to us, he always gives a lot. Instead of just a sip of his love, he promises that we will get a whole fountain, and that it will flow forever. Nobody gives better gifts than Jesus!

September 8

When is it entertaining to have your face slapped?

LUKE 6:29

In some parts of the world, as odd as it may seem, people slap each other's faces for fun. They think of it as a sport. One person slaps the other one, and then the second one slaps back. The "game" is over when one of the contestants says stop or falls down. In 1974, Los Angeles held a face-slapping contest during the oddball Olympics, and two men slapped each other for thirty-one hours.

So what?

The Bible mentions face slapping. *It says:*

If someone slaps you on one cheek, turn the other cheek.   LUKE 6:29, NLT

But the Bible isn't suggesting that you play the face-slapping game. "Turning the other cheek" means that if someone does something unkind that hurts you or makes you feel bad, try not to hurt him back to get even. Suppose a friend hurt your feelings by telling a lie about you. Instead of telling a lie about your friend, give that person another chance to tell the truth the next time. God's way is for you to be forgiving whenever you possibly can. He doesn't want you being mean to others, even if they have been mean to you. Be willing to treat people nicer than you think they deserve, and you will be on God's team.

September

Who missed a once-in-a-lifetime chance?
PROVERBS 24:17

If you've ever overslept for school, you know what an awful feeling it is to wake up and realize you've made a big mistake. But there was an athlete who felt worse than you did about oversleeping. His name was Wim Esajas, and he was a runner. He was the only athlete that his country, Dutch Guiana (now Suriname), sent to the 1960 Olympics. On the day of his competition, the eight-hundred-meter run, Wim decided to rest in the morning so that he could do his best that afternoon. He left his room at the Olympic Village in time to be at the track to start his race. It was only after he arrived that he realized he had made a big mistake. The race had taken place that morning, and Wim had been eliminated for not appearing. He then had to return to his own country without even taking part in the Olympics.

So what?

Wim must have felt awful about having made such a big mistake. Maybe some of the other runners said, "We're glad he didn't come because now we have a better chance to win." *But the Bible tells us:*

Do not rejoice when your enemies fall into trouble. Don't be happy when they stumble.   PROVERBS 24:17, NLT

When someone makes a mistake, even if it might help you to win a race or get a better grade in school, you should not be selfishly happy about it. You should try to understand what the other person is feeling and be kind to him or her. Someday it may be your turn to make a big mistake, and you will want others to be kind to you then. Kindness is always the best way to become a winner.

September

How does the telephone tell you the time?

MARK 13:32

When you make a telephone call to get the time and temperature, you hear a recording. But that's not always how it was done. Long ago, when not many people owned telephones, you could call a real operator, and she would tell you what time it was. As more and more people installed telephones, the operators got too busy to tell people the time. The phone company hired special people just to take care of the "time" calls. A person sat at a microphone for half an hour, which was about as long as she could stand it, and announced every fifteen seconds what time it was. Then a different person would take over. Finally, the tape recorder was invented. One person needed to make a recording just one time. First, he said all the numbers for the hours—one through twelve. Then he said all the numbers for minutes—zero through fifty-nine. After that, the numbers were arranged on tape in all the possible time combinations. When the phone rings, it triggers the recording, and you hear the correct numbers.

So what?

People like to know things; not only what is happening in the present time, but also what will be happening in the future. Despite what others might say, no one can tell you with certainty when the end of the world will be. The future belongs only to God. *His Son, Jesus, says:*

No one knows about that day or hour, not even the angels in heaven, nor the Son, but only the Father.   MARK 13:32, NIV

Don't put your trust in people who claim to know everything, because only God knows everything. Trust in him, and he will tell you what you need to know.

September 11

How did a spring become a toy?

JEREMIAH 20:9

Richard James was on a big ship during a war, testing to see if the ship was working correctly. All of a sudden, a spring fell to the floor and went bouncing around. Was Richard thinking that the ship was falling apart? Not at all. He was thinking about what an interesting bounce that spring had.

After he came back home, Richard couldn't forget the spring, which he thought would be fun to play with. He and his wife, Betty, made some springs out of wire and took them to a toy store. No one thought that the springs looked like very much fun. Richard and Betty asked if they could show how the springs worked. They made a slide out of a board, put one of the springs at the top, and let everyone watch as it tumbled over itself to the bottom. People were amazed when they watched this, and four hundred springs were sold in less than two hours. Richard and Betty had to make a lot more springs, so while Richard went to his job every day, Betty took care of their children, packaged and wrapped the springs, and delivered them to the stores. You have probably played with one of these toys yourself. As the commercials used to say, "Everyone loves a Slinky!"

So what?

The Jameses were so excited about their Slinky that they just had to show it to people, even if at first no one wanted to see it. When you become God's child, don't be surprised if you're so excited that you want to tell people right away. It's hard to keep your happiness to yourself. *The Bible describes this feeling when it says:*

If I say I'll never mention the LORD or speak in his name, his word burns in my heart like a fire. It's like a fire in my bones! I am weary of holding it in! JEREMIAH 20:9, NLT

Good news travels fast—faster than a Slinky!

September

Who didn't know about snow?

JOB 37:6

Once there was a king who lived in the warm country of Spain. He knew that his wife had never seen snow, and because he loved her he wanted to show her what snow was like. Did he take her to Alaska, to Switzerland, to the North Pole, or even to the mountains of his own country to look at the snow? No, because in those days it was very hard to travel so far from home. Instead, this king decided to try to "make" some snow right there in his own country.

He told some of his workers to plant almond trees all over a hillside. In the spring, almond trees grow white petals. As the petals all fell from the trees and dropped onto the ground underneath, the whole hill looked like it had been covered with white snowflakes.

So what?

Even though the king had a very clever idea, he couldn't really make it snow no matter how much he wanted to. People can never make things as well as God can. God made snow much more interesting than almond petals. Real snow can be packed into snowballs; you can slide down a snow-covered hill on a sled; and snow will melt on your tongue. You can't do any of those fun things with almond petals! And the almond petals can't fall from high up in the sky so that we can enjoy watching them swirl and tumble all the way down. *The Bible tells us this about God:*

He directs the snow to fall on the earth.   JOB 37:6, NLT

And the snow does what God says! Aren't you glad that God's idea for snow is so much better than the king's?

September 13

What makes a small gift grand?
JOHN 14:27

Everybody loves presents—usually the bigger the better! But once there was a contest to see who could give the *smallest* gift.

The country of India is famous for its tiny artwork. There were schools in India that taught people how to create miniature art. Sometimes the students had to spend ten years just watching and learning before they were even allowed to try it themselves. The art might be painted with a brush that had only one hair, or carved on the tiniest of objects.

One time, India wanted to give the Soviet Union a gift of seven elephants. That would have been a big present, except that the elephants weren't real. They were carved into a sewing needle. The Soviet Union then gave an even smaller gift back to India. It was just one human hair, hollowed out and polished, with three hundred elephants carved inside.

Miniature art is a challenge for anyone who tries it, and a wonder for everyone who sees it. At the 1939 World's Fair, an American man demonstrated how he could paint all the words of the Lord's Prayer on a grain of rice.

So what?
Unusual gifts are fun to get and interesting to look at. But no one can match the gifts that God has given us. *He says:*

I am leaving you with a gift—peace of mind and heart. And the peace I give isn't like the peace the world gives. So don't be troubled or afraid.
JOHN 14:27, NLT

All the countries that have exchanged gifts could stay friends or become enemies at any time, but Jesus never changes in his love for you. The gifts he gives are for keeps.

September 14

How did a dog help save a city?

EPHESIANS 2:14

In 1925, diphtheria, a fatal disease, was threatening the city of Nome, Alaska. The city didn't have enough medicine for its citizens. Extra medicine was a thousand miles away, but Nome was surrounded by a snowy wilderness. The only way to deliver the medicine would be by dogsled. It would take two weeks, and that would be too long. Wild Bill Shannon, a rugged trapper, thought of a solution. If each trapping town could have a fresh dog team and driver ready, the serum could be delivered by relay, cutting the time down to nine days. Within hours, Shannon was on his way from Anchorage with the medicine.

Through the outstanding efforts of four relay teams, the medicine was passed to the fifth driver, Gunnar Kaasen. Kaasen was to pass off to one more driver, but because of a blizzard, he missed the trader's cabin where they were to meet. He was on his own. His lead dog, a Siberian husky named Balto, was well known as an excellent sled dog. In the blinding blizzard, Kaasen couldn't see the trail and was forced to rely on Balto's instincts. Later, he said about Balto, "He never once faltered. The credit is his."

Balto pressed on for the next fifty-three miles. When they reached Nome, Kaasen was almost unconscious, temporarily blinded, and badly cut on his face by ice particles. He had to be chipped from his sled, and the serum was a solid frozen block. It had been delivered in only six days, which saved all but two victims from the diphtheria that could have wiped out an entire city.

So what?

You can imagine how tense people were in Nome as they waited for help. There must have been feelings of worry and helplessness. Maybe you've been having those same feelings. God doesn't want you to spend your time like that. It's not good for you, and it's not necessary. *The Bible says:*

Christ himself is our way of peace. EPHESIANS 2:14, TLB

If you find yourself wishing that you could be rescued, ask Jesus to be the Lord of your life. A blinding snowstorm, a raging fire, or an overwhelming tidal wave couldn't prevent Jesus from rescuing you from your sins. Call for him, and he will bring you the medicine for your soul without fail.

September

How did stamp collecting start?

JOHN 6:12

Before the first postal stamps were created in 1840, people had to take their letters to the post office and pay cash to have them sent. Then the letter was marked "Paid" and sent on its way. The first stamp was sold in England and was called a "Penny Black." It was decorated with a picture of the head of Queen Victoria. In 1841, one young lady started the hobby of stamp collecting for an unusual reason. She had an idea, and placed an advertisement in the *London Times*, asking people to send her their used stamps. Why would she need those? She merely wanted to change the appearance of her room—the stamps would be her new wallpaper when she glued them to her walls!

So what?

The idea of reusing stamps as wallpaper may qualify as one of the first recycling projects. Even Jesus was concerned about leftovers. Jesus fed the crowds with loaves and fishes that kept multiplying until everyone was full. *Jesus told his disciples:*

Now gather the leftovers . . . so that nothing is wasted.   JOHN 6:12, NLT

When we treat our blessings with respect and don't waste them, it shows God that we appreciate his abundant gifts.

September **16**

What secrets are some statues hiding?

PSALM 23:4

When you see a statue of a man sitting on a horse, you probably don't realize that the sculptor is giving you a clue about how the man died. Although this doesn't apply to every statue, it has long been a tradition to position the horse by a type of code. If the horse has all four feet on the ground, its rider died from natural causes. If one of the horse's hooves is raised, it indicates that the rider eventually died from wounds he received in a battle. If the horse is rearing up with both front hooves in the air, the rider died right on the battlefield.

So what?

Death is an important milestone in human history. We pay attention to how it happens to others. Maybe that's because we know it will happen to us someday—as it does to everyone—and we want to learn as much as we can. All we really need to know is that we will not be alone. God has promised that he will never leave us. *We can say with confidence:*

Even when I walk through the dark valley of death, I will not be afraid, for you are close beside me.   PSALM 23:4, NLT

Whether or not anyone ever builds a statue about you, if you're God's child, everyone will know how you died—carried securely to heaven by his love.

September

Why does the man walk next to the curb when escorting a woman?

JOB 31:4

The street can be a dangerous place. Vehicles can splash puddle water onto your clothes or drive threateningly close to the curb. City-street gutters can be full of unpleasant garbage. The custom of men walking next to the street came about because people in the early days threw trash and emptied chamber pots (before there were toilets) from the windows above. Pedestrians walking below were likely to get a dirty shower. A gentleman was expected to take the part of the sidewalk closest to the street in order to protect the lady he was accompanying from getting hurt or dirty.

So what?

It's a good idea to have someone keep an eye on every step we take so that our feet won't come down in the wrong place. Living within God's love is like that. He watches your steps carefully so you can avoid the dangers. It's God himself who will be doing the guarding. *You can turn your worries over to him, because the Bible says:*

He sees everything I do and every step I take.   JOB 31:4, NLT

What a wonderful feeling to know that God loves you so much that he's inviting you to hold on to him, watching wherever you go, and paving the way ahead of you.

September 18

How was masking tape invented?
ACTS 4:12

If people hadn't wanted to buy fancy cars, masking tape might never have been invented. In 1902, a new company was started called the Minnesota Mining and Manufacturing Company—3M for short. The people at 3M wanted to dig for a mineral called corundum and sell it to companies that would use it to make sandpaper. But 3M made two mistakes. While they were trying to mine the mineral, a better way to make sandpaper was invented. Suddenly no one needed corundum anymore. Not only that, but 3M found out that the mine they had built didn't even have corundum in it.

At that time 3M almost went out of business, but it decided instead to try to make its own sandpaper. Because 3M's biggest customers for sandpaper would be people who worked on auto bodies, 3M spent time with the car builders and found out about a big problem they had. The newest cars in the 1920s were supposed to have two different colors painted on them, but the painters couldn't get clear, straight lines between the two colors. They had tried covering one color with newspaper while they sprayed the other color on. But the newspaper had to be glued to the car and wouldn't come off without pulling the paint off too. To solve the problem, 3M invented a tan-colored tape that wouldn't take off the paint but would make a sharp line between colors. The man most responsible for this project was Richard G. Drew.

But 3M made yet another mistake. To save money, 3M didn't put enough stickiness on the back of the tape, so it tended to fall off the car. The painters said that 3M was like the Scotch people, who were said to be good at saving money. Then 3M put more stickiness onto their tape, and the workers started using what they had nicknamed "Scotch" tape. The 3M company kept that name for all of their products.

So what?

When we need tape, the name *Scotch* comes to mind. When we need hope, the name *Jesus* is what we think about if we know anything about him. *The Bible says:*

There is salvation in no one else! There is no other name in all of heaven for people to call on to save them. ACTS 4:12, NLT

September

What was brewing over the tea bag?

MARK 2:22

Making tea used to be a messy process. Thomas Sullivan was well aware of the problem and found a way to fix it. A tea salesman in the early 1900s, Sullivan sent samples of his tea to customers, either in tins or in paper packets. The loose tea leaves, once unwrapped, fell out all over, and customers never really got to try the tea. Sullivan decided to send his samples in hand-sewn miniature silk bags instead. All the customer had to do was drop the bag in boiling water and enjoy. After Sullivan sent the new bags, he got many orders for his tea—but the customers only wanted the tea if it came in the little bags. They loved the convenience, and Thomas Sullivan became the surprised inventor of the tea bag.

So what?

Jesus talked about another kind of container to help us think about how our life is changed once we invite him in. *Jesus said:*

No one puts new wine into old wineskins. The wine would burst the wineskins, spilling the wine and ruining the skins. New wine needs new wineskins. MARK 2:22, NLT

Jesus meant that his presence changes everything. We can't expect to keep the old rules or remain our old selves once his love comes to us. We are changed as completely as the tea business was changed by the appearance of the tea bag. There's no desire to go back to the old way.

September

Why do men wear neckties?

DEUTERONOMY 30:11-14

Neckties today don't really serve a purpose, except for men to add a little personality to their outfits with color and pattern. Neckties, which were more like scarves, were first worn by the soldiers of ancient Rome for a specific reason. Those neckties warmed necks in cold weather and absorbed sweat in heated climates. There was also a fluffy collar called a "ruff" before 1660. That's the year when men's neckwear changed. The new style came from Croatian soldiers who came to Paris and marched in a parade. Each soldier had a bright handkerchief around his neck, which the French began to copy. This was eventually called a *cravat*—French for "Croatian." Some cravats were worn with wire in them to make them stiff; others were filled with cushions to make them puffy. Many were worn so tightly around the neck that a man couldn't even turn his head.

During the French Revolution, ties changed again. The English attacked by surprise. The French at that time were wearing their cravats in a "slide," like the Boy Scout's scarf, which has a metal circle to hold the scarf together in front. The French didn't have time to slide the cloth through, so they quickly knotted their handkerchiefs around their necks, starting a new fad. The French won the battle, and neckties became popular for all men. The color you wore showed which side of the Revolution you supported. After that, ties became a custom. The fashionable narrower, knotted tie started in 1920.

So what?

A tie is a sign that a man is respecting the "rules" of appropriate dress. God asks us to give signs of our respect for him by obeying his commandments. *He tells us in the Bible:*

This command I am giving you today is not too difficult for you to understand or perform. It is not up in heaven, so distant that you must ask, "Who will go to heaven and bring it down so we can hear and obey it?" It is not beyond the sea, so far away that you must ask, "Who will cross the sea to bring it to us so we can hear and obey it?" The message is very close at hand; it is on your lips and in your heart so that you can obey it. DEUTERONOMY 30:11-14, NLT

In other words, the rules for pleasing God are as easy to understand as the rules about how to dress. When you put your clothes on, tuck God's words inside your heart and remember to obey him.

September

Why were wedding rings collected at a tollbooth?

1 PETER 1:18-19

Yyou have to pay to drive on some roads. A tollbooth is where they collect your money before you use the road. Imagine that it's your turn to drive up to the booth, wanting to cross the Golden Gate Bridge in San Francisco, and you discover that you don't have any money. Now what? Fortunately, you're allowed to leave something else of value in place of money, as long as it is equal to or exceeds the price of the toll. That's how the tollbooth collected such a strange collection of objects. In exchange for being allowed to cross the bridge, drivers have left a can of motor oil, a frying pan, a set of silverware, a new book, and rock-and-roll music. Wedding rings are often left, mostly by men. An older gentleman left his dentures, but he came back to claim them the next day. A diamond wristwatch worth $7,000 still hadn't been picked up years later, and was sold at an auction for $5. The only things that the tollbooth won't take are animals, uncanned food, or clothes. One man offered to leave his dog, but only the collar was kept by the tollbooth attendant. There was a young man who offered to pay with drugs. He didn't get to make the trip across the bridge; instead, he went to jail.

So what?

We understand how the tollbooth works: We give something of value in exchange for the privilege of going to another place. That's exactly what Jesus did for us: He paid the price so that we could have the privilege of going to heaven. *The Bible says:*

You know that God paid a ransom to save you from the empty life you inherited from your ancestors. And the ransom he paid was not mere gold or silver. He paid for you with the precious lifeblood of Christ, the sinless, spotless Lamb of God. 1 PETER 1:18-19, NLT

September **22**

Why does the Leaning Tower of Pisa lean?
MATTHEW 7:24-27

The Leaning Tower of Pisa is a famous Italian landmark. It was built as part of a church just before the Renaissance, which was a period of great cultural growth. The tower is round and measures 179 feet high. The tower started leaning because it was built near a riverbed on ground that was not solid. Even as it was being built, it was starting to sink. The builder tried making the upper stories taller on one side, but the tower leaned even more because of the extra weight. Building stopped completely for a hundred years while everyone studied the problem. Finally they tried adding two more stories out of line from the rest of the building, but the tower still leaned.

Many people tried to think of ways to straighten the tower. Among the letters sent to Pisa was one suggesting to tie balloons to the top of the tower to lift it up. Once, holes were dug underneath the lowest side of the tower, and the holes were filled with nine hundred tons of cement. But the building just tilted more.

In 1990 the Italian government appointed a special committee to look into the problem. These people determined that the tower was unsafe for tourists, so it was closed to the public. After many years John Burland, a professor of soil mechanics, came up with a way to remove soil from under one side of the building so it would settle back into the ground, reducing the tilt. After spending thirty million dollars, the tilt is now sixteen inches less than it was, with a total lean of eleven feet, eight inches. In 2001 the tower was again opened to the public. For now it is safe, but more major repairs may be done in the future.

So what?

Jesus used an example that we can understand. *He said:*

All who listen to my instructions and follow them are wise, like a man who builds his house on solid rock. Though the rain comes in torrents, and the floods rise and the storm winds beat against his house, it won't collapse, for it is built on rock. But those who hear my instructions and ignore them are foolish, like a man who builds his house on sand. For when the rains and floods come, and storm winds beat against his house, it will fall with a mighty crash. MATTHEW 7:24-27, TLB

Don't count on being able to lean like the Tower of Pisa. Make sure you've got your foundation straight with God.

September

Why do police cars use blue lights?

PSALM 19:7-11

Many years ago, emergency vehicles all had red and white lights only. Why did the police add blue ones? The answer is that officers encountered problems when they were signaling cars to stop. Sometimes the car would continue moving, and the driver would claim that he was "just trying to get out of the way," as drivers are supposed to do with other emergency vehicles. The most the driver could then be charged with was "failing to yield to an emergency vehicle." Because police cars have added blue flashing lights, there can be no mistaking who's behind you. Incidentally, blue was picked instead of another color because it is most easily seen.

So what?

Laws are created for your well-being. Without laws, there would be no order to anything we do. Maybe you have experienced that kind of confusion— there doesn't seem to be any order, plan, or purpose. That might be because you're not letting yourself live close enough to God to understand and obey his laws so they can protect you. We can't do the things that please God if we don't know what those things are. And we can't know God's laws unless we read the Bible and study it. *The Bible says:*

God's laws are perfect. They protect us, make us wise, and give us joy and light. God's laws are pure, eternal, just. They are more desirable than gold. They are sweeter than honey dripping from a honeycomb. For they warn us away from harm and give success to those who obey them. PSALM 19:7-11, TLB

Search the Bible to learn the rules that will protect you when you obey them.

September 24

Why couldn't the secretary of the U.S. Department of the Treasury buy dinner?

LUKE 10:20

It eventually pays to be in charge of our country's money, as Michael Blumenthal found out in 1979. Secretary Blumenthal was in an embarrassing predicament. He had just enjoyed an elaborate and expensive meal at a restaurant in San Francisco. He gave the waiter his credit card, and the waiter returned with the news that the card had expired and couldn't be used for payment. The secretary next offered to pay by check. Unfortunately, the restaurant needed a guarantee on a signature on a check from out-of-town. But instead of being worried, this is when Blumenthal could relax. Verifying his signature was easy. He pulled a dollar bill out of his wallet and showed the waiter the signature in the corner of the bill. There it was—W. M. Blumenthal. His name was printed on all the bills produced in the United States at that time. Just to be sure, the waiter compared the signatures. They were, of course, a perfect match, and the secretary's check was accepted with no further questions.

So what?

When someone recognizes your name and knows who you are, it gives you a powerful feeling. If you think earthly recognition is a thrill, think about how exciting it will be when you are acknowledged in heaven! *The Bible says:*

Rejoice because your names are registered as citizens of heaven.
LUKE 10:20, NLT

It is much more important to gain access to eternity than it is to gain entrance into a restaurant. Live your life so that when your time comes, God will say, "Yes, I recognize that name. This person belongs here with me and is entitled to all the privileges of heaven."

September

When didn't the son of the president of the United States listen to his father?

MATTHEW 13:44

Most of us are familiar with the book *Treasure Island,* written by Robert Louis Stevenson. He described his book as a story "all about a map, and a treasure, and a mutiny, and a derelict ship . . . and a sea-cook with one leg. . . ." How does an author come up with such an imaginative work, and what does it have to do with a president's son? Robert Louis Stevenson surprised even himself with his thoughts for the book. He was entertaining his stepson one rainy day by drawing a treasure map. When the child begged for explanations to match the pictures, Stevenson made up some stories. He liked what he told his stepson and made copies of the tales he told. With a few changes, these ideas became the novel *Treasure Island.* Perhaps the highest praise for Stevenson's book came from Charlie Taft, a president's son. When President Taft was making his inauguration speech, his son Charlie—obligated to attend the ceremony, but convinced he would be bored—chose to bring along a copy of *Treasure Island,* the book he thought would be more interesting than his father's presidential acceptance speech.

So what?

If Charlie liked stories about looking for treasure, there is another book he would have enjoyed reading. The most valuable thing we can "find" on earth is not gold, but the rewards of God's love. *The place to look for those is in the Bible, which says:*

The Kingdom of Heaven is like a treasure that a man discovered hidden in a field. In his excitement, he hid it again and sold everything he owned to get enough money to buy the field—and to get the treasure, too! MATTHEW 13:44, NLT

Now, that's a treasure hunt worth going on!

September

What's the story behind clean clothes?
2 CORINTHIANS 5:17

Your clothes are probably washed much more often than your ancestors' clothes were. In the seventeenth century, clothes were washed about four or five times a year. One hundred years later, washing day came every five or six weeks.

The clothes were hard to get clean. Rubbing the clothes on rocks or sand in the river and laying them out to dry was one way to do laundry. When washing clothes moved inside, water had to be hauled in, then heated over a fire and poured into several tubs. Rinsing required even more water. Then there was the scrubbing on a board, and the squeezing out of every piece of clothing.

In the early 1800s, the wringer, which was turned by a handle, appeared. In 1859 Hamilton E. Smith came up with a better idea. He patented a washtub that had paddles turned by a hand crank. Then in 1874 Bill Blackstone put six pegs in the bottom of a washtub, connected them to a rotating mechanism, and invented what's been called the first washing machine. Blackstone even presented it to his wife on her birthday (when perhaps jewelry would have been more exciting!). By 1922 America was making electric washing machines, which housewives in foreign countries used with great creativity. During World War II, Dutch women used the washers as substitute butter churns, and island women used them to tenderize their octopus dinners.

So what?
Because wash days used to be so hard, it must have been a big relief when everything was finally clean and fresh. Maybe you could have that feeling, too, by having all the bad things in your past washed away. Jesus offers you the opportunity to start over, any time you're ready to take it. *The Bible says:*

Those who become Christians become new persons. They are not the same anymore, for the old life is gone. 2 CORINTHIANS 5:17, NLT

If you haven't asked Jesus to be the Lord of your life, you're living with your sins, which is like a lot of dirty laundry. Just by telling him, "Jesus, I want you to take over now," your whole life can be clean from sin. Why not make today the most important "wash day" of your life?

September

Who wanted the same birthday present every year?

2 PETER 1:19

Everybody likes presents, but maybe the most unique gift ever received was one that an Englishman, Isambard Kingdom Brunel, gave himself. Brunel was a design engineer in the 1800s. He worked on the plans for a railroad tunnel to be built in England. He figured he could change the specifications slightly and give himself a personal treat. On only one day a year, the sun was in just the right place so that when it rose in the morning, it brilliantly lit up the inside of the tunnel. Which day was it? April 9—Brunel's birthday.

So what?

Brunel always waited eagerly for dawn on his birthday, which is when he received his special gift to himself each year. We, too, can receive a special gift of light, and we should search every bit as eagerly for it. *The Bible says:*

Pay close attention to what they [the prophets] wrote, for their words are like a light shining in a dark place—until the day Christ appears and his brilliant light shines in your hearts. 2 PETER 1:19, NLT

Imagine the most glorious early morning light, and see that light shining on yourself. That's how you look to God when you believe in his Son.

September

Why do people shake hands?

JAMES 1:22

Long ago, men often carried weapons in their right hand. If you wanted to show that you were friendly, you held out your empty right hand so that the other person could see that you weren't holding a weapon. That person held out his empty right hand to show you the same thing. To keep each other from reaching for a hidden weapon, you would grab each other's hands and hold them for a moment until you were sure of friendly feelings. Although no one knows for sure, some people think that the hands were shaken up and down so that if either man had a weapon hidden up his sleeve, it would fall out.

Shaking hands is a pleasant way to greet people, compared to the custom in Tibet. In that country, bumping heads together used to be part of the official greeting when two people met!

So what?

Holding your hand out in friendship is an action that Jesus likes. He wants us to be kind and caring toward each other. *The Bible says:*

Be doers of the word, and not hearers only. JAMES 1:22, NKJV

We share Christian love best when we *show* it instead of just *talking* about it. For example, suppose a new student was sitting all alone at your school. If you told her, "Don't worry, you'll make friends soon," and walked away, you would be telling but not showing. It would please God much more if you would ask, "Why don't you join us at our lunch table?" Offer a helping hand—not just a helping word—whenever you can.

September

Why are veins blue when blood is red?

1 JOHN 1:7

Blood in your body makes an amazing round-trip. It starts in your lungs, where it gets lots of oxygen. Within the red blood cells, the oxygen gets mixed with a protein called hemoglobin, which is also red. Now the blood, which is bright red because its color has been intensified by oxygen and hemoglobin, travels through the arteries. Arteries are thick, strong tubes that help the blood reach the rest of your body, where it delivers the oxygen it's carrying. Along the way, blood deposits oxygen to your tissues. When all the oxygen has been distributed to the different parts of your body, your blood is ready to make the return trip back to your lungs to fill itself back up with more oxygen. As blood travels to your heart and then back through your lungs, it goes through veins. Veins are thinner and more transparent than arteries, which is why you can see your blood in them. The blood appears blue or purplish because it no longer has oxygen in it. The color of blood "fades" until more oxygen is added.

So what?

Jesus had ordinary blood like ours, yet his was also one-of-a-kind. His blood is the most powerful that ever flowed. *The Bible says:*

If we are living in the light of God's presence, just as Christ is, then we have fellowship with each other, and the blood of Jesus, his Son, cleanses us from every sin. 1 JOHN 1:7, NLT

We always think of blood as making stains, yet the blood of Jesus is the only thing that can clean away the stain of sin.

September 30

Who invented Frisbees?

ECCLESIASTES 11:9

Using a pie plate to play with doesn't sound like much fun, but that's not what the students at Yale University thought. They tossed the plates back and forth to each other on the college grounds after they had bought and eaten the pies baked in the tin plates by the Frisbie Pie Company. To warn people to watch out for the flying pie plate, the students would yell out, "Frisbie!"

The first plastic toy shaped like a pie plate came from Fred Morrison in 1948, but he called it a Pluto Platter. Everyone at that time was excited about outer space, and the plastic disc looked like a flying saucer. But the name didn't work—too many people thought the toy was named after the Disney cartoon character Pluto the dog. The name was finally changed to *Frisbee,* spelled just a little bit differently than the pie company's name.

In the meantime, Mr. Morrison thought of an interesting way to sell his toy. He went to a county fair and rented a booth. Then he walked through the fairgrounds, pretending that he was stringing up a wire and yelling, "Make way! Make way for the wire!" Mr. Morrison was trying to get people's attention. He told the crowd that gathered around him that he would toss the Frisbee, which would then float magically across the wire to his assistant. That's exactly what the Frisbee appeared to do. Mr. Morrison told the crowd that he would give the Frisbee away for free, but they must buy one hundred yards of the imaginary wire for one cent a yard. Of course, people knew that the wire was just a joke, but they wanted the Frisbee anyway.

So what?

The college boys who first started throwing pie plates had no idea that they were inventing such a popular game. They thought they were just having fun. God likes to see the young people in his family playing and having a good time. *The Bible says:*

Be happy, young man, while you are young, and let your heart give you joy in the days of your youth. ECCLESIASTES 11:9, NIV

God gives us a childhood to enjoy.

October
1

Which inventions were never used?

1 TIMOTHY 4:7

People are always trying to come up with better ideas. Some inventions become famous. Some are never heard of again. Here are some ideas that never became popular. See if you can figure out why.

The Chewing Brush: It's a little brush with no handle that you pop into your mouth and chew on. It's for people whose hands are too busy to take the time to hold a regular toothbrush. (Defect—it could be swallowed.)

The Backward/Forward Shoe: The top of the shoe is normal and faces the same direction as your foot does. The sole, or bottom of the shoe, is reversed. The heel is underneath your toes. Why? Anyone following your footprints will think that you went in the opposite direction than you're really walking. The shoe makes a backwards footprint each time you step. (Defect—it won't work on a sidewalk; and, besides that, not many people would need it.)

Spike for the Bike: If someone tries to steal this bike, it could be an uncomfortable experience. There is a spike that can be raised or lowered in the middle of the seat. Raise the spike when you're away from your bike, and no one will be tempted to hop on. (Defect—the bike can just be rolled away.)

The Thumb Twiddler: A small cylinder with holes on either side for your thumbs. You rotate your thumbs around and around in this wheel, and it counts how many times you've twiddled. (Defect—who would care to know?)

So what?

The people who thought of these inventions probably spent lots of time on them. But the things they made weren't very useful. *The Bible tells us that if you really want to use your time wisely, you should:*

Spend your time and energy in training yourself for spiritual fitness.
1 TIMOTHY 4:7, NLT

What are some spiritual exercises you can do? Read the Bible. Make time to pray. Think of all the blessings that God has given you. Try to do something nice for someone else. These are exercises that will make your faith stronger and make good use of your time.

October

How was exercising turned into a game?

PSALM 125:2

Some toys can actually be good for your health. The Hula Hoop is one of them. Australian kids in 1958 were using a bamboo hoop during exercise time in school. The owners of the Wham-O Toy Company saw these hoops and decided that American kids might enjoy them. So they made some wooden hoops and went out to playgrounds in California to show kids how to twirl them around their waists. Any child who could twirl the hoop got to keep it. Soon everyone wanted to play with this new toy. The toy company thought about calling it the Swing-A-Hoop or the Twirl-A-Hoop, but finally decided on the Hula Hoop, after the Hawaiian dance. They made the hoop out of plastic in bright colors and even added little pellets inside the plastic so the hoop would make a noise as it twirled. One hundred million Hula Hoops were sold in the first two years. That's a lot of exercising!

So what?

Circles like the Hula Hoop have no beginning and no end. When you put a Hula Hoop around your waist, there is no way to break through it. That's the way God wants to surround you too. *The Bible says:*

Just as the mountains surround and protect Jerusalem, so the LORD surrounds and protects his people, both now and forever.
PSALM 125:2, NLT

You do not need to be afraid when God is surrounding you. He will always go before you and behind you just like a big Hula Hoop, keeping you from harm.

October 3

What's a "googol"?

PSALM 139:18

Each number has a name—like four, or eighty, or two million. If you were in charge, what name would you pick for a new number? Nine-year-old Milton Sirotta made up a very strange name for a new number.

Milton's uncle was a mathematician, someone who knows a lot about numbers. Milton's uncle said there was a number that was so big that it was hard to understand. Write the number one on paper, and then write one hundred zeroes after it. No one had done much thinking about a number that big, so it didn't even have a name. One day, Milton made up a silly name for the number. He called it a *googol,* just for fun. Milton's uncle told the people he worked with what Milton had said, and soon they were calling the number a googol too. In 1940 Milton's uncle wrote a book about mathematics, and he used the word *googol* in it. Now everyone knows about Milton's silly word, but it isn't considered silly anymore. And just how big is a googol? Milton's uncle said that if we counted every word ever spoken since people first began to talk, all of those words would not be enough to be even one googol.

So what?

That's a lot! *But even a googol can't measure God's love:*

I can't even count how many times a day your thoughts turn towards me. And when I waken in the morning, you are still thinking of me!
PSALM 139:18, TLB

The smartest mathematician with the most powerful computer in the whole world will never be able to think of enough numbers to start counting God's goodness to us. That's how big God is!

October

When was a canteen alive?

ISAIAH 55:1

If you were going to travel across a desert, the canteen or Thermos hadn't been invented yet, and there were no gas stations where you could buy juice or soda, how would you keep from getting thirsty? The Pima Indians had a good answer. They carried water inside an old cactus. Not just any cactus would do—it had to be a certain kind of cactus called a *saguaro.*

Strangely enough, the saguaro cactus was the favorite living place for the gila woodpecker. The woodpecker pecked at the cactus until it made a hole big enough for its nest. Then the cactus tried to heal itself by growing a layer of tissue all around the inside of the hole. The tissue looked like cork. Later, the woodpecker left, and the cactus died and rotted away. Left on the ground was the hard shell that the cactus had grown. The Indians picked this container up, filled it with water, and went on their way.

So what?

God knows that we get thirsty and must have water to keep living. That is why he made sure that the Indians had a way to carry water with them. Because water is so important to us, the Bible tells us about God by comparing him to water. *It says:*

Come, all you who are thirsty, come to the waters.   ISAIAH 55:1, NIV

This means that God will always give you what you need most of all.

October

What's it like to be swallowed by a whale?

JONAH 2:6

Once there was a sailor named James Bartley, and what happened to him in 1891 was almost unbelievable. James worked on a whaling ship—chasing whales, harpooning them, and collecting their blubber. One day, one of the men on James's boat threw a harpoon at a whale. Instead of trying to swim away, the whale attacked the boat by attempting to bite it. Every man but James jumped overboard. James waited too long: He was in charge of the boat, and he was hoping he could get the boat out of danger. Instead, he slipped into the mouth of the whale and disappeared.

His shipmates were horrified, and they decided to wait for a few hours to see if one of the whales they had hit would come back to the surface. Finally, the body of a whale did appear. The men pulled it up next to the boat and began cutting the blubber. When they got to the stomach, they noticed a lump the size of a person. It was James!

They opened the stomach and saw that James was still breathing, so they splashed him with sea water and gave him drinks to wake him up. At first, he was a little confused, but later he remembered sliding down something spongy and landing in a big "sack." It was the whale's stomach. James told of feeling fish there that wriggled away when he touched them. Although it was completely dark, there was just enough air and the whale was just warm enough for James to stay alive.

So what?

In the Bible, a man named Jonah was swallowed by a big fish, and later God told the fish to spit Jonah out. *Jonah said:*

I was locked out of life and imprisoned in the land of the dead. But you, O LORD my God, have snatched me from the yawning jaws of death!
JONAH 2:6, NLT

God saves many people from danger. If you ask him to, God will make sure that evil doesn't swallow you up. When your heart and your soul belong to God, he is always right there with you to watch over you.

October

Can a horse count?

PSALM 40:5

Professor Van Osten was excited. His horse, Hans, could count! Over and over, the professor would ask Hans different questions, and Hans would stamp the correct answer with his hoof every time. The professor was sure that Hans could not only count, but that he could read and add, too. He just knew he had the smartest horse in the world!

Finally, another scientist decided to study Hans, to find out what made the horse so smart. By carefully watching the professor, the scientist was able to figure out what was happening. The scientist discovered that Hans couldn't really count on his own. Hans was watching the professor's face whenever a question was asked. The professor didn't mean to, but he changed his expression when Hans had stamped his hoof enough times. The professor was giving away the answer to Hans, just by the way he moved his face. The proof of this was clear when the professor stepped behind a screen. Someone else asked Hans a question, but the horse didn't know the answer because he couldn't see the professor's face. The professor might have been a little sad to know that Hans couldn't add, but Hans was still a very smart horse—he could tell, just by watching his master's face, what he was supposed to do next.

So what?

Because we can speak, read, and count, we are smarter than animals. But we are not smarter than God. *The Bible says:*

Many, O LORD my God, are the wonders you have done. The things you planned for us no one can recount to you; were I to speak and tell of them, they would be too many to declare. PSALM 40:5, NIV

We could count forever and never be able to add up how many wonderful things God has done. There are not enough words to describe his greatness, even if we use a whole dictionary. And all the paper in the world wouldn't be enough to write down all the ways God is special. God made us the smartest creatures on earth, but he is much, much wiser than we are.

October 7

What do a tree frog, an ant, and a warthog all have in common?

EPHESIANS 6:17

They all use their heads to protect themselves! There is a tree frog from Mexico called the helmet frog whose head has a bony knob on it. The helmet frog needs to stay wet. So when the weather is too dry, the frog crawls into a hole in a tree and plugs up the hole with its head. The knob on its head becomes the closed door of the hole, and the frog is able to stay moist inside the hole, even during a drought.

There are also ants that live in trees. They, too, use their heads as doors. Ants that live there are allowed to go in and out, but ants that are strangers are stopped when the tree ant closes the hole with its head.

Warthogs, which are wild hogs, also depend on their heads. When they are ready to rest, warthogs back up under some rocks, into a hole in the ground, or into a cave. Warthogs are prepared to face any danger because they leave their head in the opening. Not only will they be warned if another animal comes, but just seeing the big tusks of the warthog might scare visitors away.

So what?

The Bible tells us that we can protect ourselves with our heads too, but not by poking them into a hole. We need to use our heads to think and to make a decision to follow Jesus Christ. *The Bible tells us to do this:*

Put on salvation as your helmet. EPHESIANS 6:17, NLT

A helmet, like the kind you wear when skating or riding a bike, is meant to keep your head from getting injured. Your helmet of salvation will protect your mind from doubting what God has done for you.

October

Is it "catsup" or "ketchup"?

ACTS 4:12

The Chinese invented it with fish and spices; sailors took it to England, where walnuts, cucumbers, and mushrooms were added; and Americans changed the recipe with tomatoes. But no one seems sure how to spell it. Originally, the sauce was called *ke-tsiap*, which means "pickled fish" in Chinese. Later, the spelling was changed to *kechap*, because that's the way it sounded. Finally, a mistake in printing turned the spelling to *ketchup*, which is the most common way to spell the word now.

Ketchup started in China in the 1600s, went to England in the 1700s, and was first bottled in America in 1876 by a chef whose name you may recognize: Henry Heinz.

So what?

Even though people sometimes say and spell ketchup in different ways, it's easy to understand what they mean: They want us to pass the bottle of red sauce. But if people want to get to heaven, the Bible tells us that Jesus is the only way. *It says:*

There is salvation in no one else! There is no other name in all of heaven for people to call on to save them. ACTS 4:12, NLT

Ask for ketchup, and you'll get a tasty meal. Ask for Jesus, and you'll get a great life that lasts forever!

October

Do you know what to do if you see someone choking?

ACTS 16:30-31

Long ago, no one really did. It used to be thought that if you pounded the person on the back, it would help—but sometimes that actually makes things worse. The man who figured out the best thing to do was Dr. Harry Heimlich. He was a lung specialist, and he knew that even a choking person probably has some air still in his lungs. Dr. Heimlich tried to think of a way to push the air out of the lungs quickly and forcefully enough to pop out whatever was caught in someone's windpipe. He experimented with lots of ways and finally found one that worked well.

Maybe your mom or dad or one of your teachers knows the "Heimlich maneuver" and can show you how it works. When you're older, you can learn how to do it yourself. If it doesn't work, try it again. Remember—if a person is coughing strongly and is not turning blue, that means he is getting air and probably doesn't need help. But if you see a person who cannot talk, cough, or breathe, he needs emergency help from the Heimlich maneuver.

So what?

If you were choking and no one knew what to do, you would be hoping with all your heart that someone would run to Dr. Heimlich and ask him what to do so that you could be saved. Once, some of Jesus' followers, Paul and Silas, were in jail. Their guard realized that his soul needed to be saved because he didn't belong to God. *The jailer ran to Paul and Silas in their jail cell, and this is what he did:*

He brought them out and asked, "Sirs, what must I do to be saved?"
They replied, "Believe on the Lord Jesus and you will be saved."
ACTS 16:30-31, NLT

When you understand that you need to be saved from your sins, Jesus can rescue you.

October

How does a spider weave its web?
PSALM 91:3

A spider chooses the spot for its web carefully. It must be a sturdy place so that the web won't fall down. The breeze must blow in the right direction, and underneath the web there should be grass where lots of insects live. Once the spider has found the place, the building begins.

Spiders have little tubes called *spinnerets* that squirt out liquid silk. The spider pushes its spinnerets against something hard, which makes the liquid start to flow. As soon as the liquid touches air, it turns into a thread, and the spider moves along, with the silk string following. To get started, the spider makes one long strand. The breeze blows it across, so the spider can use it as a bridge to travel on while it finishes the web. The center of the web is padded with lots of extra silk, because this is where the spider rests until insects get caught in the web. The only time the web won't catch insects is after it gets wet, because then all the stickiness is rinsed away. The spider never gets caught in its own web because it covers its legs with oil from its mouth.

So what?

After a bug flies into a spider's web, the more it struggles, the more it gets tangled. Maybe something like that has happened to you. Perhaps you made a mistake, like spilling grape juice on the new white carpet. When you tried to fix your mistake by cleaning it up, you made it worse. Now you are about to fall into a bigger trap, because you are in danger of lying or trying to hide what you did. Before you get into even deeper trouble, ask God to help you. *The Bible says:*

He will rescue you from every trap. PSALM 91:3, NLT

The best way to deal with any problem is to tell the truth, ask for forgiveness, and try your best not to make the same mistake again. Whenever you seem headed right toward another sticky web, call on God to untangle you.

October

Can you guess which instrument used by doctors was made from a flute?

ISAIAH 55:3

This helpful tool was made by a doctor who played the flute in his spare time. The doctor's name was René Laënnec, and he worked in Paris.

One day Dr. Laënnec was sitting next to the bed of a little girl who had heart problems. He had tried and tried, but he couldn't hear her heart clearly. He wondered why he could hear children playing in the street better than he could hear the little girl's heart. He looked out the window to see what the children were doing. They were talking to each other through a hollow log. The doctor had played the same game when he was little, and he remembered how the log magnified the sound of voices. He had another thought. He rolled up a piece of paper and put one end to his ear, the other against the little girl's chest. It worked! He could hear her heartbeat! And the flute? Dr. Laënnec made a permanent wooden tube to listen through by blocking up the holes in one of his flutes. Other doctors copied him, and soon the first real stethoscope was made.

So what?

It was an important step for doctors to be able to hear inside their patients' bodies. But there is something much more important that everyone needs to hear. *God says:*

Come to me with your ears wide open. Listen, for the life of your soul is at stake. ISAIAH 55:3, NLT

When you hear about Jesus and decide to follow him, it changes your life forever. There are many important ways to use your ears, but none is more important than listening to God.

October

How did people make toast in the past?

2 CORINTHIANS 1:9

If you wanted toast in the 1800s, you needed a coal stove, a toasting "cage," and time to watch the bread so it wouldn't burn. The toasting cage was made from wire and tin. If you held it over the opening of the coal stove, the fire would make the bread crisp on one side. Then the bread had to be turned over.

It wasn't until 1919 that Charles Strite invented the first electric pop-up toaster. That toaster, just like pop-up toasters today, had slots on the top so that you could slide a piece of bread into each one. Then you would select whether you preferred dark or light toast and push down a knob that made the bread go down inside the toaster. Both sides of the bread would be toasted at the same time. When your toast was browned just right, it would pop back up out of the toaster.

But how did the toaster know when to pop out the toast? Pushing the knob down to start the toasting wound up a timer inside the toaster. If you wanted light toast, the timer was wound only a little and popped the toast out sooner. Dark toast took longer to heat, and the timer took longer to unwind and pop up the bread.

So what?

Just as we know a toaster will pop up our toast for us, we trust that God will raise us up and take us to heaven after we die. *The Bible says:*

We learned not to rely on ourselves, but on God who can raise the dead. 2 CORINTHIANS 1:9, NLT

If a toaster is dependable, imagine how much more we can count on God. A toaster can pop up toast only a few inches, but God can raise us up after we die and take us right out of the world into heaven!

October 13

Did you know that your stomach has acid in it?

JOB 10:8

The body does a good job of taking care of itself. When you are about to be sick to your stomach, your mouth fills with saliva. The extra saliva is needed to protect your gums and teeth as the burning acid from your stomach comes through your mouth when you vomit. The acid usually stays in your stomach to help digest food, and the stomach protects itself from this strong acid with a coating of slime along its walls. Sometimes the stomach lining gets burned, and that's called an ulcer. Heartburn is what it's called when a small amount of the acid escapes from the stomach up through the tube that goes to your mouth. This acid, called hydrochloric acid, is so strong that if you vomit into a handkerchief and don't rinse it off, it can burn a hole right through the material.

So what?

The Bible tells us about our bodies. *And in a book of the Bible named after him, Job tells God:*

Your hands shaped me and made me.   JOB 10:8, NIV

God thought of every detail when he made our bodies. All the parts work together like a wonderful puzzle, and each part is amazing. We could never build a body that works as well as the one God has created. And even when our body gets sick, God can fix it and make it work again.

October **14**

Can animals get sunburned?
MATTHEW 17:2

Being in the intense rays of the sun too long can be uncomfortable for animals. Camels have learned to face the sun so that the rest of their bodies stay out of the sun as much as possible.

Animals without fur have an even harder time in the sun. Other than people, pigs and elephants are the only mammals that can get sunburned; and what's worse, pigs can't sweat, so they are often too hot unless they roll in the mud. Elephants also roll in the mud, but that's how they start putting on their suntan lotion. Once they're nice and muddy, they spray dust out of their trunks onto themselves. The dust sticks, and that's what protects elephants from sunburn. As an extra benefit, when the elephant rubs against a tree, the dust acts like sandpaper and squashes bugs that have landed on the elephant.

One of the few animals to enjoy the sun is the ring-tailed lemur. It needs to be warmed by the sun because its blood flows very slowly through its body. That's why ring-tailed lemurs all sunbathe together each morning, standing up and stretching out their arms.

So what?
Whether you reach for the sun or hide from it, it's obvious that it is the brightest part of our earthly life. *That's why, when Jesus went up on a mountain to meet with his heavenly Father, the three disciples with him described Jesus by saying:*

His face shone like the sun. MATTHEW 17:2, NLT

We don't need to hide ourselves from Jesus, the Son (of God), because he would never harm us like the real sun can. The closer we stay to Jesus, the more like him we get. Open your arms like the lemur, and welcome the warmth of God's Son.

October

When was a toast a test?

JOHN 7:37-38

When people raise their drinking glasses up high or clink them together, it's called a toast. They usually say something nice like "To your health!" and it's just a polite way to make everyone feel happy. But toasting wasn't always just for fun.

Long ago, a toast was a way to test whether someone was trying to kill you. Enemies sometimes put poison in each other's drinks. When someone came to visit you, you showed that you wouldn't hurt your guest by letting him pour some of his drink into your cup. Then you would each drink out of your glasses at the same time. If you were willing to swallow the same drink that he had, that was proof that you hadn't poisoned it. Before you drank it, you would say "To your health" to tell him that you wanted him to stay healthy and not be killed.

How did your guest show that he trusted you? When it came time for him to pour his drink into your cup, he didn't do it. Instead, he just touched his cup to yours and drank without expecting you to take any of his drink.

So what?

In the old days, being thirsty could be dangerous. But Jesus wants you to have another kind of thirst. *He says:*

If you are thirsty, come to me! If you believe in me, come and drink!
JOHN 7:37-38, NLT

People who are thirsty can't wait to drink, and they feel very satisfied after they've had a refreshing glass of water. Jesus knows this. He is hoping you want to belong to him even more than you would want an icy lemonade on a sizzling hot day. He promises that he can make you happier than a cup of hot chocolate during a snowstorm. Trust Jesus to give you a life that's so satisfying you won't ever thirst for anything better!

October

Why don't dogs and cats cry?
REVELATION 7:17

Most living things have moisture in their eyes. This wetness has some chemicals in it that wash the eyes and protect them from infection. The eyes are automatically washed when we blink, about every ten seconds. Most of the time, the extra liquid drains away into our tear ducts, which are tiny tubes. Then the liquid collects in the tear sacs and also in the nose. Sometimes, our eyes make more liquid than usual, like when we are sad, or yawning, or laughing hard, so our tear sacs fill up very fast. At these times, our faces are squeezed up, and muscles near our eyes push hard on the tear sac. That's why the liquid overflows down our cheeks. Dogs and cats have moisture in their eyes too. But they don't have the same muscles in their faces to squeeze the moisture out. That's why they don't cry like we do.

So what?

When people have tears rolling down their faces, most of the time it's because they're upset. As long as people live on this earth, things will happen that will make them sad. *But the Bible tells us that someday:*

God will wipe away all their tears.   REVELATION 7:17, NLT

In heaven there will be no more tears. But even now, if something is making you very sad, you can get comfort from God. He will help you through your time of sorrow, because he understands exactly how you feel.

October

Can a bird hear worms in the ground?

ISAIAH 42:20

If you watch a bird for a while, you'll notice that the bird tilts its head from side to side before pecking for food. What is it listening for? Can a bird hear worms in the ground? Absolutely not. The bird moves its head because it cannot see straight ahead. Each of its eyes are placed on the side of the head, so it must turn one side or the other toward what it wants to see.

So what?

Birds know how to find their food, even if they look a little strange while they're doing it. But people sometimes have trouble finding God, even though he is showing them the way. *The Bible says:*

You see and understand what is right but refuse to act on it. You hear, but you don't really listen. ISAIAH 42:20, NLT

To live as God's child, you can use your eyes to see the wonderful world he has created. You can use your ears to hear the truth in the Bible. But you also need to use your heart. Let God have room to live inside your heart, and you will be sure to find him there.

October 18

How did skipping a trip to the store change cookie baking forever?

PSALM 119:103

Ruth Wakefield wanted to make chocolate cookies, but she didn't have the right kind of chocolate. All she had in the cupboard was some Nestlé's semi-sweetened chocolate, which wasn't supposed to be for cookies. She decided to break it into pieces anyway, hoping that it would melt into the cookies and make them chocolate. But when Ruth baked her cookies, she was surprised to find that the chocolate stayed in little chips. The cookies were delicious!

The year was 1930, and Ruth had just invented the first chocolate chip cookie. The cookies were called "Toll House" because that was the name of the house where Ruth lived. Many years earlier, the house had been a place where stagecoaches stopped to pay a toll, or fee, to use the road nearby. Ruth and her husband had turned the old house into an inn—a small hotel.

Ruth's guests and everyone in her town of New Bedford, Massachusetts, loved the new cookies. They all began buying Nestlé's semi-sweetened chocolate. The Nestlé company noticed how much chocolate they were selling in New Bedford and went to find out why. When the people from Nestlé met Ruth, they asked her if they could print her recipe on their chocolate wrapper. She agreed, and soon the whole country was enjoying the cookies.

For the next ten years, Nestlé still made their chocolate only in a big bar, so people had to make their own "chocolate chips." Finally, in 1939, Nestlé started making chocolate in the shape of little chips. The cookies made by mistake earned their very own shape of chocolate.

So what?

We get excited when a new cookie is created, because most of us enjoy the taste of something sweet. *The Bible compares God's Word to sweetness:*

How sweet are your words to my taste; they are sweeter than honey.
PSALM 119:103, NLT

We can understand that God's promises bring us as much pleasure as a treat. If people give us cookies or candy, they know these treats will make us happy. God knows that if we read his Word and believe it, we will be even happier than if we were eating the world's best chocolate chip cookie!

October 19

What was the biggest goof never made?
PROVERBS 22:1

There is a famous news magazine called *Time* that is read by millions of people. *Time* magazine realizes how important it is to be correct, to be dependable, and also to publish on schedule. That's why it was such a problem when the employees at *Time* discovered a mistake in the magazine. Not only was it wrong, but it was displayed on the front cover, the most obvious place in the whole magazine.

The covers were being printed, and 200,000 copies were already finished when the mistake was noticed. It was a small spelling mistake. There was a headline saying "New Plan for Arms Control," but the letter *r* in the word *control* was missing. Here was the problem: It would cost the magazine a lot of money to start the printing over, and the magazine would be late getting to the newsstands to be sold. But if they didn't fix it, this would be the first time that the magazine had ever had a spelling mistake on the cover in all its history. Which way should they choose?

The editors didn't take long to decide. They ordered the presses stopped, the mistake corrected, and the cover printed again. Because of this, almost half the *Time* magazines were late being delivered, and it cost $100,000 to start over. But *Time* magazine appeared as it always had, with no mistakes on the cover.

What people think of you is called your *reputation*. If you are gentle and loving, you will have a reputation for being kind. *Time* magazine had a reputation for being accurate and correct. When a decision had to be made, *Time* wanted to keep being known for its accuracy, even if it lost money.

So what?
The Bible gives advice about this problem. *It says:*

Choose a good reputation over great riches, for being held in high esteem is better than having silver or gold. PROVERBS 22:1, NLT

It is more important to be the kind of person that others can trust than it is to be rich. It is better for people to think good thoughts about you than it is to have lots of money. Why? Because money comes and goes, but your reputation sticks with you.

October

Why is the bottom button of a man's vest left undone?

1 CORINTHIANS 1:25

Men don't button the bottom button of a vest or a suit coat. It's a custom, taught from fathers to sons. But where did it come from? All the buttons on vests and coats were buttoned until the late 1700s. It was the Prince of Wales, who was in line to become king, who started this fashion statement. He always left the bottom buttons undone, and other men copied his ways, hoping to appear more kingly themselves. The Prince of Wales wasn't trying to change the fashion industry. He was just trying to be comfortable. His large stomach wouldn't quite fit into the buttoned clothes. Because the prince was overweight, men of all sizes and shapes have been unbuttoning ever since.

So what?

When buttoning their vests, men probably don't stop to ask themselves why they're doing it. But there are many times in our lives when we want to ask God why. Why does he allow sad things to happen. Why did I lose my loved one? Why did I flunk my test? Why don't I have a family like my friend does? Often we feel that there can't be a good reason for something that hurts us so much. But our mind is limited to human thoughts. Only God can see the whole picture. *The Bible says:*

The foolishness of God is wiser than man's wisdom, and the weakness of God is stronger than man's strength. 1 CORINTHIANS 1:25, NIV

You can have peace when you accept that God is in charge, that he has knowledge and wisdom far beyond our own, and that we can trust him.

October 21

When did a solution lead to an even bigger problem?

JOHN 15:1-5

Soil was a problem in the southern United States. It was constantly eroding, or washing away. After many frustrating years, a solution seemed to appear. It was the kudzu vine, which came from Asia. This vine had deep roots that held the soil in place. It grew quickly, and it even put nitrogen back into the soil. Farmers received free cuttings of the vine from the Soil Conservation Service. Entire communities got together to plant the kudzu vine throughout their cities and towns. Everyone was excited about how the vine would save the soil. But that's not what happened. Instead, the plant made things much worse.

The kudzu vine grew so fast, it could cover a foot a day in every direction. It grew four feet into the ground. It choked gardens and crops, and it clung to buildings and utility poles—anything and everything in its path. The kudzu vine was out of control. Chain saws, chemicals, hatchets, or even fire couldn't kill the underground roots and stop it. Every spring it begins to grow again. Kudzu can be found across seven million acres in the South.

So what?

Farmers don't want the kudzu vine to be fruitful or multiply anymore. But there is a good vine that everyone should want to have grow all over the world. *Jesus says:*

I am the true vine, and my Father is the gardener. He cuts off every branch that doesn't produce fruit, and he prunes the branches that do bear fruit so they will produce even more. You have already been pruned for greater fruitfulness by the message I have given you. Remain in me, and I will remain in you. For a branch cannot produce fruit if it is severed from the vine, and you cannot be fruitful apart from me. Yes, I am the vine; you are the branches. Those who remain in me, and I in them, will produce much fruit. For apart from me you can do nothing. JOHN 15:1-5, NLT

When Jesus covers the earth like a vine, it won't be considered a problem. Instead, it will be an occasion for rejoicing—and you can join the celebration.

October

Why would a family throw glass balls at a fire?

JAMES 3:5

We really don't know how people learned to use fire. Lightning probably started a fire in a forest, and someone may have picked up a burning piece of wood and started a fire in the spot of his choosing. We do know that after humans realized fires were good for keeping warm and chasing animals away, they made sure to keep their fires going, because they didn't yet know how to start a new one.

Throughout history we have learned much more about fire. For instance, not all fires cause smoke. If you see smoke, it means that unburned materials are floating into the air. If everything in the flames is being totally consumed, there will be no smoke. We also know that the hardest fires to put out are those burning cork or rubber.

Learning how to stop a fire was a long process. In 1734, a German doctor put a saline solution into glass balls. He suggested that those who found their house on fire should throw these balls into the flames, where they would burst and start extinguishing it. Then in 1816, after witnessing a fire where no one above the fifth floor could be helped, a Scottish man invented a copper canister filled with compressed air, potassium carbonate, and water. This canister allowed people to start controlling a fire themselves until additional help could arrive.

So what?

Getting a fire under control has remained a big problem. Sometimes it can't be stopped, even though all known extinguishers are used. The Bible compares our tongues to a fire that is out of control. *It says:*

The tongue is a small thing, but what enormous damage it can do. A tiny spark can set a great forest on fire.   JAMES 3:5, NLT

Once something is said, it is almost impossible to take it back. If you are lying or gossiping, you may become the source of destruction of your own reputation or someone else's. Think carefully about what you say, because even the smallest word—the tiniest spark—can be fanned by more words until they become a raging fire that no one can control.

October

Why was someone ironing dollar bills?

JOB 5:12-13

During the years of 1912 to 1916, if someone handed you a crisp one-dollar bill, it had probably just been freshly ironed. Yes, ironed, as in what happens to clothes after they've been washed. Who would iron money? The United States Department of the Treasury. During that time, bills were in short supply. A study showed that most used bills were simply dirty, rather than unusable. To save expenses, the Treasury Department decided to wash the old money. A machine was built that could wash forty thousand bills a day with two people operating it. Two long conveyor belts moved the money into some germicide and soapy water. Then the bills were dried. Finally, the money was ironed and put back into circulation.

The next time currency became a problem was during World War I. Until that time bills had been made out of linen, which suddenly became rare. The Treasury Department made the paper money out of cotton instead, but that faded too much to be washed. After the war, it was suggested that linen money and the washing process be started again. That's when the Secret Service stepped in and announced that "washed" money was easier to mix up with counterfeit. So the Treasury Department burned old bills until the 1970s, and then switched to a shredder to remove more than fifty-one billion dollars from circulation in the next three years alone.

So what?

The Treasury Department tries its hardest to keep people from counterfeiting money. But there will always be deceitful people who are working even harder, trying to beat the system. Maybe you've run across someone who's tried to cheat you. God will deal with that person. *The Bible says:*

He frustrates the plans of the crafty, so their efforts will not succeed. He catches those who think they are wise in their own cleverness, so that their cunning schemes are thwarted. JOB 5:12-13, NLT

Don't seek revenge, because that would result in your becoming crafty yourself. God knows the best way to deal with and conquer evil.

October

Who tried to control the ocean?

PSALM 89:9

Canute was a Viking warrior who became the ruler over England and Scandinavia in the eleventh century. One day in England King Canute wanted to prove a point. He went down to the ocean shore and stood on the beach, commanding the waves not to rise. King Canute wasn't suffering from a big ego. Quite the opposite was true. He wanted his subjects to see that God has powers much greater than any man. As the king stood on the shore, the waves advanced until the incoming tide was swirling around his feet. That's when he announced to his people that no one on earth was worthy to be "king." The only king, he said, was God, "whose nod heaven and earth and sea obey under laws eternal." To emphasize the lesson, King Canute took off his crown and never wore it again. Instead, he hung it on a crucifix above the head of Jesus.

So what?

By being humble, King Canute was becoming a better ruler. *He was directing his subjects toward God, urging them to acknowledge what the Bible teaches about our Creator:*

You rule the oceans when their waves arise in fearful storms; you speak, and they lie still. PSALM 89:9, TLB

Just as he should, the king was bowing to the King of kings.

October

How did a lost cabdriver help save a life?

PSALM 40:2-3

William Cowper lived in London in 1763. He had made up his mind that his life was hopeless, and that the only way out was to commit suicide. He decided to jump off the bridge that was built over the Thames River and called a cab to take him there. After driving around, the cabdriver complained that the thick fog was making it impossible for him to figure out where they were. Not only couldn't he find the bridge, but he didn't even know how to take William home. Out of frustration, the driver demanded that William get out of the cab immediately. William obeyed. When he looked around to try to see where he'd been dropped off, William realized with amazement that he was standing in front of his own house! Gone were thoughts of suicide. Instead, William Cowper went into his house, sat down, and wrote the famous hymn "God Moves in a Mysterious Way."

So what?

God has his own way of protecting us even when we're not aware of it. *The Bible says:*

He lifted me out of the pit of despair, out of the mud and the mire. He set my feet on solid ground and steadied me as I walked along. He has given me a new song to sing, a hymn of praise to our God.
PSALM 40:2-3, NLT

Whenever you're afraid that there is no more hope, turn toward God. He's been waiting for you so that he can begin working miracles in your life.

October

What were sheep doing at the White House?
PSALM 23:1-4

There are a few things you may not know about sheep. In 1917, a small flock lived on the White House lawn. They were President Woodrow Wilson's idea, so that the lawn could stay trimmed without using valuable manpower that was needed during World War I. When the sheep also ate some of the beautiful land-scaping, like the bushes and flowers on the White House lawn, people objected. But Mrs. Wilson pointed out that the sheep had provided ninety-eight pounds of wool that had been auctioned to make a contribution to the Red Cross.

Sheep are also responsible for giving us the phrase about "knocking the tar" out of something. Long ago, when sheep received accidental cuts during shearing, tar was smeared on the wound. This helped to prevent infection, but it made a mess by sticking to the wool. Before the wool could be sold, the shearer had to "knock the tar" out of it.

Another interesting fact about sheep is that they are afraid to drink from running water. It doesn't seem reasonable for sheep to avoid a flowing stream when they're thirsty. Remember, though, that some fears of humans don't make sense either.

So what?

God understands your feelings. He wants to take your hand and take you to a stronger place. He knows your deepest fears and knows that they bother you. He wants to help you to become more trusting of his protection. He will do this in a gentle way if you'll only allow him to. Think of Jesus as a shepherd and yourself as one of those frightened sheep. The Bible tells us how Jesus will take care of you. *It says:*

The Lord is my shepherd; I have everything I need. He lets me rest in green meadows; he leads me beside peaceful streams. He renews my strength. He guides me along right paths, bringing honor to his name. Even when I walk through the dark valley of death, I will not be afraid, for you are close beside me. PSALM 23:1-4, NLT

If Jesus is so sensitive to what a sheep needs and will take such good care of it, imagine how much more precious you are to him. Let him lead you to quiet places where your soul can relax and you can be refreshed.

October

How was a whole country fooled?

MATTHEW 7:15

The little country of Albania could finally take down their "vacancy" sign! The people had been looking for a new leader, and they had asked a prince from another country to come and be their ruler. The prince said yes, and now everyone was waiting for him to arrive.

Finally, a fancy carriage drove into the city, and a tall, thin man got out and said, "Make way for the new prince!" Then a strong-looking man got out. And after him came the prince. The prince made a speech and announced that Albania would now have a whole week of celebrating. Everyone thought this was a great idea.

But one day, a mysterious letter was sent to Albania. It said, "Thank you for asking me to be your prince. Someone told me that you think I am already there. Of course, that is ridiculous. I will be coming soon."

The people asked each other, "Then who is the man who came in the coach?" They went to the palace, but he and his two friends were already gone. Later it was discovered that the false prince was really a circus performer and that his two helpers were really the strong man and the giant from the circus.

So what?

Sometimes it's easy to be fooled by people. The way they speak and act may be very convincing. *But the Bible tells us:*

Watch out for false prophets. They come to you in sheep's clothing, but inwardly they are ferocious wolves.   MATTHEW 7:15, NIV

We should not believe any person who claims to be as good as Jesus. People who try to make you admire them (or something else) more than Jesus may seem nice and gentle like sheep, but they are really mean—like wolves. Stay close to Jesus, and you won't be fooled.

October

How could you buy land from a cereal box?

PSALM 24:1-2

In 1955 you could become a landowner each time you opened a box of cereal. That's because the Quaker Oats Company tucked a piece of paper, with a free deed of sale written on it, in each box of Puffed Rice and Puffed Wheat. The only catch was that the land you just became owner of was exactly one square inch big! Quaker Oats was sponsoring a television show for children called *Sergeant Preston of the Yukon*. They arranged to buy 19.11 acres of the Yukon Territory from Canada, so that kids could own some land there. After the land was divided, 21 million numbered deeds, selling an inch each, were put into cereal boxes. Only one person actually tried to claim the property. He said he had collected enough certificates to be the owner of a seventy-five-square-foot plot. Quaker Oats checked, but found that his "inches" of land weren't even next to each other. In the end, the land was reclaimed by Canada, and all that remained was the memory of a "mini" media masterpiece.

So what?

With the exception of the one man, everyone understood that the Yukon property was just for fun, just part of an interesting promotion. But when it comes to the real property in our life, we sometimes get possessive, proudly saying that the yard or the neighborhood or thousands of acres "belong" to us. Technically, your parents may have bought it from someone else, and in the eyes of the law, it's yours. But mere humans made the laws; the fact is, we didn't make the land. Ultimately, the earth belongs to someone else. *The Bible says:*

The earth belongs to God! Everything in all the world is his! He is the one who pushed the oceans back to let dry land appear.
PSALM 24:1-2, TLB

We are entitled to use the land only because of God's generosity, in much the same way that you loan a book to a friend and tell him to keep it as long as he'd like. During the time that he uses the book, you would expect him to treat it with respect because it really belongs to you. Someday you may own land. But whether you ever own land or just enjoy living on some of it, remember to appreciate it as the blessing God intended it to be.

October

How were Life Savers saved?

1 JOHN 5:12

Even though Edward Noble didn't invent Life Savers, he is the reason that we still enjoy them today. Noble's job was to advertise products. He bought the Life Saver invention from Clarence Crane because he thought that Life Savers could be a big success. He was wrong at first. Noble found out that the mint Life Savers did not stay fresh in their paper tubes. To make things worse, the candy even began to taste like paper. Anyone who bought a pack of Life Savers didn't want to try them again. Noble made a tinfoil wrapper, but people still said, "No, thank you!"

How could Life Savers get a second chance? Noble asked store owners to put Life Savers in a special place next to the cash registers with a sign that said Five Cents. In addition, Noble asked store owners to be sure to include a nickel whenever a customer got change at the register. Because the customers had the right price for the candy in their hands, they began to try Life Savers again.

Not only were they eating Life Savers, but people began using the candy in creative ways, such as decorations for a Christmas tree or holders for candles on a birthday cake. Noble had invented a new way of selling.

People bought so many Life Savers that other companies wanted to put their products near the cash register too. Soon, Life Savers were getting lost among all the other products near the cash register. Noble got another idea. He built a special rack for holding all kinds of candy and put his Life Savers right up front. The next time you see a candy rack near the register, you'll likely notice that Life Savers are the first in line.

So what?

The only true "Lifesaver" is Jesus, and he is offering the sweet gift of salvation. The Bible makes this very clear and simple. *It says:*

Whoever has God's Son has life; whoever does not have his Son does not have life. 1 JOHN 5:12, NLT

If you were drowning and someone threw a lifeline or an inflated tube to you, you'd grab it and not let go. God is offering you his Son. Clutch him to your heart and hang on for dear life.

October

Why do birds fly in a V-formation?

PSALM 32:8

We don't often think of birds as having the ability to organize themselves. Yet they often fly in formation. How and why do they end up in a V shape? It has to do with air currents. The lead bird becomes the point of the V, slicing through the air and creating a current of V-shaped air behind it. The other birds are helped along because whirlpools of wind form within the V shape and give an extra push forward. Scientists also think that birds see better while flying that way, since their eyes are on the sides of their heads. The V gives birds the best view of the rest of their flock.

So what?

When birds have somewhere to go, they put all their energy into the journey. God has equipped them with special instincts to help them fly the fastest, surest way. People, too, need direction. God values us so much more than other living things that he wants us to do things in the best possible way. *Along with the abilities he gives us to think and to understand information, God gives us this promise:*

I will guide you along the best pathway for your life. I will advise you and watch over you. PSALM 32:8, NLT

When we see birds flying in a V-formation, looking like an arrow, we should remember that God wants to point the way for us.

October

How did a Christmas card lead to a unique advertising campaign?

PSALM 119:105

Clinton Odell heard of a chemist who had become ill and moved to Arizona for his health. Clinton sent $25 and an encouraging note to the chemist at Christmastime. A year later, in 1925, the chemist, Carl Noren, appeared at his house saying, "I'm here and I'm well, and what can I do for you?" Clinton asked Carl if he knew anything about brushless shaving cream. Carl mixed up several batches. When Clinton found a leftover batch, he tried shaving with it and liked it because it had aged a few months. Now he had a good product to advertise—Burma-Shave.

Clinton's son, Allan, saw some gas station road signs that followed one another on the roadside, telling of gas, oil, and rest rooms. These signs gave Clinton the idea for Burma-Shave's new campaign. The family painted crude signs and put them along two roads. Repeat orders started coming in from druggists whose customers drove by the signs. It took almost eighteen seconds to read a series of them, which was more time than most advertisers could expect. Also, the separated signs created suspense. And the signs used humor.

Some examples of these clever signs are: "The bearded lady/ Tried a jar/ She's now/ A famous/ Movie star/ Burma-Shave." "Avoid the store/ Which claims/ You should/ Buy something else/ That's just as good/ Burma-Shave." One sign said: "Rip a fender/ Off your car/ Send it in/ For a half-pound jar." The Odells received tiny fenders from toy cars as well as real fenders packed in them! As promised, everybody got his or her free jar of Burma-Shave.

So what?

As you travel the road of life, you will sometimes wish you could see some signs that show you how to make things better. The highway will seem dark and rough at times. But Jesus will be beside you. Talk to him. Believe in his ability to show you the way. Trust. He will lead you. *The Bible says:*

Your word is a lamp for my feet and a light for my path.
PSALM 119:105, NLT

Turn on the light by turning to Jesus.

November
1

What's the big secret behind Betty Crocker?
JOHN 20:29

Most of us are familiar with her, or have at least heard her name—the happy, skilled homemaker known as Betty Crocker. Her radio show, *The Betty Crocker Cooking School of the Air,* began in 1924, continued for twenty-four years, and had more than one million listeners. Betty Crocker has served as the official home-baker's guide by answering cooking questions and has sold more than fifty million cookbooks. One ingredient is missing, however, from her secret recipe for success—she never really existed. She's entirely made up.

It all started in 1921. The Washburn Crosby Company of Minneapolis was getting hundreds of letters each week from women who wanted baking advice. In an attempt to give their responses a personal touch, the company, which later became part of General Mills, invented a lady to answer the mail. "Crocker" was her last name in honor of a retired company director, William Crocker. "Betty" was chosen because the name sounded familiar and friendly. A secretary's handwriting won the company contest to create a signature for the fake female. When the radio show began, Betty Crocker needed a voice, so an actress was hired. Fifteen years later, a picture was needed for the cookbooks. A portrait was painted, using combined features from all of the women employees. The picture was updated over the years, giving Betty eight different images. Each version made Betty appear even younger than the picture before!

So what?

No one had ever heard of Betty Crocker before 1921. And even after that, they only saw a drawing—never an actual person. People were convinced that she really existed because they knew what she "said" in her books and radio shows.

It's amazing that people have known for centuries what Jesus said in the Bible, but they still resist him because they haven't seen him with their own eyes. Why is it easier to accept a pretend cook than it is to believe in a real-life Savior? *Jesus says:*

Blessed are those who haven't seen me and believe anyway.
JOHN 20:29, NLT

November 2

Where did Thomas Edison go on vacation?
1 TIMOTHY 4:14

Thomas Edison, inventor of the electric light and many other innovations, was well known for his intense concentration on work. At the age of twelve, he was hired to sell city newspapers and candy to people traveling by train. He outsold all the other boys and proceeded to write and sell copies of his own newspaper. During the same time, he set up a small laboratory in the back of a baggage car. The young Edison spilled some chemicals that caused a fire, and he lost his job.

As an adult, he often had trouble understanding that not everyone shared his enthusiasm for work. Once, Edison noticed that his workers were constantly checking the factory clock during business hours. He came up with a unique way to change this habit. Edison installed many clocks throughout the plant, and made sure that each clock showed a different time. The employees were so confused that they gave up trying to figure out the correct time and turned their attention back to work.

Edison's dedication to work also showed itself at home. One time his wife urged him to take a much-needed vacation, but he replied that he wouldn't know where to go. She then told him to pick the one place where he'd rather be than anywhere else on earth. He agreed and said, "I'll go tomorrow." Edison kept his word, and the next morning he went directly to the laboratory.

So what?
No one can deny that Thomas Edison had a passion for his work. He was talented, and he couldn't wait to use his abilities every day. *The Bible says:*

Be sure to use the abilities God has given you.   1 TIMOTHY 4:14, TLB

If you feel drawn toward a certain career, God may be trying to guide you. If you've been wanting to try a new craft, to be an encourager to your classmates, to write a song, or to organize things—by all means, try it! Ask God to help you know what your talents are and how you can use them for him. He'll show you things about yourself that you haven't yet discovered, and he'll help you keep improving the abilities you know are yours.

November

When was the United States ruled by an emperor?

ISAIAH 57:15

Traditionally, an emperor is thought to have wealth, power, and prestige. Joshua Norton had none of those. Norton moved from England to San Francisco to make his fortune. He did become wealthy, but lost all his money within ten years. He ended up living in a small rooming house and working in a rice factory. Norton thought that the United States was not being run correctly. He was a charming and gentle man who told lots of people about his views on how to make America a better place. One newspaper editor decided to print a story about Norton, including Norton's ideas about making himself emperor of the United States. In 1859, he did it—he proclaimed himself emperor.

Norton wore a secondhand military uniform and a hat with a feather in it. He walked around San Francisco every day, checking on his "empire." He watched to make sure gutters didn't have trash in them and that streetcars kept to their schedules. If Norton saw something he didn't like, he would "abolish" it. When asked nicely, however, Emperor Norton would change his mind. Merchants kindly accepted his own "money," which he was allowed to print. Theaters saved a special seat for him, and he ate in restaurants for free. The people of San Francisco were delighted with their emperor of the United States. They bowed when they saw him on the street, and many citizens contributed to his living expenses without his knowing. After twenty years of being emperor, Norton died, and for two days more than ten thousand of Norton's "subjects" paid respect to their lovable "leader."

So what?

It's very hard to lose all of your money. Norton couldn't really accept it, so he invented a way in which he could still seem important. Make-believe answers don't usually work in the real world. But God loves those who can accept setbacks with grace, and who continue to have faith in him. *He says:*

I refresh the humble and give new courage to those with repentant hearts. ISAIAH 57:15, NLT

God doesn't measure your importance by your popularity or your money. Let him show you how to be content with who you are and what you have.

November 4

How did some prisoners dig themselves into deeper trouble?

PROVERBS 14:22

Some prisoners in Mexico were planning a daring underground escape. They carefully calculated how far it would be to dig past the prison walls and secretly began working on a tunnel. After several months the passageway was complete, and the time to escape arrived. Seventy-five convicts traveled underground, through the tunnel, and beyond the prison boundaries. Everything went according to plan until the very last minute. As the escapees emerged, they realized that they had dug their tunnel directly into a courtroom.

So what?

It's a good guess that wherever the prisoners had come out, they wouldn't have gotten away with their escape, although justice was unusually swift in their case. We know that the people who intentionally do wrong usually bring bad things on themselves. That's one of the messages of the Bible. *It says:*

If you plot evil, you will be lost; but if you plan good, you will be granted unfailing love and faithfulness. PROVERBS 14:22, NLT

The best way to avoid trouble is to dig into God's Word and steer clear of evil.

November 5

Why does one eye work harder than the other?

MATTHEW 6:22-23

Did you know that you have a dominant eye? Your brain chooses this eye to do the work first when both of your eyes are open. You can do a simple test to find out which of your eyes is the dominant one. Hold a pencil up with your arm outstretched in front of you. With both eyes open, line the pencil up to a straight line in the distance—the edge of a wall, door, picture frame, or the trunk of a tree (any straight line will do). Now close one eye at a time. When you're looking through one eye, the pencil will appear to stay exactly where you lined it up, exactly even with the line you've chosen. But when you close that eye and open the other, you'll discover that the pencil appears to have moved—even jumped—to one side or the other. It will no longer look lined up to the edge. What does this mean? The eye that made the pencil appear to stay even with the edge is your dominant eye. That's the one your brain is using to record what you're seeing.

So what?

God wants you to understand the power of your eyes. It's a much bigger issue than simply having perfect vision. *The Bible tells us:*

If your eye is pure, there will be sunshine in your soul. But if your eye is clouded with evil thoughts and desires, you are in deep spiritual darkness. And oh, how deep that darkness can be! MATTHEW 6:22-23, TLB

If life seems blurry and confusing, adjust your soul by focusing on Jesus, and let the Son shine in!

November

What's the "hobo code"?

MATTHEW 25:40

During the Great Depression, many Americans had no jobs or money. Men desperate for work rode in the empty cars of trains, going from town to town, hoping to find a better life. When the train stopped, the men, who were often called hobos, would get off and go looking for a meal or a job. When a hobo knocked at the door, many of the townspeople would help by sharing some of their food or paying for a small chore to be done. Other people were mean and unkind. Hobos wanted to let the next trainload of men know where they would be welcomed and which places they should avoid. So before getting back on the train, the hobos would leave a secret, hidden message on a fence or wall, describing different addresses. They would leave little drawings that meant, "This man will let you sleep in his shed," or "If you're sick, this doctor will help you," or "Dishonest lady—won't pay you for work." These signals were called the "hobo code," and it was a small way that men who could barely help themselves tried to help others.

So what?

Many people today are afraid to help a stranger, especially someone with a scruffy beard, a tattered shirt, and holes in his shoes. But there are things we can do without endangering ourselves. Our families and our church leaders can put a needy person in touch with a mission or a homeless shelter. We can also offer our help at a soup kitchen, a food pantry, or a secondhand clothing store. *Jesus says:*

I assure you, when you did it to one of the least of these my brothers and sisters, you were doing it to me! MATTHEW 25:40, NLT

God wants us to treat each person we meet as if he were Jesus in disguise. Ask your dad and mom how your family can help someone in need.

November

Why do some people have naturally curly hair?

ECCLESIASTES 7:13

Have you ever noticed that no matter how hard you try to make your hair look like someone else's, you usually end up looking just like you? That's because God designed your hair especially for you. You were born with tiny holes, called follicles, all over your scalp. Your hair grows out of these holes. If your follicles are round, you have straight hair. Wavy hair comes from oval-shaped follicles, and square follicles make your hair curly. The follicles are so small that you can't see what shape they are. But God knows what shape you have because he picked it out for you.

So what?

If you try to curl your straight hair and it stays straight anyway, or if you straighten your curly hair, but the curls come bouncing back, don't be upset. *The Bible says:*

Don't fight the ways of God, for who can straighten out what he has made crooked?   ECCLESIASTES 7:13, NLT

When God had the writer of Ecclesiastes write the above verse, he probably wasn't thinking about hair! However, we know that God is pleased with his plan for you, so you can even be happy about your hair, whatever kind you have. It's part of what makes you special.

Why do horses sleep standing up?
JAMES 4:7

A horse likes to sleep on its feet because it's safer: If danger comes, the horse is already standing and can begin to run as soon as it wakes up. Horses also prefer standing because they weigh so much that if they lie down it is sometimes hard for them to breathe. Also, it takes lots of energy for the horse to lie down and get back up. Horses can lock their knees in a standing position, and that's why they don't fall down when they doze off. Something you might see is a mother and colt standing together while they doze. The colt makes sure its whiskers are touching its mother. That way, if she moves, he will know it.

So what?

When a horse sees danger, it has to run away to protect itself. But we don't have to depend on our feet or on our speed to help us. In fact, we can stand on the promises of God, and he will protect us. *The Bible tells us:*

Resist the Devil, and he will flee from you. JAMES 4:7, NLT

A horse that stands still might get attacked. But when you refuse to lie or cheat or steal, the devil is the one who has to run away! He won't even stay nearby when you refuse to go along with his evil schemes.

November

What kind of food was once sold with a pair of gloves so people could hold it?

JOHN 13:13

There are many stories about a long sausage, first invented in Germany. Some may be true; others probably are not.

We are told that Antoine Feuchtwanger started selling these sausages in America in 1880, but they were so hot, his customers' hands were getting burned. So Antoine gave them each a pair of gloves! Later, he switched to wrapping the sausages in a bread bun. While this may be true, it is likely that the people in Germany ate the sausages with bread long before that.

This sausage had several names. The first name was frankfurter, from the city where the sausage was invented—Frankfurt, Germany. Then the frankfurter got a new name after people noticed that it looked like the long, skinny dog called a dachshund. Then one time, it is said, a cartoonist drew a picture of the "dachshund sausage" in the newspaper in the early 1900s, but he didn't know how to spell *dachshund*. Instead, he just labeled the sausage a "hot dog"—and that's the name that stuck. However, it has also been reported that the "hot dog" name appeared in college magazines in the 1890s.

So what?

Names are a way to describe things and people. The hot dog got its name because of what it looks like. Our names for God describe his importance to us. *Jesus said:*

You call me "Teacher" and "Lord," and you are right, because it is true.
JOHN 13:13, NLT

What kind of a name would people use to describe you? Would they nickname you "Happy," because you are spreading the joy of belonging to Jesus? Or would you be called "Nosy," because you gossip about others? Think of a nickname for yourself that you would be proud to have, and use it as a reminder of how you want to act.

November

What are some inventions made by kids?

1 TIMOTHY 4:12

Good ideas don't come just from grown-ups. A fifth-grader named Chris invented a disposable handle for shopping carts. It just snaps onto the cart, and you throw it away when you leave. Why did he make it? So his baby brother could chew on the handle without chewing germs.

Third-grader Charlie thought of a bowling ball with holes all over it, so bowlers wouldn't have to turn the ball all around looking for the finger holes.

When Alex was in the third grade, he figured out a way for just one person to use the seesaw. He made a spring to go beneath the seat, so he could bounce up and down when he was by himself.

Daniel was in kindergarten when he invented the shoe magnet. His shoelaces had metal tips on the ends, and they stuck to magnets on his shoes. That way, even if they came untied, they wouldn't drag on the ground and trip him.

Another Daniel, an eighth-grader, invented a safer way for people on crutches to walk on icy sidewalks. He put a cap with sharp spikes over the rubber tip on each crutch. The spikes pierce the ice, and the crutches stay steady.

April noticed that her baby brother cried whenever he had his diaper changed, because their mom used wet wipes that were too cold. April, who was in third grade, invented an electrical box that heats up the baby wipes.

So what?
The Bible says:

Don't let anyone think less of you because you are young. Be an example to all believers in what you teach, in the way you live, in your love, your faith, and your purity. 1 TIMOTHY 4:12, NLT

God wants you to use your mind and heart to make the world a better place. It pleases God when you set a good example and share a good idea.

November

Why was a 107-year-old lady supposed to go to first grade?

PROVERBS 16:31

Alldora Bjarnadottir was 107 years old, living in Iceland, when she got a letter telling her how much fun she would have when she began going to first grade! Alldora was confused. Who would think that she needed to go back to school?

Finally, the mystery was solved by some people who worked for the government of Iceland. In their country, every child who turned seven needed to start school. The computer that sent out the letters to new first graders could only count people's ages up to 100. After that, it started over. Alldora was 100 plus 7, but the computer thought she was only seven!

So what?

Alldora deserved respect for the many years she had lived. *The Bible tells us:*

Gray hair is a crown of glory; it is gained by living a godly life.
PROVERBS 16:31, NLT

We should listen to older people and respect the wisdom they have gained in their lifetimes. If Alldora was really going back to school, she should have gone as a teacher rather than a student, because she had already learned 100 years' worth of extra knowledge about life.

November 12

How do animals help their friends?

ISAIAH 58:10

Animals seem to know when a friend is sick, weak, or hurt, and they try to help. Elephants keep a sick relative standing up as long as they can, but if it dies, the elephants cover the body with leaves and dirt, and then stay nearby for several days. Animals that live in water help their sick friends by swimming near them or under them, trying to keep them close to the top of the water so they won't drown. In wild dog families, the father dog goes hunting, leaving the mother dog and pups behind. When he gets back, he spits the food out of his mouth so the mother and puppies can eat it. Sometimes animal families combine, and one healthy grown-up will take care of another family's sick grown-up along with all of the babies from both families.

So what?

We can learn a lesson from the animals. *The Bible says:*

Feed the hungry and help those in trouble. Then your light will shine out from the darkness, and the darkness around you will be as bright as day. ISAIAH 58:10, NLT

If we do whatever we can to help people who need it, we will be showing the light of God's love. Being kind is a good thing for animals *and* people to do!

November

Why is fish served with lemon?

PSALM 5:12

If you have ordered fish to eat at a restaurant, you may have noticed that a slice of lemon is usually added to your plate with the fish. The cooks and servers may not know it, but they are following a custom that was started way back in history during the Middle Ages. Lemon and fish went together, but not because the lemon was squeezed over the fish to make it taste better. The lemon was served with the fish for safety reasons. In those days, people mistakenly believed that if you swallowed a fish bone, lemon juice would help to dissolve the bone.

So what?

It is sad to think that people would depend on a lemon to protect them, when we know that the lemon couldn't do any protecting at all. True protection—from swallowing fish bones or from any other danger—comes only from God. *The Bible tells us:*

You bless the godly, O LORD, surrounding them with your shield of love.
PSALM 5:12, NLT

Believing in God's power is much better than believing in the power of a piece of fruit!

November 14

What unusual tracks did a car leave on the road?

PHILIPPIANS 4:5

There was once a famous movie star named Tom Mix, and he had a very unusual car. It was a fancy Rolls-Royce with a pair of antlers on its hood. The city of Hollywood, where Tom Mix lived, was full of dirt roads at that time, so he had his initials put on the car's tires like a rubber stamp. That way, whenever he drove his car, everyone would know where he had been by following the "TM, TM, TM" tracks that he left behind his car as he drove along.

So what?

What if you had your initials stuck on the bottom of your shoes, so that every time you took a step, they made a stamp showing where you had been? Would your footprints show that you had walked out of your way to help pick up a package someone had dropped, or would they show that you ran to hide when it was time to do your chores? Would they show that you went to church every week? Would your footprints be found on the sidewalk, or could they be tracked through a neighbor's yard because you wanted to take a shortcut? *The Bible tells us:*

Let everyone see that you are considerate in all you do.
PHILIPPIANS 4:5, NLT

Each day, try to do things that are honest and fair and kind, so that if people really could see your initials left behind you, they'd say, "One of God's kids has been here."

November **15**

Why did a brand-new prison fail?

PSALM 142:7

In 1982, a new jail was built in Maryland. It was supposed to be the most modern jail in America at that time, one of the first to be run by computers, and it cost over eleven million dollars to build. But nothing seemed to work like it was supposed to.

There were remote-control cameras in the corners, to take pictures of the prisoners at all times—but the cameras could take pictures for only thirty minutes, and then they had to be shut down or the motors would burn up. The locks on most of the doors didn't work. People got stuck where they weren't supposed to be. A sliding door cut off part of a guard's finger. Guards couldn't see the prisoners from their station, and the microphones that they were supposed to use to speak to the prisoners didn't work. The jail was built with solar panels on the roof that were supposed to warm the building. Instead, they froze. Some prisoners escaped by kicking through the glass and plastic windows, which were supposed to be unbreakable.

So what?

This story is about a jail made of bricks and glass, but some prisons are not buildings. Your mind can be a prison, because if you think that you will never be successful, your thoughts can hold you back from trying. Your emotions can be a prison. If you stay angry at someone, you are holding yourself back from happiness because you won't forgive. *To get help, say to God:*

Bring me out of prison so I can thank you. The godly will crowd around me, for you treat me kindly. PSALM 142:7, NLT

You won't have to dig or kick or sneak your way out of your prison. God will throw open the door to your heart and mind, and he will free you if you just ask.

November **16**

Why won't a tire stay buried?
1 SAMUEL 2:8

If you buried a tire five feet under the ground in your backyard, would you be surprised if it came back to the top again all by itself? In about ten years, it would. Most things that are buried stay underground and slowly fall apart. But not a tire. It is made of rubber, which is so tough that it doesn't break apart, even under dirt. But how does a tire get itself up out of the ground?

Rubber expands—gets larger—when it is warm, and it contracts—gets smaller—when it is cold. As the ground gets warmer or cooler with the weather, the tire "wiggles." The dirt underneath the tire is packed very firmly, but the dirt on top of the tire is not as solid. When the tire moves ever so slightly, it causes tiny pieces of dirt from above to fall down underneath it. As these extra pieces of dirt pile up underneath the tire, they push the tire upward little by little. One day it will be up at the top again.

So what?

Maybe sometimes you feel like you're that tire. Maybe you feel that you're buried under piles of schoolbooks. Perhaps you think you're stuck down in a hole you can't climb out of because you're having problems with your friends or family that you can't do anything about. A very good way to get back on top of things is to pray. Ask God to help you, and trust that he will. Whenever you find yourself down in the dirt like that tire, start yourself "wiggling to the top" with a prayer. *The Bible promises this:*

[God] lifts the poor from the dust—yes, from a pile of ashes!
1 SAMUEL 2:8, NLT

November

Which word is used most in the English language?

PROVERBS 27:2

When people *write* in English, the word they use the most is *the*. When people *speak* English, the word they use the most is *I*.

So what?

Spend some time listening to yourself speak. If you notice that most of your sentences start with *I,* you may want to change the way you think. If you're always talking about yourself, it might seem to everyone else that you think you're the most important person you know. *The Bible has a suggestion:*

Don't praise yourself; let others do it!   PROVERBS 27:2, NLT

Spend more time asking other people how they feel or what they think. Soon they'll be saying, *"I really like talking to you!"*

Here are some other facts about words and letters that are easy to remember and fun to share at school:

- When people write in English, the letter they use the most is *e.*
- Every continent name has a first letter that matches its last letter. The continents are Africa, North and South America, Antarctica, Asia, Australia, and Europe.
- Only one state in the United States has a one-syllable name: Maine.

November 18

What treasure was found in a toolbox?

PROVERBS 12:22

Charles Dunn was a father who went to the garage sale of a sixty-four-year-old woman and bought a toolbox from her for fifteen dollars. The woman's husband had died four years before, and she was selling the things she didn't need anymore. Charles was looking for bargains because his family didn't have much money. Buying things at garage sales was a good way for his family to get what they needed without having to pay a lot.

This time, Charles got the bargain of a lifetime! When he opened the toolbox later, he discovered that it held $5,500 in cash. It crossed his mind to keep the money. After all, he had bought the toolbox fair and square. But Charles decided that it wouldn't be right. The woman would never have left the money in the toolbox if she had known it was there. Charles was honest and took the money back to the lady. She was so happy that she laughed and cried at the same time.

So what?

Charles could have said, "I found it, so I get to keep it. Finders—keepers." But Charles knew that it wouldn't have been right to keep the money. Even though Charles didn't have the $5,500 after he returned the money, he got something even more valuable. *The Bible says:*

The Lord . . . delights in men who are truthful.   PROVERBS 12:22, NIV

No matter how rich you are, you can't pay God to be happy with you. What pleases him is when you make the right choice and act the way he would. Your reward for this is much more valuable than money: You will be a child of the King.

November 19

Who was George Nissen, and why did he put a trampoline on top of his car?

PROVERBS 24:15-16

When George Nissen was young, there was no such thing as a trampoline. There were safety nets, and George loved to watch the circus performers drop from the high wire, doing tricks on the way down and then bouncing out of the net to land on their feet. The Eskimos made a "bouncing table" by pounding stakes into the ground and stretching walrus skins across the top. And a comedian hid a bouncing table in an orchestra pit, fell off the stage on purpose, and bounced back up to amaze his audience.

But George thought the safety nets and bouncing tables could be improved. He wanted to make something that all people could easily use, without having to make their own from scratch. So George took over the family garage and began to experiment. He used a piece of canvas stretched across the metal of his own bed, and he used ropes and inner tubes to make it bounce.

George named his invention after the Spanish word for bounce—*trampolin*. He took his trampoline to the YMCA to test it out. Kids abandoned everything else in the gym to stand in line to play on it. Next, George put a trampoline on top of his car and drove to anyplace he could find a crowd that would watch while he demonstrated it. Finally, lots of people wanted trampolines, for exercise as well as for fun. George still didn't give up on trying to get people's attention on the trampoline. He did crazy stunts, like teaching a kangaroo to jump on a trampoline. Because George was a good inventor and a good salesman, he became famous for his trampoline, which he invented in 1936.

So what?

Falling down and jumping back up are fun things to do on a trampoline. But when you fall down or fail when you're trying to accomplish something, that's not very fun. God doesn't want you to give up on a good project, though. *The Bible says:*

The godly . . . may trip seven times, but each time they will rise again.
PROVERBS 24:15-16, NLT

God wants you to get up again and keep trying. He will be with you every step of the way.

November

When did children need to hunt for a home?

PSALM 27:4

In the 1800s, American grown-ups from the East collected children and sent the kids away on trains. What did the children do to be sent away? Nothing. The grown-ups were trying to help these children, many of whom were homeless or living in orphanages.

They wanted these children to have a better chance at life, so the kids were sent to the wild West. Along the way, the trains would stop in towns. At each stop, the children would get out of the train and put on name tags. People in the town would come to see the children, and if they liked a child, they would adopt him. The kids who weren't chosen would get back on the train and travel to the next town. Ten thousand kids found new homes in the fifty years that the trains helped them look.

So what?

These children were sent to find an earthly home. Having a home and people who love you and care for you is something we all need while we live in this world. There is something even more important that you should look for, though. *The Bible says:*

The one thing I ask of the LORD—the thing I seek most—is to live in the house of the LORD all the days of my life, delighting in the LORD's perfections and meditating in his Temple. PSALM 27:4, NLT

No matter what kind of home you have—fancy or plain, brick or wood, small or large—you will always be welcome in God's house, which is heaven. Look for the path to heaven by reading the Bible and going to church and Sunday school, and you will find the best home—one you'll never need to leave!

November

What can go wrong with words?
PROVERBS 23:12

When people translate English into other languages, sometimes they make odd mistakes. That's because there may not be an exact word in the other language to match the English word. For example, an American company wanted to sell a dentist's drill to dentists in Italy. The drill worked by a foot pedal. English speakers rewrote the instruction book in Italian, but the directions didn't turn out very well. They said, "The dentist takes off his shoe and sock and presses the drill with his toe." Italian patients would be very surprised to see their dentists getting ready like that!

When another American company sent a computer to Indonesia, the translators wanted their booklet to talk about software. In English, *software* means the programs that help the computer run. In Indonesian, *software* means "tissue" and "underwear."

And when General Motors began selling a new car in Latin America, the results were not good. The car's name was Nova, which means "star" in English. But in Spanish, *no va* means "No go" or "It doesn't go." That's not a smart way to describe a new car!

So what?
After you make a mistake, you usually have two choices. You can ignore it or you can try to correct it. *The Bible tells us:*

Don't refuse to accept criticism; get all the help you can.
PROVERBS 23:12, TLB

The people who didn't translate some words very well could have corrected their mistakes by asking someone from each country to help them fix the language. Of course, the best thing to do is to ask for advice before you finish your work. Then you will save time and embarrassment!

November

What surprise was found in a closet?

JOB 28:17-18

It's fun to go on a treasure hunt. But it's even more fun when you find some treasure! One day in 1929, an American businessman named Ben Jaymin was visiting his nephews and nieces at the hotel in France where their parents had come on vacation. To keep the children from getting bored, Ben made up a game. He reached under cushions and looked in closets, pretending to search for treasure while the children watched eagerly. Much to his surprise, when Ben felt into the corner of a high closet shelf, he really found a box.

When he pulled the box off the shelf, the children squealed because it was so fancy. Opening the box was even more exciting. It was full of jewelry—earrings, bracelets, pins, necklaces, and rings. Ben was sure the jewels weren't real, so he let the kids play kings and queens for a while.

Later, Ben told the manager at the hotel desk about the box. The manager was shocked, because a rich guest had reported that her jewels had been stolen, and a maid had been fired for stealing them. The rich lady had put the jewelry on the shelf herself and had then forgotten about it. Imagine how Ben felt, realizing that his nieces and nephews, with his permission, were upstairs playing with $100,000 worth of valuable jewelry!

So what?

Although it's fun to dream of finding treasure and becoming rich, you may already be richer than you think. *The Bible says:*

Wisdom is far more valuable than gold and crystal. It cannot be purchased with jewels mounted in fine gold. Coral and valuable rock crystal are worthless in trying to get it. The price of wisdom is far above pearls. JOB 28:17-18, NLT

If you are listening to God, you already have some wisdom. If you search for God's plan for you, you'll find a life that's rich in joy, peace, and love.

November 23

Why did people once hold parties just to watch someone vacuum?

PSALM 24:3-4

England was having a ceremony to crown the new king, Edward VII, and the room with the thrones was being prepared for the celebration. At the last minute, it was discovered that the carpets underneath the thrones were filthy. It was too late to send the carpets out to be cleaned. What else could be done?

H. C. Booth had an idea. He was the inventor of a new kind of carpet cleaner that sucked dirt into a bag. He had invented it after he put a handkerchief to his mouth, bent over the dirt, and sucked in his breath. Dirt stuck to the handkerchief, and Mr. Booth knew he could try to build a machine that pulled the dirt in—a "vacuum" cleaner. People didn't really like the vacuum cleaner, though, because it was large and noisy. It had to be hauled on a wagon and parked outside a house. Long hoses were dragged inside to clean the carpet.

But when the king heard how Mr. Booth's vacuum had cleaned the throne room, he invited Mr. Booth to give another demonstration. The king ordered a vacuum cleaner for the palace. Then many people wanted their homes vacuumed, and Mr. Booth was very busy going from house to house. People had tea parties when Mr. Booth was coming to clean so that their guests could watch him work. Mr. Booth even made his vacuum hoses clear so that people could see the dirt being sucked into the machine.

So what?

Crowds don't gather anymore to watch someone vacuum, but long ago it was considered very entertaining. Having a clean floor is nice, but it doesn't even compare to having a clean soul. *The Bible says:*

Who may climb the mountain of the LORD? Who may stand in his holy place? Only those whose hands and hearts are pure, who do not worship idols and never tell lies. PSALM 24:3-4, NLT

The Bible is not talking about dirt that you can vacuum up or wash off. Having pure hands means that you don't use your hands to do bad things, like stealing or hitting your little brother or sister. A pure heart means that you love God more than anyone or anything else. God looks at your heart, not at your floors.

November 24

Why was Florida so cold one Christmas?

LUKE 19:10

Mr. and Mrs. Lewenetz lived in Russia. They decided to go visit Mrs. Lewenetz's father in Florida, so they bought airplane tickets and took the trip. But when they got off the plane, it wasn't sunny and warm like they expected Florida to be.

Even though they were a little confused, they didn't figure out that something was really wrong until they tried to find the house where Mrs. Lewenetz's father lived. The cabdriver knew lots of addresses in the city, but he couldn't find that one. Finally someone who could speak Russian was called to help, and Mr. and Mrs. Lewenetz found out why they were so lost and cold. The ticket seller in Russia had written *Petersburg* instead of *St. Petersburg* on their tickets. The couple's plane didn't go to Florida at all! Their plane had landed in the city of Petersburg, Alaska. They were three thousand miles away from where they were supposed to be! They finally got to Florida on Christmas Eve, just in time to be a Christmas surprise.

So what?

As soon as the Russian translator arrived to help, things got better for the Lewenetzes. After he found them, he was able to explain what had happened, and soon they weren't confused or lost anymore. *In the Bible Jesus tells us that he is like that Russian-speaking helper:*

I, the Son of Man, have come to seek and save those . . . who are lost.
LUKE 19:10, NLT

Jesus came to earth to look for us and to show us the way to heaven. That way, of course, is believing that he died for our sins and asking him to save us. Without Jesus, we would still be wandering around, not able to figure out how to get to his home.

November

How can ants help with healing?

HEBREWS 2:18

If you ever cut yourself and need stitches, be sure to ask the doctor if he has any ants—and then hope that he says no. Believe it or not, in some parts of South America, ants have been used by Brazilian Indians who had no thread or cord available to sew up a cut. The wound is just held closed, and an ant is placed on the cut. The ant bites the skin, closing the wound. Then the ant's body is twisted off, which leaves its jaws locked across the cut. The ant-stitches stay on the wound until it heals.

These ants, called "doctor ants," are interesting in another way, too. They tear off pieces of leaves from trees and move the leaves to their nests by carrying them over their heads. This gives them another nickname: "parasol ants." (*Parasol* is another word for umbrella.) Watch out for ants with umbrellas walking around in your doctor's office!

So what?

A doctor can take care of your body, but he can't heal your feelings. Jesus can. *The Bible says:*

Since he himself has now been through suffering and temptation, he knows what it is like when we suffer and are tempted, and he is wonderfully able to help us. HEBREWS 2:18, TLB

Jesus became a man so that he could understand exactly how we feel. Maybe you are unhappy because you've done something selfish or greedy. Maybe you're hurting because you're lonely, or you're sad because someone has neglected you. Tell Jesus about it, and ask him to help you. He will fix the places where you hurt or feel bad inside, and he doesn't need stitches or ants to do it.

November

What is the five-year frog?

MATTHEW 6:26

A very strange frog lives in central Australia. It's called the water-holding frog, and it has been equipped with some unique capabilities for survival. Rain, which rarely comes to the frog's desert home, is the biggest event in its life. The frog climbs out of its underground home as the rain begins. The first thing it does is to absorb the water through its specially designed skin, which causes the frog to blow up like a balloon. Next, it eats a tremendous quantity of insects. Eggs are then laid in the puddles, and the next generation begins. The tadpoles develop the ability to breathe air in just a few weeks—much faster than other frogs since the pools where they swim evaporate quickly. When all the rainwater has dried up, the adult and young frogs dig underground to make a small living space. They move in and then make an "envelope" from skin secretions that cover their bodies. The membrane helps their bodies retain the moisture they've collected. It even has an airhole for breathing. The frogs become still and don't move for up to five or six years, when the next rainfall comes and the whole process begins again.

So what?

Not too many people are aware that a creature like this even exists. We certainly haven't been personally concerned about its ability to survive. Yet God created this frog with ways to take care of itself. When we begin to inspect the world around us, we find unlimited ways in which God is very efficiently running the universe without our help. Grass grows, a cloud blows, water flows. The list is endless. But what does this mean to you? *The Bible gives a suggestion:*

Look at the birds. They don't need to plant or harvest or put food in barns because your heavenly Father feeds them. And you are far more valuable to him than they are. MATTHEW 6:26, NLT

Your survival is important to God, because he loves you and wants to take care of you. So the next time you doubt whether God can fix your problem and you try to handle it yourself—stop. Count the birds, the trees, the blades of grass. Try to make the wind blow or the rain fall. You will be reminded of who's in charge—and why.

November 27

What did gloves say about hands?
EPHESIANS 6:14-17

You can probably think of someone you know who "talks with her hands," making many gestures and movements to express her thoughts. But you may not know that throughout history, people have used gloves to "speak" for them. It began with gloves telling that the wearer was part of royalty. These gloves, as you might expect, were decorated with precious stones, jewels, and gold embroidery. Royal gloves were sometimes given to others as a show of support. On market days in Germany, the king's glove was placed in a public spot to warn thieves not to attempt a robbery. A lady would give her glove to a favorite knight as a token of her affection, and the knight would carry it with him into battle. At a king's coronation, a glove was always tossed to the ground as a challenge to anyone who wanted to capture the crown. This was known as "throwing down the gauntlet."

By the sixteenth century, gloves were perfumed in the belief that the smell would keep diseases away. That proved to be a false notion, but people still enjoyed the scent because bathing was rare. People showed concern for beauty, softening their hands at night by wearing gloves made of chicken skin. In many portraits, however, the subjects are only holding their gloves or wearing just one. What do those gloves tell us? That they weren't made very skillfully and probably didn't fit their owner. Queen Elizabeth I once had such a pair, with thumbs that measured over five inches long.

So what?
Gloves were used in history as protection for reputation, beauty, or power. But when we're feeling lonely, afraid, and threatened, a glove is no help at all. We need the armor of God. The Bible tells us about this armor. *It says:*

Stand your ground, putting on the sturdy belt of truth and the body armor of God's righteousness. For shoes, put on the peace that comes from the Good News, so that you will be fully prepared. In every battle you will need faith as your shield to stop the fiery arrows aimed at you by Satan. Put on salvation as your helmet, and take the sword of the Spirit, which is the word of God. EPHESIANS 6:14-17, NLT

How do you get all this protection? It's free for the asking. Invite Jesus to come into your life, and he will equip you with his power.

November

Why would a house have two thousand doors?

JOHN 14:2-4

If there were a prize for "Strangest House in America," the Winchester mansion in California would probably win. It was owned by Sarah Winchester, who had inherited the fortune made by her father-in-law from the Winchester Repeating Arms Company, which was famous for its rifles. Sarah Winchester was fearful, mistakenly, that she was being visited by the souls of people who had been shot by the guns her family made and sold. She thought that these souls wouldn't be able to find her if she made her house confusing enough, so renovations and construction were daily happenings at the Winchester house for thirty-eight years. What was being built? Doors that led to brick walls, stairways that didn't go anywhere, and windows that showed no view. There were 160 rooms with 48 fireplaces that took up eight stories and six acres. The final total was 10,000 windows and 2,000 doors by the time Winchester died at age eighty-five in 1922.

So what?

The Winchester house was built from the motivations of fear, dread, and anxiety. But all of those many rooms provided no comfort or sense of security to Sarah Winchester.

Jesus talked about his Father's house, which is also a mansion. *He said:*

There are many rooms in my Father's home, and I am going to prepare a place for you. If this were not so, I would tell you plainly. When everything is ready, I will come and get you, so that you will always be with me where I am. And you know where I am going and how to get there.
JOHN 14:2-4, NLT

We can't know for sure what God's house will be like until we get there, but we can be certain that it was built out of love. In his mansion, no fear, despair, dread, or anxiety will ever exist.

November

Why did the richest woman in the world eat cold oatmeal?

PROVERBS 22:1

What would you do if you inherited ten million dollars? Hetty Green, the daughter of a shipping magnate, found herself in that position. She decided to make her fortune grow, and she succeeded, acquiring one hundred million dollars by the time she died in 1916. But becoming the richest woman in the world made Hetty a poor example to follow.

Hetty was hard on her children, forcing them to wear rags. She sent her daughter away to become a nun so that others would pay her expenses. When Hetty's son developed a leg infection, she took him to the hospital's charity ward instead of to a doctor. When someone recognized her, she refused to pay for treatment and took her son home. Later his leg had to be amputated. Even then, Hetty insisted that the operation be performed in her house.

Hetty ate cold oatmeal, onions, and cold eggs rather than pay for fuel to heat her food. She once spent hours searching the street for a coin her son had lost. Rather than spend money on an office, Hetty surrounded herself with old trunks and papers and sat on the floor in the middle of a bank building to conduct her business. She wore a dirty black dress and rubber boots with money stuffed in them. Hetty worried constantly about people trying to take her money. By the time she died, her selfish ways had earned Hetty a nickname. She was called "The Witch of Wall Street."

So what?

The Bible says this about money:

If you must choose, take a good name rather than great riches; for to be held in loving esteem is better than silver and gold.   PROVERBS 22:1, TLB

Although we can't sit in judgment of Hetty, from all appearances she didn't lead a pleasant life even though she had lots of money. She put her money ahead of her children's health and comfort, as well as her own. We can only guess at how much good her money could have done for many people, including her own family. The fact that Hetty left behind great riches and a horrible nickname seems to show that she wasn't the happy person she could have been if she had lived with her values the other way around.

November

What did you get if you ordered "bossy in a bowl"?

MALACHI 1:11

If a waitress brought you "bossy in a bowl," "dog biscuits," and "nervous pudding," what would you be eating? Beef stew, crackers, and Jell-O! Before restaurants became so crowded, waitresses didn't write down your order—they just announced it over the counter to the cook. There was a special language that made things interesting for the workers, and its nickname was "hash house Greek." Descriptions for certain foods were made up, and everyone who worked in the restaurant knew which was which. "Moo juice" was milk, "brown cow" was chocolate milk, cereal was a "bowl of birdseed," and a sandwich "with grass" meant it came with lettuce. As more people began eating out, order-taking had to be streamlined, and written orders were simply hung on a carousel to be more efficient. But no one can deny that the original method was much more interesting.

So what?

Names of things and names of people are important. They're what we use when we're trying to communicate. The most important of all names, of course, is Jesus. *He says:*

All around the world they offer sweet incense and pure offerings in honor of my name. For my name is great among the nations.
MALACHI 1:11, NLT

If you didn't live in the "diner" generation or eat out a lot, you might never have heard of the strange names for food. Maybe that makes you feel like you missed out on a fun time in America. But in all generations and in all places, the wonderful name of Jesus will always be known. You'll only miss out if you don't ask him in.

Decem ber

1

How did Kleenex find out that "the nose knows"?

MATTHEW 6:8

The Kimberly-Clark Company had a problem. During World War I, they had supplied the soldiers with Cellucotton, a tissue made from a mixture of cotton and wood fibers. Cellucotton was used for dressing wounds, and as a filter for gas masks. In 1918, after the war, a huge quantity of Cellucotton remained. What could be done with it? Kimberly-Clark decided to present the tissues to the American public as a glamorous, "scientific" way to remove makeup. Many celebrities were used in the advertising campaign, and sales slowly but steadily increased. Kimberly-Clark was very surprised to receive a great deal of mail regarding their Cellucotton. Wives were reporting that their husbands were taking their makeup tissues to use as handkerchiefs. The men were wondering why the product wasn't being advertised as a disposable handkerchief.

Meanwhile, Andrew Olsen invented a new pop-up tissue box in 1921, which Kimberly-Clark began to use. The box was called Serv-a-Tissue, and it increased sales even more. Some officials at Kimberly-Clark wanted to keep Cellucotton as a makeup remover, but others wanted to market it as a disposable hand-kerchief. To settle the dispute, they went to Peoria, Illinois, to decide. The people there were given two coupons—one for the makeup tissue, one for the nose-blowing tissue. More people noticed and turned in the coupons for free hankies, and that, in 1924, was the official birth of Kleenex.

So what?

It's amazing how many products throughout history have become successful because they filled a need. It took the people of Kimberly-Clark six years and numerous hints from the public to figure out what need they were best at filling. You will never have that problem with God. *The Bible says:*

Your Father knows exactly what you need even before you ask him!
MATTHEW 6:8, NLT

No human is capable of caring so completely. God is the only one who can fill all your needs.

December 2

How did the Jeep get its name?
HEBREWS 13:5

We're all familiar with the all-purpose Ford vehicle known as the Jeep. Its design began as a contest sponsored by the United States government. A four-wheel-drive vehicle that was practical, easy to drive, and could carry at least a quarter-ton load was needed for the army troops of World War II. But the vehicle couldn't weigh more than 2,160 pounds. Three automakers submitted designs. One of the companies was Willys-Overland, but they had a problem with the weight—they were 250 pounds over the limit. At the last minute, they revised their vehicle to make it lighter. The revisions were so close that only one coat of paint could be put on their prototype. The second coat would have made the vehicle too heavy.

In the end, the army used a Jeep that was a combination of three designs from Ford, Willys, and American Bantam. Its many abilities may have helped lead to the Jeep name. The vehicle was first used as a fact-finding spy car by the army in 1940, and it arrived with the letters GP painted on its side. The letters stood for "General Purpose," and many people claim that the name was a shortened version of how the initials were said. Others, however, point to the Popeye cartoon character whose name was Eugene the Jeep. Appearing in comic strips during the late 1930s, he was a little creature who ate orchids, solved problems, and could do almost anything. Whichever of the two possibilities really gave the Jeep its name, one thing was certain—it was indeed depended upon for a variety of purposes. During the war, one Jeep that was completely buried by sand in a desert, and another that traveled underwater tied to a submarine, were still very much drivable afterward.

So what?

People were impressed by the Jeep because it was so dependable. It was also versatile, which meant that it could be counted on to perform well in a variety of situations. If that's what we're looking for in a vehicle, doesn't it make sense that we'd look for those same qualities, only magnified, in our God? Dependability and versatility are exactly what you get from God—guaranteed. Lifetime warranty, and beyond! *God makes this promise to you:*

I will never fail you. I will never forsake you.   HEBREWS 13:5, NLT

You even have his promise in writing—just check your Bible for the contract.

December

What is the history of the sandwich?
MATTHEW 11:28

He was right in the middle of a card game when his servants brought the meal. John Montague had asked that his roast be placed between two slices of toast and handed to him at the table—that way, he could eat and play at the same time. Montague did this so often that his friends began naming this special meal after him, even though he didn't invent this food. As early as Roman times, people were putting food between pieces of bread; the Romans called it *offula*. Montague just made the sandwich more popular. His birthday, November 3, is considered "Sandwich Day." Before the Hawaiian Islands had their name changed, they were called the Sandwich Islands because the discoverer, Captain James Cook, named them after Montague. What does the name "sandwich" have to do with him? John Montague was the earl of *Sandwich*. Now there are so many varieties of sandwiches, they have their own names, like "heroes," "poor boys," "hoagies," and "submarines."

So what?
The earl of Sandwich was so involved in what he was doing, he didn't even want to take time to eat. Maybe you're feeling that's the story of your life too. Homework, chores, music lessons, pop quizzes, church, school, sports practice—there never seems to be a time just to relax and be a kid. You'd like for things to be different, but you don't know how to change them. It might surprise you to know that Jesus understands. He knows what being hurried and overwhelmed feels like. He has a special invitation just for you. *He says:*

Come to me, all of you who are weary and carry heavy burdens, and I will give you rest. MATTHEW 11:28, NLT

When's the last time you got an offer of help from someone who really has the power to change things? You can test God and see for yourself. It takes only a few minutes out of your schedule each day to talk to him. If you tell him how hard it is, you will begin to feel more rested, because God will give you wisdom. He will refresh you with a reminder that you're not alone— he is your backup and will never let you down. You will begin to see new ways to use your time. If you slow down and let God feed your soul with his comfort and reassurance, that will be a meal well worth your time.

December 4

Why were windshield wipers invented?

PSALM 146:8

When rain or snow is blocking your vision through the windshield of your family's car, the driver can push a button or turn a lever, and the problem is wiped away. It wasn't always so easy. The trolley-car drivers in New York City in the early 1900s had to stop the trolley, leave their seats, step out into the bad weather, and wipe the windshield themselves. The worse the weather, the more often the trolley stopped, and the longer it took to travel anywhere. One passenger, Mary Anderson, became impatient. She knew that the trolley drivers needed a way to clear the windshield from the inside so that they wouldn't have to keep stopping the trolley. Mary thought about their problem. She always washed her own windows by tying a sponge to the end of a stick and pushing it across the glass. Mary wondered why the trolley drivers couldn't do the same thing. She experimented and finally found a long strip of hard rubber that could clear a windshield when tied to a pole. She fixed the pole to the windshield and connected it to the inside with a lever that the driver could operate from his seat. The trolley driver who first tried the wiper in 1902 found that it worked beautifully. Mary Anderson started an idea that is now part of every bus, train, car, and airplane.

So what?

You can ask God for a brand-new pair of "windshield wipers" that have nothing to do with auto parts. If you've been reading the Bible but feel you're not "seeing" and understanding the Scriptures as much as you'd like to, God can help. *The Bible says:*

The LORD opens the eyes of the blind. PSALM 146:8, NLT

Ask God to help you see more clearly what he wants you to do, where he wants you to go, and how he wants you to live each day. And he will!

December
5

What's the story behind the Taj Mahal?

PSALM 135:13

If you've ever heard someone say, "You act like you live in the Taj Mahal," maybe you've wondered what they meant. It all began in the 1600s. The emperor Shah Jahan of India built the monument as a tomb for the wife he loved and lost. She died after twenty years of a happy marriage, while giving birth to their fourteenth child. Her name was Mumtaz Mahal, and "Taj Mahal" is a shortened version of her name, which means "Chosen One of the Palace."

The palace was built on the banks of the Jumna River by twenty-two thousand men over the course of twenty-two years. The emperor planned to build his own tomb out of black marble across the river, to be connected to the Taj Mahal by a silver bridge. But that never happened because Shah Jahan was put in prison by his own son during a political fight. When the emperor died, he was laid to rest in the Taj Mahal next to his wife.

The Taj Mahal is a palace in the shape of an octagon, with six domes, fancy gardens, a long pool, a tall sandstone gate, and many decorations made from gemstones. Just one flower designed on one wall was made with as many as sixty pieces of inlaid gems. For its time, the Taj Mahal was recognized as one of the most elaborate structures in the world.

So what?

Building the Taj Mahal was the way that the emperor chose to remind people of his wife. The memory of her will last or endure as long as the building does—which won't be forever. But God does not need a building or a memorial or anything else we can see to remind people about him. *The Bible says:*

Your name, O LORD, endures forever; your fame, O LORD, is known to every generation. PSALM 135:13, NLT

Everything we know about God is passed from parent to child to grandchild. Telling our families about God, about his deeds, and about his promises is the most precious gift we can share with those we love.

December

Does spinach really make you strong?

EPHESIANS 6:10

In the old *Popeye the Sailor* cartoons, Popeye ate a can of spinach and immediately had superhuman strength. Parents told their children to eat their spinach so they'd grow up strong like Popeye. It's true that spinach contains iron, and our bodies need iron because it builds red blood cells. But spinach does not contain an especially large amount of iron. The body doesn't even absorb all the iron that is contained in one serving of spinach.

Other foods like enriched breads, lean meats, whole-grain cereals, and liver are just as beneficial in providing iron for your body. In fact, to get all our iron needs from spinach alone, we would have to eat our weight in spinach every day.

Why did spinach get such a "strong" reputation? In 1870, a food percentage table, or chart, was published, and many people read it. It compared the health benefits of different foods. The decimal point for spinach, however, was in the wrong place. The result of this mistake was that spinach seemed to have ten times more iron than other vegetables. The error stuck in people's minds, and spinach became thought of as the vegetable for strength.

So what?

It's amazing that people will believe, without question, that a vegetable can make them strong, yet doubt whether God can. God, in fact, is the only one who can make us truly strong. *The Bible says:*

Your strength must come from the Lord's mighty power within you.
EPHESIANS 6:10, TLB

The next time you're feeling weak, fuel yourself by opening the Bible instead of a can of spinach.

December 7

How did foot powder win
an election for mayor?

JOSHUA 24:15

Advertising can be powerful. In 1969, there was an election for mayor in a town in Ecuador. Around that time, newspapers began running an ad for a foot powder called Pulvapies. The ad looked just like a voting ballot, and made it look like the can of foot powder was a candidate for mayor. The ads said, "Vote for Pulvapies" and "Vote for any candidate, but if you want well-being and hygiene, vote for Pulvapies." People did. So many people used the fake ballots that the foot powder won the election!

So what?

Elections help us express our opinions about how we would like our future to be. But there is one opinion that will cause you to make a choice that will affect you for all eternity. *In the Bible Joshua wrote:*

If you are unwilling to serve the LORD, then choose today whom you will serve. . . . But as for me and my family, we will serve the LORD.
JOSHUA 24:15, NLT

Will you vote for life in heaven with Jesus that will last forever, or for the world's idea of leaving God out of your life? What do you suppose is the best choice? How about choosing to live your life with Christ at the center?

December

Does sound always travel at the same speed?
JAMES 1:19

There is a definite difference in the speed that sound can travel, depending on what it is traveling through. You would think that since air is thinner than solids, sound would travel faster through air than anything else. But that's not true at all. Air is at the bottom of the list for speedy sound. Air molecules are not tightly packed, so sound waves lose more energy when they travel through air. In one second, sound travels 1,129 feet through air. Through water, it can move about 4,760 feet per second, and through steel or glass it moves 16,000 feet per second. In other words, sound travels fastest through solids, slows down in liquids, and is slowest in gases. The denser the molecules, the faster sound goes through them.

So what?
Just as sound has different speeds, the Bible tells us that we should have different speeds in our behavior. *It says:*

My dear brothers and sisters, be quick to listen, slow to speak, and slow to get angry. JAMES 1:19, NLT

If you concentrate on listening, you will learn a lot. If you think twice before speaking, you might stop yourself from saying something unkind or untrue. And if you keep anger out of your feelings as much as possible, you will get along better with everyone you know. You'll be much happier if you learn from the Bible when to speed up, and when to slow down.

December 9

How did those sneakers get such a strange name?

PSALM 37:23-24

It's a name almost everyone is familiar with, but few know how it came to be. The product is sneakers, and the brand name is Adidas. In 1920, a German man named Adolph Dassler created the company that produces the popular athletic shoes. Known by his friends as Adi, Adolph added his nickname to his last name and formed Adidas.

So what?

We might think that a certain brand of shoes can improve our running or protect our feet. In a practical sense, that may be true. A better way to take care of our feet, though, is to ask God's blessing and guidance for their activity. *The Bible says:*

The steps of the godly are directed by the Lord. He delights in every detail of their lives. Though they stumble, they will not fall, for the Lord holds them by the hand. PSALM 37:23-24, NLT

Others will be able to recognize that God is our "brand name" if our feet follow his will.

December

Why do we call them "wisdom teeth"?

1 CORINTHIANS 1:26-28

The last four teeth that grow near the back of your mouth are called your wisdom teeth. Long ago, people really needed their wisdom teeth, because meat was very chewy and tough, and those back teeth helped people break it down. But over the centuries, the human jaw has gradually become shorter, so most people no longer have room in their mouth for those four molars. Why the name "wisdom teeth"? These teeth don't try to come in until you're at least eighteen years old, and you're supposed to be wise by then!

So what?

Being "wise" doesn't just mean being smart. It means that you have an understanding about what's important in life. *The Bible tells us what it really means to be wise:*

Remember, dear brothers and sisters, that few of you were wise in the world's eyes, or powerful, or wealthy when God called you. Instead, God deliberately chose things the world considers foolish in order to shame those who think they are wise. And he chose those who are powerless to shame those who are powerful. God chose things despised by the world, things counted as nothing at all, and used them to bring to nothing what the world considers important. 1 CORINTHIANS 1:26-28, NLT

This means that you are truly wise in God's eyes when you choose to follow Jesus, even though the rest of the world follows money or fame instead. The wisest thing you can ever do is to choose Jesus to be your leader.

December 11

What amazing number is always the same?

PSALM 40:5

You'll need a pencil and paper to perform this test and prove that it works. No matter how many times you follow these steps, you will always get the same answer! With practice, you will be able to surprise your parents, teachers, and friends with this trick.

1. Pick any three-digit number. The first number must be different from the last (975, for example).
2. Write the number you just picked in reverse (579).
3. Subtract the smaller number (579) from the bigger number (975). (Important: if the answer has only two numbers, like 99, add a zero to the beginning—099.)
4. Take the answer from Step 3 (in this case, 975 minus 579 equals 396) and write it backwards (693).
5. Add together the answer for Step 3 (396) and its reverse (693).
6. You will always end up with the number 1089!

Let's try it again. Pick a three-digit number (447). Now reverse it (744). Subtract the smaller number from the bigger one (744 minus 447 equals 297). Reverse your answer (792). Add the two new numbers together (297 plus 792 equals 1089). You did it!

So what?

We can count numbers, but no one can count all the good things God does. *His children say to him:*

O Lord my God, you have done many miracles for us. Your plans for us are too numerous to list. If I tried to recite all your wonderful deeds, I would never come to the end of them. PSALM 40:5, NLT

And the best part is that God is never tricking you.

December

Why are traffic lights red, yellow, and green?
MICAH 7:8

The first traffic lights weren't for cars—they were for trains. When railroad signals began to be used in 1830, green meant stop and white meant go. But there were all sorts of problems with the clear, white light. When conductors saw a clear light from far away, they couldn't tell if it was a go light or just a light from a house or street lamp. Also, if the tinted green glass fell out of a stop light, then it looked clear. The train could go rushing ahead, thinking the broken green light was a go instead of a stop. So new colors needed to be picked.

It was easy to pick red for stop. Red is the color of blood, which makes people think of danger. "Go" was changed to green because the color green doesn't have much effect on our emotions. Our brains tell us that we have nothing to fear; that there is no reason to stop or slow down. Yellow became "caution," mainly because yellow is the color that seems brightest when put next to red and green. This system worked much better for trains, so eventually it was copied for cars.

So what?
Traffic lights help us to travel safely. But there is another kind of light that can help you much more. This light can give you the power to change your life and overcome hardships. If you search for this light, you are guaranteed to find it. *We can read in the Bible:*

The LORD himself will be my light.   MICAH 7:8, NLT

That's right—God is like a light that will brighten your life. You don't even have to travel anywhere to see God's light. He will bring it to you if you just ask.

December

What do gold, tents, and a blacksmith have to do with your blue jeans?

MATTHEW 6:25

Each item played a part in the history of Levi's jeans. Levi Strauss was seventeen when he decided to take a ship to California, where there was a big hunt for gold going on called the Gold Rush. Levi was a salesman, so he took his merchandise along on the ship. He sold all of his goods to the passengers, except for some heavy cloth. Levi intended to make tents and wagon covers from the cloth, but when he got to San Francisco, the miners told him that what they really wanted were heavy pants that wouldn't tear while they were digging. So Levi had the canvas material sewn into pants, and everyone wanted a pair. The cloth was made in Genoa, Italy, a city the French called "Genes." Soon "jeans" became the nickname for the pants. Cowboys loved the jeans.

The rivets, or metal buttons, on the pockets were the idea of a blacksmith named Jacob Davis. One day a man named Alkali brought a pair of Levi's to Jacob. Alkali was tired of having his pockets tear when he stuffed rock samples into them. Jacob fixed Alkali's pants by putting rivets on the pockets, and the pockets never tore again. So Levi Strauss went into business with Jacob, and Levi's jeans had rivets on the back pockets until 1932, when they were taken off because teachers complained that the rivets were scratching school desks.

Another thing that was special about Levi's jeans was the curved stitching across the back pockets. The only time the stitching was left off was during World War II, when the thread couldn't be wasted just for decoration. (During those years, the curved markings were painted on!)

So what?

The story of Levi's is interesting, but if these pants are too expensive for your budget, don't feel bad. *The Bible tells us:*

Don't worry about *things*—food, drink, and clothes. For you already have life and a body—and they are far more important than what to eat and wear. MATTHEW 6:25, TLB

If you dress yourself with God's love, kindness, and generosity on the inside, what you are wearing on the outside won't matter.

December 14

Where did the dessert with the wiggle come from?

HEBREWS 7:19

Jell-O is really gelatin—a gooey, gluey liquid. People have cooked with gelatin for many years, often using it as a glue to hold foods, like meat, together. It was often flavored with wine, vinegar, or almonds. Gelatin molds used to be very fancy, shaped like fortresses and castles with windows, doors, and notched towers.

Making the gelatin itself took all day. This gluey gel was found only in the middle of the bones, antlers, knuckles, or feet of animals. To make gelatin, first you had to scrape all the hair off the animal parts. Then you had to boil the gel for hours and cook it with egg whites to remove the grease. Next, the gel had to be poured through "jelly bags" to let just the smooth part filter through. Finally, the clear gel had to be dried into sheets. What a lot of work! You can imagine how happy people were in 1890, which was the first time when they could just add water to a powder to make gelatin.

Then a lady named May Wait thought of adding sugar and fruit flavors to gelatin. She called her new mix "Jell-O," and she sold the idea to a man named Frank Woodward. To get people to buy Jell-O, Frank had to teach people what to do with it. Frank sent Jell-O salesmen out in fancy buggies, and later cars, to hand out Jell-O recipe books and visit church socials and picnics to show everyone how to make the new dessert.

So what?

When you learn of a better way to do something, it can change your mind. Once people saw how easy it was to make Jell-O, they liked it. *When Jesus came and told the people how they could be close to God, they said:*

Now we have a far better hope, for Christ makes us acceptable to God, and now we may draw near to him. HEBREWS 7:19, TLB

Because Jesus told people of a new way to live as God's children, many wanted to follow him. By telling your friends how much better your life is because of Jesus, you are giving them a chance to enjoy a better life too.

December

How can making a mistake make you money?

MATTHEW 22:29

Sometimes learning from your mistakes can make you rich. That's what happened to Bette Graham in the 1950s. She was a secretary who was a terrible typist. Bette made so many mistakes that the only way she could keep up with fixing them was to have a container of white paint in her desk. Every time she made a mistake, she would brush a little bit of white paint over the wrong letter. The other secretaries liked her idea and asked her to make little paint bottles for them, too.

Bette went to the library and researched how to make a better paint. Before she knew it, Bette was making lots of bottles of what she called "Mistake Out" in her garage, where her son helped her. They used ketchup and mustard bottles full of the new paint to fill smaller containers. Bette decided to name her paint Liquid Paper. In 1975, Bette had two hundred people working for her, and four years later she sold her Liquid Paper business for forty-seven million dollars.

So what?

The mistakes that Bette made were small spelling errors. These mistakes could easily be corrected. But there is one mistake that you don't want to make, because it could affect the rest of your life—especially after your death. *Jesus said:*

You are in error because you do not know the Scriptures or the power of God. MATTHEW 22:29, NIV

The only way to correct this mistake is to read the Bible. Get to know who God is, what he expects from you, and what he promises you. Then praise God for all the wonderful things he has done. Thank him for forgiving you, not for doing things in the wrong way (making mistakes), but for doing wrong things (committing sins). Then rejoice and thank God for making you able to smell perfume, to taste candy, and to feel a kitten's fur. The biggest bottle of Liquid Paper in the world won't help you as much as knowing God's Word will!

December

What toy was invented specifically to help students study?

JEREMIAH 29:13

In London in the 1760s, a geography teacher named John Spilsbury wanted to find a fun way to help his students remember the map of England. He glued the paper map to a flat piece of wood. Then he took the wood home and cut it into pieces with a small saw called a jigsaw. When the children came to class, they had an interesting assignment. Their job was to learn about England by putting together the first "jigsaw puzzle," which was named after the saw that Mr. Spilsbury used to make it.

So what?

If you have ever done a jigsaw puzzle, you know how disappointing it is when one piece is missing and no matter how hard you look for it, you cannot find it. Then the picture always has a hole in it.

Without Jesus, our lives have a hole in them. But God promises that he will fill our empty place if we ask him to. God tells us in the Bible:

If you look for me in earnest, you will find me when you seek me.
JEREMIAH 29:13, NLT

You will always be able to find Jesus when you look for him.

December 17

What does the *X* in "Xmas" stand for?

JOHN 1:1-3

Around Christmastime, you have probably noticed signs that say "Xmas" instead of Christmas. Maybe you thought that in our hustle-bustle world, people write the word that way to make it shorter and faster to read and write. Or maybe you thought that people were trying to leave Christ out of Christmas completely. But neither of those reasons is truly why the *X* is used. Actually, Christians themselves first started using the *X* long ago in Greece. The Greek letter for the beginning of Christ's name is *chi*, and the way to write *chi* is with an *X*. The *X* is just an old way of using Christ's initial.

So what?

The letter *X* is the symbol for Christ, who is the symbol of all beginnings. *The Bible says:*

Before anything else existed, there was Christ, with God. He has always been alive and is himself God. He created everything there is—nothing exists that he didn't make. JOHN 1:1-3, TLB

If you haven't already asked Jesus to begin his work in you, why not do so today? He will give you a whole new kind of life.

December 18

What job could you do if you couldn't hear or speak?

DEUTERONOMY 16:17

Imagine that you couldn't hear or speak. Maybe you would feel that you couldn't do anything else, either. Maybe you would feel sorry for yourself.

Once there was a young man named Leroy Columbo who was not able to hear or speak. But Leroy found something useful to do. Because Leroy depended on his eyes to show him what he couldn't hear, he always watched everything very carefully. Since Leroy's eyes became especially good from all that practice, he decided to become a lifeguard at Galveston Beach in Texas. He sat on the shore every day for fifty-seven years, searching the ocean for swimmers in trouble. Was Leroy good at his job? The people of Galveston thought so. They put a sign on the beach thanking Leroy for saving 907 people from drowning.

So what?
The Bible tells us:

Each of you must bring a gift in proportion to the way the LORD your God has blessed you. DEUTERONOMY 16:17, NIV

That means God has made sure everyone can do something well. He doesn't want us to get upset about what we *can't* do. Instead, God wants us to find our best ability and use it the best way we can, just like Leroy did.

December 19

Why did a school put a traffic light in its lunchroom?

PSALM 139:2

If you find that your ears are getting more of a workout than your mouth when you eat lunch in the school cafeteria, you might want to suggest an idea that worked in 1982 in a Tennessee elementary school. Something was added to this school's cafeteria that had never been there before: a traffic light. The light was hooked up to a machine that measured sound levels. When the talking was normal, the light stayed green, and the kids knew that they were doing a good job. Louder talking turned the light yellow, and everyone knew they were being warned. If the talking was way too loud, the light turned red. When the red light was on, no one was allowed to talk at all until it turned green again.

So what?

It's natural for people to want to talk. That's the way we explain to others how we think and feel. When we're not allowed to talk, it is harder to communicate. Imagine how special it would be if you could just think something and your friend knew exactly what you were thinking without your having to say a word. *The Bible reminds us that we do have a Friend like that:*

You know when I sit down or stand up. You know my every thought when far away. PSALM 139:2, NLT

You will always have a green light when you are praying, because God wants you to talk to him anytime—even though he already knows what you're thinking!

December

What letter is used most often in the English language?

2 TIMOTHY 3:16

As we mentioned last month, it's the letter *e*. We use it all the time to help spell what we want to say.

One man did something very hard. He wrote a whole book without ever using the letter *e*. His name was Ernest Vincent Wright, and he spent 165 days writing his book. The book was almost three hundred pages long, and it used about fifty thousand words. He had to tape down the letter *e* on his typewriter so he would remember not to use it.

Books that leave out a letter have a name of their own—they're called *lipograms*. Just to give yourself a challenge sometime, try this: Pick out a vowel. Make up a sentence. Then search each word of your sentence to see how many times the vowel is there. Now try to make up a new sentence without ever using that vowel. This is a fun game to play. Maybe someday you'll even write a lipogram of your own!

So what?

Lipograms are interesting books, but they are not very useful. They are more like games than places to find information. *If you're looking for a book that has something very important to say—something that will change the rest of your life—try the Bible:*

All Scripture is inspired by God and is useful to teach us what is true and to make us realize what is wrong in our lives. It straightens us out and teaches us to do what is right.   2 TIMOTHY 3:16, NLT

Every lipogram leaves something out, but the Bible tells you everything you need to know about being God's child.

December 21

Why wouldn't a locksmith give anyone his key?
REVELATION 3:7

Joseph Bramah loved to invent things. He especially liked making locks. In 1784 he created a lock that he was sure no one could open. He even printed a challenge on the front of the lock, saying that he would pay a reward to anyone who could figure out how to open it without a key. For sixty years, no one was able to collect the money. Three years after Joseph died, someone spent a whole week trying to get the lock open but had to give up. In 1851 there was a big fair in London, and a locksmith named Alfred Hobbs decided he would work on the lock in front of everyone. Alfred spent a few hours every day tinkering with the lock. He had to use many tools, but finally, after a whole month, he opened the lock.

So what?
Sometimes people's hearts have locks on them. They don't want to open their hearts to hear about God. But the Bible tells us that God can open people's hearts and minds. *It says:*

[God] opens doors, and no one can shut them; he shuts doors, and no one can open them. REVELATION 3:7, NLT

So don't be discouraged if you talk about Jesus and your friend doesn't want to listen. God can use your words as a key to open your friend's closed heart, even if your friend is trying hard to keep it shut.

December 22

Why did someone who never had to wash dishes invent the automatic dishwasher?

TITUS 3:4-6

You would think that the dishwasher would have been invented by someone who hated doing dishes and had to do a lot of them. But the woman who invented the dishwasher never washed dishes. She was very wealthy and had servants to do all her kitchen work. So why would she care about a dishwasher? The lady, Josephine Cochrane, was married to a famous man, and it was her job to be the hostess at many fancy dinners given in her home. Mrs. Cochrane liked to serve these banquets on her best delicate china dishes. She was upset because several times her china pieces were broken while the maids were washing them. Mrs. Cochrane wished for a machine that could be depended on not to break her dishes. There wasn't one, so she decided to invent it. She entered her machine in the Chicago World's Fair of 1893, which was an exhibit to display the world's newest ideas, and the dishwasher won the highest award.

So what?

What if, after the dishes were cleaned in the dishwasher, they were automatically filled with the most delicious food as a special bonus? That's what God does with us when we come to him! First he washes us clean from sin. Then he pours the Holy Spirit into our hearts, giving us spiritual refreshment that's even better than a big serving of our favorite food. *The Bible says it this way:*

Then God our Savior showed us his kindness and love. He saved us, not because of the good things we did, but because of his mercy. He washed away our sins and gave us a new life through the Holy Spirit. He generously poured out the Spirit upon us because of what Jesus Christ our Savior did. TITUS 3:4-6, NLT

All you have to do is ask God for spiritual washing, and you'll be clean from all sin!

How did Velcro get invented?

ROMANS 8:39

One day in the 1940s, a Swiss engineer went on a hunting trip in the foot-hills of the Alps, and that's why you can fasten your sneakers with Velcro. It didn't happen quite that fast, but the trip that George de Mestral took started him thinking. He was very annoyed by all the burrs that stuck to his socks and pants. He wondered what made them stick so well, so he examined some under a microscope. George saw that each burr had little hooks on the end and that the hooks stuck to the loops in the material of his clothes.

George wondered if he could copy the burrs. He worked on this project for eight years before he figured it out. Finally, he had a weaver make two strips of cotton cloth. One was rough and had hooks like the burr. The other was smooth and had tiny loops like the material in his pants. When the two strips were pressed together, they locked until they were pulled apart again.

Why do we call this fastener Velcro? It comes from two French words. *Vel* is short for *velours,* which means "velvet." That was the name for the smooth cotton strip. The name for the rough strip was *cro,* which was short for the French word *crochet,* meaning "hook."

So what?

God's love sticks even more strongly than Velcro. *The Bible tells us:*

Whether we are high above the sky or in the deepest ocean, nothing in all creation will ever be able to separate us from the love of God that is revealed in Christ Jesus our Lord. ROMANS 8:39, NLT

No matter how hard the world tries to keep you from God, nothing will be able to pull you away from him if you ask him to stay close to you.

December 24

Why do we call up-to-the-minute information the "news"?

LUKE 2:10-11

News is reported from all around the world, and that's why some people think that the letters in the word *news* stand for *north, east, west,* and *south.* But that's not really where the word came from. In the Old English language, there was a word spelled *niwe.* It meant "something you haven't heard before," and it was pronounced the same way we say *new* today. We just changed the spelling to make it more modern.

So what?

Sometimes watching or listening to the news from around the world can be depressing. It seems as if there's only bad news, and the more you hear, the worse it gets. Bad news can make you feel helpless to change it and hopeless that it will ever change on its own. But remember that the nightly news report is only telling about humans and the way they behave. Humans don't have the power that God has. God's Good News will always be true, helpful, and healing to every human being.

The Bible tells of this special news. *It was not brought to us by television or radio, but by an angel:*

Don't be afraid! . . . I bring you good news of great joy for every-one! The Savior—yes, the Messiah, the Lord—has been born tonight in Bethlehem, the city of David! LUKE 2:10-11, NLT

Jesus came to earth so that you would always have good news in your life—news that lasts a lot longer than a television program. If you tell Jesus that you want to be his child, you will have his promise that he will be with you forever—now on this earth and forever in heaven. And that's the kind of news you'll want to spread!

December 25

How did a broken church organ inspire the creation of a Christmas carol?

PSALM 61:8

The church organ was broken, the repairman couldn't come, and the upcoming Christmas Eve services for December 24, 1818, needed some music. These were excellent reasons for Franz Gruber, the organist, and the priest, Josef Mohr, to get to work. Franz composed the melody, and Josef wrote the words, and three-and-a-half hours later, the song "Silent Night" was completed. The children's choir sang with Franz and Josef as they were accompanied by guitar on Christmas Eve. The parishioners enjoyed the song immensely.

Is that the way it really happened? That's how the story is often told. However, some sources now reveal that Mohr probably wrote the words in 1816. He asked Gruber to add music to them for the 1818 service, but no one knows for sure if the organ was broken. Perhaps Josef Mohr simply liked guitar music.

The story continues by saying that when the organ repairman came, he was given a copy of "Silent Night," which he shared from town to town. After thirteen years of being passed from person to person, "Silent Night" was listed as "author unknown." Then, since people couldn't remember, they began to say it was the work of one famous composer or another.

Quite unexpectedly the confusion was straightened out. One day, a choir director at an Austrian school received a letter asking for a copy of "Silent Night." The director—at random—asked one of his students, Felix Gruber, to find a copy. Felix went home and got one from his father, Franz, who had written the music! After twenty-six years of neglect, the real composers finally began to get the proper credit.

So what?

It's exciting to create a song that everyone enjoys and finds meaningful. But you don't have to be a composer to please God. He is as pleased with the praises from your own heart as he is with the songs of a whole choir—of people or angels! *Say to him:*

Then I will always sing praises to your name as I fulfill my vows day after day. PSALM 61:8, NLT

Take some time each day to tell God how much you appreciate his blessings. Even if you sing off-key, God will know if the message comes from your heart.

December

What unusual item was once found in a bag of potato chips?

PSALM 32:8

Ginger Stewart was hungry. She bought a bag of potato chips and reached inside. What her hand brought out of the bag was certainly not what she expected. It was square. It was smooth. It was something no one could ever eat. It was a wallet!

How in the world did a wallet get sealed into a potato chip bag? The wallet contained twenty-seven dollars, some credit cards, and the name of the owner—Thomas Kelley. When he was located, he said he thought he would never see his wallet again. He knew it had ended up in a potato chip bag because he worked in the potato chip factory. The wallet fell out of his pocket and onto the moving ramp that carried the chips down to be bagged.

So what?

Thomas saw his wallet going down the wrong path in the potato chip factory, but he couldn't do anything to change where the wallet went. *With God guiding you, you won't ever become lost like the wallet did:*

I will guide you along the best pathway for your life. I will advise you and watch over you. PSALM 32:8, NLT

God won't just sit back and watch you go the wrong way if you ask him to help you. He will get you back on track, and then he'll keep track of everything you do.

December 27

Why is the White House white?

PSALM 51:7

It wasn't always. At first, the president's house was gray, because that was the color of the stone that was used to build it. The house may have been called the White House, though, because the gray stone looked white next to the other Washington buildings, which were all made of red brick. Also, the stone was a soft sandstone, which began to crumble. To keep water from getting into the cracks, the house was whitewashed many times, which did give it a white appearance.

Then in 1814, the stone house was burned by British soldiers who captured it during a war with the Americans. Later, it came time to fix up the house again. Perhaps because the outside walls had dark smoke stains on them, white seemed to be the sensible color to paint the house to cover up the stains. Even though it had been called the White House much earlier, now the paint matched the name. Theodore Roosevelt made the name official in 1901.

So what?

God's forgiveness is like a big bucket of fresh white paint that he pours over our hearts when we ask him to forgive us. He not only covers the stains of the bad things we do, but he erases them completely and forgets all about them. *Ask God, like King David did:*

Purify me from my sins, and I will be clean; wash me, and I will be whiter than snow.   PSALM 51:7, NLT

Do you want God to erase and forget? He will!

December
28

Why would anyone collect chicken bones?
EPHESIANS 5:20

Lots of people collect things for a hobby, but no one collected what Martha Beaulieu did. What did she collect, and why did she pick such an unusual hobby?

When Martha was little, times were tough for her family. It was during the Great Depression, and almost everybody was poor. But Martha's family some-how managed to have a chicken dinner every Sunday. When Martha grew up, she remembered how special those chicken dinners were, and she decided to do something to remind herself to always be thankful. She began by hanging a wishbone on a peg in her kitchen, so that when she saw it, she would think about how much God had blessed her family. Then the next time Martha had chicken, she hung that wishbone up too. Soon she was saving the wishbones from all her poultry. Once she counted them and found that she had wish-bones from 201 turkeys, 493 chickens, 37 pheasants, 43 ducks, and 4 partridges on her wall. The total came to 778 reasons to be thankful!

So what?
The Bible says this is what we should do:

You will always give thanks for everything to God the Father in the name of our Lord Jesus Christ. EPHESIANS 5:20, NLT

Just think of all the reminders you could hang on your wall for the blessings you have had! Maybe you are grateful for your favorite pair of sneakers, a soft pillow, an ice cream cone, your puppy, or a snowflake. If you could hang these things up, it would be a strange wall to look at, but it would help you remember to be thankful every time you saw it.

December 29

What was so wacky about old-time wigs?
LUKE 7:38

If you were a woman in Europe in the eighteenth century, you would soon find out that wearing a wig, which everyone was doing, was a lot of trouble. Wigs could be very tall—so high that they almost touched the chandeliers on the ceilings—so you had to be careful where and how you walked. Your wig might be decorated with models of ships, fruits, gardens, or birds, and because your wig was so fancy, you wouldn't take it off for months. To keep your wig from falling apart, you would smear it with melted fat and pat it with flour. When you went to sleep, you had to have a special pillow to keep your wig attached to your head, and you had to cover your wig with a special metal cage so that mice or bugs would not try to crawl into it. Yuck!

Why would you want to wear a wig in the first place? Because you were a copycat. When the ruler of England, Queen Elizabeth I, was twenty-nine years old, she had a disease called smallpox that made all her hair fall out. After that she was completely bald, so she always wore a wig. Since everyone wanted to be like the queen, other women put wigs on too.

So what?

Most people like their hair, or their wigs, to look nice, because hair is one of the first things people notice about you. If you are proud of your hair, you probably wouldn't wipe the ground with it, or rub mud into it. But there was a woman in the Bible who used her hair like a towel to show Jesus how much she loved him. *The Bible tells us:*

Then she knelt behind him at his feet, weeping. Her tears fell on his feet, and she wiped them off with her hair. Then she kept kissing his feet and putting perfume on them. LUKE 7:38, NLT

Jesus likes it when we use what we have to praise him. Be willing to do something unusual for Jesus, or something ordinary. Whatever you do, he will be pleased that you found a way to show your love for him.

December 30

Since earthworms have no legs, how do they move?

EZEKIEL 34:26

A worm has different segments, or sections, from its head to its tail. Each segment can be stretched out, or pulled shorter, and each section has little bristles on it. When the section is squeezed short, the bristles pop out. When the section expands and gets longer, the bristles go back inside and the segment becomes smooth again. As the earthworm starts to move, it scrunches up one segment at a time, starting near the head. While the first section gets long and smooth, it is able to glide through the soil because the scrunched-up segment behind it is gripping the soil with bristles. Then the second segment smooths out and pushes through the soil while the next segment is holding the soil with its bristles. This way, the worm can push and stretch its way along.

When it rains, you can see lots of worms on the sidewalk. Are they coming out of the ground to get a drink? No, they are trying to survive. When rainwater runs down into the ground, worms will die if they don't get out of the dirt. That's because worms breathe through their skin.

So what?
God says:

I will send showers, showers of blessings, which will come just when they are needed. EZEKIEL 34:26, NLT

The next time there is a rain shower or snow shower, look at all the raindrops or snowflakes. There will be too many to count. Then imagine that each raindrop or snowflake stands for a blessing from God. Try to name some. If you don't have a toothache today, that's a blessing. If someone smiled at you, that was a gift from God to make you cheerful. A rainbow, the taste of something sweet, the soft fur of a pet, a pretty song: These are all blessings. You don't even have to get wet like the worm to receive your shower of blessings—so that's a blessing too!

December 31

How did a weapon become a toy?

HOSEA 6:1

You probably think that your parents would never let you play with a weapon. But if you've ever used a yo-yo, you've used a weapon.

Yo-yos have been around for thousands of years, but they weren't brought to America until 1929. The people of the Philippines made yo-yos with vines tied to pieces of flint. They would throw the flint to kill an animal, and then they would pull the flint back with the vine.

The first yo-yos in America were made of wood. Donald Duncan had the idea of asking Filipino people to show off the yo-yos in department stores, and that's how Americans learned that the yo-yo could be used as a toy. Eventually yo-yos were made out of colorful plastic and became available in every toy store. The yo-yo got its name from the Philippine Tagalog language. *Yo-yo* means "come, come."

So what?

Many times every day, Christians all over the world are saying:

Come, let us return to the LORD! HOSEA 6:1, NLT

No matter what you've done wrong, God is willing to forgive you and welcome you back, just as you are glad to have your yo-yo return to you. If you feel that you are getting too far away from God and the way he wants you to live, think of the yo-yo. Return to him quickly, and start again.

Bibliography

JANUARY 1
What money mistake did America make?
Flexner, Stuart Berg. *Listening to America.* New York: Simon and Schuster, 1982.
Goldberg, M. Hirsh. *The Blunder Book.* New York: William Morrow and Co., 1984.

JANUARY 2
When can you buy an antique by scratching your nose?
Polley, Jane, ed. *Stories Behind Everyday Things.* New York: Reader's Digest Association, 1980.

JANUARY 3
What's the background on "backlog"?
Claiborne, Robert. *Loose Cannons and Red Herrings.* New York: W. W. Norton and Co., 1988.

JANUARY 4
When do you "let the cat out of the bag"?
Claiborne, Robert. *Loose Cannons and Red Herrings.* New York: W. W. Norton and Co., 1988.
Funk, Charles Earle. *A Hog on Ice and Other Curious Expressions.* New York: Harper and Row, 1948.
McLoone-Basta, Margo, and Alice Siegel. *The Second Kids' World Almanac of Records and Facts.* New York: World Almanac Publications, 1987.
Morris, William, and Mary Morris. *Morris Dictionary of Word and Phrase Origins.* 2d ed. New York: HarperCollins, 1988.
Paisner, Milton. *One Word Leads to Another: A Light History of Words.* New York: Dembner Books, 1982.
Smith, Douglas B. *Ever Wonder Why?* New York: Fawcett Gold Medal, 1992.
Vanoni, Marvin. *Great Expressions.* New York: William Morrow and Co., 1989.

JANUARY 5
How did a bathtub help solve a mystery?
Clements, Gillian. *The Picture History of Great Inventors.* New York: Alfred A. Knopf, 1994.
Giscard d'Estaing, Valerie-Anne. *The World Almanac Book of Inventions.* New York: World Almanac Publications, 1985.
Goodenough, Simon. *1500 Fascinating Facts.* London: Treasure Press, 1987.

JANUARY 6
How did cowboys get their meals "to go"?
Flexner, Stuart Berg. *Listening to America.* New York: Simon and Schuster, 1982.
Sanders, Deidre, et al. *Would You Believe This, Too?* New York: Sterling Publishing Co., 1976.
Smith, Douglas B. *Ever Wonder Why?* New York: Fawcett Gold Medal, 1992.

JANUARY 7
Why are girls' and boys' bikes different?
Feldman, David. *Why Do Clocks Run Clockwise? and Other Imponderables.* New York: Harper and Row, 1987.
Lurie, Susan, ed. *The Big Book of Amazing Knowledge.* New York: Playmore, Inc., 1987.
McCutcheon, Marc. *The Writer's Guide to Everyday Life in the 1800s.* Cincinnati, Ohio: Writer's Digest Books, 1993.

JANUARY 8
How did dead fish help improve frozen foods?
Aaseng, Nathan. *The Rejects.* Minneapolis: Lerner Publications, 1989.
Buchman, Dian Dincin, and Seli Groves. *What If? Fifty Discoveries That Changed the World.* New York: Scholastic, Inc., 1988.
Campbell, Hannah. *Why Did They Name It . . . ?* New York: Fleet Publishing, 1964.
Fabell, Walter C. *Nature's Clues.* New York: Hastings House, 1964.
Flexner, Stuart Berg. *Listening to America.* New York: Simon and Schuster, 1982.
Giscard d'Estaing, Valerie-Anne. *The World Almanac Book of Inventions.* New York: World Almanac Publications, 1985.
Landau, Irwin, ed. *I'll Buy That.* New York: Consumer Reports, 1986.
Montagu, Ashley, and Edward Darling. *The Prevalence of Nonsense.* New York: Harper and Row, 1967.
Perko, Marko. *Did You Know That . . . ?* New York: Berkley Books, 1994.
Polley, Jane, ed. *Stories Behind Everyday Things.* New York: Reader's Digest Association, 1980.
Robertson, Patrick. *The Book of Firsts.* New York: Bramhall House, 1974.
Sanders, Deidre, et al. *Would You Believe This, Too?* New York: Sterling Publishing Co., 1976.

JANUARY 9
What's up with eyebrows?
Tuleja, Tad. *Curious Customs.* New York: Harmony Books, 1987.

JANUARY 10
How do you build a skyscraper with matchsticks?
Buchman, Dian Dincin, and Seli Groves. *What If? Fifty Discoveries That Changed the World.* New York: Scholastic, Inc., 1988.
Burnam, Tom. *The Dictionary of Misinformation.* New York: Ballantine Books, 1975.
Harris, Harry. *Good Old-Fashioned Yankee Ingenuity.* Chelsea, Mich.: Scarborough House, 1990.
Meyers, James. *Amazing Facts.* New York: Playmore, Inc., 1986.

JANUARY 11
What really makes a bull charge at a red cape?
Blumberg, Rhoda, and Leda Blumberg. *Simon and Schuster's Book of Facts and Fallacies.* New York: Simon and Schuster, 1983.
Burnam, Tom. *The Dictionary of Misinformation.* New York: Ballantine Books, 1975.
McLoone-Basta, Margo, and Alice Siegel. *The Second Kids' World Almanac of Records and Facts.* New York: World Almanac Publications, 1987.
Meyers, James. *Amazing Facts.* New York: Playmore, Inc., 1986.
Perko, Marko. *Did You Know That . . . ?* New York: Berkley Books, 1994.
Simon, Seymour. *Animal Fact/Animal Fable.* New York: Crown Publishers, 1979.
Smith, Douglas B. *Ever Wonder Why?* New York: Fawcett Gold Medal, 1992.

Tuleja, Ted. *Fabulous Fallacies.* South Yarmouth, Mass.: John Curley and Associates, Inc., 1982.

Varasdi, J. Allen. *Myth Information.* New York: Ballantine Books, 1989.

JANUARY 12
When can books become a bother?
Adams, Simon, and Lesley Riley, eds. *Reader's Digest Facts and Fallacies.* New York: Reader's Digest Association, 1988.

JANUARY 13
How did a medicine bottle turn into a toy?
Schreiber, Brad. *Weird Wonders and Bizarre Blunders.* New York: Simon and Schuster, 1989.

JANUARY 14
How did a church leader help invent bowling?
Ellwood, Ann, and Carol Orsag. *Macmillan Illustrated Almanac for Kids.* New York: Macmillan, 1981.

Giscard d'Estaing, Valerie-Anne. *The World Almanac Book of Inventions.* New York: World Almanac Publications, 1985.

McCutcheon, Marc. *The Writer's Guide to Everyday Life in the 1800s.* Cincinnati, Ohio: Writer's Digest Books, 1993.

Morris, Scot. *The Emperor Who Ate the Bible and More Strange Facts and Useless Information.* New York: Doubleday, 1991.

Smith, Douglas B. *More Ever Wonder Why?* New York: Fawcett Gold Medal, 1994.

Wallechinsky, David, and Irving Wallace. *The People's Almanac Presents the Book of Lists 2.* New York: Bantam Books, 1978.

Wulffson, Don L. *How Sports Came to Be.* New York: Lothrop, Lee, and Shepard, 1980.

JANUARY 15
What can you do with a useless tunnel?
Ferrell, David. *Los Angeles Times.* Los Angeles, California, January 3, 2002.

Wallace, Irving, Amy Wallace, and David Wallechinsky. *Significa.* New York: E. P. Dutton, Inc., 1983.

JANUARY 16
How could treason be committed during dinner?
Morris, Scot. *The Emperor Who Ate the Bible and More Strange Facts and Useless Information.* New York: Doubleday, 1991.

JANUARY 17
What causes bad breath?
Feldman, David. *Why Do Dogs Have Wet Noses? and Other Imponderables of Everyday Life.* New York: HarperCollins, 1990.

Murphy, Jim. *Guess Again: More Weird and Wacky Inventions.* New York: Bradbury Press, 1986.

Owl magazine, eds. *The Kids' Question and Answer Book Three.* New York: Grosset and Dunlap, 1990.

Rovin, Jeff. *The Unbelievable Truth!* New York: The Penguin Group, 1994.

Varasdi, J. Allen. *Myth Information.* New York: Ballantine Books, 1989.

JANUARY 18
Why were the police called to an exercise class?
Sobol, Donald, and Rose Sobol. *Encyclopedia Brown's Book of Strange but True Crimes.* New York: Scholastic, 1991.

JANUARY 19
Why isn't the bald eagle bald?
Perko, Marko. *Did You Know That . . . ?* New York: Berkley Books, 1994.

Smith, Douglas B. *More Ever Wonder Why?* New York: Fawcett Gold Medal, 1994.

Varasdi, J. Allen. *Myth Information.* New York: Ballantine Books, 1989.

Vogel, Malvina G., ed. *The Big Book of Amazing Facts.* New York: Playmore, Inc. 1980.

JANUARY 20
Why does a contest usually have first-, second-, and third-place winners?
Smith, Douglas B. *Ever Wonder Why?* New York: Fawcett Gold Medal, 1992.

JANUARY 21
When was a sunny day bad for baseball?
Goldberg, M. Hirsh. *The Blunder Book.* New York: William Morrow and Co., 1984.

JANUARY 22
Which fish takes aim at its lunch?
Simon, Seymour. *Animal Fact/Animal Fable.* New York: Crown Publishers, 1979.

JANUARY 23
What did people do about their cuts before Band-Aids?
Buchman, Dian Dincin, and Seli Groves. *What If? Fifty Discoveries That Changed the World.* New York: Scholastic, Inc., 1988.

Caney, Steven. *Steven Caney's Invention Book.* New York: Workman Publishing, 1985.

Felder, Deborah G. *The Kids' World Almanac of History.* New York: Pharos Books, 1991.

Garrison, Webb. *Why Didn't I Think of That? From Alarm Clocks to Zippers.* Englewood Cliffs, N. J.: Prentice Hall, 1977.

Harris, Harry. *Good Old-Fashioned Yankee Ingenuity.* Chelsea, Mich.: Scarborough House, 1990.

McKenzie, E. C. *Salted Peanuts: 1800 Little-Known Facts.* Grand Rapids, Mich.: Baker Book House, 1972.

McLoone-Basta, Margo, and Alice Siegel. *The Kids' World Almanac of Records and Facts.* New York: World Almanac Publications, 1985.

Polley, Jane, ed. *Stories Behind Everyday Things.* New York: Reader's Digest Association, 1980.

JANUARY 24
How did a little girl's letter change history?
McLoone-Basta, Margo, and Alice Siegel. *The Second Kids' World Almanac of Records and Facts.* New York: World Almanac Publications, 1987.

Thompson, C. E. *101 Wacky Facts about Kids.* New York: Scholastic, Inc.,1992.

Varasdi, J. Allen. *Myth Information.* New York: Ballantine Books, 1989.

JANUARY 25
Why are barns red?
Johnny Wonder Question and Answer Book. New York: Playmore, 1984.

Smith, Douglas B. *Ever Wonder Why?* New York: Fawcett Gold Medal, 1992.

JANUARY 26
Which sport started with a fruit basket?
Blumberg, Rhoda, and Leda Blumberg. *Simon and*

Schuster's Book of Facts and Fallacies. New York: Simon and Schuster, 1983.

Caney, Steven. Steven Caney's Invention Book. New York: Workman Publishing, 1985.

King, Norman. The Almanac of Fascinating Beginnings. New York: Citadel Press, 1994.

Smith, Don. How Sports Began. New York: Franklin Watts, 1977.

Varasdi, J. Allen. Myth Information. New York: Ballantine Books, 1989.

Zotti, Ed. Know It All! New York: Ballantine Books, 1993.

JANUARY 27
Who was Chester Greenwood, and why did he cover his ears?
Caney, Steven. Steven Caney's Invention Book. New York: Workman Publishing, 1985.

Gray, Ralph, ed. Small Inventions That Make a Big Difference. Washington, D.C.: The National Geographic Society, 1984.

Harris, Harry. Good Old-Fashioned Yankee Ingenuity. Chelsea, Mich.: Scarborough House, 1990.

McKenzie, E. C. Salted Peanuts: 1800 Little-Known Facts. Grand Rapids, Mich.: Baker Book House, 1972.

McLoone-Basta, Margo, and Alice Siegel. The Second Kids' World Almanac of Records and Facts. New York: World Almanac Publications, 1987.

JANUARY 28
Where did the first little red wagon come from?
Asakawa, Gil, and Leland Rucker. The Toy Book. New York: Alfred A. Knopf, 1992.

JANUARY 29
Who made the first metal detector?
Wallace, Irving, Amy Wallace, and David Wallechinsky. Significa. New York: E. P. Dutton, Inc., 1983.

JANUARY 30
When is it good manners to wipe your fingers on the tablecloth?
Felder, Deborah G. The Kids' World Almanac of History. New York: Pharos Books, 1991.

Giblin, James Cross. From Hand to Mouth, or, How We Invented Knives, Forks, Spoons, and Chopsticks, and the Table Manners to Go with Them. New York: Thomas Y. Crowell, 1987.

JANUARY 31
Why do we call our favorite shopping place the "mall"?
Burnam, Tom. More Misinformation. New York: Ballantine Books, 1980.

Muschell, David. Where in the Word? Roseville, Calif.: Prima Publishing, 1990.

FEBRUARY 1
How did a mistake start the invention of the match?
Ardley, Bridget, and Neil Ardley. The Random House Book of 1001 Questions and Answers. New York: Random House, 1989.

Felder, Deborah G. The Kids' World Almanac of History. New York: Pharos Books, 1991.

Louis, David. 2201 Fascinating Facts. New York: Crown Publishing, 1983.

McKenzie, E. C. Salted Peanuts: 1800 Little-Known Facts. Grand Rapids, Mich.: Baker Book House, 1972.

Robertson, Patrick. The Book of Firsts. New York: Bramhall House, 1974.

FEBRUARY 2
When was a little girl sent through the mail?
Wallace, Irving, Amy Wallace and David Wallechinsky. Significa. New York: E. P. Dutton, Inc., 1983.

Wulffson, Don L. Amazing True Stories. New York: Scholastic, Inc., 1991.

FEBRUARY 3
Why did America destroy its own spaceship?
Goldberg, M. Hirsh. The Blunder Book. New York: William Morrow and Co., 1984.

Harvey, Edmund, ed. Reader's Digest Book of Facts. New York: Reader's Digest Association, 1987.

Leokum, Arkady. The Curious Book. New York: Sterling Publishing Co., 1976.

Louis, David. 2201 Fascinating Facts. New York: Crown Publishing, 1983.

Nussbaum, Hedda, ed. Charlie Brown's Fifth Super Book of Questions and Answers. New York: Random House, 1981.

Sobol, Donald J. Encyclopedia Brown's Second Record Book of Weird and Wonderful Facts. New York: Delacorte Press, 1981.

Williams, Brenda, and Brian Williams. The Random House Book of 1001 Wonders of Science. New York: Random House, 1990.

FEBRUARY 4
Why did a sculptor carve his statues smaller and smaller?
Harvey, Edmund, ed. Reader's Digest Book of Facts. New York: Reader's Digest Association, 1987.

FEBRUARY 5
What should you know about mistletoe?
Blumberg, Rhoda, and Leda Blumberg. Simon and Schuster's Book of Facts and Fallacies. New York: Simon and Schuster, 1983.

Johnny Wonder Question and Answer Book. New York: Playmore, Inc., 1984.

Perko, Marko. Did You Know That . . . ? New York: Berkley Books, 1994.

Smith, Douglas B. More Ever Wonder Why? New York: Fawcett Gold Medal, 1994.

Vogel, Malvina G., ed. The Big Book of Amazing Facts. New York: Playmore, Inc., 1980.

FEBRUARY 6
When was the last time you dropped your pencil and found $40,000?
Sobol, Donald J. Encyclopedia Brown's Third Record Book of Weird and Wonderful Facts. New York: William Morrow and Co., 1985.

FEBRUARY 7
Why would two brothers booby-trap their house?
Adams, Simon, and Lesley Riley, eds. Reader's Digest Facts and Fallacies. New York: Reader's Digest Association, 1988.

Smith, Richard, and Edward Decter. Oops! The Complete Book of Bloopers. New York: The Rutledge Press, 1981.

FEBRUARY 8
Who called 9-1-1?
Felton, Bruce. One of a Kind. New York: William Morrow and Co., 1992.

FEBRUARY 9
What can you do with a pack of camels?
Felton, Bruce. *One of a Kind*. New York: William Morrow and Co., 1992.
Felton, Bruce, and Mark Fowler. *Felton and Fowler's Best, Worst, and Most Unusual*. New York: Thomas Y. Crowell, 1975.
Lurie, Susan, ed. *The Big Book of Amazing Knowledge*. New York: Playmore, Inc., 1987.
Morris, Scot. *The Emperor Who Ate the Bible and More Strange Facts and Useless Information*. New York: Doubleday, 1991.
Perl, Lila. *It Happened in America*. New York: Henry Holt and Co., 1992.
Vogel, Malvina G., ed. *The Big Book of Amazing Facts*. New York: Playmore, Inc., 1980.

FEBRUARY 10
Why are a cat's whiskers better than a man's?
Louis, David. *2201 Fascinating Facts*. New York: Crown Publishing, 1983.
Squire, Dr. Ann. *101 Questions and Answers about Pets and People*. New York: Macmillan Publishing Co., 1988.

FEBRUARY 11
Why do movie scenes start with a black-and-white-striped clapboard?
Smith, Douglas B. *More Ever Wonder Why?* New York: Fawcett Gold Medal, 1994.

FEBRUARY 12
When can colors be confusing?
Goldwyn, Martin M. *How a Fly Walks Upside Down . . . and Other Curious Facts*. New York: Wings Books, 1995.
Meyers, James. *Amazing Facts*. New York: Playmore, Inc., 1986.
———. *The Best Amazing Question and Answer Book*. New York: Playmore, Inc., 1987.
Vogel, Malvina G., ed. *The Big Book of Amazing Facts*. New York: Playmore, Inc., 1980.

FEBRUARY 13
How did clay flowerpots help make buildings better?
Harvey, Edmund, ed. *Reader's Digest Book of Facts*. New York: Reader's Digest Association, 1987.

FEBRUARY 14
Could you be found guilty by reason of rice?
Felton, Bruce, and Mark Fowler. *Felton and Fowler's Best, Worst, and Most Unusual*. New York: Thomas Y. Crowell, 1975.
Fullerton, Timothy T. *Triviata: A Compendium of Useless Information*. New York: Hart Publishing, 1975.

FEBRUARY 15
Why were people buying raccoon tails?
Asakawa, Gil, and Leland Rucker. *The Toy Book*. New York: Alfred A. Knopf, 1992.
Panati, Charles. *Panati's Parade of Fads, Follies, and Manias*. New York: HarperCollins, 1991.

FEBRUARY 16
How are crossword puzzles connected with Christmas?
Burnam, Tom. *The Dictionary of Misinformation*. New York: Ballantine Books, 1975.
Giscard d'Estaing, Valerie-Anne. *The World Almanac Book of Inventions*. New York: World Almanac Publications, 1985.
Harris, Harry. *Good Old-Fashioned Yankee Ingenuity*. Chelsea, Mich.: Scarborough House, 1990.
King, Norman. *The Almanac of Fascinating Beginnings*. New York: Citadel Press, 1994.
Lurie, Susan, ed. *The Big Book of Amazing Knowledge*. New York: Playmore, Inc., 1987.
Panati, Charles. *Panati's Parade of Fads, Follies, and Manias*. New York: HarperCollins, 1991.
Robertson, Patrick. *The Book of Firsts*. New York: Bramhall House, 1974.

FEBRUARY 17
Why did farmers have curfews?
Ayto, John. *Dictionary of Word Origins*. New York: Arcade Publishing, 1990.
Claiborne, Robert. *Loose Cannons and Red Herrings*. New York: W.W. Norton and Co., 1988.
Justice, Dr. David B., ed. *Webster's Word Histories*. Springfield, Mass.: Merriam-Webster, Inc., 1989.
Muschell, David. *Where in the Word?* Roseville, Calif.: Prima Publishing, 1990.
Soukhanov, Anne H., ed. *Word Mysteries and Histories*. Boston: Houghton Mifflin, 1986.
Vanoni, Marvin. *Great Expressions*. New York: William Morrow and Co., 1989.

FEBRUARY 18
Where were houses built roof-first and books read back to front?
Leokum, Arkady. *The Curious Book*. New York: Sterling Publishing, 1976.
Louis, David. *2201 Fascinating Facts*. New York: Crown Publishing, 1983.

FEBRUARY 19
Why did a priest decide to live with lepers?
McLoughlin, E. V., ed. *The Book of Knowledge*, Vol. 7. New York: The Grolier Society, Inc., 1946.
Varasdi, J. Allen. *Myth Information*. New York: Ballantine Books, 1989.

FEBRUARY 20
Why did the United States have a one-day president?
Lurie, Susan, ed. *The Big Book of Amazing Knowledge*. New York: Playmore, Inc., 1987.
Perko, Marko. *Did You Know That . . . ?* New York: Berkley Books, 1994.
Vogel, Malvina G., ed. *The Big Book of Amazing Facts*. New York: Playmore, Inc., 1980.

FEBRUARY 21
Where does dew come from if it doesn't fall from the sky?
Burnam, Tom. *More Misinformation*. New York: Ballantine Books, 1980.
Goldwyn, Martin M. *How a Fly Walks Upside Down . . . and Other Curious Facts*. New York: Wings Books, 1995.
Varasdi, J. Allen. *Myth Information*. New York: Ballantine Books, 1989.

FEBRUARY 22
When can you strike a nerve at the dentist's office?
Burnam, Tom. *The Dictionary of Misinformation*. New York: Ballantine Books, 1975.

FEBRUARY 23
Which president had a giant bathtub?
Asimov, Isaac. *Would You Believe?* New York: Grosset and Dunlap, 1982.
McKenzie, E. C. *Salted Peanuts: 1800 Little-Known Facts.* Grand Rapids, Mich.: Baker Book House, 1972.
Meyers, James. *Eggplants, Elevators, Etc.: An Uncommon History of Common Things.* New York: Hart Publishing Co., 1978.
Sloane, Eric. *ABC Book of Early Americana.* New York: Henry Holt and Co., 1963.

FEBRUARY 24
Can you tell what a bird eats by looking at the bird?
Blumberg, Rhoda, and Leda Blumberg. *Simon and Schuster's Book of Facts and Fallacies.* New York: Simon and Schuster, 1983.
Nussbaum, Hedda, ed. *Charlie Brown's Fifth Super Book of Questions and Answers.* New York: Random House, 1981.

FEBRUARY 25
How was the toothbrush invented?
Felder, Deborah G. *The Kids' World Almanac of History.* New York: Pharos Books, 1991.
McLoone-Basta, Margo, and Alice Siegel. *The Kids' World Almanac of Records and Facts.* New York: World Almanac Publications, 1985.
Owl magazine, eds. *The Kids' Question and Answer Book Two.* New York: Grosset and Dunlap, 1988.
Wulffson, Don L. *Extraordinary Stories Behind the Invention of Ordinary Things.* New York: Lothrop, Lee, and Shepard Books, 1981.

FEBRUARY 26
What makes a Mexican jumping bean jump?
Blumberg, Rhoda, and Leda Blumberg. *Simon and Schuster's Book of Facts and Fallacies.* New York: Simon and Schuster, 1983.
Goldwyn, Martin M. *How a Fly Walks Upside Down . . . and Other Curious Facts.* New York: Wings Books, 1995.
Manchester, Richard B. *Incredible Facts.* New York: Galahad Books, 1985.

FEBRUARY 27
What did a president of the United States, a candy seller, and a stuffed animal have to do with a favorite children's toy?
Asakawa, Gil, and Leland Rucker. *The Toy Book.* New York: Alfred A. Knopf, 1992.
Harris, Harry. *Good Old-Fashioned Yankee Ingenuity.* Chelsea, Mich.: Scarborough House, 1990.
Sanders, Deidre, et al. *Would You Believe This, Too?* New York: Sterling Publishing Co., 1976.

FEBRUARY 28
Why do farmers want their calves to swallow magnets?
Chrystie, Frances N. *The First Book of Surprising Facts.* New York: Franklin Watts, 1956.
Louis, David. *2201 Fascinating Facts.* New York: Crown Publishing, 1983.

MARCH 1
Can a beaver make a tree fall in just the right spot?
Blumberg, Rhoda, and Leda Blumberg. *Simon and Schuster's Book of Facts and Fallacies.* New York: Simon and Schuster, 1983.

Burnam, Tom. *The Dictionary of Misinformation.* New York: Ballantine Books, 1975.
Owl magazine, eds. *The Kids' Question and Answer Book Three.* New York: Grosset and Dunlap, 1990.
Rosenbloom, Joseph. *Bananas Don't Grow on Trees: A Guide to Popular Misconceptions.* New York: Sterling Publishing Co., 1978.
Tison, Annette, and Talus Taylor. *The Big Book of Amazing Animal Behavior.* New York: Grosset and Dunlap, 1986.

MARCH 2
Why keep a broken bell?
Giblin, James Cross. *Fireworks, Picnics, and Flags: The Story of Fourth of July Symbols.* New York: Houghton Mifflin Co., 1983.
Wallace, Irving, Amy Wallace, and David Wallechinsky. *Significa.* New York: E. P. Dutton, Inc., 1983.

MARCH 3
Why did a dog want to live in a graveyard?
Asimov, Isaac. *Would You Believe?* New York: Grosset and Dunlap, 1982.
Wallace, Irving, Amy Wallace, and David Wallechinsky. *Significa.* New York: E. P. Dutton, Inc., 1983.

MARCH 4
Why would a bird need goggles?
Johnny Wonder Question and Answer Book. New York: Playmore, Inc., 1984.

MARCH 5
How did Monopoly become a game?
Aaseng, Nathan. *The Rejects.* Minneapolis: Lerner Publications, 1989.
Asakawa, Gil, and Leland Rucker. *The Toy Book.* New York: Alfred A. Knopf, 1992.
Elwood, Ann, and Carol Orsag. *Macmillan Illustrated Almanac for Kids.* New York: Macmillan Publishing Co., 1981.
Felder, Deborah G. *The Kids' World Almanac of History.* New York: Pharos Books, 1991.
Goldberg, M. Hirsh. *The Blunder Book.* New York: William Morrow and Co., 1984.
Harris, Harry. *Good Old-Fashioned Yankee Ingenuity.* Chelsea, Mich.: Scarborough House, 1990.
Harvey, Edmund, ed. *Reader's Digest Book of Facts.* New York: Reader's Digest Association, 1987.
King, Norman. *The Almanac of Fascinating Beginnings.* New York: Citadel Press, 1994.
Martinet, Jeanne. *The Year You Were Born: A Day-to-Day Record of 1985.* New York: Tambourine Books, 1992.
Martinet, Jeanne. *The Year You Were Born: A Day-to-Day Record of 1986.* New York: Tambourine Books, 1993.
McLoone-Basta, Margo, and Alice Siegel. *The Second Kids' World Almanac of Records and Facts.* New York: World Almanac Publications, 1987.
Panati, Charles. *Panati's Extraordinary Origins of Everyday Things.* New York: Harper and Row, 1987.
Polley, Jane, ed. *Stories Behind Everyday Things.* New York: Reader's Digest Association, 1980.
Robertson, Patrick. *The Book of Firsts.* New York: Bramhall House, 1974.

MARCH 6
Why is the Oscar named after a farmer?
Morris, Scot. *The Emperor Who Ate the Bible and More Strange Facts and Useless Information.* New York: Doubleday, 1991.

Rosenbloom, Joseph. *Polar Bears Like It Hot.* New York: Sterling Publishing Co., 1980.

MARCH 7
Is there air pollution in outer space?
Wallace, Irving, Amy Wallace, and David Wallechinsky. *Significa.* New York: E. P. Dutton, Inc., 1983.

MARCH 8
Why do people always get onto a horse from the left side?
Smith, Douglas B. *Ever Wonder Why?* New York: Fawcett Gold Medal, 1992.
Tuleja, Tad. *Curious Customs.* New York: Harmony Books, 1987.
Vogel, Malvina G., ed. *The Big Book of Amazing Facts.* New York: Playmore, 1980.

MARCH 9
What would you do if you went to a restaurant and the menu offered steamed kangaroo and rhinoceros pie?
Lurie, Susan, ed. *The Big Book of Amazing Knowledge.* New York: Playmore, Inc., 1987.

MARCH 10
Why does a pencil have six sides?
Chrystie, Frances N. *The First Book of Surprising Facts.* New York: Franklin Watts, 1956.
Guinness Book of Trivia Records. New York: Sterling Publishing Co., 1985.
McKenzie, E. C. *Salted Peanuts: 1800 Little-Known Facts.* Grand Rapids, Mich.: Baker Book House, 1972.
Smith, Douglas B. *Ever Wonder Why?* New York: Fawcett Gold Medal, 1992.
Wulffson, Don L. *Extraordinary Stories Behind the Invention of Ordinary Things.* New York: Lothrop, Lee, and Shepard Books, 1981.

MARCH 11
Why do we have white half-moon-shaped marks at the base of our fingernails?
Ardley, Bridget, and Neil Ardley. *The Random House Book of 1001 Questions and Answers.* New York: Random House, 1989.
Burnam, Tom. *The Dictionary of Misinformation.* New York: Ballantine Books, 1975.
Feldman, David. *Why Do Clocks Run Clockwise? and Other Imponderables.* New York: Harper and Row, 1987.
Louis, David. *2201 Fascinating Facts.* New York: Crown Publishing, 1983.
McKenzie, E. C. *Salted Peanuts: 1800 Little-Known Facts.* Grand Rapids, Mich.: Baker Book House, 1972.
McLoone-Basta, Margo, and Alice Siegel. *The Second Kids' World Almanac of Records and Facts.* New York: World Almanac Publications, 1987.
Rowan, Peter. *Can You Get Warts from Touching Toads? Ask Dr. Pete.* New York: Julian Messner, 1986.

MARCH 12
Why is a bunch of lions called a "pride"?
Achenbach, Joel. *Why Things Are: Answers to Every Essential Question in Life.* New York: Ballantine Books, 1991.
Louis, David. *2201 Fascinating Facts.* New York: Crown Publishing, 1983.

MARCH 13
Who was Dr. Pepper?
Campbell, Hannah. *Why Did They Name It . . . ?* New York: Fleet Publishing, 1964.
Caney, Steven. *Steven Caney's Invention Book.* New York: Workman Publishing, 1985.
Feldman, David. *Do Penguins Have Knees?* New York: HarperCollins, 1991.

MARCH 14
Why were the first napkins as big as towels?
Felder, Deborah G. *The Kids' World Almanac of History.* New York: Pharos Books, 1991.
Panati, Charles. *Panati's Extraordinary Origins of Everyday Things.* New York: Harper and Row, 1987.

MARCH 15
What's the spin on revolving doors?
Zotti, Ed. *Know It All!* New York: Ballantine Books, 1993.

MARCH 16
Why do we drive on the right side of the road?
McCutcheon, Marc. *The Writer's Guide to Everyday Life in the 1800s.* Cincinnati, Ohio: Writer's Digest Books, 1993.
Smith, Douglas B. *Ever Wonder Why?* New York: Fawcett Gold Medal, 1992.
Tuleja, Tad. *Curious Customs.* New York: Harmony Books, 1987.
Vogel, Malvina G., ed. *The Big Book of Amazing Facts.* New York: Playmore, Inc., 1980.

MARCH 17
How did a brilliant man's name develop into "dunce"?
Perko, Marko. *Did You Know That . . . ?* New York: Berkley Books, 1994.
Smith, Douglas B. *Ever Wonder Why?* New York: Fawcett Gold Medal, 1992.
Wallace, Irving, Amy Wallace, and David Wallechinsky. *Significa.* New York: E. P. Dutton, Inc., 1983.

MARCH 18
Why did the Dutch build a memorial for a person who never existed?
Morris, Scot. *The Emperor Who Ate the Bible and More Strange Facts and Useless Information.* New York: Doubleday, 1991.
Tuleja, Tad. *Fabulous Fallacies.* New York: Harmony Books, 1982.

MARCH 19
Which country has a pancake party every year?
Martinet, Jeanne. *The Year You Were Born: A Day-to-Day Record of 1984.* New York: Tambourine Books, 1992.
Nussbaum, Hedda, ed. *Charlie Brown's Fifth Super Book of Questions and Answers.* New York: Random House, 1981.

MARCH 20
What do roofs and ears have in common?
Editors of American Heritage Dictionaries. *Word Mysteries and Histories.* Boston: Houghton Mifflin, 1986.
Funk, Charles Earle. *Horsefeathers and Other Curious Words.* New York: Harper and Row, 1958.
Smith, Douglas B. *More Ever Wonder Why?* New York: Fawcett Gold Medal, 1994.

MARCH 21
Why would a man be glad to live in a cabinet?
Wallace, Irving, Amy Wallace, and David Wallechinsky. *Significa.* New York: E. P. Dutton, Inc., 1983.

MARCH 22
When did paying a library fine make history?
Lee, Stan. *Stan Lee Presents the Best of the Worst.* New York: Harper and Row, 1979.
Pile, Stephen. *The Book of Heroic Failures.* London: Routledge and Kegan Paul, Ltd., 1979.

MARCH 23
What plant grows only after being burned by a fire?
Harvey, Edmund, ed. *Reader's Digest Book of Facts.* New York: Reader's Digest Association, 1987.

MARCH 24
What did a flag at half-mast used to mean?
Rovin, Jeff. *The Unbelievable Truth!* New York: The Penguin Group, 1994.
Smith, Douglas B. *Ever Wonder Why?* New York: Fawcett Gold Medal, 1992.
Tuleja, Tad. *Curious Customs.* New York: Harmony Books, 1987.

MARCH 25
Why aren't there any fleas at a flea market?
Smith, Douglas B. *More Ever Wonder Why?* New York: Fawcett Gold Medal, 1994.

MARCH 26
Are you seeing things?
Zotti, Ed. *Know It All!* New York: Ballantine Books, 1993.

MARCH 27
Which flower looks like a lion's teeth?
Editors of American Heritage Dictionaries. *Word Mysteries and Histories.* Boston: Houghton Mifflin, 1986.
Muschell, David. *Where in the Word?* Roseville, Calif.: Prima Publishing, 1990.

MARCH 28
When did people let their fingers do the talking?
Blumberg, Rhoda, and Leda Blumberg. *Simon and Schuster's Book of Facts and Fallacies.* New York: Simon and Schuster, 1983.
Fabell, Walter C. *Nature's Clues.* New York: Hastings House, 1964.
Lurie, Susan, ed. *The Big Book of Amazing Knowledge.* New York: Playmore, Inc., 1987.
Robertson, Patrick. *The Book of Firsts.* New York: Bramhall House, 1964.
Rosenbloom, Joseph. *Polar Bears Like It Hot.* New York: Sterling Publishing Co., 1980.

MARCH 29
Why did W. C. Fields open so many bank accounts?
Wallace, Irving, Amy Wallace, and David Wallechinsky. *Significa.* New York: E. P. Dutton, Inc., 1983.

MARCH 30
Why was the general always absent during roll call?
Wallace, Irving, Amy Wallace, and David Wallechinsky. *Significa.* New York: E. P. Dutton, Inc., 1983.

MARCH 31
Why would people be accused of stealing their own car?
Sobol, Donald J. *Encyclopedia Brown's Book of Wacky Cars.* New York: William Morrow and Co., 1987.

APRIL 1
When did spaghetti grow on trees?
Adams, Simon, and Lesley Riley, eds. *Reader's Digest Facts and Fallacies.* New York: Reader's Digest Association, 1988.

APRIL 2
Why did a cookbook include a recipe for an explosion?
Goldberg, M. Hirsh. *The Blunder Book.* New York: William Morrow and Co., 1984.

APRIL 3
Can someone be double-jointed?
Blumberg, Rhoda, and Leda Blumberg. *Simon and Schuster's Book of Facts and Fallacies.* New York: Simon and Schuster, 1983.
Gottlieb, William P. *Science Facts You Won't Believe.* New York: Franklin Watts, 1983.

APRIL 4
How can you read when you can't even see?
Buchman, Dian Dincin, and Seli Groves. *What If? Fifty Discoveries That Changed the World.* New York: Scholastic, Inc., 1988.
Gray, Ralph, ed. *Small Inventions That Make a Big Difference.* Washington, D.C.: The National Geographic Society, 1984.
McLoone-Basta, Margo, and Alice Siegel. *The Kids' World Almanac of Records and Facts.* New York: World Almanac Publications, 1985.
McLoone-Basta, Margo, and Alice Siegel. *The Second Kids' World Almanac of Records and Facts.* New York: World Almanac Publications, 1987.

APRIL 5
When do parents want their kids to make noise?
Elwood, Ann, and Carol Orsag. *Macmillan Illustrated Almanac for Kids.* New York: Macmillan Publishing Co., 1981.

APRIL 6
How could the idea of bungee jumping be over one hundred years old?
De Vries, Leonard. *Victorian Inventions.* New York: American Heritage Press, 1971.
Murphy, Jim. *Guess Again: More Weird and Wacky Inventions.* New York: Bradbury Press, 1986.

APRIL 7
If you burn your hand, what is the best thing to do?
Simon, Seymour. *Body Sense/Body Nonsense.* New York: J. B. Lippincott, 1981.

APRIL 8
How did electricity surprise a whole crowd?
De Vries, Leonard. *Victorian Inventions.* New York: American Heritage Press, 1971.

APRIL 9
Why do boys' and girls' shirts button on different sides?
Panati, Charles. *Panati's Extraordinary Origins of Everyday Things.* New York: Harper and Row, 1987.

Smith, Douglas B. *Ever Wonder Why?* New York: Fawcett Gold Medal, 1992.

APRIL 10
Why were M&M's invented?
Choron, Sandra. *The Big Book of Kids' Lists.* New York: World Almanac Publications, 1985.
Felder, Deborah G. *The Kids' World Almanac of History.* New York: Pharos Books, 1991.
Harris, Harry. *Good Old-Fashioned Yankee Ingenuity.* Chelsea, Mich.: Scarborough House, 1990.
King, Norman. *The Almanac of Fascinating Beginnings.* New York: Citadel Press, 1994.
Louis, David. *2201 Fascinating Facts.* New York: Crown Publishing, 1983.
McLoone-Basta, Margo, and Alice Siegel. *The Kids' World Almanac of Records and Facts.* New York: World Almanac Publications, 1985.
Varasdi, J. Allen. *Myth Information.* New York: Ballantine Books, 1989.

APRIL 11
Why can't you feel your foot when it falls asleep?
Zotti, Ed. *Know It All!* New York: Ballantine Books, 1993.

APRIL 12
Why are piano keys black and white?
Smith, Douglas B. *Ever Wonder Why?* New York: Fawcett Gold Medal, 1992.

APRIL 13
Which cartoon was also a puzzle?
Morris, Scot. *The Emperor Who Ate the Bible and More Strange Facts and Useless Information.* New York: Doubleday, 1991.

APRIL 14
What really makes those noises you hear at night?
Chrystie, Frances N. *The First Book of Surprising Facts.* New York: Franklin Watts, 1956.
Vogel, Malvina G., ed. *The Big Book of Amazing Facts.* New York: Playmore, 1980.

APRIL 15
How was a person caught by a plane?
Felton, Bruce. *One of a Kind.* New York: William Morrow and Co., 1992.
Manchester, Richard B. *Incredible Facts.* New York: Galahad Books, 1985.

APRIL 16
How did noodles get their names?
Felder, Deborah G. *The Kids' World Almanac of History.* New York: Pharos Books, 1991.
Muschell, David. *Where in the Word?* Roseville, Calif.: Prima Publishing, 1990.

APRIL 17
Why do our noses have little hairs in them?
Louis, David. *2201 Fascinating Facts.* New York: Crown Publishing, 1983.
Whitfield, Philip and Ruth. *Why Do Our Bodies Stop Growing? Questions About Human Anatomy Answered by the Natural History Museum.* New York: Viking Kestrel, 1988.

APRIL 18
Who froze the first Popsicle?
Choron, Sandra. *The Big Book of Kids' Lists.* New York: World Almanac Publications, 1985.

Felder, Deborah G. *The Kids' World Almanac of History.* New York: Pharos Books, 1991.
Jones, Charlotte Foltz. *Mistakes That Worked.* New York: Doubleday, 1991.
McLoone-Basta, Margo, and Alice Siegel. *The Kids' World Almanac of Records and Facts.* New York: World Almanac Publications, 1985.

APRIL 19
Why can dogs smell things better than people can?
Louis, David. *2201 Fascinating Facts.* New York: Crown Publishing, 1983.
Owl magazine, eds. *The Kids' Question and Answer Book Two.* New York: Grosset and Dunlap, 1988.

APRIL 20
Does an ostrich really bury its head in the sand?
Blumberg, Rhoda, and Leda Blumberg. *Simon and Schuster's Book of Facts and Fallacies.* New York: Simon and Schuster, 1983.
Manchester, Richard B. *Incredible Facts.* New York: Galahad Books, 1985.
Simon, Seymour. *Animal Fact/Animal Fable.* New York: Crown Publishers, 1979.
Varasdi, J. Allen. *Myth Information.* New York: Ballantine Books, 1989.
Vogel, Malvina G., ed. *The Big Book of Amazing Facts.* New York: Playmore, Inc., 1980.

APRIL 21
How did riches escape a man who started a gold rush?
Harvey, Edmund, ed. *Reader's Digest Book of Facts.* New York: Reader's Digest Association, 1987.

APRIL 22
Why don't we eat goldfish?
Panati, Charles. *The Browser's Book of Beginnings.* Boston: Houghton Mifflin, 1984.

APRIL 23
How did golf courses end up with eighteen holes?
Feldman, David. *Why Do Clocks Run Clockwise? and Other Imponderables.* New York: Harper and Row, 1987.
Perko, Marko. *Did You Know That . . . ?* New York: Berkley Books, 1994.
Phillips, Louis. *A Kids' Book of Lists: The World by Sevens.* New York: Franklin Watts, 1981.
Smith, Douglas B. *Ever Wonder Why?* New York: Fawcett Gold Medal, 1992.

APRIL 24
How did a fruit ruin a publicity stunt?
Felton, Bruce. *One of a Kind.* New York: William Morrow and Co., 1992.

APRIL 25
What causes gray hair?
Alway, Carol, et al. *Strange Stories, Amazing Facts.* New York: Reader's Digest Association, 1976.
Montagu, Ashley, and Edward Darling. *The Prevalence of Nonsense.* New York: Harper and Row, 1967.
Rovin, Jeff. *The Unbelievable Truth!* New York: The Penguin Group, 1994.
Smith, Douglas B. *Ever Wonder Why?* New York: Fawcett Gold Medal, 1992.
Varasdi, J. Allen. *Myth Information.* New York: Ballantine Books, 1989.

Vogel, Malvina G., ed. *The Big Book of Amazing Facts.* New York: Playmore, Inc., 1980.

APRIL 26
Why were two security guards hired to stare up all day?
Lee, Stan. *Stan Lee Presents the Best of the Worst.* New York: Harper and Row, 1979.
Louis, David. *2201 Fascinating Facts.* New York: Crown Publishing, 1983.
Pringle, Laurence. *"The Earth Is Flat" and Other Great Mistakes.* New York: William Morrow and Company, 1983.
Smith, Richard, and Edward Decter. *Oops! The Complete Book of Bloopers.* New York: The Rutledge Press, 1981.

APRIL 27
What are some predictable differences in people's hands?
Louis, David. *2201 Fascinating Facts.* New York: Crown Publishing, 1983.
Rovin, Jeff. *The Unbelievable Truth!* New York: The Penguin Group, 1994.
Sobol, Donald J. *Encyclopedia Brown's Third Record Book of Weird and Wonderful Facts.* New York: William Morrow and Co., 1985.

APRIL 28
When was Hollywood a happy little hamlet?
Flexner, Stuart Berg. *Listening to America.* New York: Simon and Schuster, 1982.
Harris, Harry. *Good Old-Fashioned Yankee Ingenuity.* Chelsea, Mich.: Scarborough House, 1990.
Louis, David. *2201 Fascinating Facts.* New York: Crown Publishing, 1983.
Smith, Douglas B. *More Ever Wonder Why?* New York: Fawcett Gold Medal, 1994.
Varasdi, J. Allen. *Myth Information.* New York: Ballantine Books, 1989.
Watkins, T. H. *California, An Illustrated History.* Palo Alto, Calif.: American West Publishing Company, 1973.

APRIL 29
Why doesn't humble pie taste good?
Alway, Carol, et al. *Strange Stories, Amazing Facts.* New York: Reader's Digest Association, 1976.
Burnam, Tom. *The Dictionary of Misinformation.* New York: Ballantine Books, 1975.
Limburg, Peter R. *Stories Behind Words.* New York: H. W. Wilson, 1986.
Smith, Douglas B. *Ever Wonder Why?* New York: Fawcett Gold Medal, 1992.

APRIL 30
How can you get to sleep without counting sheep?
Boyd, L. M. *Boyd's Book of Odd Facts.* New York: Sterling Publishing, 1979.
Florman, Monte. *1,001 Helpful Tips, Facts, and Hints from Consumer Reports.* Mount Vernon, N.Y.: Consumers Union of U.S., Inc., 1989.

MAY 1
What do the letters IOU mean?
Boyd, L. M. *Boyd's Book of Odd Facts.* New York: Sterling Publishing, 1979.
Varasdi, J. Allen. *Myth Information.* New York: Ballantine Books, 1989.

MAY 2
Why has ironing always been a chore?
Felder, Deborah G. *The Kids' World Almanac of History.* New York: Pharos Books, 1991.
Panati, Charles. *Panati's Extraordinary Origins of Everyday Things.* New York: Harper and Row, 1987.

MAY 3
How did the Jacuzzi get its name?
Adams, Simon, and Lesley Riley, eds. *Reader's Digest Facts and Fallacies.* New York: Reader's Digest Association, 1988.
Harris, Harry. *Good Old-Fashioned Yankee Ingenuity.* Chelsea, Mich.: Scarborough House, 1990.

MAY 4
When did a painting turn into a puzzle?
Louis, David. *2201 Fascinating Facts.* New York: Crown Publishing, 1983.

MAY 5
Is it possible to learn a language overnight?
Louis, David. *2201 Fascinating Facts.* New York: Crown Publishing, 1983.
Meyers, James. *The Best Amazing Question and Answer Book.* New York: Playmore, Inc., 1987.

MAY 6
How could you commit a crime with a pillow?
Smith, Douglas B. *Ever Wonder Why?* New York: Fawcett Gold Medal, 1992.

MAY 7
How can you move an elephant?
Lurie, Susan, ed. *The Big Book of Amazing Knowledge.* New York: Playmore, Inc., 1987.

MAY 8
How did a toy stop an army?
Wallace, Irving, Amy Wallace, and David Wallechinsky. *Significa.* New York: E. P. Dutton, Inc., 1983.

MAY 9
How did the propeller of a ship help invent the cash register?
Buchman, Dian Dincin, and Seli Groves. *What If? Fifty Discoveries That Changed the World.* New York: Scholastic, Inc., 1988.
Gray, Ralph, ed. *Small Inventions That Make a Big Difference.* Washington, D.C.: The National Geographic Society, 1984.
Harris, Harry. *Good Old-Fashioned Yankee Ingenuity.* Chelsea, Mich.: Scarborough House, 1990.
Robertson, Patrick. *The Book of Firsts.* New York: Bramhall House, 1974.
Smith, Douglas B. *Ever Wonder Why?* New York: Fawcett Gold Medal, 1992.

MAY 10
What haven't you noticed when watching the clock?
Leokum, Arkady. *The Curious Book.* New York: Sterling Publishing Co., 1976.
Zotti, Ed. *Know It All!* New York: Ballantine Books, 1993.

MAY 11
Why does a cat lick like that?
Squire, Ann. *101 Questions and Answers about Pets and People.* New York: Macmillan Publishing Co., 1988.

MAY 12
When did a softball player catch a flying baby?
Wulffson, Don L. *Amazing True Stories.* New York: Scholastic, 1991.

MAY 13
Since fish are always in schools, aren't they smart?
Achenbach, Joel. *Why Things Are: Answers to Every Essential Question in Life.* New York: Ballantine Books, 1991.

MAY 14
How did the cavemen build their caves?
Goldwyn, Martin M. *How a Fly Walks Upside Down . . . and Other Curious Facts.* New York: Wings Books, 1995.
Nussbaum, Hedda, ed. *Charlie Brown's Fifth Super Book of Questions and Answers.* New York: Random House, 1981.

MAY 15
Why do chickens wear contact lenses?
Sobol, Donald J. *Encyclopedia Brown's Second Record Book of Weird and Wonderful Facts.* New York: Delacorte Press, 1981.

MAY 16
If someone told you to be quiet, would you never speak again?
Manchester, Richard B. *Incredible Facts.* New York: Galahad Books, 1985.

MAY 17
If you lived before locks were invented, how could you keep yourself and your things protected?
Jupo, Frank. *The Story of Things.* New Jersey: Prentice Hall, 1972.

MAY 18
What kind of fire alarm would be foolproof?
Felton, Bruce. *One of a Kind.* New York: William Morrow and Co., 1992.

MAY 19
What is a passport?
Adams, Simon, and Lesley Riley, eds. *Reader's Digest Facts and Fallacies.* New York: Reader's Digest Association, 1988.

MAY 20
Why are the letters on a computer keyboard all mixed up?
Meyers, James. *Eggplants, Elevators, Etc.: An Uncommon History of Common Things.* New York: Hart Publishing Co., 1978.
Pringle, Laurence. *"The Earth Is Flat" and Other Great Mistakes.* New York: William Morrow and Co., 1983.

MAY 21
Why were people lined up just to buy a ballpoint pen?
Buchman, Dian Dincin, and Seli Groves. *What If? Fifty Discoveries That Changed the World.* New York: Scholastic, Inc., 1988.
Caney, Steven. *Steven Caney's Invention Book.* New York: Workman Publishing, 1985.
Gray, Ralph, ed. *Small Inventions That Make a Big Difference.* Washington, D.C.: The National Geographic Society, 1984.
Kaufman, Joe. *Joe Kaufman's What Makes It Go? What Makes It Work? What Makes It Fly? What Makes It Float?* New York: Golden Press, 1971.
Morris, Scot. *The Emperor Who Ate the Bible and More Strange Facts and Useless Information.* New York: Doubleday, 1991.
Polley, Jane, ed. *Stories Behind Everyday Things.* New York: Reader's Digest Association, 1980.
Robertson, Patrick. *The Book of Firsts.* New York: Bramhall House, 1974.
Rosenbloom, Joseph. *Polar Bears Like It Hot.* New York: Sterling Publishing Co., 1980.

MAY 22
Which two letters have been left off the telephone, and why?
Rovin, Jeff. *The Unbelievable Truth!* New York: Penguin Books, 1994.
Smith, Douglas B. *More Ever Wonder Why?* New York: Fawcett Gold Medal, 1994.
Zotti, Ed. *Know It All!* New York: Ballantine Books, 1993.

MAY 23
Why do rabbits wiggle their noses?
Owl magazine, eds. *The Kids' Question and Answer Book Two.* New York: Grosset and Dunlap, 1988.
People, Places, and Things. Illinois: Publications International, Ltd., 1992.
Squire, Ann. *101 Questions and Answers about Pets and People.* New York: Macmillan Publishing Co., 1988.

MAY 24
What misunderstanding created the piggy bank?
Jones, Charlotte Foltz. *Mistakes That Worked.* New York: Doubleday, 1991.

MAY 25
How can a plant get its own water?
Harvey, Edmund, ed. *Reader's Digest Book of Facts.* New York: Reader's Digest Association, 1987.
Manchester, Richard B. *Incredible Facts.* New York: Galahad Books, 1985.

MAY 26
When did the whole world have recess at the same time?
Felton, Bruce. *One of a Kind.* New York: William Morrow and Co., 1992.
McLoone-Basta, Margo, and Alice Siegel. *The Second Kids' World Almanac of Records and Facts.* New York: World Almanac Publications, 1987.

MAY 27
When did an umbrella make people laugh?
Buchman, Dian Dincin, and Seli Groves. *What If? Fifty Discoveries That Changed the World.* New York: Scholastic, Inc., 1988.
Felder, Deborah G. *The Kids' World Almanac of History.* New York: Pharos Books, 1991.
Gray, Ralph, ed. *Small Inventions That Make a Big Difference.* Washington, D.C.: The National Geographic Society, 1984.
Meyers, James. *Amazing Facts.* New York: Playmore, Inc., 1986.
Meyers, James. *Eggplants, Elevators, Etc.: An Uncommon History of Common Things.* New York: Hart Publishing Co., 1978.
Robertson, Patrick. *The Book of Firsts.* New York: Bramhall House, 1974.

MAY 28
What lieutenant wouldn't stop fighting World War II?
Meyers, James. *Amazing Facts.* New York: Playmore, Inc., 1986.
Pile, Stephen. *The Book of Heroic Failures.* London: Routledge and Kegan Paul, Ltd., 1979.
Pringle, Laurence. *"The Earth Is Flat" and Other Great Mistakes.* New York: William Morrow and Co., 1983.

MAY 29
Why did one letter take seven years to reach the White House?
Sobol, Donald J. *Encyclopedia Brown's Second Record Book of Weird and Wonderful Facts.* New York: Delacorte Press, 1981.

MAY 30
What American pastime started with a garage door and a projector?
Harris, Harry. *Good Old-Fashioned Yankee Ingenuity.* Chelsea, Mich.: Scarborough House, 1990.
King, Norman. *The Almanac of Fascinating Beginnings.* New York: Citadel Press, 1994.
Tuleja, Tad. *Curious Customs.* New York: Harmony Books, 1987.

MAY 31
What is the surprise ingredient in your cereal?
Adams, Cecil. *Return of the Straight Dope.* New York: Ballantine Books, 1994.
Felton, Bruce. *One of a Kind.* New York: William Morrow and Co., 1992.

JUNE 1
When was delivering mail a challenge for mail carriers?
Schreiber, Brad. *Weird Wonders and Bizarre Blunders.* New York: Simon and Schuster, 1989.
Smith, Douglas B. *More Ever Wonder Why?* New York: Fawcett Gold Medal, 1994.

JUNE 2
What can happen if you have only one copy of your manuscript?
Goodenough, Simon. *1500 Fascinating Facts.* London: Treasure Press, 1987.
Pile, Stephen. *The Book of Heroic Failures.* London: Routledge and Kegan Paul, Ltd., 1979.
Smith, Richard, and Edward Decter. *Oops! The Complete Book of Bloopers.* New York: The Rutledge Press, 1981.

JUNE 3
How did a nose and fingertips create measurements?
Alway, Carol, et al. *Strange Stories, Amazing Facts.* New York: Reader's Digest Association, 1976.
Feldman, David. *Why Do Clocks Run Clockwise? and Other Imponderables.* New York: Harper and Row, 1987.
How Things Change. Chicago: Field Enterprises Educational Corporation, 1971.
Lurie, Susan, ed. *The Big Book of Amazing Knowledge.* New York: Playmore, Inc., 1987.
Panati, Charles. *The Browser's Book of Beginnings.* Boston: Houghton Mifflin, 1984.
Sanders, Deidre, et al. *Would You Believe This, Too?* New York: Sterling Publishing Co., 1976.

Seuling, Barbara. *You Can't Sneeze with Your Eyes Open.* New York: E. P. Dutton, Inc., 1986.
Smith, Douglas B. *Ever Wonder Why?* New York: Fawcett Gold Medal, 1992.
Vogel, Malvina G., ed. *The Big Book of Amazing Facts.* New York: Playmore, Inc., 1980.

JUNE 4
Why does metal feel colder than wood?
Ardley, Bridget, and Neil Ardley. *The Random House Book of 1001 Questions and Answers.* New York: Random House, 1989.

JUNE 5
What billion-dollar industry was created from paper cups and milk shakes?
Aaseng, Nathan. *The Unsung Heroes.* Minneapolis: Lerner Publications, 1989.
Giscard d'Estaing, Valerie-Anne. *The World Almanac Book of Inventions.* New York: World Almanac Publications, 1985.
Harris, Harry. *Good Old-Fashioned Yankee Ingenuity.* Chelsea, Mich.: Scarborough House, 1990.
Landau, Irwin, ed. *I'll Buy That.* New York: Consumer Reports, 1986.
Meyers, James. *Eggplants, Elevators, Etc.: An Uncommon History of Common Things.* New York: Hart Publishing Co., 1978.
McLoone-Basta, Margo, and Alice Siegel. *The Kids' World Almanac of Records and Facts.* New York: World Almanac Publications, 1985.
Morgan, Hal. *Symbols of America.* New York: Viking, 1986.
Patton, Phil. *Made in U.S.A.: The Secret Histories of the Things That Made America.* New York: Grove/Atlantic Monthly, 1992.
Sutton, Caroline. *How Did They Do That?* New York: William Morrow and Co., 1984.

JUNE 6
What popular game began on the grounds of a hotel?
Garrison, Webb. *Why Didn't I Think of That? From Alarm Clocks to Zippers.* Englewood Cliffs, N.J.: Prentice Hall, Inc., 1977.
Harris, Harry. *Good Old-Fashioned Yankee Ingenuity.* Chelsea, Mich.: Scarborough House, 1990.
Panati, Charles. *Panati's Parade of Fads, Follies, and Manias.* New York: HarperCollins, 1991.

JUNE 7
Where does the term "hangnail" come from?
Burnam, Tom. *The Dictionary of Misinformation.* New York: Ballantine Books, 1975.
Morris, William, and Mary Morris. *Morris Dictionary of Word and Phrase Origins.* 2d ed. New York: HarperCollins, 1988.

JUNE 8
Where would you find a nest egg?
Morris, William, and Mary Morris. *Morris Dictionary of Word and Phrase Origins.* 2d ed. New York: HarperCollins, 1988.

JUNE 9
How did a captive audience escape from the singing emperor?
Asimov, Isaac. *Would You Believe?* New York: Grosset and Dunlap, 1982.

Tuleja, Tad. *The New York Public Library Book of Popular Americana*. New York: Macmillan, 1994.

JUNE 10
When was Heidi the most unpopular movie on television?
Goldberg, M. Hirsh. *The Blunder Book*. New York: William Morrow and Co., 1984.

JUNE 11
Why don't doctors wear white like nurses?
Feldman, David. *Why Do Clocks Run Clockwise? and Other Imponderables*. New York: Harper and Row, 1987.

JUNE 12
What do checkers and cookies have in common?
Varasdi, J. Allen. *Myth Information*. New York: Ballantine Books, 1989.

JUNE 13
How did chop suey get its name?
Harris, Harry. *Good Old-Fashioned Yankee Ingenuity*. Chelsea, Mich.: Scarborough House, 1990.
Louis, David. *2201 Fascinating Facts*. New York: Crown Publishing, 1983.
Perko, Marko. *Did You Know That . . . ?* New York: Berkley Books, 1994.
Rovin, Jeff. *The Unbelievable Truth!* New York: Penguin Books, 1994.
Varasdi, J. Allen. *Myth Information*. New York: Ballantine Books, 1989.
Vogel, Malvina G., ed. *The Big Book of Amazing Facts*. New York: Playmore, Inc., 1980.

JUNE 14
Why did Cinderella wear glass slippers?
Goldberg, M. Hirsh. *The Blunder Book*. New York: William Morrow and Co., 1984.
Jones, Charlotte Foltz. *Mistakes That Worked*. New York: Doubleday, 1991.
Rawson, Hugh. *Devious Derivations*. New York: Crown Trade Paperbacks, 1994.
Varasdi, J. Allen. *Myth Information*. New York: Ballantine Books, 1989.

JUNE 15
What made feeding babies more fun?
Aaseng, Nathan. *The Problem Solvers*. Minneapolis: Lerner Publications, 1989.
Burnam, Tom. *More Misinformation*. New York: Ballantine Books, 1980.
Harris, Harry. *Good Old-Fashioned Yankee Ingenuity*. Chelsea, Mich.: Scarborough House, 1990.

JUNE 16
How did people wake up on time before alarm clocks?
Adams, Simon, and Lesley Riley, ed. *Reader's Digest Facts and Fallacies*. New York: Reader's Digest Association, 1988.
Lurie, Susan, ed. *The Big Book of Amazing Knowledge*. New York: Playmore, Inc., 1987.
Murphy, Jim. *Weird and Wacky Inventions*. New York: Crown Publishers, 1978.

JUNE 17
How can you tell where a coin was made?
Louis, David. *2201 Fascinating Facts*. New York: Crown Publishing, 1983.

Smith, Douglas B. *Ever Wonder Why?* New York: Fawcett Gold Medal, 1992.
Sobol, Donald J. *Encyclopedia Brown's Second Record Book of Weird and Wonderful Facts*. New York: Delacorte Press, 1981.
Vogel, Malvina G., ed. *The Big Book of Amazing Facts*. New York: Playmore, Inc., 1980.

JUNE 18
Why aren't there more green flowers?
Ardley, Bridget, and Neil Ardley. *The Random House Book of 1001 Questions and Answers*. New York: Random House, 1989.
Owl magazine, eds. *The Kids' Question and Answer Book Two*. New York: Grosset and Dunlap, 1988.

JUNE 19
Are you feeling red, pink, or yellow today?
Aylward, Jim. *Your Burro Is No Jackass! And Over 100 Other Things No One Ever Told You*. New York: Holt, Rinehart and Winston, 1981.
Simon, Seymour. *Body Sense/Body Nonsense*. New York: J. B. Lippincott, 1981.
Sobol, Donald J. *Encyclopedia Brown's Third Record Book of Weird and Wonderful Facts*. New York: William Morrow and Co., 1985.

JUNE 20
What bird gives its babies up for adoption?
Cobb, Vicki. *Why Doesn't The Earth Fall Up?* New York: E. P. Dutton, 1988.

JUNE 21
Why do golfers yell "fore"?
Smith, Douglas B. *Ever Wonder Why?* New York: Fawcett Gold Medal, 1992.

JUNE 22
What happens when you grab a crab?
Blumberg, Rhoda, and Leda Blumberg. *Simon and Schuster's Book of Facts and Fallacies*. New York: Simon and Schuster, 1983.
Nussbaum, Hedda, ed. *Charlie Brown's Fifth Super Book of Questions and Answers*. New York: Random House, 1981.
Rosenbloom, Joseph. *Polar Bears Like It Hot*. New York: Sterling Publishing Co., 1980.

JUNE 23
Why was a soft clay invented?
Asakawa, Gil, and Leland Rucker. *The Toy Book*. New York: Alfred A. Knopf, 1992.
Harris, Harry. *Good Old-Fashioned Yankee Ingenuity*. Chelsea, Mich.: Scarborough House, 1990.

JUNE 24
How did a bookmark become a special notepad?
Jones, Charlotte Foltz. *Mistakes That Worked*. New York: Doubleday, 1991.

JUNE 25
How did Ping-Pong get its strange name?
Robertson, Patrick. *The Book of Firsts*. New York: Bramhall House, 1974.
Wulffson, Don L. *How Sports Came to Be*. New York: Lothrop, Lee and Shepard, 1980.

JUNE 26
What did kids in the past pay for their toys?
Choron, Sandra. *The Big Book of Kids' Lists*. New York: World Almanac Publications, 1985.

JUNE 27
Why is purple the royal color?
Smith, Douglas B. *Ever Wonder Why?* New York: Fawcett Gold Medal, 1992.

JUNE 28
Does your kitchen contain this invention?
Aaseng, Nathan. *Better Mousetraps.* Minneapolis: Lerner Publications, 1990.
Giscard d'Estaing, Valerie-Anne. *The World Almanac Book of Inventions.* New York: World Almanac Publications, 1985.
Harris, Harry. *Good Old-Fashioned Yankee Ingenuity.* Chelsea, Mich.: Scarborough House, 1990.
King, Norman. *The Almanac of Fascinating Beginnings.* New York: Citadel Press, 1994.
Publishers of *Yankee Magazine. The Inventive Yankee.* Dublin, N.H.: Yankee Books, 1989.
Tuleja, Tad. *Curious Customs.* New York: Harmony Books, 1987.

JUNE 29
Did you know that you've probably played with a toy called Gooey Gupp?
Asakawa, Gil, and Leland Rucker. *The Toy Book.* New York: Alfred A. Knopf, 1992.
Felder, Deborah G. *The Kids' World Almanac of History.* New York: Pharos Books, 1991.
Flatow, Ira. *They All Laughed . . .* New York: HarperCollins, 1992.
Goldberg, M. Hirsh. *The Blunder Book.* New York: William Morrow and Co., 1984.
Jones, Charlotte Foltz. *Mistakes That Worked.* New York: Doubleday, 1991.
McLoone-Basta, Margo, and Alice Siegel. *The Second Kids' World Almanac of Records and Facts.* New York: World Almanac Publications, 1987.
Morris, Scot. *The Emperor Who Ate the Bible and More Strange Facts and Useless Information.* New York: Doubleday, 1991.

JUNE 30
How can animals warn people of coming disaster?
Sobol, Donald J. *Encyclopedia Brown's Third Record Book of Weird and Wonderful Facts.* New York: William Morrow and Co., 1985.

JULY 1
What would you do if you were rolling across a slippery floor on skates that couldn't be stopped?
Caney, Steven. *Steven Caney's Invention Book.* New York: Workman Publishing, 1985.
Gray, Ralph, ed. *Small Inventions That Make a Big Difference.* Washington, D.C.: The National Geographic Society, 1984.
Harris, Harry. *Good Old-Fashioned Yankee Ingenuity.* Chelsea, Mich.: Scarborough House, 1990.
Murphy, Jim. *Guess Again: More Weird and Wacky Inventions.* New York: Bradbury Press, 1986.
Robertson, Patrick. *The Book of Firsts.* New York: Bramhall House, 1974.

JULY 2
Will quicksand really swallow you up?
Adams, Simon, and Lesley Riley, eds. *Reader's Digest Facts and Fallacies.* New York: Reader's Digest Association, 1988.
Owl magazine, eds. *The Kids' Question and Answer Book Three.* New York: Grosset and Dunlap, 1990.
Rosenbloom, Joseph. *Bananas Don't Grow on Trees:*

A Guide to Popular Misconceptions. New York: Sterling Publishing Co., 1978.
Varasdi, J. Allen. *Myth Information.* New York: Ballantine Books, 1989.

JULY 3
How does a mosquito choose its victims?
Harris, Harry. *Good Old-Fashioned Yankee Ingenuity.* Chelsea, Mich.: Scarborough House, 1990.
Louis, David. *2201 Fascinating Facts.* New York: Crown Publishing, 1983.
Perko, Marko. *Did You Know That . . . ?* New York: Berkley Books, 1994.
Ripley's Believe It Or Not! Mind Teasers Far and Wide. Mankato, Minn.: Capstone Press, 1991.
Tuleja, Tad. *The New York Public Library Book of Popular Americana.* New York: Macmillan, 1994.

JULY 4
How could someone lose a three-mile-long painting?
Felton, Bruce, and Mark Fowler. *Fenton and Fowler's Best, Worst, and Most Unusual.* New York: Thomas Y. Crowell, 1975.
Fullerton, Timothy T. *Triviata: A Compendium of Useless Information.* New York: Hart Publishing, 1975.
Louis, David. *2201 Fascinating Facts.* New York: Crown Publishing, 1983.
Manchester, Richard B. *Incredible Facts.* New York: Galahad Books, 1985.
Morris, Scot. *The Emperor Who Ate the Bible and More Strange Facts and Useless Information.* New York: Doubleday, 1991.
Perko, Marko. *Did You Know That . . . ?* New York: Berkley Books, 1994.
Wallace, Irving, Amy Wallace, and David Wallechinsky. *Significa.* New York: E. P. Dutton, Inc., 1983.

JULY 5
Why wasn't the perfect book perfect?
Goldberg, M. Hirsh. *The Blunder Book.* New York: William Morrow and Co., 1984.

JULY 6
How are "scratch 'n' sniff" products made?
Hawkes, Nigel, et al. *How in the World?* New York: Reader's Digest Association, 1990.

JULY 7
What were cats once accused of causing?
Buchman, Dian Dincin, and Seli Groves. *What If? Fifty Discoveries That Changed the World.* New York: Scholastic, Inc., 1988.
Lee, Stan. *Stan Lee Presents the Best of the Worst.* New York: Harper and Row, 1979.
Lurie, Susan, ed. *The Big Book of Amazing Knowledge.* New York: Playmore, Inc., 1987.
Simon and Schuster Color Illustrated Book of Questions and Answers. New York: Simon and Schuster, 1986.
Urton, Andrea. *Now Entering Weirdsville!* Los Angeles: Lowell House, 1992.
Varasdi, J. Allen. *Myth Information.* New York: Ballantine Books, 1989.

JULY 8
Why did the barber need a pole?
Flexner, Stuart Berg. *Listening to America.* New York: Simon and Schuster, 1982.
McCutcheon, Marc. *The Writer's Guide to Everyday*

Life in the 1800s. Cincinnati, Ohio: Writer's Digest Books, 1993.

McLoughlin, E. V., ed. *The Book of Knowledge.* Vol. 13. New York: The Grolier Society, 1947.

Smith, Douglas B. *Ever Wonder Why?* New York: Fawcett Gold Medal, 1992.

Tuleja, Tad. *Curious Customs.* New York: Harmony Books, 1987.

Vogel, Malvina G., ed. *The Big Book of Amazing Facts.* New York: Playmore, Inc., 1980.

JULY 9
Why are the sides of the boat called "port" and "starboard"?
Charlie Brown's 'Cyclopedia. Vol. 5 New York: Random House, 1980.

Claiborne, Robert. *Loose Cannons and Red Herrings.* New York: W. W. Norton and Co., 1988.

Funk, Charles Earle. *Horsefeathers and Other Curious Words.* New York: Harper and Row, 1958.

Parker, Steve. *How Things Are Made.* New York: Random House, 1993.

Smith, Douglas B. *Ever Wonder Why?* New York: Fawcett Gold Medal, 1992.

JULY 10
Which city was named by the toss of a coin?
Felton, Bruce. *One of a Kind.* New York: William Morrow and Co., 1992.

JULY 11
Why wasn't Miss National Smile Princess smiling?
Pile, Stephen. *The Book of Heroic Failures.* London: Routledge and Kegan Paul, Ltd., 1979.

JULY 12
Why was a statue dedicated to a bug?
Felton, Bruce. *One of a Kind.* New York: William Morrow and Co., 1992.

JULY 13
How is Thomas Jefferson connected to the potato chip?
Campbell, Hannah. *Why Did They Name It . . . ?* New York: Fleet Publishing, 1964.

Caney, Steven. *Steven Caney's Kids' America.* New York: Workman Publishing, 1978.

Choron, Sandra. *The Big Book of Kids' Lists.* New York: World Almanac Publications, 1985.

Felder, Deborah G. *The Kids' World Almanac of History.* New York: Pharos Books, 1991.

Flexner, Stuart Berg. *Listening to America.* New York: Simon and Schuster, 1982.

Gray, Ralph, ed. *Small Inventions That Make a Big Difference.* Washington, D.C.: National Geographic Society, 1984.

Harris, Harry. *Good Old-Fashioned Yankee Ingenuity.* Chelsea, Mich.: Scarborough House, 1990.

Jones, Charlotte Foltz. *Mistakes That Worked.* New York: Doubleday, 1991.

King, Norman. *The Almanac of Fascinating Beginnings.* New York: Citadel Press, 1994.

McLoone-Basta, Margo, and Alice Siegel. *The Kids' World Almanac of Records and Facts.* New York: World Almanac Publications, 1985.

Panati, Charles. *Panati's Extraordinary Origins of Everyday Things.* New York: Harper and Row, 1987.

Sutton, Caroline. *How Did They Do That?* New York: William Morrow and Co., 1984.

Taylor, Barbara. *Weekly Reader Presents Be an Inventor.* Orlando, Fla.: Harcourt Brace Jovanovich, 1987.

Tuleja, Tad. *Curious Customs.* New York: Harmony Books, 1987.

JULY 14
Why are detectives called "private eyes"?
Flexner, Stuart Berg. *Listening to America.* New York: Simon and Schuster, 1982.

Sperling, Susan Kelz. *Tenderfeet and Ladyfingers.* New York: The Penguin Group, 1981.

Wallechinsky, David, and Irving Wallace. *The People's Almanac Presents the Book of Lists 2.* New York: Bantam Books, 1978.

JULY 15
What kind of puzzle took five years to solve?
May, John. *Curious Facts.* New York: Holt, Rhinehart, and Winston, 1980.

JULY 16
What is the dollar bill saying with symbols?
Baecher, Charlotte, ed. "Money Talks." *Zillions.* January, 1996.

Smith, Douglas B. *More Ever Wonder Why?* New York: Fawcett Gold Medal, 1994.

JULY 17
How did an ocean liner get the wrong name?
Harvey, Edmund, ed. *Reader's Digest Book of Facts.* New York: Reader's Digest Association, 1987.

JULY 18
How did the question mark get its strange shape?
Meyers, James. *Amazing Facts.* New York: Playmore, Inc., 1986.

Smith, Douglas B. *Ever Wonder Why?* New York: Fawcett Gold Medal, 1992.

JULY 19
What's the fastest-growing fungus in the world?
Harvey, Edmund, ed. *Reader's Digest Book of Facts.* New York: Reader's Digest Association, 1987.

JULY 20
How did frogs fall from the sky?
Branley, Franklyn M. *It's Raining Cats and Dogs: All Kinds of Weather and Why We Have It.* Boston: Houghton Mifflin Co., 1987.

JULY 21
Why isn't a fan really cooling the air?
Burnam, Tom. *The Dictionary of Misinformation.* New York: Ballantine Books, 1975.

Rosenbloom, Joseph. *Bananas Don't Grow on Trees: A Guide to Popular Misconceptions.* New York: Sterling Publishing, 1978.

Rovin, Jeff. *The Unbelievable Truth!* New York: The Penguin Group, 1994.

Vogel, Malvina G., ed. *The Big Book of Amazing Facts.* New York: Playmore, Inc., 1980.

JULY 22
Did George Washington really have wooden teeth?
Felton, Bruce. *One of a Kind.* New York: William Morrow and Co., 1992.

Gray, Ralph, ed. *Small Inventions That Make a Big Difference.* Washington, D.C.: The National Geographic Society, 1984.

JULY 23
Why do we call it the "funny bone" when it definitely isn't?
Blumberg, Rhoda, and Leda Blumberg. *Simon and Schuster's Book of Facts and Fallacies.* New York: Simon and Schuster, 1983.
Owl magazine, eds. *The Kids' Question and Answer Book Three.* New York: Grosset and Dunlap, 1990.
Smith, Douglas B. *Ever Wonder Why?* New York: Fawcett Gold Medal, 1992.
Varasdi, J. Allen. *Myth Information.* New York: Ballantine Books, 1989.

JULY 24
Which dogs were asked to dinner?
Manchester, Richard B. *Incredible Facts.* New York: Galahad Books, 1985.

JULY 25
Did you know that you've probably used a cup named after a doll factory?
Campbell, Hannah. *Why Did They Name It . . .?* New York: Fleet Publishing, 1964.
Caney, Steven. *Steven Caney's Invention Book.* New York: Workman Publishing, 1985.
Garrison, Webb. *Why Didn't I Think of That? From Alarm Clocks to Zippers.* Englewood Cliffs, N. J.: Prentice Hall, 1977.
King, Norman. *The Almanac of Fascinating Beginnings.* New York: Citadel Press, 1994.

JULY 26
If a marble and a bowling ball raced down a ramp, which one would win?
Cobb, Vicki. *Why Doesn't the Earth Fall Up?* New York: E. P. Dutton, 1988.

JULY 27
Who had the biggest dollhouse ever?
Glubok, Shirley. *Dolls' Houses: Life in Miniature.* New York: Harper and Row Publishers, 1984.
Jacobs, Flora Gill. *A World of Doll Houses.* New York: Gramercy Publishing Co., 1965.
Polley, Jane, ed. *Stories Behind Everyday Things.* New York: Reader's Digest Association, 1980.

JULY 28
When did a dog deliver mail?
Wallace, Irving, Amy Wallace, and David Wallechinsky. *Significa.* New York: E. P. Dutton, Inc., 1983.

JULY 29
Who invented raincoats?
Buchman, Dian Dincin, and Seli Groves. *What If? Fifty Discoveries That Changed the World.* New York: Scholastic, Inc., 1988.

JULY 30
How does a toad change its skin?
Ranger Rick's Answer Book. National Wildlife Federation, 1981.

JULY 31
What does the pack rat pack?
Ranger Rick's Answer Book. National Wildlife Federation, 1981.

AUGUST 1
How was the disposable razor invented?
Campbell, Hannah. *Why Did They Name It . . . ?* New York: Fleet Publishing, 1964.

Felder, Deborah G. *The Kids' World Almanac of History.* New York: Pharos Books, 1991.
Hawkes, Nigel, et al. *How in the World?* New York: Reader's Digest Association, 1990.
King, Norman. *The Almanac of Fascinating Beginnings.* New York: Citadel Press, 1994.
Taylor, Barbara. *Weekly Reader Presents Be an Inventor.* Orlando, Fla.: Harcourt Brace Jovanovich, 1987.

AUGUST 2
How are a lemon seed and a drinking straw connected?
Caney, Steven. *Steven Caney's Invention Book.* New York: Workman Publishing, 1985.

AUGUST 3
What do some of our nursery rhymes really mean?
Burnam, Tom. *More Misinformation.* New York: Ballantine Books, 1980.
Lurie, Susan, ed. *The Big Book of Amazing Knowledge.* New York: Playmore, Inc., 1987.
Tuleja, Tad. *Curious Customs.* New York: Harmony Books, 1987.

AUGUST 4
When did one man with a good idea change an entire country?
Blumberg, Rhoda, and Leda Blumberg. *Simon and Schuster's Book of Facts and Fallacies.* New York: Simon and Schuster, 1983.
Harris, Harry. *Good Old-Fashioned Yankee Ingenuity.* Chelsea, Mich.: Scarborough House, 1990.
Louis, David. *2201 Fascinating Facts.* New York: Crown Publishing, 1983.
Robertson, Patrick. *The Book of Firsts.* New York: Bramhall House, 1974.
Varasdi, J. Allen. *Myth Information.* New York: Ballantine Books, 1989.
Webster's Unabridged Dictionary Third Edition. New York: Simon and Schuster, 1983.

AUGUST 5
Do boys and girls study differently?
Sobol, Donald J. *Encyclopedia Brown's Third Record Book of Weird and Wonderful Facts.* New York: William Morrow and Co., 1985.

AUGUST 6
Why was a man in a diving outfit working at a church?
Adams, Simon, and Lesley Riley, ed. *Reader's Digest Facts and Fallacies.* New York: Reader's Digest Association, 1988.

AUGUST 7
What invention made grocery shopping easier?
Buchman, Dian Dincin, and Seli Groves. *What If? Fifty Discoveries That Changed the World.* New York: Scholastic, Inc., 1988.
Harris, Harry. *Good Old-Fashioned Yankee Ingenuity.* Chelsea, Mich.: Scarborough House, 1990.
Ripley's Believe It or Not! Mind Teasers Far and Wide. Mankato, Minn.: Capstone Press, 1991.
Wulffson, Don L. *Extraordinary Stories Behind the Invention of Ordinary Things.* New York: Lothrop, Lee, and Shepard Books, 1981.

AUGUST 8
Why did the rainmaker lose his job?
Adams, Simon, and Lesley Riley, eds. *Reader's Digest*

Facts and Fallacies. New York: Reader's Digest Association, 1988.

Alway, Carol, et al. *Strange Stories, Amazing Facts.* New York: Reader's Digest Association, 1976.

Felton, Bruce, and Mark Fowler. *Felton and Fowler's More Best, Worst, and Most Unusual.* New York: Fawcett Crest, 1976.

Vogel, Malvina G., ed. *The Big Book of Amazing Facts.* New York: Playmore, Inc., 1980.

AUGUST 9
How was a wedding ring reclaimed after it was lost at sea?
Alway, Carol, et al. *Strange Stories, Amazing Facts.* New York: Reader's Digest Association, 1976.

AUGUST 10
Where does the asphalt go from a pothole?
Feldman, David. *Why Do Clocks Run Clockwise? and Other Imponderables.* New York: Harper and Row, 1987.

Rovin, Jeff. *The Unbelievable Truth!* New York: The Penguin Group, 1994.

Smith, Douglas B. *Ever Wonder Why?* New York: Fawcett Gold Medal, 1992.

Williams, Brian, and Brenda Williams. *The Random House Book of 1001 Wonders of Science.* New York: Random House, 1990.

AUGUST 11
Why was a bank alarmed about a withdrawal?
Sobol, Donald J. *Encyclopedia Brown's Book of Wacky Crimes.* New York: E. P. Dutton, Inc., 1982.

AUGUST 12
How do rocks travel in Death Valley?
Adams, Simon, and Lesley Riley, eds. *Reader's Digest Facts and Fallacies.* New York: Reader's Digest Association, 1988.

Robbins, Pat, ed. *Why in the World?* Washington, D.C.: National Geographic Society, 1985.

AUGUST 13
How did a fire alarm improve baking bread?
Campbell, Hannah. *Why Did They Name It . . . ?* New York: Fleet Publishing, 1964.

Jones, Charlotte Foltz. *Mistakes That Worked.* New York: Doubleday, 1991.

AUGUST 14
How do seeds always know to send their roots downward?
Goldwyn, Martin M. *How a Fly Walks Upside Down . . . and Other Curious Facts.* New York: Wings Books, 1995.

Robbins, Pat, ed. *Why in the World?* Washington, D.C.: National Geographic Society, 1985.

Vogel, Malvina G., ed. *The Big Book of Amazing Facts.* New York: Playmore, Inc., 1980.

AUGUST 15
How did a war start the idea of a menu?
Flexner, Stuart Berg. *Listening to America.* New York: Simon and Schuster, 1982.

Meyers, James. *Eggplants, Elevators, Etc.: An Uncommon History of Common Things.* New York: Hart Publishing Co., 1975.

AUGUST 16
Why is the ocean so salty?
Feldman, David. *Do Penguins Have Knees?* New York: HarperCollins, 1991.

Fullerton, Timothy T. *Triviata: A Compendium of Useless Information.* New York: Hart Publishing, 1975.

Goldwyn, Martin M. *How a Fly Walks Upside Down . . . and Other Curious Facts.* New York: Wings Books, 1995.

Johnny Wonder Question and Answer Book. New York: Playmore, Inc., 1984.

Louis, David. *2201 Fascinating Facts.* New York: Crown Publishing, 1983.

Rosenbloom, Joseph. *Polar Bears Like It Hot.* New York: Sterling Publishing Co., 1980.

Simon and Schuster Color Illustrated Book of Questions and Answers. New York: Simon and Schuster, 1986.

Smith, Douglas B. *Ever Wonder Why?* New York: Fawcett Gold Medal, 1992.

Vogel, Malvina G., ed. *The Big Book of Amazing Facts.* New York: Playmore, Inc., 1980.

Williams, Brian, and Brenda Williams. *The Random House Book of 1001 Wonders of Science.* New York: Random House, 1990.

AUGUST 17
Why is it impossible to buy fresh sardines?
Burnam, Tom. *The Dictionary of Misinformation.* New York: Ballantine Books, 1975.

Feldman, David. *Imponderables.* New York: William Morrow and Co., 1986.

Fullerton, Timothy T. *Triviata: A Compendium of Useless Information.* New York: Hart Publishing, 1975.

Varasdi, J. Allen. *Myth Information.* New York: Ballantine Books, 1989.

AUGUST 18
How do you return the favor of a rescue?
Wulffson, Don L. *Amazing True Stories.* New York: Scholastic, Inc., 1991.

AUGUST 19
Why don't birds seem frightened by scarecrows?
Vogel, Malvina G., ed. *The Big Book of Amazing Facts.* New York: Playmore, Inc., 1980.

AUGUST 20
When were dirty tennis shoes helpful?
Jones, Charlotte Foltz. *Mistakes That Worked.* New York: Doubleday, 1991.

AUGUST 21
What does it mean to give someone the cold shoulder?
Alway, Carol, et al. *Strange Stories, Amazing Facts.* New York: Reader's Digest Association, 1976.

Flexner, Stuart Berg. *Listening to America.* New York: Simon and Schuster, 1982.

McLoone-Basta, Margo, and Alice Siegel. *The Second Kids' World Almanac of Records and Facts.* New York: World Almanac Publications, 1987.

Rovin, Jeff. *The Unbelievable Truth!* New York: The Penguin Group, 1994.

Smith, Douglas B. *Ever Wonder Why?* New York: Fawcett Gold Medal, 1992.

Sperling, Susan Kelz. *Tenderfeet and Ladyfingers.* New York: The Penguin Group, 1981.

AUGUST 22
How did sideburns get their name?
Burnam, Tom. *The Dictionary of Misinformation.* New York: Ballantine Books, 1975.

Flexner, Stuart Berg. *Listening to America.* New York: Simon and Schuster, 1982.

Limburg, Peter R. *Stories Behind Words*. New York: H. W. Wilson, 1986.

Morris, William, and Mary Morris. *Morris Dictionary of Word and Phrase Origins*. 2d ed. New York: HarperCollins, 1988.

Smith, Douglas B. *More Ever Wonder Why?* New York: Fawcett Gold Medal, 1994.

AUGUST 23
Why don't birds get electrocuted when they sit on wires?
Johnny Wonder Question and Answer Book. New York: Playmore, Inc., 1984.

Zotti, Ed. *Know It All!* New York: Ballantine Books, 1993.

AUGUST 24
Who was Simon in the game "Simon Says"?
Rovin, Jeff. *The Unbelievable Truth!* New York: The Penguin Group, 1994.

Smith, Douglas B. *More Ever Wonder Why?* New York: Fawcett Gold Medal, 1994.

AUGUST 25
Why do giraffes need such long necks?
Ardley, Neil, et al. *Why Things Are*. New York: Simon and Schuster, 1984.

McGrath, Susan. *The Amazing Things Animals Do*. Washington, D.C.: The National Geographic Society, 1989.

AUGUST 26
How was a sinking ship saved by a comic book?
Wallace, Irving, Amy Wallace, and David Wallechinsky. *Significa*. New York: E. P. Dutton, Inc., 1983.

AUGUST 27
What's so great about grass?
Felder, Deborah G. *The Kids' World Almanac of History*. New York: Pharos Books, 1991.

Feldman, David. *Why Do Clocks Run Clockwise? and Other Imponderables*. New York: Harper and Row, 1987.

Giscard d'Estaing, Valerie-Anne. *The World Almanac Book of Inventions*. New York: World Almanac Publications, 1985.

Goldwyn, Martin M. *How a Fly Walks Upside Down . . . and Other Curious Facts*. New York: Wings Books, 1995.

Panati, Charles. *Panati's Extraordinary Origins of Everyday Things*. New York: Harper and Row, 1987.

Panati, Charles. *Panati's Parade of Fads, Follies, and Manias*. New York: HarperCollins, 1991.

Tuleja, Tad. *Curious Customs*. New York: Harmony Books, 1987.

AUGUST 28
When does a board game take a test?
Asakawa, Gil, and Leland Rucker. *The Toy Book*. New York: Alfred A. Knopf, 1992.

AUGUST 29
How did they build a bridge across Niagara Falls?
Hicks, Donna E. *The Most Fascinating Places on Earth*. New York: Sterling Publishing Co., 1993.

AUGUST 30
What trapped a fire truck?
Sobol, Donald J. *Encyclopedia Brown's Second Record Book of Weird and Wonderful Facts*. New York: Delacorte Press, 1981.

AUGUST 31
What's the good of garlic?
Morris, Scot. *The Emperor Who Ate the Bible and More Strange Facts and Useless Information*. New York: Doubleday, 1991.

Robbins, Pat, ed. *More Far-Out Facts*. Washington, D.C.: The National Geographic Society, 1982.

SEPTEMBER 1
How do flies walk on the ceiling?
Burnam, Tom. *More Misinformation*. New York: Ballantine Books, 1980.

Goldwyn, Martin M. *How a Fly Walks Upside Down . . . and Other Curious Facts*. New York: Wings Books, 1995.

Perko, Marko. *Did You Know That . . . ?* New York: Berkley Books, 1994.

Varasdi, J. Allen. *Myth Information*. New York: Ballantine Books, 1989.

Vogel, Malvina G., ed. *The Big Book of Amazing Facts*. New York: Playmore, Inc., 1980.

SEPTEMBER 2
Why does aluminum foil have a shiny side and a dull side?
Feldman, David. *Why Do Clocks Run Clockwise? and Other Imponderables*. New York: Harper and Row, 1987.

SEPTEMBER 3
Why do people say, "I'll eat my hat if I'm wrong"?
Smith, Douglas B. *Ever Wonder Why?* New York: Fawcett Gold Medal, 1992.

SEPTEMBER 4
How is a pizza like the Italian flag?
McLoone-Basta, Margo, and Alice Siegel. *The Second Kids' World Almanac of Records and Facts*. New York: World Almanac Publications, 1987.

SEPTEMBER 5
Why do you shrink?
Hagerman, Paul Stirling. *It's a Mad Mad World*. New York: Sterling Publishing Co., 1978.

Morris, Scot. *The Emperor Who Ate the Bible and More Strange Facts and Useless Information*. New York: Doubleday, 1991.

Wallace, Irving, Amy Wallace, and David Wallechinsky. *Significa*. New York: E. P. Dutton, Inc., 1983.

SEPTEMBER 6
When did a fish lunch cost someone a big prize?
Sobol, Donald J. *Encyclopedia Brown's Third Record Book of Weird and Wonderful Facts*. New York: William Morrow and Co., 1985.

SEPTEMBER 7
How does a beetle get a drink in the desert?
Harvey, Edmund, ed. *Reader's Digest Book of Facts*. New York: Reader's Digest Association, 1987.

SEPTEMBER 8
When is it entertaining to have your face slapped?
McWhirter, Norris, and Ross McWhirter. *Guinness Book of Astounding Feats and Events*. New York: Sterling Publishing Co., 1975.

Vogel, Malvina G., ed. *The Big Book of Amazing Facts*. New York: Playmore, Inc., 1980.

SEPTEMBER 9
Who missed a once-in-a-lifetime chance?
Goldberg, M. Hirsh. *The Blunder Book.* New York:
William Morrow and Co., 1984.

SEPTEMBER 10
How does the telephone tell you the time?
Zotti, Ed. *Know It All!* New York: Ballantine Books,
1993.

SEPTEMBER 11
How did a spring become a toy?
Asakawa, Gil, and Leland Rucker. *The Toy Book.* New
York: Alfred A. Knopf, 1992.
Felder, Deborah G. *The Kids' World Almanac of History.*
New York: Pharos Books, 1991.
Harris, Harry. *Good Old-Fashioned Yankee Ingenuity.*
Chelsea, Mich.: Scarborough House, 1990.
Jones, Charlotte Foltz. *Mistakes That Worked.* New York:
Doubleday, 1991.

SEPTEMBER 12
Who didn't know about snow?
Harvey, Edmund, ed. *Reader's Digest Book of Facts.* New
York: Reader's Digest Association, 1987.

SEPTEMBER 13
What makes a small gift grand?
Louis, David. *2201 Fascinating Facts.* New York: Crown
Publishing, 1983.
Morris, Scot. *The Emperor Who Ate the Bible and More
Strange Facts and Useless Information.* New York:
Doubleday, 1991.

SEPTEMBER 14
How did a dog help save a city?
Alway, Carol, et al. *Strange Stories, Amazing Facts.* New
York: Reader's Digest Association, 1976.
McLoughlin, E. V., ed. *The Book of Knowledge.* Vol. 15.
New York: The Grolier Society, Inc., 1947.

SEPTEMBER 15
How did stamp collecting start?
Vogel, Malvina G., ed. *The Big Book of Amazing Facts.*
New York: Playmore, Inc., 1980.

SEPTEMBER 16
What secrets are some statues hiding?
Rovin, Jeff. *The Unbelievable Truth!* New York: The
Penguin Group, 1994.
Smith, Douglas B. *More Ever Wonder Why?* New York:
Fawcett Gold Medal, 1994.

SEPTEMBER 17
*Why does the man walk next to the curb when
escorting a woman?*
Smith, Douglas B. *More Ever Wonder Why?* New York:
Fawcett Gold Medal, 1994.
Tuleja, Tad. *Curious Customs.* New York: Harmony
Books, 1987.
Vogel, Malvina G., ed. *The Big Book of Amazing Facts.*
New York: Playmore, Inc., 1980.

SEPTEMBER 18
How was masking tape invented?
Alway, Carol, et al. *Strange Stories, Amazing Facts.* New
York: Reader's Digest Association, 1976.
Campbell, Hannah. *Why Did They Name It . . . ?* New
York: Fleet Publishing, 1964.

Caney, Steven. *Steven Caney's Invention Book.* New
York: Workman Publishing, 1985.
Giscard d'Estaing, Valerie-Anne. *The World Almanac
Book of Inventions.* New York: World Almanac
Publications, 1985.
Harris, Harry. *Good Old-Fashioned Yankee Ingenuity.*
Chelsea, Mich.: Scarborough House, 1990.
Landau, Irwin, ed. *I'll Buy That.* New York: Consumer
Reports, 1986.
Lurie, Susan, ed. *The Treasury of Amazing Knowledge.*
New York: Playmore, Inc., 1988.
Rovin, Jeff. *The Unbelievable Truth!* New York: The
Penguin Group, 1994.
Smith, Douglas B. *More Ever Wonder Why?* New York:
Fawcett Gold Medal, 1994.
Sutton, Caroline. *How Did They Do That?* New York:
William Morrow and Co., 1984.

SEPTEMBER 19
What was brewing over the tea bag?
Buchman, Dian Dincin, and Seli Groves. *What If? Fifty
Discoveries That Changed the World.* New York:
Scholastic, Inc., 1988.
Flexner, Stuart Berg. *Listening to America.* New York:
Simon and Schuster, 1982.
Jones, Charlotte Foltz. *Mistakes That Worked.* New York:
Doubleday, 1991.
Smith, Douglas B. *More Ever Wonder Why?* New York:
Fawcett Gold Medal, 1994.

SEPTEMBER 20
Why do men wear neckties?
Giscard d'Estaing, Valerie-Anne. *The World Almanac
Book of Inventions.* New York: World Almanac
Publications, 1985.
Harris, Harry. *Good Old-Fashioned Yankee Ingenuity.*
Chelsea, Mich.: Scarborough House, 1990.
Lurie, Susan, ed. *A Treasury of Amazing Knowledge.*
New York: Playmore, Inc., 1987.
Meyers, James. *Amazing Facts.* New York: Playmore,
Inc., 1986.
Panati, Charles. *Panati's Extraordinary Origin of Everyday
Things.* New York: Harper and Row, 1987.
Rovin, Jeff. *The Unbelievable Truth!* New York: The
Penguin Group, 1994.
Smith, Douglas B. *Ever Wonder Why?* New York:
Fawcett Gold Medal, 1992.
Sutton, Caroline. *How Did They Do That?* New York:
William Morrow and Co., 1984.

SEPTEMBER 21
Why were wedding rings collected at a tollbooth?
Wallace, Irving, Amy Wallace, and David Wallechinsky.
Significa. New York: E. P. Dutton, Inc., 1983.

SEPTEMBER 22
Why does the Leaning Tower of Pisa lean?
Adams, Simon, and Lesley Riley, eds. *Reader's Digest
Facts and Fallacies.* New York: Reader's Digest
Association, 1988.
Goldberg, M. Hirsh. *The Blunder Book.* New York:
William Morrow and Co., 1984.
Goodenough, Simon. *1500 Fascinating Facts.* London:
Treasure Press, 1987.
Jones, Charlotte Foltz. *Mistakes That Worked.* New York:
Doubleday, 1991.
Pringle, Laurence. *"The Earth Is Flat" and Other Great
Mistakes.* New York: William Morrow and Co.,
1983.

Smith, Douglas B. *More Ever Wonder Why?* New York: Fawcett Gold Medal, 1994.

Smithsonian Magazine, June 2001.

Tuleja, Tad. *Fabulous Fallacies.* New York: Harmony Books, 1982.

Vogel, Malvina G., ed. *The Big Book of Amazing Facts.* New York: Playmore, Inc., 1980.

Wallace, Irving, Amy Wallace, and David Wallechinsky. *Significa.* New York: E. P. Dutton, Inc., 1983.

SEPTEMBER 23
Why do police cars use blue lights?

Smith, Douglas B. *Ever Wonder Why?* New York: Fawcett Gold Medal, 1992.

SEPTEMBER 24
Why couldn't the secretary of the U.S. Department of the Treasury buy dinner?

Morris, Scot. *The Emperor Who Ate the Bible and More Strange Facts and Useless Information.* New York: Doubleday, 1991.

SEPTEMBER 25
When didn't the son of the president of the United States listen to his father?

Louis, David. *2201 Fascinating Facts.* New York: Crown Publishing, 1983.

Perko, Marko. *Did You Know That . . .?* New York: Berkley Books, 1994.

Seuling, Barbara. *The Last Cow on the White House Lawn and Other Little Known Facts about the Presidency.* New York: Doubleday, 1978.

Stevenson, Robert Louis. *Treasure Island.* New York: Henry Holt and Co., 1993.

SEPTEMBER 26
What's the story behind clean clothes?

Aylward, Jim. *Your Burro Is No Jackass! And Over 100 Other Things No One Ever Told You.* New York: Holt, Rinehart, and Winston, 1981.

Ewing, Elizabeth. *Everyday Dress.* New York: Chelsea House Publishers, 1984.

Felder, Deborah G. *The Kids' World Almanac of History.* New York: Pharos Books, 1991.

Giscard d'Estaing, Valerie-Anne. *The World Almanac Book of Inventions.* New York: World Almanac Publications, 1985.

Harris, Harry. *Good Old-Fashioned Yankee Ingenuity.* Chelsea, Mich.: Scarborough House, 1990.

Landau, Irwin, ed. *I'll Buy That.* New York: Consumer Reports, 1986.

SEPTEMBER 27
Who wanted the same birthday present every year?

Harvey, Edmund, ed. *Reader's Digest Book of Facts.* New York: Reader's Digest Association, 1987.

SEPTEMBER 28
Why do people shake hands?

Leokum, Arkady. *The Curious Book.* New York: Sterling Publishing Co., 1976.

Smith, Douglas B. *Ever Wonder Why?* New York: Fawcett Gold Medal, 1992.

SEPTEMBER 29
Why are veins blue when blood is red?

Tuleja, Tad. *Fabulous Fallacies.* New York: Harmony Books, 1982.

Varasdi, J. Allen. *Myth Information.* New York: Ballantine Books, 1989.

Whitfield, Philip, and Ruth Whitfield. *Why Do Our Bodies Stop Growing? Questions About the Human Anatomy Answered by the Natural History Museum.* New York: Viking Kestrel, 1988.

SEPTEMBER 30
Who invented Frisbees?

Asakawa, Gil, and Leland Rucker. *The Toy Book.* New York: Alfred A. Knopf, 1992.

Caney, Steven. *Steven Caney's Invention Book.* New York: Workman Publishing, 1985.

Elwood, Ann, and Carol Orsag. *Macmillan Illustrated Almanac for Kids.* New York: Macmillan Publishing Co., 1981.

Felder, Deborah G. *The Kids' World Almanac of History.* New York: Pharos Books, 1991.

Harris, Harry. *Good Old-Fashioned Yankee Ingenuity.* Chelsea, Mich.: Scarborough House, 1990.

Johnny Wonder Question and Answer Book. New York: Playmore, Inc., 1984.

Jones, Charlotte Foltz. *Mistakes That Worked.* New York: Doubleday, 1991.

King, Norman. *The Almanac of Fascinating Beginnings.* New York: Citadel Press, 1994.

McLoone-Basta, Margo, and Alice Siegel. *The Second Kids' World Almanac of Records and Facts.* New York: World Almanac Publications, 1987.

Rovin, Jeff. *The Unbelievable Truth!* New York: The Penguin Group, 1994.

OCTOBER 1
Which inventions were never used?

Time-Life Books, eds. *Inventive Genius.* Alexandria, Va.: Time-Life, 1991.

OCTOBER 2
How was exercising turned into a game?

Asakawa, Gil, and Leland Rucker. *The Toy Book.* New York: Alfred A. Knopf, 1992.

Harris, Harry. *Good Old-Fashioned Yankee Ingenuity.* Chelsea, Mich.: Scarborough House, 1990.

Panati, Charles. *Panati's Parade of Fads, Follies, and Manias.* New York: HarperCollins, 1991.

OCTOBER 3
What's a "googol"?

Elwood, Ann, and Carol Orsag. *Macmillan Illustrated Almanac for Kids.* New York: Macmillan Publishing Co., 1981.

Louis, David. *2201 Fascinating Facts.* New York: Crown Publishing, 1983.

Vogel, Malvina G., ed. *The Big Book of Amazing Facts.* New York: Playmore, Inc., 1980.

Wallace, Irving, Amy Wallace, and David Wallechinsky. *Significa.* New York: E. P. Dutton, Inc., 1983.

OCTOBER 4
When was a canteen alive?

Harvey, Edmund, ed. *Reader's Digest Book of Facts.* New York: Reader's Digest Association, 1987.

OCTOBER 5
What's it like to be swallowed by a whale?

McCormick, Donald. *The Master Book of Escapes.* New York: Franklin Watts, 1975.

Tallarico, Tony. *I Didn't Know That! About Strange But True Mysteries.* Illinois: Kidsbooks, 1992.

Wallace, Irving, Amy Wallace, and David Wallechinsky. *Significa.* New York: E. P. Dutton, Inc., 1983.

OCTOBER 6
Can a horse count?
Tison, Annette, and Talus Taylor. *The Big Book of Amazing Animal Behavior.* New York: Grosset and Dunlap, 1986.

OCTOBER 7
What do a tree frog, an ant, and a warthog all have in common?
Feldman, Eve B. *Animals Don't Wear Pajamas: A Book about Sleeping.* New York: Henry Holt, 1992.
Harvey, Edmund, ed. *Reader's Digest Book of Facts.* New York: Reader's Digest Association, 1987.

OCTOBER 8
Is it "catsup" or "ketchup"?
Felder, Deborah G. *The Kids' World Almanac of History.* New York: Pharos Books, 1991.
Feldman, David. *Who Put the Butter in Butterfly?* New York: Harper and Row, 1989.
McLoone-Basta, Margo, and Alice Siegel. *The Kids' World Almanac of Records and Facts.* New York: World Almanac Publications, 1985.

OCTOBER 9
Do you know what to do if you see someone choking?
Buchman, Dian Dincin, and Seli Groves. *What If? Fifty Discoveries That Changed the World.* New York: Scholastic, Inc., 1988.
Kunz, Jeffery R. M., ed. *Family Medical Guide.* New York: Random House, 1982.

OCTOBER 10
How does a spider weave its web?
Goldwyn, Martin M. *How a Fly Walks Upside Down . . . and Other Curious Facts.* New York: Wings Books, 1979.
Johnny Wonder Question and Answer Book. New York: Playmore, Inc., 1984.
Lurie, Susan, ed. *The Big Book of Amazing Knowledge.* New York: Playmore, Inc., 1987.
Perko, Marko. *Did You Know That . . . ?* New York: Berkley Books, 1994.
Vogel, Malvina G., ed. *The Big Book of Amazing Facts.* New York: Playmore, Inc., 1980.

OCTOBER 11
Can you guess which instrument used by doctors was made from a flute?
Buchman, Dian Dincin, and Seli Groves. *What If? Fifty Discoveries That Changed the World.* New York: Scholastic, Inc., 1988.

OCTOBER 12
How did people make toast in the past?
Felder, Deborah G. *The Kids' World Almanac of History.* New York: Pharos Books, 1991.
Harris, Harry. *Good Old-Fashioned Yankee Ingenuity.* Chelsea, Mich.: Scarborough House, 1990.
Nussbaum, Hedda, ed. *Charlie Brown's Fifth Super Book of Questions and Answers.* New York: Random House, 1981.

OCTOBER 13
Did you know that your stomach has acid in it?
Rowan, Peter. *Can You Get Warts from Touching Toads? Ask Dr. Pete.* New York: Julian Messner, 1986.

OCTOBER 14
Can animals get sunburned?
Blumberg, Rhoda, and Leda Blumberg. *Simon and Schuster's Book of Facts and Fallacies.* New York: Simon and Schuster, 1983.
McLoone-Basta, Margo, and Alice Siegel. *The Second Kids' World Almanac of Records and Facts.* New York: World Almanac Publications, 1987.
Owl magazine, eds. *The Kids' Question and Answer Book Three.* New York: Grosset and Dunlap, 1990.

OCTOBER 15
When was a toast a test?
Leokum, Arkady. *The Curious Book.* New York: Sterling Publishing Co., 1976.
Smith, Douglas B. *Ever Wonder Why?* New York: Fawcett Gold Medal, 1992.
Tuleja, Tad. *Curious Customs.* New York: Harmony Books, 1987.

OCTOBER 16
Why don't dogs and cats cry?
Ardley, Neil, et al. *Why Things Are.* New York: Simon and Schuster, 1984.
Blumberg, Rhoda, and Leda Blumberg. *Simon and Schuster's Book of Facts and Fallacies.* New York: Simon and Schuster, 1983.

OCTOBER 17
Can a bird hear worms in the ground?
Blumberg, Rhoda, and Leda Blumberg. *Simon and Schuster's Book of Facts and Fallacies.* New York: Simon and Schuster, 1983.
Varasdi, J. Allen. *Myth Information.* New York: Ballantine Books, 1989.

OCTOBER 18
How did skipping a trip to the store change cookie baking forever?
Caney, Steven. *Steven Caney's Invention Book.* New York: Workman Publishing, 1985.
Felder, Deborah G. *The Kids' World Almanac of History.* New York: Pharos Books, 1991.
Jones, Charlotte Foltz. *Mistakes That Worked.* New York: Doubleday, 1991.
King, Norman. *The Almanac of Fascinating Beginnings.* New York: Citadel Press, 1994.
Panati, Charles. *Panati's Extraordinary Origins of Everyday Things.* New York: Harper and Row, 1987.

OCTOBER 19
What was the biggest goof never made?
Felton, Bruce. *One of a Kind.* New York: William Morrow and Co., 1992.
Morris, Scot. *The Emperor Who Ate the Bible and More Strange Facts and Useless Information.* New York: Doubleday, 1991.

OCTOBER 20
Why is the bottom button of a man's vest left undone?
Tuleja, Tad. *Curious Customs.* New York: Harmony Books, 1987.

OCTOBER 21
When did a solution lead to an even bigger problem?
Goldberg, M. Hirsh. *The Blunder Book.* New York: William Morrow and Co., 1984.
Pringle, Laurence. *"The Earth Is Flat" and Other Great Mistakes.* New York: William Morrow and Co., 1983.

OCTOBER 22
Why would a family throw glass balls at a fire?
Giscard d'Estaing, Valerie-Anne. *The World Almanac Book of Inventions.* New York: World Almanac Publications, 1985.
Leokum, Arkady. *The Curious Book.* New York: Sterling Publishing, 1976.
Louis, David. *2201 Fascinating Facts.* New York: Crown Publishing, 1983.
Robertson, Patrick. *The Book of Firsts.* New York: Bramhall House, 1974.
Vogel, Malvina G., ed. *The Big Book of Amazing Facts.* New York: Playmore, Inc., 1980.
Williams, Brenda, and Brian Williams. *The Random House Book of 1001 Wonders of Science.* New York: Random House, 1990.

OCTOBER 23
Why was someone ironing dollar bills?
Wallace, Irving, Amy Wallace, and David Wallechinsky. *Significa.* New York: E. P. Dutton, Inc., 1983.

OCTOBER 24
Who tried to control the ocean?
Harvey, Edmund, ed. *Reader's Digest Book of Facts.* New York: Reader's Digest Association, 1987.

OCTOBER 25
How did a lost cabdriver help save a life?
Morris, Scot. *The Emperor Who Ate the Bible and More Strange Facts and Useless Information.* New York: Doubleday, 1991.

OCTOBER 26
What were sheep doing at the White House?
Louis, David. *2201 Fascinating Facts.* New York: Crown Publishing, 1983.
McKenzie, E. C. *Salted Peanuts: 1800 Little-Known Facts.* Grand Rapids, Mich.: Baker Book House, 1972.
Smith, Douglas B. *More Ever Wonder Why?* New York: Fawcett Gold Medal, 1994.
Wallace, Irving, Amy Wallace, and David Wallechinsky. *Significa.* New York: E. P. Dutton, Inc., 1983.

OCTOBER 27
How was a whole country fooled?
Manchester, Richard B. *Incredible Facts.* New York: Galahad Books, 1985.

OCTOBER 28
How could you buy land from a cereal box?
Wallace, Irving, Amy Wallace, and David Wallechinsky. *Significa.* New York: E. P. Dutton, Inc., 1983.

OCTOBER 29
How were Life Savers saved?
Campbell, Hannah. *Why Did They Name It . . . ?* New York: Fleet Publishing, 1964.
Caney, Steven. *Steven Caney's Invention Book.* New York: Workman Publishing, 1985.
Harris, Harry. *Good Old-Fashioned Yankee Ingenuity.* Chelsea, Mich.: Scarborough House, 1990.

OCTOBER 30
Why do birds fly in a V-formation?
Robbins, Pat, ed. *Why in the World?* Washington, D.C.: National Geographic Society, 1985.
Smith, Douglas B. *Ever Wonder Why?* New York: Fawcett Gold Medal, 1992.

OCTOBER 31
How did a Christmas card lead to a unique advertising campaign?
Campbell, Hannah. *Why Did They Name It . . . ?* New York: Fleet Publishing, 1964.
Flexner, Stuart Berg. *Listening to America.* New York: Simon and Schuster, 1982.
Morgan, Hal. *Symbols of America.* New York: Viking, 1986.
Rowsome, Frank Jr. *The Verse by the Side of the Road.* Brattleboro, Vt.: Stephen Greene Press, 1990.
Wallechinsky, David, and Irving Wallace. *The People's Almanac.* New York: Doubleday, 1975.

NOVEMBER 1
What's the big secret behind Betty Crocker?
Boyd, L. M. *Boyd's Book of Odd Facts.* New York: Sterling Publishing, 1979.
Campbell, Hannah. *Why Did They Name It . . . ?* New York: Fleet Publishing, 1964.
Morgan, Hal. *Symbols of America.* New York: Viking, 1986.
Panati, Charles. *Panati's Extraordinary Origins of Everyday Things.* New York: Harper and Row, 1987.
Tuleja, Tad. *The New York Public Library Book of Popular Americana.* New York: Macmillan, 1994.
Varasdi, J. Allen. *Myth Information.* New York: Ballantine Books, 1989.

NOVEMBER 2
Where did Thomas Edison go on vacation?
Humes, James C. *Speaker's Treasury of Anecdotes about the Famous.* New York: Harper and Row, 1978.
Pim, Paul. *Telling Tommy about Famous Inventors.* New York: Cupples and Leon Co., 1942.
Thompson, C. E. *101 Wacky Facts about Kids.* New York: Scholastic, Inc., 1992.

NOVEMBER 3
When was the United States ruled by an emperor?
Felton, Bruce, and Mark Fowler. *Felton and Fowler's Best, Worst, and Most Unusual.* New York: Thomas Y. Crowell, 1975.
Lurie, Susan, ed. *A Treasury of Amazing Knowledge.* New York: Playmore, Inc., 1988.
Lyon, Ron, and Jenny Paschall. *Beyond Belief.* New York: Villard Books, 1993.
Urton, Andrea. *Now Entering Weirdsville!* Los Angeles: Lowell House, 1992.

NOVEMBER 4
How did some prisoners dig themselves into deeper trouble?
Pile, Stephen. *The Book of Heroic Failures.* London: Routledge and Kegan Paul, Ltd., 1979.
Pringle, Laurence. *"The Earth Is Flat" and Other Great Mistakes.* New York: William Morrow and Co., 1983.
Smith, Richard, and Edward Decter. *Oops! The Complete Book of Bloopers.* New York: The Rutledge Press, 1981.

NOVEMBER 5
Why does one eye work harder than the other?
Vogel, Malvina G., ed. *The Big Book of Amazing Facts.* New York: Playmore, Inc., 1980.

NOVEMBER 6
What's the "hobo code"?
Mulvey, Deb, ed. *We Had Everything But Money.* Greendale, Wis.: Reiman Publications, 1992.

NOVEMBER 7
Why do some people have naturally curly hair?
Ardley, Bridget, and Neil Ardley. *The Random House Book of 1001 Questions and Answers.* New York: Random House, 1989.

Elwood, Ann, and Carol Orsag. *Macmillan Illustrated Almanac for Kids.* New York: Macmillan Publishing Co., 1981.

Goldwyn, Martin M. *How a Fly Walks Upside Down . . . and Other Curious Facts.* New York: Wings Books, 1995.

Vogel, Malvina G., ed. *The Big Book of Amazing Facts.* New York: Playmore, Inc., 1980.

NOVEMBER 8
Why do horses sleep standing up?
Blumberg, Rhoda, and Leda Blumberg. *Simon and Schuster's Book of Facts and Fallacies.* New York: Simon and Schuster, 1983.

Chrystie, Frances N. *The First Book of Surprising Facts.* New York: Franklin Watts, 1956.

Louis, David. *2201 Fascinating Facts.* New York: Crown Publishing, 1983.

Squire, Ann. *101 Questions and Answers about Pets and People.* New York: Macmillan Publishing Co., 1988.

Zotti, Ed. *Know It All!* New York: Ballantine Books, 1993.

NOVEMBER 9
What kind of food was once sold with a pair of gloves so people could hold it?
Felder, Deborah G. *The Kids' World Almanac of History.* New York: Pharos Books, 1991.

McLoone-Basta, Margo, and Alice Siegel. *The Kids' World Almanac of Records and Facts.* New York: World Almanac Publications, 1985.

Morris, Scot. *The Emperor Who Ate the Bible and More Strange Facts and Useless Information.* New York: Doubleday, 1991.

Smith, Douglas B. *Ever Wonder Why?* New York: Fawcett Gold Medal, 1992.

Sutton, Caroline. *How Did They Do That?* New York: William Morrow and Co., 1984.

NOVEMBER 10
What are some inventions made by kids?
Taylor, Barbara. *Weekly Reader Presents Be an Inventor.* Orlando, Fla.: Harcourt Brace Jovanovich, 1987.

NOVEMBER 11
Why was a 107-year-old lady supposed to go to first grade?
Sobol, Donald J. *Encyclopedia Brown's Third Record Book of Weird and Wonderful Facts.* New York: William Morrow and Co., 1985.

NOVEMBER 12
How do animals help their friends?
Tison, Annette, and Talus Taylor. *The Big Book of Amazing Animal Behavior.* New York: Grosset and Dunlap, 1986.

NOVEMBER 13
Why is fish served with lemon?
Louis, David. *2201 Fascinating Facts.* New York: Crown Publishing, 1983.

Rovin, Jeff. *The Unbelievable Truth!* New York: The Penguin Group, 1994.

NOVEMBER 14
What unusual tracks did a car leave on the road?
Louis, David. *2201 Fascinating Facts.* New York: Crown Publishing, 1983.

NOVEMBER 15
Why did a brand-new prison fail?
Goldberg, M. Hirsh. *The Blunder Book.* New York: William Morrow and Co., 1984.

NOVEMBER 16
Why won't a tire stay buried?
Smith, Douglas B. *Ever Wonder Why?* New York: Fawcett Gold Medal, 1992.

NOVEMBER 17
Which word is used most in the English language?
Ardley, Bridget, and Neil Ardley. *The Random House Book of 1001 Questions and Answers.* New York: Random House, 1989.

Lopshire, Robert. *The Biggest, Smallest, Fastest, Tallest Things You've Ever Heard Of.* New York: Thomas Y. Crowell, 1980.

Louis, David. *2201 Fascinating Facts.* New York: Crown Publishing, 1983.

McKenzie, E. C. *Salted Peanuts: 1800 Little-Known Facts.* Grand Rapids, Mich.: Baker Book House, 1972.

NOVEMBER 18
What treasure was found in a toolbox?
Sobol, Donald J. *Encyclopedia Brown's Third Record Book of Weird and Wonderful Facts.* New York: William Morrow and Co., 1985.

NOVEMBER 19
Who was George Nissen, and why did he put a trampoline on top of his car?
Caney, Steven. *Steven Caney's Invention Book.* New York: Workman Publishing, 1985.

Harris, Harry. *Good Old-Fashioned Yankee Ingenuity.* Chelsea, Mich.: Scarborough House, 1990.

NOVEMBER 20
When did children need to hunt for a home?
Elwood, Ann, and Carol Orsag. *Macmillan Illustrated Almanac for Kids.* New York: Macmillan Publishing Co., 1981.

NOVEMBER 21
What can go wrong with words?
Goldberg, M. Hirsh. *The Blunder Book.* New York: William Morrow and Co., 1984.

NOVEMBER 22
What surprise was found in a closet?
Sobol, Donald J. *Encyclopedia Brown's Third Record Book of Weird and Wonderful Facts.* New York: William Morrow and Co., 1985.

NOVEMBER 23
Why did people once hold parties just to watch someone vacuum?
Felder, Deborah G. *The Kids' World Almanac of History.* New York: Pharos Books, 1991.

Gray, Ralph, ed. *Small Inventions That Make a Big Difference.* Washington, D.C.: The National Geographic Society, 1984.

Martinet, Jeanne. *The Year You Were Born: A Day-to-Day Record of 1985.* New York: Tambourine Books, 1992.

Robertson, Patrick. *The Book of Firsts.* New York: Bramhall House, 1974.

Williams, Brenda, and Brian Williams. *The Random House Book of 1001 Wonders of Science.* New York: Random House, 1990.

Wulffson, Don L. *Extraordinary Stories Behind the Invention of Ordinary Things.* New York: Lothrop, Lee, and Shepard Books, 1981.

NOVEMBER 24
Why was Florida so cold one Christmas?

Goldberg, M. Hirsh. *The Blunder Book.* New York: William Morrow and Co., 1984.

Sobol, Donald J. *Encyclopedia Brown's Third Record Book of Weird and Wonderful Facts.* New York: William Morrow and Co., 1985.

NOVEMBER 25
How can ants help with healing?

Louis, David. *2201 Fascinating Facts.* New York: Crown Publishing, 1983.

Wallace, Irving, Amy Walllace, and David Wallenchinsky. *Significa.* New York: E. P. Dutton, Inc., 1983.

NOVEMBER 26
What is the five-year frog?

Harvey, Edmund, ed. *Reader's Digest Book of Facts.* New York: Reader's Digest Association, 1987.

NOVEMBER 27
What did gloves say about hands?

Polley, Jane, ed. *Stories Behind Everyday Things.* New York: Reader's Digest Association, 1980.

NOVEMBER 28
Why would a house have two thousand doors?

Asimov, Isaac. *Would You Believe?* New York: Grossett and Dunlap, 1982.

Harvey, Edmund, ed. *Reader's Digest Book of Facts.* New York: Reader's Digest Association, 1987.

Manchester, Richard B. *Incredible Facts.* New York: Galahad Books, 1985.

Meyers, James. *The Best Amazing Question and Answer Book.* New York: Playmore, Inc., 1987.

NOVEMBER 29
Why did the richest woman in the world eat cold oatmeal?

Alway, Carol, et al. *Strange Stories, Amazing Facts.* New York: Reader's Digest Association, 1976.

Felder, Deborah G. *The Kids' World Almanac of History.* New York: Pharos Books, 1991.

Felton, Bruce, and Mark Fowler. *Felton and Fowler's Best, Worst, and Most Unusual.* New York: Thomas Y. Crowell, 1975.

McWhirter, Norris, and Ross McWhirter. *Guinness Book of Astounding Feats and Events.* New York: Sterling Publishing Co., 1975.

Morris, Scot. *The Emperor Who Ate the Bible and More Strange Facts and Useless Information.* New York: Doubleday, 1991.

Publishers of *Yankee Magazine. The Inventive Yankee.* Dublin, N. H.: Yankee Books, 1989.

NOVEMBER 30
What did you get if you ordered "bossy in a bowl"?

Choron, Sandra. *The Big Book of Kids' Lists.* New York: World Almanac Publications, 1985.

Flexner, Stuart. *Listening to America.* New York: Simon and Schuster, Inc., 1982.

Panati, Charles. *Panati's Parade of Fads, Follies, and Manias.* New York: HarperCollins, 1991.

DECEMBER 1
How did Kleenex find out that "the nose knows"?

Caney, Steven. *Steven Caney's Invention Book.* New York: Workman Publishing, 1985.

Giscard d'Estaing, Valerie-Anne. *The World Almanac Book of Inventions.* New York: World Almanac Publications, 1985.

King, Norman. *The Almanac of Fascinating Beginnings.* New York: Citadel Press, 1994.

Panati, Charles. *Panati's Extraordinary Origins of Everyday Things.* New York: Harper and Row, 1987.

Wallace, Irving, Amy Wallace, and David Wallechinsky. *Significa.* New York: E. P. Dutton, Inc., 1983.

DECEMBER 2
How did the Jeep get its name?

Alway, Carol, et al. *Strange Stories, Amazing Facts.* New York: Reader's Digest Association, 1976.

Caney, Steven. *Steven Caney's Invention Book.* New York: Workman Publishing, 1985.

Epstein, Sam, and Beryl Epstein. *What's Behind the Word?* New York: Scholastic, Inc., 1964.

Guttmacher, Peter. *Jeep.* New York: Macmillan, 1994.

Harris, Harry. *Good Old-Fashioned Yankee Ingenuity.* Chelsea, Mich.: Scarborough House, 1990.

Landau, Irwin, ed. *I'll Buy That.* New York: Consumer Reports, 1986.

Lurie, Susan, ed. *A Treasury of Amazing Knowledge.* New York: Playmore, Inc., 1987.

Patton, Phil. *Made in U.S.A.: The Secret Histories of the Things That Made America.* New York: Grove/Atlantic Monthly, 1992.

Robertson, Patrick. *The Book of Firsts.* New York: Bramhall House, 1974.

Smith, David, and Sue Cassin. *The Amazing Book of Firsts.* London: Victoria House Publishing, Ltd., 1990.

Smith, Douglas B. *Ever Wonder Why?* New York: Fawcett Gold Medal, 1992.

DECEMBER 3
What is the history of the sandwich?

Alway, Carol, et al. *Strange Stories, Amazing Facts.* New York: Reader's Digest Association, 1976.

Buchman, Dian Dincin, and Seli Groves. *What If? Fifty Discoveries That Changed the World.* New York: Scholastic, Inc., 1988.

Epstein, Sam, and Beryl Epstein. *What's Behind the Word?* New York: Scholastic, Inc., 1964.

Felder, Deborah G. *The Kids' World Almanac of History.* New York: Pharos Books, 1991.

Flexner, Stuart Berg. *Listening to America.* New York: Simon and Schuster, 1982.

Goodenough, Simon. *1500 Fascinating Facts.* London: Treasure Press, 1987.

Jones, Charlotte Foltz. *Mistakes That Worked.* New York: Doubleday, 1991.

Limburg, Peter R. *Stories behind Words.* New York: H. W. Wilson, 1986.

McLoone-Basta, Margo, and Alice Siegel. *The Kids' World Almanac of Records and Facts.* New York: World Almanac Publications, 1985.

Panati, Charles. *Panati's Extraordinary Origins of Everyday Things.* New York: Harper and Row, 1987.

Perko, Marko. *Did You Know That . . . ?* New York: Berkley Books, 1994.

Rovin, Jeff. *The Unbelievable Truth!* New York: The Penguin Group, 1994.

Vogel, Malvina G., ed. *The Big Book of Amazing Facts.* New York: Playmore, Inc., 1980.

DECEMBER 4
Why were windshield wipers invented?

Buchman, Dian Dincin, and Seli Groves. *What If? Fifty Discoveries That Changed the World.* New York: Scholastic, Inc., 1988.

DECEMBER 5
What's the story behind the Taj Mahal?

Hicks, Donna E. *The Most Fascinating Places on Earth.* New York: Sterling Publishing Co., 1993.

Lurie, Susan, ed. *A Treasury of Amazing Knowledge.* New York: Playmore, Inc., 1988.

DECEMBER 6
Does spinach really make you strong?

Adams, Simon, and Lesley Riley, ed. *Reader's Digest Facts and Fallacies.* New York: Reader's Digest Association, 1988.

Harvey, Edmund, ed. *Reader's Digest Book of Facts.* New York: Reader's Digest Association, 1987.

McKenzie, E. C. *Salted Peanuts: 1800 Little-Known Facts.* Grand Rapids, Mich.: Baker Book House, 1972.

Rowan, Peter. *Can You Get Warts from Touching Toads? Ask Dr. Pete.* New York: Julian Messner, 1986.

Simon, Seymour. *Body Sense/Body Nonsense.* New York: J. B. Lippincott, 1981.

Smith, Douglas B. *More Ever Wonder Why?* New York: Fawcett Gold Medal, 1994.

Tuleja, Tad. *Fabulous Fallacies.* New York: Harmony Books, 1982.

DECEMBER 7
How did foot powder win an election for mayor?

Felton, Bruce, and Mark Fowler. *Felton and Fowler's More Best, Worst, and Most Unusual.* New York: Fawcett Crest, 1976.

Felton, Bruce. *One of a Kind.* New York: William Morrow and Co., 1992.

Wullfson, Don L. *Amazing True Stories.* New York: Scholastic, Inc., 1991.

DECEMBER 8
Does sound always travel at the same speed?

Goldwyn, Martin M. *How a Fly Walks Upside Down . . . and Other Curious Facts.* New York: Wings Books, 1995.

Perko, Marko. *Did You Know That . . . ?* New York: Berkley Books, 1994.

Varasdi, J. Allen. *Myth Information.* New York: Ballantine Books, 1989.

DECEMBER 9
How did those sneakers get such a strange name?

Smith, Douglas B. *More Ever Wonder Why?* New York: Fawcett Gold Medal, 1994.

DECEMBER 10
Why do we call them "wisdom teeth"?

Feldman, David. *Why Do Clocks Run Clockwise? and Other Imponderables.* New York: Harper and Row, 1987.

Meyers, James. *Amazing Facts.* New York: Playmore, Inc., 1986.

DECEMBER 11
What amazing number is always the same?

Harvey, Edmund, ed. *Reader's Digest Book of Facts.* New York: Reader's Digest Association, 1987.

DECEMBER 12
Why are traffic lights red, yellow, and green?

Smith, Douglas B. *Ever Wonder Why?* New York: Fawcett Gold Medal, 1992.

Zotti, Ed. *Know It All!* New York: Ballantine Books, 1993.

DECEMBER 13
What do gold, tents, and a blacksmith have to do with your blue jeans?

Buchman, Dian Dincin, and Seli Groves. *What If? Fifty Discoveries That Changed the World.* New York: Scholastic, Inc., 1988.

Caney, Steven. *Steven Caney's Invention Book.* New York: Workman Publishing, 1985.

Felder, Deborah G. *The Kids' World Almanac of History.* New York: Pharos Books, 1991.

Garrison, Webb. *Why Didn't I Think of That? From Alarm Clocks to Zippers.* Englewood Cliffs, N. J.: Prentice Hall, 1977.

Gray, Ralph, ed. *Small Inventions That Make a Big Difference.* Washington, D.C.: The National Geographic Society, 1984.

Harris, Harry. *Good Old-Fashioned Yankee Ingenuity.* Chelsea, Mich.: Scarborough House, 1990.

Morris, Scot. *The Emperor Who Ate the Bible and More Strange Facts and Useless Information.* New York: Doubleday, 1991.

Robertson, Patrick. *The Book of Firsts.* New York: Bramhall House, 1974.

Time-Life Books, eds. *Inventive Genius.* Alexandria, Va.: Time-Life, 1991.

Wallace, Irving, Amy Wallace, and David Wallechinsky. *Significa.* New York: E. P. Dutton, Inc., 1983.

DECEMBER 14
Where did the dessert with the wiggle come from?

Campbell, Hannah. *Why Did They Name It . . . ?* New York: Fleet Publishing, 1964.

Harris, Harry. *Good Old-Fashioned Yankee Ingenuity.* Chelsea, Mich.: Scarborough House, 1990.

Meyers, James. *Eggplants, Elevators, Etc.: An Uncommon History of Common Things.* New York: Hart Publishing Co., 1978.

DECEMBER 15
How can making a mistake make you money?

Vare, Ethlie Ann, and Greg Ptacek. *Women Inventors and Their Discoveries.* Minneapolis, Minn.: Oliver Press, 1993.

DECEMBER 16
What toy was invented specifically to help students study?

Asakawa, Gil, and Leland Rucker. *The Toy Book.* New York: Alfred A. Knopf, 1992.

Gray, Ralph, ed. *Small Inventions That Make a Big Difference.* Washington, D.C.: The National Geographic Society, 1984.

Martinet, Jeanne. *The Year You Were Born: A Day-by-Day Record of 1987.* New York: Tambourine Books, 1993.

Wullfson, Don L. *Extraordinary Stories Behind the Invention of Ordinary Things.* New York: Lothrop, Lee, and Shepard Books, 1981.

DECEMBER 17
What does the X in "Xmas" stand for?
Burnam, Tom. *The Dictionary of Misinformation.* New York: Ballantine Books, 1975.
Feldman, David. *Why Do Clocks Run Clockwise? and Other Imponderables.* New York: Harper and Row, 1987.
Louis, David. *2201 Fascinating Facts.* New York: Crown Publishing, 1983.
Perko, Marko. *Did You Know That . . . ?* New York: Berkley Books, 1994.
Rovin, Jeff. *The Unbelievable Truth!* New York: The Penguin Group, 1994.
Smith, Douglas B. *More Ever Wonder Why?* New York: Fawcett Gold Medal, 1994.
Tuleja, Tad. *Curious Customs.* New York: Harmony Books, 1987.

DECEMBER 18
What job could you do if you couldn't hear or speak?
McWhirter, Norris, and Ross McWhirter. *Guinness Book of Phenomenal Happenings.* New York: Sterling Publishing Co., 1976.

DECEMBER 19
Why did a school put a traffic light in its lunchroom?
Sobol, Donald J. *Encyclopedia Brown's Third Record Book of Weird and Wonderful Facts.* New York: William Morrow and Co., 1985.

DECEMBER 20
What letter is used most often in the English language?
Adams, Simon, and Lesley Riley, eds. *Reader's Digest Facts and Fallacies.* New York: Reader's Digest Association, 1988.
Felton, Bruce. *One of a Kind.* New York: William Morrow and Co., 1992.
Perko, Marko. *Did You Know That . . . ?* New York: Berkley Books, 1994.
Wulffson, Don L. *Extraordinary Stories Behind the Invention of Ordinary Things.* New York: Lothrop, Lee, and Shepard Books, 1981.

DECEMBER 21
Why wouldn't a locksmith give anyone his key?
Polley, Jane, ed. *Stories Behind Everyday Things.* New York: Reader's Digest Association, 1980.

DECEMBER 22
Why did someone who never had to wash dishes invent the automatic dishwasher?
Aaseng, Nathan. *The Problem Solvers.* Minneapolis: Lerner Publications, 1989.
Felder, Deborah G. *The Kids' World Almanac of History.* New York: Pharos Books, 1991.
Robertson, Patrick. *The Book of Firsts.* New York: Bramhall House, 1974.

DECEMBER 23
How did Velcro get invented?
Buchman, Dian Dincin, and Seli Groves. *What If? Fifty Discoveries That Changed the World.* New York: Scholastic, Inc., 1988.
Felder, Deborah G. *The Kids' World Almanac of History.* New York: Pharos Books, 1991.
Flatow, Ira. *They All Laughed.* New York: HarperCollins, 1992.

Gray, Ralph, ed. *Small Inventions That Make a Big Difference.* Washington, D.C.: The National Geographic Society, 1984.
McLoone-Basta, Margo, and Alice Siegel. *The Second Kids' World Almanac of Records and Facts.* New York: World Almanac Publications, 1987.

DECEMBER 24
Why do we call up-to-the-minute information the "news"?
Burnam, Tom. *The Dictionary of Misinformation.* New York: Ballantine Books, 1975.

DECEMBER 25
How did a broken church organ inspire the creation of a Christmas carol?
Louis, David. *2201 Fascinating Facts.* New York: Crown Publishing, 1983.
Wallace, Irving, Amy Wallace, and David Wallechinsky. *Significa.* New York: E.P. Dutton, Inc., 1983.

DECEMBER 26
What unusual item was once found in a bag of potato chips?
Sobol, Donald J. *Encyclopedia Brown's Third Record Book of Weird and Wonderful Facts.* New York: William Morrow and Co., 1985.

DECEMBER 27
Why is the White House white?
Hagerman, Paul Stirling. *It's a Mad Mad World.* New York: Sterling Publishing Co., 1978.
Harvey, Edmund, ed. *Reader's Digest Book of Facts.* New York: Reader's Digest Association, 1987.
Johnny Wonder Question and Answer Book. New York: Playmore, Inc., 1984.

DECEMBER 28
Why would anyone collect chicken bones?
McLoone-Basta, Margo, and Alice Siegel. *The Second Kids' World Almanac of Records and Facts.* New York: World Almanac Publications, 1987.

DECEMBER 29
What was so wacky about old-time wigs?
Louis, David. *2201 Fascinating Facts.* New York: Crown Publishing, 1983.
Morris, Scot. *The Emperor Who Ate the Bible and More Strange Facts and Useless Information.* New York: Doubleday, 1991.
Sanders, Deidre, et al. *Would You Believe This, Too?* New York: Sterling Publishing Co., 1976.
Weil, Lisl. *New Clothes: What People Wore, from Cavemen to Astronauts.* New York: Antheneum, 1987.

DECEMBER 30
Since earthworms have no legs, how do they move?
Ardley, Neil, et al. *Why Things Are.* New York: Simon and Schuster, 1984.
Blumberg, Rhoda, and Leda Blumberg. *Simon and Schuster's Book of Facts and Fallacies.* New York: Simon and Schuster, 1983.
McLoone-Basta, Margo, and Alice Siegel. *The Second Kids' World Almanac of Records and Facts.* New York: World Almanac Publications, 1987.

DECEMBER 31
How did a weapon become a toy?
Asakawa, Gil, and Leland Rucker. *The Toy Book.* New York: Alfred A. Knopf, 1992.

Blumberg, Rhoda, and Leda Blumberg. *Simon and Schuster's Book of Facts and Fallacies.* New York: Simon and Schuster, 1983.

Choron, Sandra. *The Big Book of Kids' Lists.* New York: World Almanac Publications, 1985.

Elwood, Ann, and Carol Orsag. *Macmillan Illustrated Almanac for Kids.* New York: Macmillan Publishing Co., 1981.

Gray, Ralph, ed. *Small Inventions That Make a Big Difference.* Washington, D.C.: The National Geographic Society, 1984.

Harris, Harry. *Good Old-Fashioned Yankee Ingenuity.* Chelsea, Mich.: Scarborough House, 1990.

McLoone-Basta, Margo, and Alice Siegel. *The Second Kids' World Almanac of Records and Facts.* New York: World Almanac Publications, 1987.

Sobol, Donald J. *Encyclopedia Brown's Second Record Book of Weird and Wonderful Facts.* New York: Delacorte Press, 1981.

Scripture Index

Genesis 1:21. . . . . Jan. 22

Leviticus 19:13 . . . . .May 9

Deuteronomy 5:32-33 . . . . . Aug. 24
Deuteronomy 7:9 . . . . .Feb. 18
Deuteronomy 16:17 . . . . Dec. 18
Deuteronomy 30:11-14 . . . . Sept. 20
Deuteronomy 30:19-20 . . . . Aug. 15
Deuteronomy 33:27 . . . . . . .May 12

Joshua 24:15 . . . . Dec. 7

1 Samuel 2:8 . . . . Nov. 16

2 Samuel 24:14 . . . . .Apr. 6

1 Chronicles 29:11 . . . . Aug. 23

Job 5:12-13 . . . . .Oct. 23
Job 10:8 . . . . .Oct. 13
Job 11:13-17 . . . . Mar. 27
Job 11:18-19 . . . . .Apr. 14
Job 12:10 . . . . Jan. 17
Job 18:7-10 . . . . .Apr. 23
Job 28:12-13 . . . . .Apr. 28
Job 28:17-18 . . . . Nov. 22
Job 29:15 . . . . Aug. 4
Job 31:4 . . . . Sept. 17
Job 37:6 . . . . Sept. 12

Psalm 1:3 . . . . .Feb. 5
Psalm 3:4-6 . . . . .Apr. 30
Psalm 4:8 . . . . .May 17
Psalm 5:12 . . . . Nov. 13
Psalm 8:3-4 . . . . July 1
Psalm 9:9 . . . . .Apr. 20
Psalm 17:5 . . . . Sept. 1
Psalm 19:1 . . . . Mar. 7
Psalm 19:1, 3-4 . . . . July 8
Psalm 19:7-11 . . . . Sept. 23
Psalm 19:12 . . . . .Apr. 2
Psalm 23:1-4 . . . . .Oct. 26
Psalm 23:4 . . . . Sept. 16
Psalm 24:1-2 . . . . .Oct. 28
Psalm 24:3-4 . . . . Nov. 23
Psalm 24:7 . . . . Aug. 30
Psalm 27:4 . . . . Nov. 20
Psalm 27:5 . . . . July 2
Psalm 27:9 . . . . .Apr. 13
Psalm 27:10 . . . . .June 20
Psalm 30:11 . . . . .June 19
Psalm 31:23 . . . . .June 28
Psalm 32:8 . . . . .Oct. 30, Dec. 26
Psalm 32:9 . . . . .May 7
Psalm 34:1-2 . . . . .Feb. 25
Psalm 34:11 . . . . .May 22
Psalm 37:23 . . . . Jan. 31
Psalm 37:23-24 . . . . Dec. 9

Psalm 40:2-3 . . . . .Oct. 25
Psalm 40:5 . . . . .Oct. 6, Dec. 11
Psalm 46:1-3 . . . . .Apr. 26
Psalm 49:15 . . . . Aug. 9
Psalm 51:7 . . . . Dec. 27
Psalm 55:22 . . . . .Feb. 9
Psalm 59:9 . . . . .Feb. 22
Psalm 61:8 . . . . Dec. 25
Psalm 65:7 . . . . July 21
Psalm 69:7 . . . . .May 27
Psalm 71:5 . . . . .June 15
Psalm 71:17 . . . . .Apr. 5
Psalm 89:9 . . . . .Oct. 24
Psalm 90:17 . . . . .June 23
Psalm 91:3 . . . . .Oct. 10
Psalm 91:11-13 . . . . Aug. 20
Psalm 91:14-16 . . . . .June 10
Psalm 93:4 . . . . Aug. 26
Psalm 94:16-19 . . . . . . .Jan. 3, July 5
Psalm 95:4-5 . . . . Jan. 7
Psalm 102:25 . . . . .Apr. 27
Psalm 103:2 . . . . .May 13
Psalm 104:14 . . . . Aug. 31
Psalm 104:24 . . . . . . Feb. 10, Apr. 17
Psalm 107:23-31 . . . . July 9
Psalm 119:103 . . . . .Oct. 18
Psalm 119:105 . . . . .Oct. 31
Psalm 119:117 . . . . . .Apr. 15, Aug. 16
Psalm 119:126 . . . . .Feb. 11
Psalm 124:7 . . . . .Feb. 7
Psalm 125:2 . . . . .Oct. 2
Psalm 130:6 . . . . July 14
Psalm 135:13 . . . . . . .Feb. 27, Dec. 5
Psalm 139:2 . . . . Dec. 19
Psalm 139:13 . . . . Mar. 31
Psalm 139:14 . . . . .Feb. 4
Psalm 139:18 . . . . .Oct. 3
Psalm 142:7 . . . . Nov. 15
Psalm 145:13 . . . . Aug. 19
Psalm 145:16 . . . . Mar. 1
Psalm 146:8 . . . . .May 15, Dec. 4
Psalm 147:3 . . . . Jan. 23

Proverbs 1:23 . . . . Mar. 13
Proverbs 2:6 . . . . .May 5
Proverbs 3:3 . . . . .May 21
Proverbs 3:9-10 . . . . Jan. 25
Proverbs 3:24-26 . . . . Mar. 29
Proverbs 12:10 . . . . July 24
Proverbs 12:22 . . . . Nov. 18
Proverbs 14:22 . . . . Nov. 4
Proverbs 14:29 . . . . Jan. 11
Proverbs 15:3 . . . . July 16
Proverbs 15:4 . . . . Jan. 2
Proverbs 16:16 . . . . .Feb. 6
Proverbs 16:28 . . . . Jan. 27
Proverbs 16:31 . . . . .Apr. 25, Nov. 11
Proverbs 16:33 . . . . July 10

Proverbs 17:22 . . . . July 23
Proverbs 18:10 . . . . Jan. 10
Proverbs 20:11 . . . . Mar. 28
Proverbs 20:15 . . . . Apr. 22
Proverbs 22:1 . . . . . Oct. 19, Nov. 29
Proverbs 23:12 . . . . Nov. 21
Proverbs 24:5 . . . . Aug. 5
Proverbs 24:15-16 . . . . Nov. 19
Proverbs 24:17 . . . . Sept. 9
Proverbs 24:27 . . . . Aug. 7
Proverbs 25:17 . . . . Aug. 21
Proverbs 25:19 . . . . July 22
Proverbs 25:25 . . . . Apr. 18
Proverbs 26:21 . . . . Feb. 1
Proverbs 27:2 . . . . Nov. 17
Proverbs 27:9 . . . . July 6
Proverbs 27:23 . . . . Feb. 28

Ecclesiastes 3:1 . . . . May 10
Ecclesiastes 3:1, 7 . . . . May 16
Ecclesiastes 7:1 . . . . June 13
Ecclesiastes 7:8 . . . . June 29
Ecclesiastes 7:13 . . . . Nov. 7
Ecclesiastes 9:10 . . . . June 14
Ecclesiastes 11:9 . . . . Sept. 30
Ecclesiastes 12:1 . . . . Jan. 26

Isaiah 1:18 . . . . Feb. 23, June 11
Isaiah 2:11-12 . . . . Jan. 9
Isaiah 6:8 . . . . May 19
Isaiah 7:14 . . . . Mar. 18
Isaiah 9:2 . . . . Apr. 8
Isaiah 9:6 . . . . Mar. 12
Isaiah 34:16 . . . . Jan. 12
Isaiah 35:8-10 . . . . Aug. 10
Isaiah 40:8 . . . . Aug. 27
Isaiah 40:12 . . . . June 3
Isaiah 40:31 . . . . Jan. 19
Isaiah 42:16 . . . . Apr. 4, July 7
Isaiah 42:20 . . . . Oct. 17
Isaiah 43:2 . . . . Mar. 23
Isaiah 44:3-4 . . . . Feb. 21
Isaiah 44:22 . . . . Feb. 26
Isaiah 49:15-16 . . . . Mar. 30
Isaiah 52:12 . . . . June 21
Isaiah 55:1 . . . . Oct. 4
Isaiah 55:3 . . . . Oct. 11
Isaiah 57:15 . . . . Aug. 3, Nov. 3
Isaiah 58:10 . . . . Nov. 12
Isaiah 58:11 . . . . July 25
Isaiah 60:1 . . . . June 16
Isaiah 61:11 . . . . June 18

Jeremiah 20:9 . . . . Sept. 11
Jeremiah 29:13 . . . . . Feb. 12, Dec. 16
Jeremiah 31:3 . . . . May 31

Ezekiel 34:16 . . . . May 4
Ezekiel 34:26 . . . . Aug. 8, Dec. 30

Hosea 1:7 . . . . Mar. 8
Hosea 6:1 . . . . Dec. 31

Joel 2:25 . . . . July 12

Amos 5:24 . . . . Aug. 29

Jonah 2:6 . . . . Oct. 5

Micah 7:8 . . . . June 7, Dec. 12

Malachi 1:11 . . . . Nov. 30

Matthew 1:23 . . . . Apr. 16
Matthew 4:4 . . . . July 13, Sept. 4
Matthew 4:19 . . . . Aug. 17
Matthew 5:40 . . . . July 29
Matthew 6:3-4 . . . . Apr. 9
Matthew 6:8 . . . . Dec. 1
Matthew 6:19-21 . . . . Apr. 29
Matthew 6:22-23 . . . . Nov. 5
Matthew 6:25 . . . . Dec. 13
Matthew 6:26 . . . . . . Feb. 24, Nov. 26
Matthew 7:1-5 . . . . Mar. 26
Matthew 7:7-8 . . . . May 29
Matthew 7:9-11 . . . . Aug. 13
Matthew 7:13-14 . . . . Mar. 16
Matthew 7:14 . . . . Jan. 29
Matthew 7:15 . . . . Oct. 27
Matthew 7:24-27 . . . . Sept. 22
Matthew 10:29-31 . . . . June 22
Matthew 11:28 . . . . Dec. 3
Matthew 13:44 . . . . Sept. 25
Matthew 16:19 . . . . July 1
Matthew 17:2 . . . . Oct. 14
Matthew 18:10 . . . . Jan. 24
Matthew 22:29 . . . . Dec. 15
Matthew 23:26 . . . . May 11
Matthew 24:13 . . . . Jan. 15
Matthew 24:35 . . . . June 2
Matthew 24:42 . . . . May 23
Matthew 25:40 . . . . Nov. 6
Matthew 28:2 . . . . Aug. 12

Mark 2:22 . . . . Sept. 19
Mark 4:23-24 . . . . May 6
Mark 4:26-27 . . . . Mar. 11
Mark 13:32 . . . . Sept. 10
Mark 13:37 . . . . Sept. 2

Luke 2:10-11 . . . . Dec. 24
Luke 6:29 . . . . Sept. 8
Luke 6:38 . . . . Aug. 18
Luke 7:38 . . . . Dec. 29
Luke 9:56 . . . . July 17
Luke 10:20 . . . . Sept. 24
Luke 11:23 . . . . Jan. 16
Luke 12:2-3 . . . . May 28
Luke 12:15 . . . . June 26
Luke 12:34 . . . . June 8
Luke 18:25 . . . . Mar. 5
Luke 19:10 . . . . Nov. 24
Luke 24:38-39 . . . . Sept. 6

John 1:1-3 . . . . June 12, Dec. 17
John 1:5 . . . . Feb. 17

John 3:14-17 . . . . Mar. 22
John 3:16 . . . . Mar. 3
John 4:14 . . . . Sept. 7
John 5:7 . . . . .May 3
John 6:12 . . . . Sept. 15
John 6:40 . . . . Mar. 6
John 7:37-38 . . . . .Oct. 15
John 8:12 . . . . .Feb. 15
John 8:31-32 . . . . April 1
John 9:4 . . . . .Feb. 20
John 10:11 . . . . .Feb. 19
John 13:13 . . . . Nov. 9
John 14:2 . . . . July 27
John 14:2-4 . . . . Nov. 28
John 14:6 . . . . Mar. 15
John 14:13-14 . . . . .Feb. 8
John 14:27 . . . . Sept. 13
John 15:1-5 . . . . .Oct. 21
John 15:9-11 . . . . July 11
John 16:33 . . . . Jan. 13
John 17:3 . . . . Aug. 2
John 19:2-3 . . . . .June 27
John 20:29 . . . . Nov. 1
John 20:30-31 . . . . .June 1
John 21:25 . . . . Mar. 10

Acts 1:24 . . . . Jan. 18
Acts 3:6 . . . . .June 17
Acts 4:12 . . . . Sept. 18, Oct. 8
Acts 16:30-31 . . . . .Oct. 9

Romans 2:6-7. . . . . July 15
Romans 2:7 . . . . Jan. 20
Romans 6:4 . . . . Mar. 24
Romans 8:28 . . . . .June 24
Romans 8:39 . . . . Dec. 23
Romans 10:16-17 . . . . Mar. 20
Romans 12:2 . . . . Jan. 1
Romans 12:10 . . . . Jan. 30
Romans 12:15 . . . . .Apr. 24
Romans 13:8 . . . . .May 1
Romans 14:17 . . . . Mar. 9

1 Corinthians 1:25 . . . . .Oct. 20
1 Corinthians 1:26-28 . . . . . Dec. 10
1 Corinthians 3:8 . . . . .June 25
1 Corinthians 3:11 . . . . Aug. 6
1 Corinthians 4:7 . . . . .Apr. 19
1 Corinthians 13:4-7 . . . . . . .Feb. 14
1 Corinthians 14:40 . . . . July 31

2 Corinthians 1:3-4. . . . . .Feb. 3
2 Corinthians 1:9 . . . . .Oct. 12
2 Corinthians 4:8-9. . . . . .May 2
2 Corinthians 4:14 . . . . .May 25
2 Corinthians 5:1 . . . . Mar. 21
2 Corinthians 5:7 . . . . Mar. 4
2 Corinthians 5:17 . . . . Sept. 26
2 Corinthians 6:4-5. . . . . Mar. 19
2 Corinthians 12:9 . . . . .Feb. 13

Galatians 5:13-14 . . . . Mar. 2
Galatians 5:22-23 . . . . .June 9

Galatians 6:2 . . . . Jan. 28
Galatians 6:9 . . . . .Apr. 21

Ephesians 2:14 . . . . Sept. 14
Ephesians 3:12 . . . . Aug. 25
Ephesians 3:17-19. . . . . Aug. 14
Ephesians 4:4. . . . . .May 26
Ephesians 4:24 . . . . July 30
Ephesians 4:31-32. . . . . Jan. 6
Ephesians 5:19 . . . . .Apr. 12
Ephesians 5:20 . . . . Dec. 28
Ephesians 5:30 . . . . .Apr. 3
Ephesians 6:1. . . . . Sept. 5
Ephesians 6:10 . . . . Dec. 6
Ephesians 6:14-17 . . . . Nov. 27
Ephesians 6:17 . . . . .Oct. 7

Philippians 2:4 . . . . .Feb. 2
Philippians 2:9 . . . . .Apr. 10
Philippians 2:14-16 . . . . July 3
Philippians 4:5 . . . . Nov. 14

Colossians 1:20-23 . . . . Aug. 11
Colossians 1:28 . . . . .June 30

1 Thessalonians 5:14 . . . . July 28
1 Thessalonians 5:17 . . . . . . .Apr. 11

1 Timothy 4:7 . . . . .Oct. 1
1 Timothy 4:12 . . . . Nov. 10
1 Timothy 4:14 . . . . July 20, Nov. 2
1 Timothy 4:14-16 . . . . .May 30
1 Timothy 6:18 . . . . .May 24

2 Timothy 1:13 . . . . Sept. 3
2 Timothy 2:15 . . . . Mar. 25
2 Timothy 3:16 . . . . Dec. 20

Titus 2:7. . . . . Jan. 8
Titus 3:4-6 . . . . Dec. 22

Hebrews 2:18 . . . . Nov. 25
Hebrews 6:12 . . . . Aug. 22
Hebrews 7:19 . . . . Dec. 14
Hebrews 12:1 . . . . July 26
Hebrews 13:5 . . . . .June 5, Dec. 2
Hebrews 13:6 . . . . .May 8
Hebrews 13:8 . . . . .June 6

James 1:5 . . . . July 18
James 1:12 . . . . Jan. 5
James 1:19 . . . . Dec. 8
James 1:22 . . . . Sept. 28
James 2:8 . . . . .May 20
James 3:5 . . . . .Oct. 22
James 3:5-6 . . . . .May 18
James 4:7 . . . . Nov. 8
James 4:7-8 . . . . Jan. 14
James 5:7 . . . . July 19

1 Peter 1:18-19 . . . . Sept. 21
1 Peter 2:1 . . . . Jan. 4
1 Peter 2:4 . . . . .May 14
1 Peter 4:12-14 . . . . Mar. 17

2 Peter 1:19. . . . . Sept. 27

1 John 1:7. . . . . Sept. 29
1 John 1:9. . . . . Jan. 21, Mar. 14
1 John 4:1-2. . . . . Aug. 28
1 John 5:12 . . . . .Oct. 29

Jude 1:20 . . . . Aug. 1

Revelation 3:7 . . . . Dec. 21
Revelation 3:15-18 . . . . .June 4
Revelation 3:20. . . . . .Feb. 16
Revelation 7:17. . . . . .Oct. 16
Revelation 22:17. . . . . .Apr. 7

Topical Index

Adidas . . . . Dec. 9
Air-conditioning duct full of money . . . . .Feb. 6
Alaska isn't Florida! . . . . Nov. 24
Albania gets the wrong prince . . . . Oct. 27
Aluminum foil . . . . Sept. 2
Animal groups . . . . Mar. 12
Animals help friends . . . . Nov. 12
Animals know when disaster is coming . June 30
Animals with a sunburn? . . . . Oct. 14
Animals with heads that protect them . . Oct. 7
Antique auctions . . . . Jan. 2
Ants from Brazil . . . . Nov. 25
Archer fish . . . . Jan. 22
Astrodome in Houston: skylights . . . . . . Jan. 21

Backlog . . . . Jan. 3
Bad breath . . . . Jan. 17
Bald eagle . . . . Jan. 19
Ballpoint pens . . . . May 21
Band-Aids . . . . Jan. 23
Bank withdrawal or holdup? . . . . Aug. 11
Barber poles . . . . July 8
Barns painted red . . . . Jan. 25
Basketball and peach baskets . . . . Jan. 26
Beavers . . . . Mar. 1
Beef jerky . . . . Jan. 6
Beetle in the desert . . . . Sept. 7
Bicycle crossbars . . . . Jan. 7
Birds' beaks .Feb. 24
Birds Eye frozen foods . . . . Jan. 8
Birds find worms . . . . Oct. 17
Birds' goggles . . . . Mar. 4
Birds in V-formation . . . . Oct. 30
Birds on electric wires . . . . Aug. 23
Black Plague . . . . July 7
Board games are tested . . . . Aug. 28
Boats: starboard and port sides . . . . July 9
Boll weevil . . . . July 12
Booby-trapped house . . . . .Feb. 7
Book collecting . . . . Jan. 12
Book with no errors . . . . July 5
Bowling . . . . Jan. 14
Braille . . . . .Apr. 4
Bridges and clay flowerpots . . . . .Feb. 13
Bulls and the color red . . . . Jan. 11
Bungee jumping . . . . .Apr. 6
Burma-Shave . . . . Oct. 31
Burns need water . . . . .Apr. 7
Buttons on the right or the left? . . . . . . .Apr. 9

Cabdriver gets lost, saves a life . . . . Oct. 25
Cactus becomes a canteen . . . . Oct. 4
Calves swallow magnets . . . . .Feb. 28
Camels in Texas . . . . .Feb. 9
Carlyle, Thomas, rewrites whole book . . . June 2
Cartoons with a hidden name . . . . .Apr. 13
Cash registers . . . . May 9
Cats' tongues . . . . May 11

Cat whiskers .Feb. 10
Caves . . . . May 14
Cereal box prize: Canadian land . . . . . . Oct. 28
Chicken bone collection . . . . Dec. 28
Chickens with contact lenses . . . . May 15
China's backward customs . . . . .Feb. 18
Chinese checkers and fortune cookies . . June 12
Chocolate chip cookies . . . . Oct. 18
Choking . . . . Oct. 9
Chop suey . . . . June 13
Cinderella's glass slippers . . . . June 14
Clapboards and filmmakers . . . . .Feb. 11
Clocks . . . . May 10
Coins . . . . June 17
Cold shoulder . . . . Aug. 21
Color blindness . . . . .Feb. 12
Colors affect moods . . . . June 19
Cowbird babies . . . . June 20
Crabs . . . . June 22
Crocker, Betty . . . . Nov. 1
Crossword puzzles . . . . .Feb. 16
Crying with tears . . . . Oct. 16
Cupboard home . . . . Mar. 21
Curfews for farmers . . . . .Feb. 17

Dandelions . . . . Mar. 27
Death Valley rocks . . . . Aug. 12
Dentist, enamel, and dentin . . . . .Feb. 22
Dew point . . . . .Feb. 21
Dishwashers . . . . Dec. 22
Dixie cups . . . . July 25
Dog delivers mail . . . . July 28
Dog in a graveyard . . . . Mar. 3
Dogs at the table . . . . July 24
Dog saves Nome, Alaska . . . . Sept. 14
Dogs' noses .Apr. 19
Dollhouse for Queen Mary . . . . July 27
Dollar bill . . . . July 16
Dollar coins (Susan B. Anthony) . . . . Jan. 1
Double joints .Apr. 3
Drinking straws . . . . Aug. 2
Drive-in theaters . . . . May 30
Driving on the right side . . . . Mar. 16
Dr Pepper . . . . Mar. 13
Drum messages in Africa . . . . .Apr. 5
Dunce . . . . Mar. 17
Dutch boy who never existed . . . . Mar. 18

Earmuffs . . . . Jan. 27
Earthworms . . . . Dec. 30
Eating strange foods . . . . Mar. 9
Eavesdropping . . . . Mar. 20
Edison, Thomas . . . . Nov. 2
Electricity lights up a helmet . . . . .Apr. 8
Elephants . . . . May 7
Emergency call from a tomato . . . . .Feb. 8
Emperor rules America . . . . Nov. 3
Exercise class: "Stick 'em up!" . . . . Jan. 18

Eyebrows . . . . Jan. 9
Eye: dominant one . . . . Nov. 5

Face-slapping contest . . . . Sept. 8
False fire alarms . . . . May 18
Fans . . . . July 21
Feet can't really sleep . . . . .Apr. 11
Fields, W. C. and his bank accounts . . . Mar. 29
Fingernails with white spots . . . . Mar. 11
Fingerprinting. . . . . Mar. 28
Fire extinguishers . . . . Oct. 22
Fire station door . . . . Aug. 30
Fish. . . . . May 13
Fish lunch destroys evidence. . . . . Sept. 6
Fish with lemon . . . . Nov. 13
Flag at half-mast. . . . . Mar. 24
Flea markets . . . . Mar. 25
Flies on the ceiling . . . . Sept. 1
Floaters in your eye. . . . . Mar. 26
Flower colors . . . . June 18
Foot powder wins election . . . . Dec. 7
Frisbees. . . . . Sept. 30
Frog needs water every five years . . . . Nov. 26
Frogs from the sky . . . . July 20
Funny bone . . . . July 23

Garlic . . . . Aug. 31
Gerber baby foods . . . . June 15
Gillette disposable razors . . . . Aug. 1
Giraffes. . . . . Aug. 25
Glasses clinking in a toast . . . . Oct. 15
Gloves . . . . Nov. 27
Goldfish . . . . .Apr. 22
Gold rush in South Africa . . . . .Apr. 21
Gold weighed in a bathtub. . . . . .Jan. 5
Golf courses . . . . .Apr. 23
Golfers shout "Fore!" . . . . June 21
Googol: a very big number. . . . . Oct. 3
Grapefruit replaces baseball . . . . .Apr. 24
Grass needs to be mowed. . . . . Aug. 27
Gravity . . . . July 26
Gray hair . . . . .Apr. 25
Grocery shopping carts. . . . . Aug. 7

Hair with natural curls. . . . . Nov. 7
Hands. . . . . .Apr. 27
Hangnails . . . . June 7
Hobo code . . . . Nov. 6
Hollywood . . . . .Apr. 28
Horse that can count? . . . . Oct. 6
Horses sleep standing up . . . . Nov. 8
Horses, swords, and left-sided
    mounting . . . . Mar. 8
Hot dogs . . . . Nov. 9
Hula Hoops. . . . . Oct. 2
Humble pie. . . . . .Apr. 29

Iceland woman, 107, in school? . . . . . . Nov. 11
"I'll eat my hat" . . . . Sept. 3
Inventions by kids. . . . . Nov. 10
Inventions that didn't become famous . . Oct. 1
IOU . . . . May 1

Iron in cereal. . . . . May 31
Ironing . . . . May 2

Jacuzzi . . . . May 3
Jail where nothing worked right . . . . . . Nov. 15
Japanese lieutenant waits 29 years to
    surrender . . . . May 28
Jeep . . . . Dec. 2
Jell-O . . . . Dec. 14
Jewels in a hotel closet . . . . Nov. 22
Jigsaw puzzle . . . . Dec. 16
John Hancock Tower in Boston . . . . . . .Apr. 26

Ketchup . . . . Oct. 8
King Canute wouldn't wear his crown . Oct. 24
Kleenex. . . . . Dec. 1
Kudzu vines take over. . . . . Oct. 21

Languages: a cardinal who knew
    thirty-eight . . . . May 5
Leaning Tower of Pisa . . . . .Sept. 22
Lepers and a priest . . . . .Feb. 19
"Let the cat out of the bag" . . . . .Jan. 4
Letter arrives at White House after 7 years
    . . . . May 29
Letter *e*. . . . . Dec. 20
Letters on computer keyboards. . . . . . . May 20
Letters on telephones . . . . May 22
Levi's jeans . . . . Dec. 13
Liberty Bell . . . . Mar. 2
Library fine . . . . Mar. 22
Lifeguard saves 907 people. . . . . Dec. 18
Life Savers. . . . . Oct. 29
Lincoln's beard . . . . .Jan. 24
Liquid Paper . . . . Dec. 15
Locksmith locks everyone out . . . . Dec. 21
Locks: protecting your things . . . . May 17
Lunchroom traffic light. . . . . Dec. 19

M&M's. . . . . .Apr. 10
MacArthur, Douglas, absent during
    roll call . . . . Mar. 30
Mailing a little girl. . . . . .Feb. 2
Mariner 1 spaceship . . . . .Feb. 3
Masking tape . . . . .Sept. 18
Matches . . . . .Feb. 1
McDonald's . . . . June 5
Medicine bottle caps . . . . .Jan. 13
Metal detectors. . . . . .Jan. 29
Metals feels colder than wood . . . . June 4
Metric system. . . . . June 3
Mexican jumping beans . . . . .Feb. 26
Millionaire eats cold oatmeal . . . . Nov. 29
Miniature art . . . . .Sept. 13
Miniature golf. . . . . June 6
Mistletoe . . . . .Feb. 5
Money: laundered or counterfeit?. . . . . Oct. 23
Monopoly. . . . . Mar. 5
Mosquitoes. . . . . July 3

Napkins the size of towels. . . . . Mar. 14
National Smile Princess. . . . . July 11

Neckties . . . . Sept. 20
Nero, the singing emperor . . . . June 9
Nest eggs . . . . June 8
News . . . . Dec. 24
Niagara Falls bridge . . . . Aug. 29
Noises at night . . . . Apr. 14
Noodles . . . . Apr. 16
Noses . . . . Apr. 17
Number that never changes . . . . Dec. 11
Nursery rhymes . . . . Aug. 3

Ocean liner which queen's name? . . . . . July 17
Olympic athlete oversleeps . . . . Sept. 9
Oscar statues . . . . Mar. 6
Ostriches . . . . Apr. 20

Pack rats . . . . July 31
Painting by da Vinci disappears . . . . May 4
Painting of the Mississippi . . . . July 4
Pancake party . . . . Mar. 19
Passports . . . . May 19
Pencils with six sides . . . . Mar. 10
Piano keys in black and white . . . . Apr. 12
Piggy bank . . . . May 24
Pillow tags . . . . May 6
Ping-Pong . . . . June 25
Pizza . . . . Sept. 4
Plane catches person . . . . Apr. 15
Plant needs fire to grow . . . . Mar. 23
Play-Doh . . . . June 23
Police cars and blue lights . . . . Sept. 23
Popsicles . . . . Apr. 18
Portland, Oregon . . . . July 10
Post-it notes . . . . June 24
Potato chips . . . . July 13
Potholes . . . . Aug. 10
President for a day . . . . Feb. 20
President Taft's giant bathtub . . . . Feb. 23
Prisoners escape to courtroom . . . . Nov. 4
Private eyes . . . . July 14
Purple: a royal color . . . . June 27
Puzzle from Egypt . . . . July 15

Question mark . . . . July 18
Quicksand . . . . July 2

Rabbits' noses . . . . May 23
Raccoon tails and Davy Crockett . . . . . . Feb. 15
Railroad tunnel lit by the sun once
   a year . . . . Sept. 27
Raincoats called mackintoshes . . . . July 29
Rainmaker in San Diego . . . . Aug. 8
Recess around the world: Project
   ACES . . . . May 26
Recipe for an explosion . . . . Apr. 2
Rescued boy rescues a man . . . . Aug. 18
Restaurants . . . . Aug. 15
Resurrection plant . . . . May 25
Revolving doors . . . . Mar. 15
Rice and guilt . . . . Feb. 14
Rickshaws . . . . Aug. 4
Roller skates . . . . July 1

Rolls ready to bake . . . . Aug. 13
Roots grow down . . . . Aug. 14
Rural Free Delivery . . . . June 1

Salt in the ocean . . . . Aug. 16
Sandwiches . . . . Dec. 3
Sardines . . . . Aug. 17
Scarecrows . . . . Aug. 19
Scotchgard . . . . Aug. 20
Scratch 'n' sniff . . . . July 6
Secretary of the Treasury . . . . Sept. 24
Shaking hands . . . . Sept. 28
Ship saved by plastic balls . . . . Aug. 26
Shopping malls . . . . Jan. 31
Shrinking backbones . . . . Sept. 5
Sideburns . . . . Aug. 22
Sidewalk customs . . . . Sept. 17
Silent forever . . . . May 16
Silent Night . . . . Dec. 25
Silly Putty . . . . June 29
Simon Says . . . . Aug. 24
Skyscrapers . . . . Jan. 10
Sleep without counting sheep . . . . Apr. 30
Slinky toys . . . . Sept. 11
Snow in Spain . . . . Sept. 12
Softball player catches baby . . . . May 12
Sound travels at different speeds . . . . . . Dec. 8
Spaghetti on trees . . . . Apr. 1
Spider's web . . . . Oct. 10
Spinach . . . . Dec. 6
Sports broadcasting blunder . . . . June 10
Stamp collecting . . . . Sept. 15
Statues in matchboxes . . . . Feb. 4
Statues of man on horse hold secrets . . Sept. 16
Stealing their own car . . . . Mar. 31
Stethoscope . . . . Oct. 11
Stinkhorn . . . . July 19
Stomach acid . . . . Oct. 13
Studying . . . . Aug. 5
Surgeons don't wear white . . . . June 11

Table manners . . . . Jan. 30
Taft's inauguration and Treasure
   Island . . . . Sept. 25
Taj Mahal . . . . Dec. 5
Tea bags . . . . Sept. 19
Teddy bears . . . . Feb. 27
Telephone recording: the time is . . . . . Sept. 10
The: most common English word . . . . . Nov. 17
Time magazine cover . . . . Oct. 19
Tires with initials . . . . Nov. 14
Tire won't stay buried . . . . Nov. 16
Toads . . . . July 30
Toaster . . . . Oct. 12
Tollbooths . . . . Sept. 21
Toolbox treasure . . . . Nov. 18
Toothbrushes . . . . Feb. 25
Toy cannon . . . . May 8
Toy prices from long ago . . . . June 26
Traffic lights . . . . Dec. 12
Trains: take kids out West to be
   adopted . . . . Nov. 20

Trampoline . . . . Nov. 19
Translations change words . . . . Nov. 21
Trash in outer space . . . . Mar. 7
Treason and water bowls . . . . Jan. 16
Trophies: first, second, and third place . . Jan. 20
Tunnel to gold claim. . . . . Jan. 15
Tupperware . . . . June 28

Umbrellas . . . . May 27

Vacuum cleaner . . . . Nov. 23
Veins are blue, arteries are red . . . . Sept. 29
Velcro . . . . Dec. 23
Vest buttons . . . . Oct. 20

Wagons for kids . . . . Jan. 28
Waitresses and hash house Greek . . . . . Nov. 30

Waking up before alarm clocks . . . . . . June 16
Wallet in a bag of potato chips . . . . Dec. 26
Washing machines . . . . Sept. 26
Washington's teeth . . . . July 22
Wedding ring lost in Black Sea . . . . Aug. 9
Whale swallows man. . . . . Oct. 5
White House color . . . . Dec. 27
White House sheep. . . . . Oct. 26
Wigs . . . . Dec. 29
Winchester Cathedral sinking . . . . Aug. 6
Winchester rifles and a mansion . . . . . . Nov. 28
Windshield wipers. . . . . Dec. 4
Wisdom teeth . . . . Dec. 10

Xmas . . . . Dec. 17

Yo-yo . . . . Dec. 31